Thomas Gent

Gent´s History of Hull

Salzwasser

Thomas Gent

Gent´s History of Hull

1. Auflage | ISBN: 978-3-84605-134-4

Erscheinungsort: Frankfurt, Deutschland

Erscheinungsjahr: 2020

Salzwasser Verlag GmbH

Reprint of the original, first published in 1869.

GENT'S

HISTORY OF HULL

(*Annales Regioduni Hullini,*)

RE-PRINTED

IN FAC-SIMILE OF THE ORIGINAL
OF 1735.

TO WHICH IS APPENDED

Notices of the Life and Works

OF

THOMAS GENT,

PRINTER, of YORK.

HULL.

M. C. PECK AND SON, 10 MARKET-PLACE,

—

1869.

TO THE RIGHT HONORABLE

THE

EARL DE GREY AND RIPON,

(Lord High Steward of Hull,)

THIS VOLUME IS,

WITH HIS LORDSHIP'S ESPECIAL PERMISSION,

MOST RESPECTFULLY DEDICATED,

BY HIS

OBEDIENT SERVANTS,

THE PUBLISHERS.

ADVERTISEMENT.

THE Publishers arc induced to undertake the present Reprint, from the extreme rarity and value of the original work, of which very few copies are now extant, and these so eagerly sought after as to have become a costly property, confined almost exclusively to the Libraries of a few antiquaries and connoisseurs. No reprint of this curious and quaint old volume has ever yet been made, and it is therefore comparatively unknown to the Inhabitants of Hull generally, to whom it is believed the present publication will be most welcome, as well as to the residents of Scarborough, Whitby, and Bridlington, the History of which Towns is also treated of in the same work.

GENT'S HISTORY OF HULL has ever been a favorite book with the "ingenious Lovers of Antiquity," (to whom the author dedicated it), not only on account of its great merit as a literary composition, but also from the curious and fanciful illustrations which embellish it. The work has additional claims upon the Inhabitants of Hull as being the most valuable and comprehensive early History of the Town, its Churches, Monasteries, King's Palace, &c. which has ever been published. The very great amount of interesting and valuable matter contained in its pages, ſhows the object of the author has been to crowd as much anecdote and narrative into his book as poſſible, (even the index is full of amusement), and this is carried out in a manner totally different from that adopted in the present age of *book-making.*

Liſts of the Mayors, Sheriffs, and Chamberlains, with ample chronological details of all great events in the Annals of Hull from the earlieſt times to 1735,—many facts and incidents throwing light upon the career of "Mr. A. Marvell" and his family, —the Founders of the Charter-House, the Hospitals, and the ancient Charities, are given; as also the original list of Subscribers to Mr. Gent's book, in which will be found the name of "Mr. Eugenius Aram," afterwards so celebrated as the "Eugene Aram" of Bulwer's Novel and the hero of Hood's Poem.

This Book alſo is superior in execution to the greater part of Gent's other publications, the larger Illuſtrations being executed by the beſt artiſts of that day, and are remarkable for their accuracy and elegance—unlike the engravings in the hiſtories of Ripon, York, &c. which, although exceedingly curious and quaint, are far from reliable pictures of the objects represented.

A minute examination of many copies of the original, has discovered the intereſting fact that Gent publiſhed *two* editions of this work, a circumſtance before unknown. The variations occur (Preface V, pp 164, 172, 176,) and it is from the *firſt* and rarer edition that the present reprint has been made ; the illuſtrations are reproduced in exact fac-simile, together with the entire text in its integrity, both editions having been carefully collated.

The large and influential List of Subscribers they have received to the present edition, has enabled the Publiſhers to include the intereſting *"Notices of the Life and Works of THOMAS GENT,"* which has been kindly contributed by the Rev. GEO. OHLSON, B.A., Maſter of the Hull Grammar School.

LIST OF SUBSCRIBERS.

A

A. O. Atkinson, M.A.
H. J. Atkinson
Joseph Atkinson
Wm. Atkin
Wm. Adams (3 copies)
W. E. Ashby
Mrs. Atkinson
E. Addey

B

W. H. H. Broadley, M.P. *Welton*
Rev. Canon Brooke, M.A.
Major Bannister, *Hessle*
J. P. Bell, M.D.
W. P. Burkinshaw
K. K. Brochner
Robt. Blyth
Rev. G. O. Browne, M.A. *Torquay*
W. P. Burch, *London*
H. W. Ball, *Barton* (8 copies)
W. W. Batty
Rev. A. J. Bennoch, M.A.
Jno. Brooke
Wm. Bernard
J. Brownridge
Jas. Baynes
W. Consitt Boulter
Thos. Bailey, *Grimsby*
Wm. Bromby
Thos. Bache
R. Beal
Mrs. Briggs
W. B. Bellerby, *Selby*
Wm. Briggs
Thos. Buckton (2 copies)
Geo. Bowlby
Joseph Baker
Richard Bell
A. Brown
Henry Brown
E. Bainton

J. Bryson, *Mayor of Hull.*
Chas. B. Bell
R. Battarbee
S. Birkett
Thos. Brown
J. Blackburn
Richard Baxter
Geo. Bell

C

James Clay, M.P. *London*
Henry Cook
Thos. Cook, *Chief Constable*
C. S. Clarke
Wm. Cross
W. R. Cross
T. F. Champney, *Beverley*
G. W. Carlton, Jun.
T. Craddock, *Organist Holy Trinity*
Edwd. Chapman
T. W. Clarke
Thos. Cooper, *York*
W. E. Carpendale
H. W. Chambers
M. Carlin
J. S. Campion
J. M. Cuthbert, *Bedford*
W. Casson
J. P. Chatham
Wm. Chatham
Miss Coulson
E. J. Cook
John Cook
Jas. Cochrane
G. Cussons (6 copies)
Mrs. Curtis
M. W. Clarke
R. J. Chaffer
C. C. Clark
J. Charter
I. Colley (6 copies)
Geo. Cobb
T. B. Carr

D

The Rt. Hon. Earl de Grey & Ripon
Wm. Dryden
Wm. Denison
W. T. Dibb
J. Dalton, *Withernsea*
R. Dean
J. H. Donaldson
R. D'Orscy
Thos. Dixon
W. E. Dixon, *Beverley*
J. R. Duncan
Wm. Dowsing
N. F. Dobree
W. Day
W. Dyson, jun.
H. Dring
W. H. Drew
R. Davidson, *Bridlington*
C. J. Donnison

E

Rev. R. J. Ellis
Thos. Empringham
J. Ehlers
J. S. Easterby
John Egginton
G. H. Earle

F

Col. Francis
Jno. Fountain
W. W. Fletcher
J. P. Fea, *West Hartlepool*
J. Farrell (2 copies)
James Fargus
J. R. Ford, *West Hartlepool*
C. J. Fox
J. Farr
E. Foster
Thos. Foster

G

Rev. F. F. Goe, M.A.
Rev. J. Gurnhill, B.A. *Hornsea*
W. R. Gibbons, *Brigg*
Robt. Garton
Chas. P. Gibson
Jno. Gubbins
D. Gibson
Robt. Galtress
F. B. Grotrian
Richard Glover
J. Gough
H. C. Gleadow
Miss Gleadow
A. Gemmell
H. Gates
W. L. Grantham
J. Guest, *Rotherham*

H

Hull Subscription Library
Hull Church Institute
Hull Young People's Christian &
    Literary Institute.
Hull Exchange Company
Hull Savings Bank
Lient. Col. Haworth, *Malton*
C. Heaven
F. F. Hewitt
Geo. Hardy
Wm. Hunt
J. F. Holden
Arthur Hewitt
H. Haigh
Thos. Haller
G. W. Hart
E. Hart
J. W. Hill
J. W. Holder
Thos. Howdle
E. E. Heslewood, *Hessle*
Thos. Hodgson
Richard Holder
Wm. Holdsworth
A. G. T. Heckling
H. R. Hall
Thos. B. Holmes
W. H. Humington
Thos. Holmes
J. Holiday
J. Hamilton
W. Halley
C. W. Holdich (12 copies)
Wm. Harvatt (3 copies)
E. Haller
G. H. Howden
W. H. Hearfield
Wm. Holt
C. E. Hewitt
J. S. Hawkins
Edwd. Harker
C. A. Hornstedt
S. H. H. Hodgson

I

Robert Jameson, *Sheriff of Hull*
R. W. Jameson, *Cottingham*
J. L. Jacobs
F. Ingleby
Wm. Jacklin
Geo. Jinman
R. Johnson
Miss Jackson
W. Jackman
J. Jackson
J. B. Johnson
Geo. Johnson

K.

Rev. H. W. Kemp, B.A.
W. R. King
A. Kitching, M. D.
Martin Kemp
Rev. H. G. Kinnear, M.A. *Nafferton*
Castle Kelsey
J. F. Kruger
Richard Kemp, *Anlaby* (2 copies)
F. King
Thos. Kershaw
Henry Kirk

L

The Rt. Hon. Lord Londesborough
John Loft,
Rev. E. A. Lane, M.A.
Rev. T. Lester
L. W. Longstaff
Wm. Lawton
J. Linwood
Henry Leffler
C. Leggott (2 copies)
Capt. P. R. Lempriere
J. W. Leng (6 copies)
H. Lamb
J. Leggott, Jun.
Geo. Leggott
Jas. Leslie
Thos. Luty, *York*
Thos. Leest
J. Lockwood
J. Laxton
Mrs. Lambert
E. W. Lister
Jos. Laverack
Thos. Liggins
Jos. Lyons, *Manchester*
A. Loftus
D. Love

M

Geo. Manners, F.S.A. *Croydon*
Jno. Malam, *Holmpton*
Capt. W. P. McBride
E. P. Maxsted, *Hessle*
John Malcolm
Robt. Middlemiss
J. R. Mortimer, *Fimber*
D. Middlemist
John Maw
Thos. Mapplebeck
Jas. Mortimer, *Elloughton*
M. C. Marshall
S. Musgrave
Thos. Massam
Ed. Mackrill
G. G. Mitchell
C. L. Metcalfe
S. Marsden
J. S. Moody

B. Mills
B. B. Mason
B. Moor
W. Moore, *Grimsby*
Geo. Myers
J. Minty
Geo. Midgeley
Wm. Marshall

N

C. M. Norwood, M.P. *London*
J. F. Norwood
Rev. H. Newmarch, M.A. *Hessle*
W. H. North
Capt. Newton, H.V.A.
P. Newton (6 copies)
W. Nettleship
A. Norman
W Needler
T. S. Nicholson

O

Rev. Geo. Ohlson, B.A.
Jas. Oldham, C.E.
Edwin J. Officer
J. S. Oliver
D. Ouston
R. Oxtoby

P

Lieut. Col. Pease
Rev. R. H. Parr, M.A. *Scarbro'*
Jas. Pyburn, M.D.
C. H. Phillips
Robt. P. Priest
W. J. Pearson
J. C. Pettingell
Wm. Pybus
T. J. Peck
Jas. Patrick
Geo. Peacock
A. C. Prissick
Charles Pool
G. H. Pentermann
Thos. Peck
J. Procter
Jas. Plaxton
Mrs. Phillips

R

G. C. Roberts, *Ex-Mayor*
A. Reinold
Walter Reynolds
John Rollit
W. J. Redpath
Capt. Riches
Thos. Ross
W. T. Robinson
Fredk. Ross, *London*
E. Redfern
Thos. Rymer
Jno. Robertson
Henry Rust

H. Rivett
J. Rose
W. W. Robinson, *Oxford*, (2 copies)
Jas. Rutter
J. Raby, *London*
W. Ramsey
G. Redfearn
R. Richardson
W. Rawson, jun.
I. Reckitt
A. Raines
George Raven
R. Raines, jun.
W. R. Ridsdale
James Reckitt
R. Reynolds

S

Chris. Sykes, M.P. *Brantingham*
Rev. John Scott, M.A.
Major T. Skinner, *Bath*
Rev. T. Sutton, *Withernsea*
Rev. C. Sheffield, *Burton Stather*
J. L. Seaton
G. A. Shee
Edmund Smith
John Saner
W. Sylvester
Jas. Sowerby, *London*
John Symons
Wm. Sissons
H. S. Sharp
S. Shields, *Patrington*
J. Shepherd
C. F. Smithson
S. A. Samson
E. G. Starr
B. T. Smith
T. A. Smithson
Geo. Spink
J. Saltmer
Thos. Sanderson
J. Sampson, *York* (8 copies)
Edwin Squires, *York*
Thos. Smith
Jno. Stamp
E. Shearsmith
J. Stephenson
Thos. Stratten
E. Seaman
Jas. Stevenson
R. C. F. D'O. Stephenson
E. Spink
J. C. Serres
Dr. Sharpe
R. Sollitt
Thos. Shields, *Scarbro'*
Jno. Simpson
J. A. Storry
J. B. Smith
J. Sanderson

F. Sutton
J. N. Scherling

T

Thos. Thompson, F.S.A.
C. S. Todd, F.S.A.
Jas. Thompson
Jos. Temple
S. W. Theakston, *Scarbro'* (3 copies)
T. T.
G. H. Todd
J. J. Thorney, *Coroner*
J. Thirkell
Edwin Taylor
W. B. Tarbotton

V

Henry Vise
H. E. Voight

W

Robt. Wells, *Town Clerk*
Rev. T. Westmorland, M.A.
S. Woodhouse
E. S. Wilson, F.S.A.
Thos. Wilson, *Cottingham*
Rev. J. Waltham, M.A. *Broomfleet*
Rev. E. J. Wilkinson
J. H. Walker
Gilbert Wilkinson, *Ferriby*
Charles Wells
S. Walliker
John Walker
Thos. Walton
Geo. Waugh
W. E. Woolf
Geo. Wood
Robt. Weatherley, *Sunderland*
J. B. Ward
Geo. Wilson
B. B. Walker
C. L. Warwick
Robt. Watson, *London*
Robt. Wilson
J. Wilkinson
Geo. Wright
Jno. Wright
Jas. Walker
Fras. Welburn
Wm. Watson, *Hedon*
Jas. Watson
Wm. Wood
J. K. Waddilove
Jas. Wray
A. Wallis
Joseph Weatherill
A. Wray
Alfred West

Y

John Yule, *Scarbro'* (3 copies)
H. J. F. Young
G. D. Young, *Edinburgh*

NOTICES

OF

THE LIFE AND WORKS

OF

THOMAS GENT,

PRINTER, OF YORK.

 PLEASANT task lies before me. I have to evoke from the fhadowy portals of the paft, an image upon which the duft of centuries has begun to accumulate—to bring it back, re-clothed in its own individuality, amid wonted fcenes of life and action—to trace the current of a life, at times calm and uniform in its flow, at others fwollen by ftreams of care and forrow.

There are points of difficulty in the appreciation of every life; but they are confiderably leffened as regards the fubject of the prefent Memoir, from the fact that we poffefs many of the details of the life of THOMAS GENT, written by his own hand. His early youth, which is miffing in the narrative part of the Manufcript, is detailed in fome "attempts to invoke the Mufes," who appear to have looked a little coldly upon their afpiring devotee.   We learn that he was born in Ireland, in the year 1693, "of meek and gentle parents,—rich in grace, though not in fhining ore."

The stanzas that pourtray the image of his mother glow with the true verve of poefy.   She was a gracious and gentle Matron, and one who appears to have ruled well her children, for " fhe would not," he fays,

> "........excufe the least offence I'd done :
> She'd make me bring the rod, right ufed with art,
> Not furiously, as fimple mothers ufe it,
> But mild, correct, and never once abuse it.
> Nor ever did she whip her children dear,
> But she would wound us with her kinder fpeech ;
> Ne'er gave a ftripe, but we might fee a tear
> In her fwoln eye, as if she would befeech
> That, for the future, we might take great care
> No more t'offend, that she the birch might fpare."

At the age of fourteen, Gent was removed from maternal influence, and apprenticed to a Dublin Printer, whom he pourtrays in his verfe as a "Turk," a "Tyrant," a very "Nero."   After three years of ill ufage, the young apprentice formed the defperate refolution of abandoning his Mafter, his Parents, and his Country; and fet out for London, with two or three penny loaves, feventeen-pence in his pocket, and his Sunday suit.

His voyage was rife with adventure.   Being anxious to efcape detection before the ftarting of the veffel, he crept down into the hold, where he lay very fick, and without any to help or comfort him.   A three days' voyage reduced him to fuch miferable plight, that the Captain, far from infifting on his paffage-money, gave him fixpence, with the admonition to "take to good ways."

From the moment that the young Printer turned his back upon Ireland, life opened before him as an earneft and fober reality.   He quickly found employment in London with a Mr.

Edward Midwinter, of Pie Corner, Smithfield, with whom he remained three years. He fpeaks in grateful terms of his mafter, and left him, with his full confent, when he had ferved feven years at his trade, to feek advancement.

He had already worked for feveral Printers, and done a little on his own account, when he heard from his firft master, Midwinter, that Mr. White, Printer, of York, was willing to engage him for the tempting fum of eighteen pounds a year, "besides board, lodging, and wafhing." Thefe terms were agreed to, and on Sunday, twenty-fifth of April, 1714, a glow of enthufiafm fired the breaft of the now weary traveller, as he came within fight of the walls and towers of ancient Ebor.

"The firft houfe I entered, to inquire for my new mafter, was "in a Printer's, at Petergate, the very dwelling that is now my "own by purchafe; but not finding Mr. White therein, a child "brought me to his door, which was opened by the head maiden, "that is now my dear fpoufe. She ufhered me into the chamber, "where Mrs. White lay fomething ill in bed; but the old Gentle- "man was at his dinner, by the firefide, fitting in a noble arm- "chair, with a good large pie before him, and made me partake "heartily with him."

The " head maiden," whom Gent mentions here, was henceforth to be the rifing fun of his affections. Love gives wings to the hours, and the twelve months of his engagement with the York Printer glided rapidly by. He could not be induced to renew it until he had feen his friends in Ireland, although the profpeɛt of feparation from the "lovely Miftrefs Alice," was a fource of great regret to him. He refolved, however, upon the journey; and, after some mifhaps both by land and sea, reached Dublin Harbour in fafety.

"When I came to my father's house, as our dutiful cuftom is there, I fell on my knees to ask his bleffing. The good old man took me up, with tears in his eyes, kiffed me, saying "Tommy, I fcarcely knew thee." His mother received him with no lefs affection, undutiful as he had been.   Not fo, however, his former mafter, who employed officers to feize him for abfconding from his apprenticefhip.

This induced Gent again to leave his native country, and refpond to a letter that he had received from " his deareft at York," inviting him thither.   Of this fecond period of his refidence in York, we poffefs fcarcely any details.

We meet with him a fhort time after in London, in the employ of his former mafter, Midwinter, through whose influence he was admitted a freeman of the Company of Stationers in the year 1717. On the 9th of October in the fame year, he was enrolled a freeman and citizen of London, and he appears to have been alfo a member of the fociety of Freemafons, from his many allufions to the Fraternity, into which he was probably received during his refidence at York.

His chief afpiration now was towards a fettlement in life ; but motives of prudence forbade him to enter into Matrimony, " fearing fo great an expenfe as that ftate of life requires." Work was not fo brisk as could have been defired, and " I was fometimes at a loss" says Gent, " how to fpend my time well, and procure an honeft livelihood, in a troublefome world." After fome time fpent in cafual labour, Gent again vifited Ireland at the requeft of his parents, who were now old and infirm.   He obtained employment there, though not on fuch favourable terms as in London.

On his return to the great city, we meet with him in the employ of a Mr. Clifton, a Roman Catholic, whofe fervice was far more profitable than fafe.   Clifton undertook to print pamphlets for perfons under fufpicion of the Government ; and Gent relates a curious adventure that befel him while in Clifton's employ.

Some sheets fresh from the prefs had been entrusted to his care ; and accompanied by his master, he was driven in a coach to a monastic-looking building in Westminster. "Being ushered into "a spacious room," says Gent," we sat near a large table cover- "ed with an ancient carpet of curious work, and whereon was soon "laid a bottle of wine for our entertainment. In a little time we "were visited by a grave Gentleman in a black lay habit, who en- "tertained us with one pleasant difcourfe or other, and bid us be "fecret." Not long after, Dr. Atterbury, Bishop of Rochefter, was being driven in a coach, guarded, to the Tower, and Gent recog- nised in him his former pleasant and hofpitable entertainer.

Gent was now strongly preffed by his former master, Midwin- ter, to return to his employ ; but although he experienced much trouble and annoyance in Clifton's fervice, he could not be in- duced to abandon it. He fometimes frequented the Affize Courts, as fpecial correfpondent, taking notes of the trials, and forwarding them to his master to be prepared for publication.

At length the inextricable difficulties, both pecuniary and po- litical, in which Clifton became involved, obliged our author to feek work elfewhere, and he renewed his engagement with Mr. Midwinter. This revived in him the hope that he might fhortly become his own master, and fettle with "his dearest " in London. His little stock of cash however, was exhaufted by the purchafe of two new founts of Pica, with a view to having a Prefs of his own, and he was obliged still to look upon matrimony as a future contingency.

An event, too, happened at this time, which quenched his ten- der afpirings, and was likely to be attended with ferious refults. He had retired to reft one night, ill in health, and depreffed in fpirits on account of a dream he had had, which he thought fore- boded evil. A fweet slumber crept upon him, bringing with it the oblivion of all his cares and miferies. In the dead of night, however, he was ftartled by a ftrange thundering noife at the door of his chamber. Before he had time for parley, his room was forcibly entered, and he found himfelf in the grafp of a King's Meffenger, who informed him that his concurrence in certain treafonable publications required his immediate removal to prifon.

"I called him, blockhead," fays Gent, "and told him, had I "been in another condition, I might, perhaps, have laid him by "the heels; at which he fcornfully faid, he never fhould fear a "ghoft, intimating, that I feemed little better than a fpirit at "that time."

All spirit that he was, poor Gent had to hurry on his clothes, and prepare for removal. He befought his intruders to fee the door faftened which they had broken, that he might not be robbed during his confinement, "of what he had fo honeftly and painfully earned." On defcending the ftairs, he found the paffages below, and the court-yard, filled to the very gate, with conftables, watchmen, and others ; and, with one of thofe gleams of religious feeling, which brighten at intervals the pages of his memoir, he records, that the fight of thefe men, and the circumftances of his arreft, "called to my remembrance, my injured "Saviour's apprehenfion in the garden of Gethfemane."

Gent was hurried into a coach, and driven towards Newgate. On the way he was joined by other prifoners, amongft whom, to his great aftonifhment, were Clifton, and his mafter, Midwinter. They were finally taken to Manchefter Court, a large houfe in Weftminfter, from Gent's defcription of it, and near the Thames, fince, from the room in which he was confined, he could hear the plafh of its waters, as they laved the lower part of the edifice.

Gent's imprifonment lasted five days; at the expiration of which, as nothing could be proved againft him, he was honourably difcharged.

He ftill continued to work for himfelf, and for Mr. Midwinter, who feems to have been imprifoned upon a falfe fufpicion. Things were now fo profperous with him, that he hoped in a very fhort time to have occafion to invite "his dear" to London. Alas! for human frailty, Phillis proved faithlefs. A friend, who had been on a vifit to York, happening to meet Gent in the ftreet, broke to him the cruel tidings that the "lovely Alice" had given her hand to a Mr. Charles Bourne, the grandfon of the Printer for whom Gent had worked at York.

"I was fo thunderftruck," he fays, " that I could fcarcely return "an anfwer, all former thoughts crowding into my mind. My "old vein of poetry flowed in upon me, and I wrote a copy of "verfes agreeing to the tune of " Such charms has Phillis," then "much in requeft, and proper for the flute, that I became ac- "quainted with." Thefe verfes are not to be ranked among Gent's happieft efforts, fuffice the reader to know that they contain a proper amount of fentimentality.

Soon after this event, the affairs of Mr. Midwinter became involved, and he was forced to remove within the liberties of the Fleet. Gent continued to work at his own Prefs, feeking occafional employment to fill up his leifure. His laft epoch of fervice was with a widow named Dodd, and it would feem that more tender relations than thofe of bufinefs were on the point of fpringing up between them, when an unforeseen event entirely changed his pofition in the world, and opened up a wider and more promifing fphere for the developement of his energies.

It fhall be told in his own words : " It was one Sunday morn- "ing, that Mr. Philip Wood, a quondam partner at Mr. Midwin- "ter's, entering my chambers, "Tommy," said he, "all thefe fine "materials of yours muft be moved to York :" at which, wonder- "ing, "What mean you ? " said I, "Aye," faid he, "and you muft "go too, for your firft fweetheart is now at liberty, and left in

"good circumſtances by her dear ſpouſe, who deceaſed but of
"late." Gent did not think it expedient to "trifle with a widow,
as he had done with a maid," ſo he ordered all his goods to be
privately packed up, that they might be forwarded to him, if
neceſſary, and ſet out for York.

Ten years had elapsed since they laſt met, during which, the
ſcythe of time had reaped much of the bloom, and many of the
graces of the Alice of his youth. Still, he loved her, and the tide
of her returning affeſtion inundated his ſoul with a tranquil peace
and ſerenity, which he had never experienced amid the ſtruggles
of his former unquiet exiſtence. A few months were allowed to
paſs, and the dim twilight of a December morning, though ſcarcely
able, through the rich deep tints of the windows of the Minſter, to
chaſe the ſhadows that lingered within, yet revealed the performance of a bridal ceremony, which cemented a union long deferred,
now happily conſummated.

Gent had now reached the climax of all his hopes and aſpira-
tions. The buſineſs eſtabliſhed by his wife's late husband in
York, was now become his own, and the working power of the
eſtabliſhment was conſiderably increaſed by the addition of the
stock-in-trade that he had purchaſed in London. Thus a new
career was opened under the happieſt auſpices, Gent became pro-
prietor of the only Newspaper as yet publiſhed in the County of
York, the "*Original York Journal, or Weekly Courant,*" and his
was the only Preſs that had been ſet up, as yet, in thoſe parts.

Unfortunately, Gent was not the man to improve opportunities.
His unyielding and irascible temper brought upon him many
miſeries, that otherwiſe he need not have experienced. He began
by quarrelling with the ſervants of his new establiſhment, who
were reluſtant to acknowledge his authority; and he ſeems to
intimate that his "lovely Alice," who had been the angel of his
youthful dreams, had ſomehow been transformed into an Eve.—

"I found her temper," he says, "much altered from that fweet natural foftnefs, and most tender affection, that rendered her fo amiable to me while I was more juvenile, and fhe a maiden."

Another fource of difcomfort to him, was the oppofition he experienced on the part of his wife's uncle, a Mr. White, Printer, of Newcaftle. It appears, that on the death of Bourne, he had caft a longing eye on the York eftablifhment, and endeavoured to diffuade his niece from entering into a fecond marriage. Failing in this, he fet up a Prefs at York, and endeavoured in every way to thwart Gent's honeft endeavours. This evoked on the part of Gent an implacable bitternefs of fpirit, and fruftrated every attempt of his wife to bring about a reconciliation. The fruits of fuch a courfe were foon apparent. The rival Prefs continued to make rapid advances, while Gent could fcarcely find work for his own. He refolved to try the chances of Authorfhip—"I was obliged to contrive fome bufinefs," he says, "rather than go back in the world ; and by an almoft unheard-of attempt, to feek a living, by recalling the dead, as it were, to life," (referring to his Hiftory of the Antiquities of York) "to afford me and mine, that fuftenance which the living seemed to deny me." This leads me to notice the principal works of Gent, which I fhall do in chronological order, touching upon thofe points that I may deem of fpecial intereft to the readers of this little treatise.

Gent publifhed his Hiftory of York, in the year 1730. "Poor indeed, as it comes into the world," he says in his preface, "without fo much as one dedication, one patron to defend it ; nay, rather cenfures and menaces in the room thereof: fo that it flies to the umbrage of the courteous reader, to be favourable in its reception, and to the juftice of the world in defence of its compiler." The work contains tranfcriptions from the various Monuments, fhort notices of the lives of fome of the Archbifhops and Bifhops, fome details of the Religious Houses that exifted in and near the City, mention of the chief benefactors of the Cathedral Church of St. Peter, a minute defcription of its ftained windows, and translations of the epitaphs and inscriptions of the monuments. There is a little dafh of the fhowman in Gent's manner of prefenting things, due, rather perhaps to the cuftom of the times, than to any affe&ation on his part. The prolixity of his general style robs it of all power, but there is a fimplicity in the narrative, a quaintness in the touches, and often a vividness of colouring, which charm and intereft the reader. It is worth notice that his firft account of Hull is given at page 246.

The hiftory of Ripon next appeared in 1733. In the preface, Gent reminds his readers, that the feveral "portraitures and views exhibited in the book" are fomewhat wanting in "the prospe&ive," a fa& that the courteous reader foon found out for himfelf upon examination. " Yet I humbly conceive," says Gent, "they are sufficient to give great ideas to the diftant readers, or to remind thofe who have seen the originals." This Hiftory of Ripon is conceived much upon the fame plan as that of York. It is introduced by a poem on the furprifing beauties of Studley Park, with a defcription of the venerable ruins of Fountains Abbey. It then proceeds to treat, in minute detail; of the ecclefiaftical and civic antiquities of the town of Ripon. There are alfo notices of the Churches of Beverley, Wakefield, Leeds, and of feveral Towns of intereft near York. "Faithfully and painfully colle&ed by the Author."

It muft not be omitted, that in this work occurs the firft advertifement of the forthcoming Hiftory of Hull, which was set forth in thefe terms : "In a little time, God willing, will be undertaken the Hiftory of Kingfton-upon-Hull, both as to its ecclefiaftical and civil government (authentick manufcripts being obtained for that purpofe) which, as it has been always a princely and opulent town, as well as remarkable for various furprifing transa&ions, will, with its prefent happy conftitution, afford the moft agreeable entertainment to the Reader." I cannot refrain from tranfcribing fome verfes from this work, which have reference to Hull, not from any inherent poetical merit they poffefs, but because they fhow the spirit that animated the writer in his appreciation of the contingencies of all human things.—

> "FAR hence my Eye with distant View surveys
>   A Bulwark'd Town wade out into the Seas,
> Half Isle, Half Continent : Whofe narrow Neck
> Withstands the Waves, and does their Inroads check ;
> Whofe restlefs Rage affaults with fruitless Shocks
> And vainly storms the unrelenting Rocks.
> But what could *Belgia's* Naval Pow'r sustain,
> And with its Cannon clear th'infested Main ;
> What stood th' Insults of War and raging Tides,
> In Pride's o'erwhelming Insolence fubfides.
> Pride has most Pow'rful Empires overthrown ;
> Pride fank in Dust the Glorious Babylon !
> Whofe Rival Fame in Story boasts no more
> In all the Tract that Time has travell'd o'er ;
> Which now so waste a Wildernefs is made,
> That e'en its Ruin's Ruins are decay'd.
> Warn'd by my Verfe, let other Ports beware,
> And with their Trade RELIGION make their Care:
> This Place, by Trade, like others, rear'd its Brow,
> Grew rich and vain, and then (just Fate !) grew low.
> (Unerring Vengeance will Offenders find,
> However slow it seems to limp behind.)
> Its Church in Ruins, once its grace and Boast,
> Its Beauty buried in Time's Grave and lost ;
> Till to past Crimes discharg'd the Forfeit due,
> Good Heav'n forgave,, and rais'd His HOUSE anew,
> Restor'd it stands, another Yet the same,
> We may this Change its Resurrection name.
> So when the Grave shall render back its Trust,
> And our fled Souls shall re-affume their Dust,
> Tho' not our Bodies their old Form forsake,
> Our Flesh refin'd, a purer Mould shall take.
> Now Trade returns, and Heav'n vouchsafes to show
> He'll raise, on Penitence, the humbled Brow,
> Thou, favour'd Town, shalt lift once more thy Head,
> And Summon back thy former Fortune fled.

See thy own Sc—rb—r—gh, a Man approv'd,
His Country's Friend, and of his Prince belov'd,
Dear to the Muses, who can Worth endear ;
What may'st thou hope, if thou may'st claim his Care ;
If thro' his Eyes, or thro' the Muse, the Grace
Of Majesty should lighten on the Place ?
Built for a Mart, thou challengest the choice,
Bespeak'st the Merchant, and prevent'st his Voice.
The Ocean's paffing Trade thou dost invite,
Stand'st out to View, and court'st the ships to light ;
While with a bending Arm, thy Port provides
A common refuge from the Rage of Tides.
Blazed in my Verse, the World thy Site shall see,
And thou shalt own thy open'd Trade to me ;
Thy Name the Earth's remotest Ends may pierce,
By Ships convey'd ; to Heav'n advanc'd in Verse."

*** "As I humbly conceive this to be the strongest Place for Fortification upon these Coasts, and which in case of Apprehenfion from a Foreign Invafion might be made excellent use of, methinks 'tis pity its Fortifications should have been neglected, and suffer'd to lie in Ruins ; or that any of the Fortifications upon this Coast should not be supported ; and for this Reason : The *French*, by their Contraband Trade with our Smugglers for these late years, are now well acquainted with this Coast, which in their late Wars would have been of bad Consequence to us ; for it was only owing to their apprehenfions of our Rocks, which they now know how to avoid, that we were safe from their Depredations."

Of the Hiftory of Hull, publifhed in 1735, little need be said beyond commending it to the courteous appreciation of the reader. It has its defects, no doubt, both of conception and execution, but to any one thoroughly acquainted with Hull and its institutions, it cannot fail to be a valuable and interesting text-book.   Its details concerning the Churches of Holy Trinity and St. Mary, the faithful transcriptions of the Monuments, and their quaint translations for the benefit of the English reader, are proofs that Gent spared no pains to please and to instruct his readers.— Even were the book meritless on all other points, it would still remain a monument of the most careful and scrupulous labour. "Gent's performances were not, like too many modern books of topography, mere bundles of pillage from the works of ingenious and painstaking authors, but contained matter honestly colleded and not, before his time, made public by the press."

It is interesting to note that the old Plan of Hull, given in this work at page 82, exhibits the Market Crofs which had not yet been replaced by the Statue of King William the 3rd.—The old Crofs appears to have been removed whilft this work was in pro-grefs, as the other plates represent the Statue. Gent's East View of the Town, and also his Plan, furnish us with a sketch of the Old Sugar House, the calamitous fall of which caused so much consternation a short time since.

There is much interefting matter to be found in the Addenda to Gent's Hiftory of Hull. Some of the scientific opinions there-in advanced are of the moft curious nature, and may give an idea of what paffed current for fcience in those days. A correspond-ent from Whitby (p. 216) endeavours to account for the origin of the fingular foffils now known as "ammonites" that are found upon the beach there. "One will have it," he says, "that they pro-ceed thro' the meer frolicks of nature;" a second ascribes them "to some occult quality of the earth"—another says, "they are the spiral petrifactions which the ground produces thro' a Fer-mentation peculiar to Alum Mines."—"I procured my engraver," says Gent, "to exhibit the form of one of these Serpentine Stones in a vacancy of the copper-plate, from which the following Pros-peét of Scarborough is taken off." Among the details at the end of the work are many curious articles that will repay perusal.

The curious portrait of Gent prefixed to the present volume, is after a scarce print occafionally found in copies of his works.— Although but indifferently executed, it is very charaéteristic, representing the venerable figure of the old man with his snowy hair, and around him the mufical instruments in which he de-lighted. He is seated, it may be supposed, in his quaint apartment in Petergate,

> "Where, Heaven be praifed! he built his Printing Room,
> Covered with lead, a Turret for a Dome."

In the same year Gent printed, and it is supposed partly edited a literary serial entitled " Miscellanea Curiosa," confisting of enigmas and mathematical problems in prose and verse.   It contains verses by Gent, on the Statue of King William the 3rd, at Hull, which had then been lately erected.   The work proved very unattractive and soon died out.

A quaint old volume is Gent's History of England, (1741) and still quainter his History of Rome.   In the appendix to the latter is found an account of the demolishing of Pontefract Castle in 1649, and a note records that, "Col. Overton, by an order from the Lord General, for the Publick Service for Drawbridges, for Hull, had iron teams delivered to him of the value of, in money, 2£ 17s 8d. and for timber, value 8£ 6s od."

Other works from the pen of our author, are his History of the East Window in York Minster, (1762) tolerably printed, although there are many points about it that give evidence of his failing fortunes—a Tract entitled " Judas Iscariot " (1772)—"The Holy life and death of S. Winifred,"(1742) " a poem writ by a sort of infpiration on recovery from fickness"—"The Gospel of Nicodemus,"—"The History of the Ancient Militia in Yorkshire, (1760) on the title page of which is inscribed: "Written under cruel disappointment, and waiting for paper."   In this book he thus alludes to Hull:—

> " Or who is ignorant how Hull increas'd,
> To prove the Key or Fortress of the East ?
> Both can to Glory make a just Pretence ;
> Though this Superiour for a strong Defence:
> And by its Harbour nothing them annoys;
>   *   *   *   *
> When *Hothams, Gees,* and *Moyfers* mingling gain'd
> Afcending Power o'er all their Swelling Hearts,
> Like neighbouring Worthies by the mildeft arts;
> They learn't fuch Forms as gave them full content;
> Of War, wife Laws, and happy Government."

The illustrations to these latter works are most deplorable, and betray the state of indigence to which the writer was reduced.

Slowly but surely, the shades of adverfity began to close around him. His press came to be less and less in demand. "Having but too much time to spare," he writes, "rather than be indolent, I studied music on the harp, flute, and other instruments."[*]　It was not Gent's only misfortune to be surpaffed by other and more enterprifing printers, he lost poffeffion of a house in Stonegate which had been the property of his wife's late husband, and which he hoped to have tenanted when he should be obliged to leave his present premises in Coffee Yard.　These he might, no doubt, have retained until his death, but he quarrelled with the owners, and had to remove to a house in Petergate, from whence he iffued the following quaint Advertifement :—

"*To all Ingenious Lovers of Art and Industry.*—Having in the Year 1724,
"removed my Printing Prefs and Letters from *London* to this ancient City, on
"the occasion of efpoufing the Widow of Mr. *Charles Bourne*, Printer, Grandfon
"to the memorable Mr. *John White;* and fince then followed my lawful Profeffion,
"for the preservation of my Family, with uncommon Care and Induftry, to the
"prefent Time:　I take this happy opportunity in giving Notice, that I am now
"removed into PETER-Gate, (that which is called the *Lower Part* of it) but a
"little way from *Stone-Gate.*—I humbly hope, thro' Divine assistance, that the
"favourable munificence of my friends, confidering the Contingencies in Life,
"will generously extend to the place of my new Settlement, *repair'd* to withftand
"the *Inclemency* of the weather, *freed* from all *filthy* Incumbrances, and by *credible*
"Apartments fit to entertain the better Sort of *well-bred* Lodgers, or Cuftomers that
"rightly encourage the true Typographical Artists; those only that become fuch
"by virtue of *lawful* Indentures, *&c.* and not by *interloping furreptitious* Methods,
"to the Ruin of honest Practitioners!　Which Houfe in *Petergate* is made as
"neceffary for a *Printing Office*, as tho' it had been contrived *Two* Hundred Years
"ago:　Where Books in *Greek, Latin* and *English;* also *Mathematical* Work;
"Warrants, Hand Bills, *&c.* may be printed in a neat and correct manner.—
"Likewife all Sorts of curious Printing Work, that Gentlemen and others shall
"have occafion to use, can artfully be done to Satisfaction;　Travellers furnished
"with Various Sorts of Chapmen's Books; Paper, Pens and Ink to be Sold ; as
"also the Celebrated *Daffey's* Elixer, with Pictures, and various other forts of
"Goods.

---

[*] In his "Hiftory of Rome," is a Poem on the Harp and Music, p. 59, and a singular Cut and Gamut of the Harp, p. 376.

In order to set before the public the extremities to which he was reduced, he composed and afterwards printed a prologue to the tragedy of " Jane Shore " that was performed for his benefit in 1761.   The poor, infirm old man mounted the stage, to pronounce this prologue, which he entitled, " The contingencies, viciffitudes, or changes of this tranfitory life."   I cannot refrain from quoting a few lines :—

> "Strange that a Printer, near worn out thro' age,
> Should be impell'd, fo late, to mount the Stage,
> In silver'd hairs, with Heart nigh fit to break,
> Thus to amuse, who fcarce has words to fpeak!
> ......To know such judges that I'm sure are here
> Might strike a bold Demosthenes with fear!
> To fee an audience so illuftrious shine
> Like Constellations, by the Power Divine.....
> Free of four Cities, thus my state to view,
> My fervants gone, fcarce anything to do:
> My deareft friends laid in the filent grave
> And me o'erpower'd, funk well nigh to a slave!....
> Depriv'd of Business, tho' with little left,
> And even that, for wishing well, bereft:....
> And here, methinks, amongst you 'tis I spy,
> As when kind Pity grac'd the tender Eye:
> When pence, spontaneous, but by you made willing,
> Were dropt, a tester, or a splendid Shilling.
> " How does your Spoufe? To folace her, give that—
> Don't stand uncover'd ! Pray, put on your hat—
> There, take, and drink—to comfort you—a gill "—
> (O how my foul with gratitude did fill !)
> " Let's see your ware—Come, be with Fate content—
> Get fomething warm, fo farewell, Mr. Gent."
> If in deep ficknefs, fovereign Balm could eafe ;
> If, in dejection, any Comforts please :
> 'Tis certain, from fuch tender Words they came,
> That blew the dying Sparks of Life to flame."

Between the recitation, and the printing of the Prologue, Gent was thrown into a still deeper affliction by the loss of his wife,— "It was, " he says, " on Wednesday, April 1, 1761, between the hours of X and XI in the night, that my beloved dear, Mrs. Alice Gent, meekly refigned up her precious soul (that curious and unsearchable part of Divinity) to its Maker: leaving me in a disconsolate Condition."

Poor Gent was forced at last, to become the recipient of charity, and to depend often for his food upon the bounty of the few friends that remained to him. It was a sad termination to a life that opened so fair, and with such promifing anticipations.

An unyielding and irascible temper doubtless produced many bitter fruits, still we cannot but admire the fimple piety, the honesty of principle, and the unswerving loyalty that characterised the man. He was generous even to a fault, and would often protect and relieve, in distress, those who had shown themselves his greatest enemies. In the last years of his life, as he saw the "things that are shaken" totter and fall, there is no doubt but that he learned to plant his feet more firmly, beyond the waves of time, upon the Eternal rock, among the "things that cannot be shaken."

We have no circumstantial account of his death, which took place at his house in Petergate, on the 19th of May, 1778. He was in the 87th year of his age. The old man sleeps in the filent shade of the Church of St. Michael-le-Belfrey,—" Where the wicked cease from troubling, and where the weary are at rest."

Grammar School, Hull,   GEO. OHLSON.
     May, 1869.

e of Mr Tho: Gent. Engrav'd & Prin
Engrav'd & Pri

Annales Regioduni Hullini :
OR, THE
HISTORY

Of the ROYAL and *Beautiful* TOWN of

Kingston-upon-Hull,

From the Original of it, thro' the Means of its Illuſtrious
FOUNDER, King *EDWARD* the Firſt : Who (being pleas'd with its
·beautiful Situation whilſt hunting with his Nobles on the pleaſant
Banks of the River) erected the TOWN *Anno Dom.* 1296 : And
from that remarkable Æra, the Viciſſitudes of it are diſplay'd, 'till
this preſent Year, 1735.

IN WHICH ARE INCLUDED,

All the moſt remarkable Tranſactions Eccleſiaſtical, Civil,
and Military.

The Erection of Churches, Convents, and Monaſteries ; with
the Names of their Founders,
and Benefactors : Alſo a ſuc-
cinct Relation of the *De la
POLE's* Family, from the firſt
MAYOR of that Name, to his
Succeſſors, who were advanc'd
to be Earls and Dukes of *Suffolk.*

The Monuments, Inſcriptions,
&c. in the Churches of HOLY
TRINITY, and St. MARY.

The Names of the MAYORS,
SHERIFFS, and *Chamberlains :*
with what remarkable Acci-
dents have befallen ſome of
them in the Courſe of their
LIVES : Interſpers'd with a
Compendium of *British* Hiſtory,
eſpecially what alludes to the
Civil Wars, (for the better Il-
luſtration of ſuch Things as
moſt particularly concern'd the
Town in thoſe troubleſome
Times ;) and ſince then, with
Regard to the *Revolution.*

𝔄𝔡𝔬𝔯𝔫𝔢𝔡 𝔴𝔦𝔱𝔥 ℭ𝔲𝔱𝔰.

AS LIKEWISE

Various CURIOSITIES in ANTIQUITY, HISTORY, TRAVELS, *&c.*
Alſo a neceſſary and compleat INDEX to the Whole.
Together with ſeveral LETTERS, containing ſome Accounts of the
ANTIQUITIES of *BRIDLINGTON, SCARBOROUGH,
WHITBY,* &c. for the Entertainment of the curious Travellers,
who viſit the North-Eaſt Parts of *Yorkshire.*

Dî probos mores docili juventæ,
Dî ſenectuti placidæ quietem,
Oppido HULLINO *date, remque prolem-*
que et decus omne. HOR. Car. Sæc.

Faithfully collected by THOMAS GENT, *Compiler of the* Hiſtory *of*
YORK, *and the moſt remarkable Places of that large* County.

SOLD at the Printing-Office, near the *Star* in *Stone-Gate,* YORK ;
by WARD and CHANDLER, Bookſellers, in *Scarborough,* and at
their Shop in *Fleet-ſtreet,* LONDON ; by GEORGE FERRABY, Book-
ſeller, in *HULL* ; at other Places in the Country ; and by
J. WILFORD, behind the Chapter-Houſe in *St. Paul's* Church-
Yard, LONDON. M DCC XXXV.

To All
Ingenious LOVERS
OF
ANTIQUITY
AND
HISTORY:
THIS
WORK
Is Dedicated by
Their Moſt Obſequious
And Humble Servant,

THOMAS GENT.

The PREFACE.

*MONGST the many Writers of* English *Hiſtory in general, as to the affairs of the Kingdom, and of ſome of them relating to the particular Places of it; I have often wonder'd, that the Subjects, I have treated of, should not, through their greater Capacities, have been brought from their* Cimmerian *Darkneſs, to have ſeen the Light before, but fallen to my Share to introduce them to their pleaſing* AURORA. *Works, that, for their Fidelity and Induſtry, have been candidly received by the moſt ingenuous and* ſenſible *Perſons in theſe Parts; whoſe kind Letters to me are as ſo many fair Teſtimonials of their entire Approbation: To oblige whom, I have endeavour'd, in this* Third Book, *not only to give an impartial* HISTORY *of a moſt Renowned Sea-Port* TOWN, *throughout all the ſtrange Viciſſitudes of it; but alſo, by a neceſſary and pleaſing Interſperſion of ſeveral remarkable Tranſactions, compleat in a great meaſure what I had attempted before: For their Sake have I valu'd no Labour, or Expence; no Diſcouragements could anticipate my Deſigns, in regard to the force of* TRUTH, *under its various Appearances in the World, whether fortunate or unhappy.*

If any Motive can induce a Reader to have a tender Regard for a labouring Author; certainly the Work of Antiquity (relating either to the Riſe of States, or Families) demand a favourable Attention. To know what has paſt in ſo many shining Ages before our glimmering Dawn of Life; and to conſider the Origin and Decay, the Virtue or Vice of illuſtrious and unfortunate Perſons, long ſince departed to the eternal Regions of Joy *or* Miſery; *are to a contemplative Mind as differently entertaining, as tho' we were now prophetically to be ſenſible of what should follow many Years after our Bodies were laid in the Mold. Alas! the Knowledge of the latter, might, in many reſpects, be a great Addition to our preſent certain Sorrows of Life: But by Retroſpection, we learn to imitate whatever was commendable in our Anceſtors; and to shun the contrary, equal to what Futurity would teach us, by our Succeſſors. With mighty Pleaſure we can behold the*

one;

*one; with profitable Contempt, despise the other: We are made to understand the Customs and Manners of former Ages, the better to have a greater Relish for the Improvements of our own: Our Offspring will become wise, free from the Scorn of Foreigners, when they can discourse knowingly of their Original: And, being conversant concerning their fading Earthly Habitations, have a greater Gust for their more lasting and * Cælestial.*

What exceeding Transports of Delight are afforded to us in many Passages of the Sacred Scriptures! The Creation of the World, the Formation of Human Bodies, the Building of Towers, the Ark, &c. fill us with Pleasure and Surprize: Nay, we are pleas'd with the Invention of the † Poet, who imitates some of these Things, in his Accounts of the first Formation from a Chaos, Promethean *Fires, and* Deucalion's *Flood. The Renown of* Troy, *even by its Fall, is become more glorious, than ever perhaps it was in Reality, thro' its being mournfully celebrated by the immortal* HOMER: *And* JERUSALEM, *once a most renowned City, now scarce any more than a little Village, how sweetly is it lamented and commemorated by the most mellifluous and inspired Writers! So that it seems to have a Being, tho' in miserable Ruins, as it is deliver'd down to us, thro' the powerful Charms of* ANTIQUITY.

If we descend only to Britain, *we even relish the unsavory Accounts, when the Natives are said to have worn little or no Garments,.had no Houses to dwell in; but. rude Skins of wild Beasts served for the former, shady Trees and Forests the latter. As we find how their Politeness and Felicity increas'd, our Joy rises in Proportion at the Recital: The Valour of the Kings* ‡ Caractacus *and* Casibelanus,

---

* A Rev. Gentleman, writing of the pious and learned *Mr. BOEHM,* (who, in the Year 1686, was Secretary to Prince GEORGE of *Denmark,* and after his Resignation of that Employment had travell'd to *Russia, Constantinople, Smyrna, Jerusalem, Alexandria,* &c.) has this most beautiful Passage concerning him. "How "often have I heard him withdraw from that *Jerusalem* which is *below,* to that which "is *above!* How often did he improve the Sepulchre which enclosed our Lord's *dead* "Body, towards framing the Hearts of Christians, wherein the *living* Christ is to "dwell by Faith! At least did his Journey to the Holy Land afford him many a fair "Opportunity to an holy Discourse. The earthly *Canaan,* which he had view'd with "the eyes of his Body, proved but introductory to the heavenly.—What he had begun, "he would frequently end with some noble instructive Direction; and silently move "away to the *Spiritual* Part, which is to be contemplated by Faith only, and to "which all our Actions ought to tend. And in this he endeavour'd to copy after the "Pattern of his blessed Master; who, whilst he was talking about *Jacob's* Well with "the Woman of *Samaria,* drew away by little and little into the spiritual Sphere; "and laying aside the *natural* Water, discoursed her about the Well which *springs* "up into *Life everlasting.*"

† Pub. OVID. Nasonis Metam. Lib. I.

‡ Some of the Brass Heads, which belong'd to the antient British Spears, or Javelins, curiously made, were found lately between *Tadcaster* and *Weatherby;* with two or three large Rings, and other Matters of Antiquity.

Cafibelanus, *with the unexampled Courage of Queen* Boadicea, *raife us to a Pitch of Admiration: Pleas'd, we behold the Expertnefs of their Succeffors in War; their Wifdom, and Piety, in Policy, or Religion; and admire them for all the neceffary Laws, either contrived by them, or copy'd after other Nations, for the common Good of Human Society.*

As to the following Work, I had an intention to perform fomething relating to Kingfton-upon-Hull *about four or five Years ago, foon after my fuccefsful Publication of the Hiftory of* YORK. *On purpofe I vifited the Town, took down the Infcriptions that were within the Church, with what I found remarkable in other Places, as the firft Foundation, whereon I might lay a ftronger, the better to erect my Superftructure. Afterwards, by Application, I met with fundry Manufcripts; which, tho' exceeding ufeful as to Matters of Fact contained in them, were yet confounded by an unhappy Difcordancy: Befides, their Incorrectnefs plung'd me into almoft infuperable Difficulties, thro' which it would have been impoffible for me to have extricated my felf, had I not perfonally perform'd what I did, and carefully confulted our lateft Hiftorians. The Prolixity of thofe tedious Writings were more fit for tirefome Volumes to be Clofetted, and laboriously turn'd over, than what was ufeful for a pleafant Pocket Companion, plain to the meaneft Capacity; lefs troublefome to the Learned themfelves; and, above all, at an eafy Price, confidering the great Expence and Labour of fuch an Enterprize: So that when I had ferioufly ponder'd on every thing neceffary, with the utmoft Impartiality, I was refolv'd to write an entire Piece, which I might more truly call my own; and adorn it with whatever could be productive from a ftudious Application.*

FIRST, I was determin'd to follow the Methods of the beft Authors, by dividing the Book into certain Periods, or Chapters; that fo the Reader might have the greater Relaxation, and more pleafantly refume the Perufal at proper Opportunities.

SECONDLY, I defign'd to exhibit the Names of the Right Worshipful the * Magiftrates, with other Officers of the Corporation, in or near the fame Pages, which alphabetically refer to what Tranfactions happen'd whilft They were in Power; that fo, as it were

* As I proceeded, in the nearer Centuries following the Town's Erection, I ventur'd to fuppofe how many times fome of the Gentlemen had been Mayors, by taking Notice of their firft Advancement to inferior Offices; and therefore numerated them accordingly, as to me they appeared moft reafonable: But of thofe in later Ages I became more afcertain'd, thro' my Examination of the Infcriptions over their Graves within the Churches. And where I had the leaft Reason to doubt of the true Spelling of Names, thro' their being differently written, I have inferted them both Ways, according to my two calculated Manufcripts, (which I had collated out of many) that fo the Truth might be found in one, or the other.

were at one Sight, there might be a pleafing Cohærency one with
another.

THIRDLY, Digeft what was * neceffary, in the fame Manner,
under the feveral Heads of Difcourfe.

And, LASTLY, By a compleat Index, bring the collateral
Branches to a clofer Union, that every Thing might be found out
as eafy as poffible by the curious Enquirer.

*Well—Thus fix'd, as I thought, in my Refolution, I fet about
the Work: But, alas! I had not proceeded far, before I found the
Subjects to grow upon me, by an improving Imagination; yet
attended with fuch a Charge, and Confumption of Time, that were
in no manner fuitable to one Perfon alone, efpecially in my Station
of Life. I feem'd much in the defponding Condition of the unfortunate Sir* John Hotham, *as related in the* 155*th Page of this
Book; who, having no friendly Bark to attend him, was ftopt by
a deep River, whilft he thought through Flight to attain to an
Afylum of Safety, which then was his fortify'd Houfe at* Scarborough. *Tho' the Knight had not the Valour of* Alexander,
who fwam over the Hydafpes *to face a powerful Army; yet he
had a View of meeting with fome Affiftance, which might have
reviv'd his Courage, could he have but crofs'd thofe rapid Streams:
My Profpect, over the* BITTER *Waters of* UNCOMMON *Induftry,
was nothing but a melancholly Scene of almoft infinite Labour and
Expence, I fcarce could fay, I knew to what End. Only there was
this Difference (which raifed my Hope) between the diftreffed
Knight's Cafe, and mine: He was deferting the Town of* Hull; *I
flying for Protection to it. Whether this Thought might prove of
Effect or no, I was refolved to wait with Patience and Refigna-
tion. As I knew the Copioufnefs of the Subjects might require
greater Labours, my Defign was to make* This *as comprehenfive
and acceptable as I could for the prefent; and, where I fell fhort,
fupply Deficiencies, fome time or other, by* a careful and faithful
SUPPLEMENT to the Whole.

*And here, I muft humbly beg of the more curious Reader, to
fufpend a while his Judgment, 'till he has given the Book a careful
Perufal, and confider'd juftly the indefatigable Pains of fuch a
Compofition:*

---

* Among the many Epitaphs, there are fome that are really affecting and
religious, efpecially in the Towns along the Sea Shore: They feem like preaching
Lectures to prepare us for thofe immenfe Regions of Immortality, *before we go hence,
no more to be feen* in this World! Some are placed according to the Wills of the
Deceafed; others of 'em thro' tender Refpect of their furviving Friends; and all for
the due Contemplation of Human Nature, which furely muft, one time or other, be
laid within the earth, in order to appear at the General Refurrection, to Life or Death
eternal: Of which the Poet writes,

*Judicis extremâ fententia luce vocabit
Ad fua Regna bonos,* Phlegethonta *Malos.*

Compofition: For without Candour, I am almoft certain, no true Character can be given. If afterwards it can be prov'd that I have been defective and exceedingly *erroneous, as few Authors this way can be entirely free; if I have corrupted Hiftory by defigned Partiality, and not related Things as they have been acted: Why then, should any Perfon, after a decent Manner, with the Spirit of Meeknefs, employ the Prefs, by doing of* a Better *within the like Compafs; or to confute me, and put his Name thereto, (for the* *unknown Envious *or* Ignorant, *which are* † *fynonimous, are either not worth regarding, or to be anfwer'd in another Method) if I find the Arguments are of any Validity, I shall be very willing for the Publick Good, to own all the Errors in the Book, were it poffible there should be an Infinity of them: But otherwife, I shall return a modeft Anfwer, in the fame Spirit, by way of defending what ought to be defended, fuch as, I hope, will give no Reafon for any Perfon juftly to complain againft me. For indeed, as to the Civil Wars, when* England *was ftain'd with the Blood of its Nobility and Gentry, I think fcarce any can mention thofe dreadful Times, without raifing the Paffions of the Mind, in one, or another, according to the different Principles of Mankind: In which, tho' I ever approv'd of Moderation, I was to consider myfelf as an Hiftorian, and confequently ought not to recede from Truth a Tittle. I knew I was exempt from the Objections of Persons in the prefent Age, whom I had nothing to do with (at leaft little to fear from) in this Refpect; fince the beft and greater Number of us, I truft, are so firmly attach'd to Regal Dignity, for the Sake of our Prefent* Gracious SOVEREIGN, *as never to be led to approve of fuch wicked Actions, as were formerly perpetrated, to the Downfal of the Reform'd Epifcopal Church of* England, *and the well-fettled State of the Nation, by the unparallel'd Murder of one of the beft of Kings! Events, which poffibly might have been prevented, was it not for the undutiful Behaviour of Sir* John Hotham *to his highly injur'd Majefty; for which Crime divine Vengeance feem'd to purfue him, whilft he fcarcely enjoy'd the Benefit of Repentance.*

I

---

* Were even fuch *fenfelefs,* unkilling *Satyrifts to be known,* who should happen with other *natural* and *endemic* Diftempers to be troubled with the *Scribling* ITCH, and *write* (in meer *Malice*) againft what they had never the *Glorious Spirit* to *undertake;* the wifeft of Sovereign Princes, King SOLOMON had given Advice to Mankind in both the Cafes above-mentioned, *Prov.* vi. 4, 5. the laft of which feems very proper: *Refponde* Stolido *fecundum ftultitiam ejus, &c.* In like manner should all *Ill·Vill—ns* or *Sc—bby Sc—d—ls* whatever be ferv'd, who might elfe abufe their own *Fathers* and *Mothers;* nay, facrifice their very Religion for Intereft Sake! 'Tis the part of *charitable Doctors* to cure fuch filthy Wretches, who should offer to *poifon* what is defign'd to be ufeful to the World, and which *may* flourish in fpite of the whole Race of *l—fy, beggarly* SOTS, who (like horrid *Letter-Droppers*) might fuppofe their wicked *Dulnefs* and impious *Impudence* would frighten Mankind from their *Free* Habitations.

† *ENVY* slayeth the *Silly One.* JOB V. 2.

I could have wish'd there had been no Occasion for me to mention the dismal Catastrophe of either ; but I could not avoid it, as they concern'd this History in a very particular Manner.

To lay aside therefore such melancholly Remarks, let us turn our Thoughts towards the TOWN *as in its former State.* 'Twas *such, that, as it were, might, for its Gates, Walls, Towers, &c. gain the Appellation of a Pretty* CITY. *Mr.* Camden *has long since made Report of its being famous for* † *stately Edifices, strong Fortifications, &c. abounding with Opulency and Plenty. Nay, he stiles the Inhabitants* * Citizens, *who inform'd him how they were first govern'd by a Warden ; and confirm'd what was before his Time, as I have related in the following Sheets.*

Pleasant would the Prospect have been, had it been taken in those Times, when Buildings were more pompous, tho' perhaps less useful, than at present : For Religious Houses seldom wanted the Ornaments of Towers, Turrets, Spires, Contraforts and Battlements, to make 'em look more venerable : But, Thanks be to GOD, *there are now two fair Churches, that give Lustre to the Town ; which have escaped the Rage of wicked Men, and become the Places where our most Holy and Orthodox Religion is profess'd. To ornament this Work, I caused two Copper-Plates to be engraved : One a South Prospect of the largest and most beautiful Edifice, dedicated to the* Holy Trinity ; *the other, an East View of the Town which in part exhibits that consecrated to St.* Mary : *In both of which, so many Right Worshipful and Honourable Persons (whose Memories ought ever to be held in Veneration for that Piety, Virtue, and Charity, which adorn'd their Lives) now lie reposited. Other Matters I have only inserted as common Ornaments of the Press ; of which, tho' I cannot utter much, yet I am satisfy'd are not to be discommended ; and might be a Crime if omitted, (especially the* Plan, *which shews the Streets, Lanes, &c.) because instructive to distant Readers.*

And what can appear more beautiful, or be more refreshing, than the Haven, resembling for Colour as it were an Ocean of Silver, into which so many Rivers discharge themselves ! Here I must inform my Readers what Camden *has mention'd concerning it.* Ptolomy, *he says, call'd it the* Æstuary Abus ; *the* Saxons, HUMBER ; *and consequently, the Land, lying North of it,* North-Humber-Land, *which became a great Kingdom in the* Heptarchy.
But

---

† Ut magnificis ædificiis, firmis propugnaculis, navibus instructissimis, mercatorum copiâ, & rerum omnium affluentiâ sit nunc emporium hujus tractus longè celeberrimum.   *CAM. Pag.* 579.

* Pro Magistratu (ut à *Civibus* accepi) primum Custodem habuit, inde Ballivos, postea Majorem cum Ballivis, &c.   *ibid.*

But the Names of ‡ both, he thinks, are derived from Aber, *a British Word, which denotes the Mouth of a River ; and perhaps might be given to this by Way of Eminence, (writes his excellent Improver) because the* Eurus, *or* Ouse, *with all those Streams that flow into it, and other great Rivers of Note, come tumbling in here. An * Æstuary, which certainly is the largest belonging to* Britain, *and most abounding with the Finny Race.* Alexander Necham, *a Poet, is quoted, who agrees with what is written, as to the Name of* Humber, *and the Danger it threatens Mariners with at certain Times : All which I shall thus paraphrase.*

> Each Flux and Reflux seems more dreadful far
>   To Careful Pilots, than *Neptunian* † Waves ;
> Rapid the Streams, the Murmurs frightful are,
>   Which seem to point to them their wat'ry Graves !
> Proudly it passes Towns, with lofty Spires ;
>   Far in the Country force the flowing Tides :
> Nor less seems dreadful, when it back retires,
>   And borrow'd Streams within the Ocean hides.

As †† Necham, *and* ** *another Poet, intimate, that the first Syllable of* Humber *was properly to be deriv'd from a Country or People that belong'd to a Prince, who (flying from a* British *King that pursu'd him) perish'd in the Streams; I shall thus alter the Translation.*

> †† The Prince of *Hunns* turns Back to King *Locrine* :
>   Flying, the Waters stop him with his Breath ;
> *Humber !* his Fate gave thee that Name of thine ;
>   And thou can'st boast of giving him his Death.

But I hope this famous Æstuary is not so dangerous now, as it
was

---

‡ Utrumque nomen ex *Aber* Britannico deflexum videatur, quod fluminis ostium illis denotat, & huic igitur impositum existimem, quòd *Urus*, sive *Ousa* plurimos fluvios suo hospitio exceptos in hoc deducit, aliáque maximi nominis flumina in illud evolvuntur.   *CAM. Pag.* 577.

* Et certe totius Britanniæ æstuarium est amplissimum, & piscosissimum.

   † *Fluctibus æquoreis nautis suspectior Humber,*
     Dedignans urbes visere, rura colit.

A Reverend Antiquary tells us, That the Sea has swallow'd up several Towns that were in *Holdernefs,* whose Names were *Frismerk, Tharlethorp, Redmayr, Penysthorp,* and *Ravenspurn.* To which some have added, *Botevante* and *Grimston.*

   †† *Hunnorum princeps ostendens terga Locrino,*
     Submersus nomen contulit Humbris aquæ.

   ** *Dum fugit, obstat ei flumen, submergitur illic,*
     Deque suo tribuit nomine, nomen aquæ.

CAM. Pag. 577.

was in antient Times; at leaſt, that our Mariners, growing more expert in Navigation, know better how to avoid or paſs by what might otherwiſe precipitately prove their Deſtruction.   The River HULL, whoſe Riſe is from the Woulds, *has a near vicinity to this Conflux, along with* Little-Ouſe, Aire, Calder, || Wharfe, *and* Eure; *alſo* Trent, Darwent-manifold, *and* Ankham, *out of* Lincolnshire: *All of which empty themſelves into the* German *Ocean.*

I have thus dwelt upon theſe Deſcriptions, becauſe neceſſary to illuſtrate the Proſpects mention'd a little before, which were chiefly deſign'd to preſerve the fair Ideas to diſtant Readers, who dwell upon the Land; or for the Entertainment of thoſe Mariners, who are Lovers of this Port *and* Town, *whilſt they are pleaſantly ſailing (ſwiftly before the Wind) with fresh and proſperous Gales: When (in being exempted from foaming Billows and raging Storms, which require the utmoſt Labour to preſerve the tottering Veſſels) they may have little elſe to do, than divert themſelves by peruſing this Hiſtory; and conſequently, being better furnish'd with the Knowledge of what they have but tranſiently ſeen, their Diſcourſe may be render'd more delightful, in thoſe Towns abroad, whoſe Inhabitants are Lovers of* Kingſton-upon-Hull, *when they have paſs'd the Ocean, and shall be ſafely arrived on the* Belgic *or* German *Shores.*

And here I muſt take ſome Notice of what makes not one of the leaſt Parts in this Work; and that is, an Account of the Family of the De la POLES, *with their ſurprizing Actions, ſince, by* * *One of them, who obtained great Priviledges for the Town, it was*
                                                                    firſt

---

|| Tho' there are many pretty Rivers in *England*, charming the Eyes, and captiva‑ting the Thoughts by their limpid Streams; yet, I think, none can exceed the *Wharfe* for Beauty, as I took Notice of it in travelling to viſit my Relations in the Weſtern Parts of *Yorkshire*. The Solitude, and pleaſant Murmuring of the Waters, with the delightful Banks on either Side, wou'd as well become the Seats of the Muſes, as ever *Cam*, *Iſis*, or *Thames*, were repreſented to adorn thoſe renowned for Learning. Nobody has taken Notice of it, as I have perceiv'd, except the ingenious and attract‑ing Mrs. *Mary Maiſters*, on Occaſion of her journey from *Otley* to *Wakefield*; who, having gain'd the Summit of a high Mountain, and ſurvey'd the pleaſing Variety of Nature below, beſtows this Encomium on the River, in a modeſt deſire, which might raiſe another in the Publick, that she would but endeavour to compleat the lovely Deſcription, which this Gentlewoman hinted at in theſe Lines.

"What vaſt Variety the Proſpect yields
"Of Rocks, and Woods, and Lawns, and flow'ry Fields!
"The winding *Wharfe*, the diff'rent Shades of Green,
"Houſes and Hills diverſify the Scene.
"Oh! could my Thoughts in riſing Numbers flow,
"Sprightly as *Wharfe*, and as delightful too;
"Strong, but yet clear, the wand'ring Stream should glide,
"Rush o'er its ſtoney Bed, and pour a Silver Tide,
"With diff'rent Courſes, thro' the verdant Vale,
"The Chiefeſt Beauty of the beauteous Dale."

* Quæ omnia accepta ferunt Cives partim Michaeli *De-la-Pole*, qui privilegia huic impetravit, &c.   *CAM. Pag.* 577.

firſt partly raised to its Grandeur, and ſoon after enabled to build a † Brick Wall, with many Towers, on that Side which was not defended by the River.   Indeed his Father, Sir William, *(who obtain'd of King* EDWARD *the Third that never-to-be-forgotten Honour of having been the firſt* MAYOR *of* HULL) *had piously begun the famous Work of the Charter-Houſe, with other ſtately Buildings; but Death cloſing his Eyes before the Deſires of his Heart were accomplished, his glorious Son* MICHAEL *Lord of* Wingfield *finiſh'd it, gave a Charter thereto as hereafter mention'd, and built a moſt ſtately Palace for his Reſidence, of which there is a remarkable Account of the Manner of its Structure : Yet, for all his good Deeds, his being a faithful Subject, an able Stateſman, true to his King, and a lover of his Country, he was forced into* France, *where he obſcurely ended his Days.   His Succeſſors were ſeveral of them unfortunate thro' their Attachment to their Prince, for which they ſuffer'd the greateſt Calamities, even Death itſelf, and frequently murder'd in their Reputations, in being made the Sport of every inſipid Writer, or gingling Poetaſter.   A Family ſo unfortunately remarkable, and by whoſe Influence this happy Town received ſo many ſignal Favours, I have traced, as far as I was able, almoſt from their Beginning to the Period of their Glory ! From whom this ſerious Reflection may be drawn, That, to our Vigilance, we should add Contentment in every Station of Life ; ſince neither Virtue, Honour, Riches, Palaces, or fair Eſtates, are ſo durable, as to enſure us from the Force of Vice, Slander, Decay, Deſtruction, or the Snares of deſigning Perſons :   So that by ſeriously conſidering the unhappy Fall of this once Great Family, we may leſs wonder at, and endeavour more chearfully to bear, whatever Afflictions may happen to ourſelves.*

I think I have but little more to add, fearing that I have enlarg'd too much already.   What further I wou'd remark, is, That a Book of this famous Town, having never been fully publiſhed before, may be an Inducement to a kind Reception.   I would not have it, or any other Production of mine, prevent the Grand Deſigns of thoſe more capable, (I hope I may add more induſtrious) *when ever they shall be heartily intended by* ſuch *Perſons.   May all imaginable Succeſs, I ſincerely pray, attend them, purely for the Sake of their Labours ! Certainly what I've done, to prevent Diſchroniſm, or Errors relating to Matters of Fact, and ſmoothing out the overgrown and almoſt untrodden Paths of Antiquity, muſt be a very great Aſſiſtance to further Enquiries.   Without Vanity, I*

may

---

† Unde brevi admodum ſpatio lateritio muro, crebrisque turribus urbem ſuam fepſerunt, qua flumine non defenditur.   *CAM. Pag.* 577.

*may affirm, that far lefs Pains have (from learned Pens) met
with greater Approbation than ever, God knows, I shall either
expect or defire.   But 'till fuch fublimer Works do appear in
shining Luftre, whofe glittering Beams shall as it were quite
eclipfe the fading Glories of mine ; I hope I may fay to every kind
Reader what the ingenious Poet faid to his advifed Friend, which
is often juftly quoted in the like Cafes.*

    * Live, *and* farewell.   If any Thing you know
        Better than thefe, I pray you now be free :
        Fairly impart them ; *make your Wit to flow ;*
        If not, then ufe thefe Rules along with me.

*And as I defign'd this to be the laft Work I should ever under-
take in Search of Things of this Nature, (unlefs perhaps to reprint
fome of my former Editions) I have communicated to the World,
in feveral Letters, what have been fent me from various Places :
Wherein there is fuch a pleafant Intermixture of Wit among the
ferious Thoughts of Antiquity, that I hope will be look'd upon as
confiderable Additions ; and prove very delightful to thofe curious
Perfons, who travel to* Whitby, Scarborough, *and other. Towns
along the Shore.   I return my hearty Thanks to thofe generous
Encouragers, from whom I had the leaft Affiftance towards promoting this Work, or have been Well-Wishers to it.   Nor have
my Enquiries been wanting as I had Opportunities to gather what
was remarkable : Thus have I done myfelf the Honour to commem-
orate the late Reverend, Pious and Learned Dr.* CHARLES
BLAKE, † *Subdean of* York, &c. *in Refpect that I was one of
his Parishioners when he was the worthy Minifter of* S.
Sepulchre's *Church in* London *: And thro' the great Efteem the
late famous Sir* WILLIAM DAWES, *Bart. had for that excellent Divine (as mention'd in the Infcription wrote of him by his
Friends) have, by inferting it, given a Sanction to my Page, as
being adorn'd with the Name of One of the moft glorious Prelates,
once belov'd and admir'd, and whofe Memory will ever be precious,
for the Bleffings he was endow'd, with, both for Prefence of Body
and Mind, with every Ornament of Virtue becoming his venerable
Character, as ever yet adorn'd the Throne of this Archiepifcopal See.
To conclude this (I fear) too long a Preface : If all the Pains I
have taken, will prove of any Service or Delight to the Reader ; if
bringing the Glory of our Anceftors in paft Ages, as it were from*
                                        their

---

    * Vive, vale. Si quid novifti rectius iftis,
      Candidus imperti : fi non, his utere mecum.   *HOR.*

  † He lies intomb'd under a handfome Monument in St. *Helen's* Church-Yard
at *Wheldrake,* near *York.* See Page 63, &c. of this Book.

*their Tombs and Sepulchres, will be pleasant to be remember'd by
the present: I shall then think my Labours happily compensated,
and bless kind Providence for enabling me to perform whatever can
be acceptable to the World. Nay, should it prove the contrary, I
do not in the least doubt of receiving that reciprocal Kindness from
it, in being suffer'd silently to slide away into that dark Obscurity,
from which I thought to withdraw the Veil, that the glorious
Actions of others might appear afresh for our Imitation. I write
this, not that I court the Favour of the Envious: For none, who
may think to gain any Advantage by (or satisfy their unreason-
able Malice in) running down any authentick Labours, as tho' my
Destruction alone was intended, shall never by me be own'd as competent Judges. But to the far Better and Disinterested Part of the
World, in each Sex, and every Degree; who are not to be deceiv'd
by the gilded Folly of ridiculous Calumniators; can perceive by
candid and impartial Examination where there is real true Merit
from pretended; and, by considering the Greatness of the Design,
will tenderly excuse some almost unavoidable Errors that may
happen in a first, but laudable Attempt: To These, (These only) do
I submit myself, and lay this my Performance at their Feet: who,
I trust in GOD, as they are to be my Judges on this Occasion, will
have just Reason to prove my Advocates too. But, let the Consequences be whatever they will, my Respect, whilst I have Breath,
shall continue steadfast to the Town of* Kingston-upon-Hull: *May
its flourishing Inhabitants be ever happy, and never suffer such like
wretched Contingencies, to which they have been formerly expos'd!
May Prosperity be continually flowing with the welcome Tides
towards their celebrated Haven, and safely land upon the happy
Shore! May their late Gratitude to the Memory of their Glorious
Deliverer, meet with a just Regard from their Royal Defender!
Harmony and Union adorn the Magistrates; Love and Obedience
be the glory of the People: That so, after many comfortable Ages,
and happy successions, both in Church and Civil Government, the
Corporation may still flourish more and more, without the least
Interruption, or Declension, 'till the End of the World.*

YORK, *June*
11, 1735.   THOMAS GENT:

THE

THE
CONTENTS
OF THE
CHAPTERS.

CHAP. I. *Of the Nature and Situation of the Land, before the* TOWN *was erected; and of its fuccefsful Beginning, in the Reign of King* EDWARD *the Firft, thro' Means of that Monarch's being wonderfully taken with the delightful Profpects, both by Land and Water, as he was hunting along the Shore with his Nobles.*   Page 1

CHAP. II. *Of the Building of the* High-Church, *dedicated to the* HOLY TRINITY : *With the Monuments and Infcriptions, at prefent therein, and in the Church-Yard : Likewife thofe of St.* MARY'S, *called the* Low-Church.   P. 13

CHAP. III. *Of the* MONASTERIES, *and other* Religious Houfes *in* Kingfton-upon-HULL ; *With an Account of their Benefactors ;*

[*⁎*]

Benefactors; but more especially of the Family of De la POLE, *some of whom came at last to be of Royal Blood.* P. 66

C H A P . IV. *An Account of the* Streets, Lanes, &c. *that are in* Kingston-upon-Hull. P. 82

C H A P . V. *Containing some few Incidents from the Foundation of the Churches, 'till the Time when the first* M A Y O R *of* Kingston-upon-Hull *was elected, in the Year* 1332. P. 86

C H A P . VI. *An Account of the Mayors, from the Year* 1332, *'till* 1439, *when a* Sheriff *was appointed: With what remarkable Accidents happened, relating to* HULL. P. 89

C H A P . VII. *A Continuation of the* MAYORS, *and Beginning of the* Sheriffs, *'till the Year of* CHRIST, 1561. P. 99

C H A P . VIII. *Continuation of the* MAYORS, *and* SHERIFFS, *together with some Account of the* Chamberlains, *and what Transactions have happened, relating to* Kingston-upon-Hull, *until the Year of* CHRIST, 1611. P. 121

C H A P . IX. *The Accounts carried down from the aforesaid Year, 'till the Death of King* CHARLES *the First.* P. 130

C H A P . X. *From thence to the Restoration of King* CHARLES II. *and so to the Beginning of the Reign of King* JAMES II. P. 169

C H A P . XI. *The Succession of* MAGISTRATES, &c. *brought down to the Revolution: With what remarkable Transactions happened thereupon.* P. 181

C H A P . XII. *Continuation of the* MAYORS, SHERIFFS, *and* Chamberlains, *with other Affairs, and Remarks, down to the present Times.* P. 190

A EX-

EXPLANATION

OF THE

Eaſt PROSPECT of the Royal Town of *Kingston-upon-Hull*.

[Which precedes the 𝕿𝖎𝖙𝖑𝖊-𝕻𝖆𝖌𝖊.]

AT the Top, on the Left Hand, is a Repreſentation of Part of an old Monaſtery, as ſuppoſing it to have been *Meaux* Abbey; becauſe from the Abbot of that Place, the Royal Founder King EDWARD the Firſt purchaſed the Ground where *Kingſton-upon-Hull* now ſtands: The King is alſo portray'd as hunting with his Nobles, *&c.*

On the Right Hand is delineated the Effigy of King *WILLIAM* III. of Ever-Glorious Memory.

Beneath is the Proſpect of the Town itſelf: And the Figures 1, 2, 3, *&c.* interſpers'd here and there, denote the following Particulars, *viz.*

1. *PArt of* Lincoln-shire.
2. HUMBER.
3. *South Block-House.*
4. *The Garriſon.*
5. *Governour's Houſe.*
6. *Soldiers Barracks.*
7. *H. Trinity Church.*
8. *Old Guard Houſe.*
9. *St.* Mary's *Church.*
10. *The Magazine.*
11. *North-Bridge.*
12. *Sugar-Houſe.*
13. Drypool *Church.*
14. *New-Cut.*

ERRATA. The literal *Errata* in the Book, I humbly ſubmit to my Readers; and hope they will be ſo kind, as to amend them with the Pen, where ever they ſhall find any.

THE

The ANTIENT *and* MODERN
H I S T O R Y
Of the TOWN, and COUNTY, of
KINGSTON-upon-*HULL*.

CHAP. I.

Of the Nature and Situation of the Land, before the Town was erected ; and of its successful Beginning in the Reign of King EDWARD *the First.*

HE Glorious Gospel of our Blessed REDEEMER, (first established in the *Northern* Parts, thro' Means of the exemplary Life, and powerful Preaching of PAULINUS, Archbishop of *York*, who converted *Edwin*, (Son of ALLA, the First Ruler of *Deira*) King of *Northumberland*, about the Year Six Hundred after CHRIST) was in seeming Perfection, according to the Devotion of that Age, in which the valourous King EDWARD the First magnificently ruled over this Realm ; and when,

A. D. 624, *&c.* EACH. *Hist. of* Engl.

thro'

thro' the Encouragement of that triumphant Monarch, the rich Town of *HULL* began to have its Rife. Surely this feemed, to the confiderate Perfons, then living, a moft happy Prefage of its future Glory, thro' the Graces and Ornaments of a Royal Prince, a devout Chriftian, and one of the moft renowned and victorious Heroes, that was then to be found throughout the whole Universe.

BUT, to look further back, and confider the Nature and Situation of the Place, it may not be improper to suppofe, That, in antient Times, all that Ground, whereon this Royal TOWN now ftands, was but a low barren Point of Land, extending itfelf, as an acute Angle, between the Rivers *Humber* and *Hull;* 'till, at length, their Streams, thro' a continual Overflowing, had caft up fo much Sand and Earth upon the fame, as raifed it to a competent Height and Drinefs. And, as Nature, unaffifted by Art, is often very flow in fuch defirable Improvements ; fo, we may reafonably give her the Time of fome Ages, fuppofing two or three hundred Years, for raifing this very Point, from its low Condition, unto the fufficient Height of being fafe and ufeful both to Man, or Beaft.

WHEN *Julius Cæfar*, the firft *Roman* Emperor, (after having conquer'd the powerful *Gauls*, either fir'd with the Prospect of New Glories in being alfo Sovereign of the Weftern World, or provok'd by the *Britains* fending Supplies to his Enemies in his late Wars) made two Expeditions into this Realm, which were between Fifty and Sixty Years before the Incarnation of the SON of GOD ; then the *Northern Parts* of *Great-Britain*, began to flourish from its former low Condition, and were in the large Kingdom of the *Brigantes*.

A. ant. C.
53.
52.

SOON after, the *Romans*, being called home, to defend their own Territories from the Incurfions of
the

the *Gothes, Swedes,* and *Vandals ;* the *Saxons* landed, and poffefs'd themfelves of the whole Island ; divided it into Kingdoms ; making themfelves Governors thereof ; and then, this Part fell to be in the Kingdom call'd *Deira,* which was afterwards by Conqueft united to that of *Northumberland.*

IT was, in thofe Times, that the *Danes* often invading the Land, us'd to vifit *Humber,* and the adjacent Shore, then but poor and almoft naked ! There they ferved the laborious Fishermen, with their humble Cottages, juft as thofe cruel, inhuman and bloody Wretches had before done, to thofe Perfons and Places, over whom, and where, they ever had obtain'd an arbitrary Power : That, in short, was, burning, murdering, ranfacking and deftroying all before them !

BUT, about One Hundred Years after thefe terrible Depopulations, the *Danes* being all driven out of the Realm ; by the wife and pacifick Management of King EDWARD the Confeffor, this Nation then enjoy'd a pretty conftant Peace, 'till the Death A. D. of the valiant King HAROLD ; which concluded the 1066. Empire of the *English Saxons,* in this Nation, (begun by HENGIST and HORSA, and fuftain'd with fome little Interruptions for about 617 Years) when WILLIAM, Duke of *Normandy,* by overthrowing his Army in Battle, in which that Hero was slain with an Arrow, obtain'd this Kingdom by Conqueft, and fo advanc'd himfelf to the Throne, Crown and Dignity of that unfortunate Prince.

THIS Monarch enjoy'd not his Victory above Four Years, before he was difturb'd by SWEYN, King of *Denmark :* Who, coming with a great Fleet into the *Humber ;* and, with his Soldiers, having deftroy'd all that was in the leaft valuable in the Country on both Sides the River, they proceeded to YORK, took and plunder'd that antient City, and miferably ruin'd the circumjacent Parts for feveral
Miles

Miles together. Among thofe, near *Hull*, that fuffer'd fuch lamentable Deftruction, an antient Manufcript has particularly recorded the Villages of *Ferriby, Drypool, Sculcotes*, and *Myton:* Which laft appears to have been a Hamlet, confifting of a few ftragling Houfes upon the Banks of *Humber;* and that this Part of the Country was then a kind of INGS, open Pafture, or Common. In the Fifteenth Year of the Reign of the Conqueror, he commanded a Survey to be taken (call'd *Doomfday-Book*, as tho' it fhould laft for authentic Truth to the Day of Judgment) of every City, Town, Village, Hamlet, Monaftry, Church, Chapel, Mill, *&c.* in the whole Kingdom; of all Land, Tillage, Meadow or Wafte; who were Owners and Tenants thereof; what they had been taxed at by the *Danes*, in the Reign of King EDWARD *the Confeffor*, or in the Time fince his afcending to the Throne. And this Survey certify'd his Majefty of every Place in this Part of the Country, as follows.

IN the Eaft-Riding of *Yorkshire*, (*Haffel*-Hundred) FERRIBY is mention'd as a Manor, in which EDINA " enjoys almoft 1000 Acres, that had been affeffed " at the *Dane-Gelt*, or Great Tax of the *Danes*, for " no more than 500*d.* RALPH *de* MORTIMER was " Lord of the Manor, and had there under him " 14 * Villains, or small Farmers, occupying 3 " Caracutes of Land, which amounted to 300 Acres. " There was alfo a Church, and a Minifter belong- " ing to it, in the Time of King EDWARD *the Con-* " *feffor:* The whole Manor, and all the Villa- " ages therein, were affeffed at One Hundred Pounds; " but afterwards, confidering the great Ravages " made by the *Danes*, it was only tax'd at Sixty."

---

* *Call'd fuch in thofe Days, as being Servants to the Lord, and accounted as Members annexed to his Manor.*

" To

"To the fame Manor of FERRIBY belonged
"then the following Villages, and Hamlets:
"*Kirk-Elley*, in which were only two Bovates
"of Land, that contained about 30 Acres of Til-
"lage; *Wandby*, 100 Acres for the fame Ufe;
"*Yeokfleet*, about the fame Number; *Riplingham*,
"120; *Myton*, about 140; *Wolferton*, much the
"fame; and about 100 in *Haffel.*" In the *Danish*
Tax, thefe were reckoned at 6 Caracutes and a half
(each being 125 Acres) befides thofe in *Ferriby*.
But moft of it lay wafte, thro' their cruel Divefta-
tions. Four Petty Farmers occupy'd one Cara-
cute in *Haffel*: The Archbishop of *York* had about
100 Acres in the Manor of *Sculcotes*, (or *Cowfcotes*)
and near 20 in that of *Drypool*. OTE and RAVEN-
HILL likewife poffeft about 130 Acres of Land;
which alfo were tax'd fo heavily at the *Dane-
Gelt*, that two of them lay ufelefs as the former;
'till, in the Time of King EDWARD *the Confeffor*, they were rated in a more reafonable
Manner.

FROM all which, it may be concluded, That this
Country was but very thinly inhabited before the
Norman Conqueft: That, as the *Danes* had, from
Time to Time, deftroy'd moft Part of it; fo, it lay
wafte and untill'd, in many Places, even to the
Time of this Survey, and perhaps for a long while
after: That *Ferriby*, tho' it contained not above
thirty Houfes, was then the chiefeft Town of this
Part of the Country; thofe leffer, fcarcely exceeding Twelve each: RALPH *de* MORTIMER
being the Lord, was likewife Owner of *Nechafom,
Spillington, Grypton, Briflon, Honvilgeton, Fulcarthorp,
Cheteleftorn, Middleburn*, &c. with feveral Territories in *Yorkshire*, as well as other Eftates in moft
Counties of *England*, from whofe Loins afterwards defcended the famous and renowned Earls
of MARCH.

IT

IT is alſo evident, that all the aforeſaid Towns, particularly *Riplingham*, *Sculcotes*, and *Drypool*, were in the Pariſh and Manor of *Ferriby*: And it is very probable, all the Inhabitants reſorted there to hear Divine Service, the Mother CHURCH being in that Place.   There was then no ſuch Town, or Hamlet, as *Wyke*, in Being; for, if it had, it would never have been omitted in the Survey.   *Myton* was then the only Hamlet, that ſtood on this Neck of Land; which conſiſted but of a few mean Cottages, for poor People to dwell in, who got their Livings by Fishing, Grazing, or little Tillage.

BUT, in Proceſs of Time, all the aforeſaid Towns began to be inhabited, and flourish more than ever. It happened, that the Lord of *Holderneſs*, WILLIAM *le* GROSS, who was Earl of *Albemarle*, and of Royal Blood, had made a Vow to viſit *Jeruſalem*:   But Age and Corpulency rendering him unable, he was ſo very much disturb'd in his Mind, that he apply'd himſelf to *Adam*, a Monk of FOUNTAINS-ABBEY, to know what might be done to diſengage himſelf from his Vow? *Sir,* ſaid the Prieſt, *if you pleaſe to erect a Monaſtry of the* Ciſtercian *Order, I will engage to obtain Abſolution for you from the* Roman *Pontiff,* EUGENIUS III.   The Earl conſented, and ADAM was as good as his Word.   *Melſa,* then overgrown with Woods, and environed with marshy Ground, was the Place, where the Monk choſe to erect that venerable Building: And on a little Eminence, call'd St. *Mary's* Hill, he fix'd his Staff, pronouncing theſe Words: *May this Place hereafter be ſtyl'd the King's Court, the Vineyard of Heaven; and let there be a People created to worship the* SAVIOUR *of the World.* The Monaſtry (which was call'd MEAUX from a Place in *Normandy,* from whence thoſe that peopled it came over with the Conqueror) was begun in the Year 1150, and adorned with ſtately Pinacles and

Towers :

Towers: Monks were brought from FOUNTAINS; and *Adam* became their Abbot. The Country People flock'd to give their Affiftance in the Work, along with the laborious Priefts, from whofe Doctrines they were taught the Means of Salvation; and feveral rich Perfons, (as HAWISIA, the Earl's Daughter; Sir JOHN FRIBOYS, Knight; PETER *de* MALOLACU; and RICHARD *de* OTTRINGHAM, Rector of *Shelford,* in *Ely* Diocefe) gave, and bequeath'd, what might enable them to perform the Parts belonging to their Sacred Function.

THIS Monastry flourishing, in so surprizing a Manner, the Abbot and Monks became able to purchafe Estates, additional to what they enjoy'd. MAUD CAMIN, a Gentlewoman, fold to them two Parts of Land that she had in the Village of *Myton,* which included feven Stengs, four Bovates, Pafture for eight Sheep, a Toft, and a Hall: They also bought of her a Fishery in *Humber,* two Parts of her Salt Pits, as many of Land-Croft, with all her Lordship, for ninety one Marks of Silver; which she folemnly confirm'd by laying her Hand on the Gofpels, in Prefence of RICHARD, Son of SCHERUS, or Lord SAYER, of *Sutton* in *Holdernefs;* whose Monument is to be seen at this Day. Other Witneffes were, WILLIAM *de* Limmingburgh; THOMAS, Prieft of *Wawgn;* THOMAS, the Brother of BENEDICT of *Sculcotes;* with ADAM and ALEXANDER, Relations of JOHN the Priest.

IN the Year 1174, the little Hamlet of *Wyke,* then given to the Monastry, is thus recorded.

"IN the Time of PHILIP the Abbot, the Son of "JOHN of *Meaux,* gave, to the Abbey, four Ox- "gangs of Land in *Myton,* Pasture for four hun- "dred Sheep, the Seat of one Fishery in *Humber,* "two Parts of the Salt-Pits there, a Toft, and a "Hall, two Parts of his Lands in *Wyke,* and all "their Appurtenances. WILLIAM of *Sutton,* and

B   " BENEDICT

" BENEDICT of *Sculcotes,* gave them the other
" Part of *Wyke,* within the Water-Furrows, to the
" Bounds of *Old-Hull,* where formerly was a Grange,
" or Farm-Houfe, divided from the South Part of
" *Old-Hull* and *Humber.*   And be it known further,
" that, in old Times, *New-Hull* was nothing but a
" great Dyke, or Sewer, originally made to drain
" the Country ;   which, in Procefs of Time, both
" by the Descent of all the Waters that Way, and
" by the Warping up of the old River, *Hull* grew
" exceeding deep and wide.   Hereupon it was
" called some Times *New-Hull,* and at other
" Times *Sayer-Cryk,* from the Lord SAYER of *Sutton :*
" Who did not only first cause the same to be cut,
" but alfo had several Rights therein :   The Grange-
" Houfe, before-mentioned, ought to be reckoned
" within *Wyke* aforesaid ; but nothing of it now re-
" mains :   The Place, whereon it stood, which was
" converted into a feeding Pasture, is at present
" known by the Name of *Grange-Wyke,* and made
" a new Manor in *Myton,* call'd *Tripcotes,* or *Tupcotes.*"

FROM hence, Two Things seem remarkable.

1. THAT even then appear'd some small Hamlet on this Point of Land, confisting of five or six
mean Cottages call'd *Wyke,* from their stragling
Situation :   Which, undoubtedly, belong'd to, and
were Part of *Myton ;* tho' it was not in the very
Place where *Kingfton*-upon-*Hull* now stands, but a-
bout a Quarter of a Mile West of it :   The Grange
of which, was afterwards made the Manor-House,
and call'd by the Name of *Tupcotes,* &c.

2. THERE was then an *Old-Hull,* and a *New.*
The former feems to have run into the *Humber,*
(about half a Mile beyond *Drypool*) to have
broke its Paffage into it, by fome rapid Flood ; and,
having continued its Course, was grown into a great
River, which now commonly goes by the Name of
Hull, and is indeed the Haven of the Town.

FOR

FOR about 123 Years, it appears, that *Wyke* made but a very poor Figure : There was little else to be seen, but Kine and Sheep, Cribs and Folds, with perhaps some Places of Shelter, to defend the Shepherds from the Extremities of the Seasons. In the Year 1296, King EDWARD I. being justly provok'd Reg. $\frac{24}{25}$ at the bold Defiance of the *Scots,* in declaring themselves free from former Obligations to him, march'd with a courageous Army against them, and in a bloody Battle slaying 28000, put the rest to flight : He also took *Barwick, Dunbar, Edinborough,* with other Places ; forc'd JOHN BALIOL their 96th Monarch, as a Prisoner, to refign all *Scotland,* by a Charter, dated at *Brechin,* the 10th of *July ;* seiz'd upon his Crown, Scepter, *Regalia,* Coronation Marble Chair from the Monastry of *Scone,* (now in *Weftminfter-Abbey)* with the Records ; all which were sent to *England,* as Trophies of his Victory. After that, returning from thence, attended by several of his martial Nobility, and coming thro' *Holdernefs,* he was pleased to ftay some Days at *Baynard-* *The King* *Caftle,* at *Cottingham,* (a few Miles from *Wyke)* which *vifits Lord* was then the Seat of the Lord WAKE ; who receiv'd WAKE *at his* and entertain'd him, and his noble Retinue, with the *Caftle in* Cottingham. greateft Magnificence. One Morning, the Monarch and his Retinue rode a Courfing, and started a Hare. The Creature led them along the pleasant Banks of *He rides a* the River *Hull,* and ran amongft the Cattle and *hunting.* Shepherds at *Wyke* for Safety. Here the King, being struck with the Advantageoufnefs of the Situa- *He is taken* tion, an Object far more delightful to his Eye than *with the Sit-* the Sport, quickly conceiv'd a glorious Thought ; *uation of* which was, to contrive a fortify'd Town, and a safe Wyke. commodious Harbour. Whilst his Attendants were otherwise employ'd, he rode to the Shepherds, and ask'd, *How deep was the River, to what Height the Tydes flowed, and who was the Owner of the Soil?* In all which, being fully satisfy'd, the King liberally rewarded

those

those Men, and return'd exceedingly pleas'd to the Castle ; from whence he immediately sent to the Monastry of † *Meaux* for the Lord Abbot, and gave him equivalent, or rather more Lands in *Lincoln-shire*, in Exchange for the Ground so neceſſary for the Splendour, as well as Defence of his Kingdom, and with which he was so much in Admiration.

† Five Miles North of HULL.

NOR, was it a Wonder the King should be so charm'd with it : For this Piece of Land was ſitua-ted between the *Humber*, (so call'd, as Historians write, from a Prince of the *Huns ;* who, flying from King LOCRINE, was drowned therein ; which is in-deed a great Arm of the Sea, in some Places above a Mile over, running near twenty Miles from the Ocean to the South of it) and the River *Hull*, on the North, which, with its fresh limpid Streams, de-scending from *Driffield*, (a Town of Note, for having been the Burial-Place of King ALFRED) as also from *Yorkshire* Woulds, mix'd with that famous Æstuary, allaying the Salt Waters thereof. This Conflux, or Union, more conducing to the Monarch's De-ſign, by the high flowing of the Tides, seem'd na-turally to afford not only a convenient Harbour where Ships might safely cast Anchor, without the Mariners fearing the Rage of Storms, or Tempests ; but also a Place where Veſſels of the greatest Bur-den might sail very near to the Shore, and eaſily depart, to lade, or be unladen. The other Side of the * Land, no Ways washed by either of these Ri-vers, seemed fitting for strong Walls, Towers, and Moats, for its Ornament, as well as its Defence.

ALFRED, the learned K. of Northum-berland, *dy'd about the Be-ginning of the 8th Century.*

** The whole very near the Form of a Triangle.*

THE Agreement, with the Abbot, being thus hap-pily concluded, Proclamation was issued forth in two Months Time, *That whoever pleas'd to build, and inhabit there, should have great Freedoms, Priviledges and Im-munities.* To confirm the King's great Deſire towards a general Encouragement, he order'd a Manor-Hall to be erected for his own Use, at the same time com-manding

The Manor Hall built.

manding the Place to be call'd *Kingſton-upon-Hull.* Afterwards, the Harbour was finished by his Order : *When* (as 'tis recorded) *that Monarch gave Freedom to the Town, whoſe Inhabitants from thence became Free-Burgeſſes; having Liberty granted, to them and their Heirs for ever, to diſpoſe of their Eſtates by their Laſt Wills and Teſtaments; to have the Return of Writs, with an Exemption from the Execution of any by the King's Officers, except in Vacancy of the Warden, or chief Magiſtrate: That no where elſe they should plead, or be impleaded, for Treſpaſſes, Tranſgreſſions, Contracts, or Tenures, acted or made within their Bounds: That they, or their Succeſſors, by Writs of Chancery, might chuſe a Coroner of their own, to be preſented to, (and take the Oath of his Office before) the Warden: That a Priſon should be built for various Offenders, particularly* Thieves, who were to be judged by the Head Ruler: That the Inhabitants should be free over* England *from paying to Bridges, or to the King's Forreſters for Wood uſed in building Ships, or towards feeding Swine; or Murage, a Toll for repairing the Walls of a City or Town, paid by the Owners of every Horſe and Cart that enter'd therein: nay, freed from the Payment of their own Merchandizes: That two Markets should be kept Weekly;* Monday *appointed for the one, and* Friday *the other: Likewiſe one † Fair, annually, to begin at ‡ St.* Austin's *Day, and hold* 29 *Days after, except in that Time, which might prejudice a neighbouring Market.* These were the substantial Heads of the Charter, ſigned by WILLIAM, Bishop of *Coventry* and *Litchfield;* HENRY *de* LACY, Earl of *Lincoln;* HENRY *de* PERCY; JOHN GREGORY; WALTER *de* BEAUCHAMP, Steward of the King's Palace; ROGER BRABAZON; JOHN *de* METTINGHAM; PETER MALLORE; WALTER *de* GLOCESTER; and Others. Dated at *Weſtminſter,* in the Year 1299.

WHAT could be the Conſequence of such Munificence from the King, but a willing Obedience from thoſe Subjects, who, by yielding to his Deſire, promoted

A. D.
1299.
The Town's Charter given by the King.

* *The Warden had the Power, on Conviction, to put them to Death.*

† *To begin ſoon after* Eaſter.
‡ *May* 29.

Reg. 21/11

moted their own Intereſt ? Numbers came from all Parts: The Shepherds and Folds were ſcarcely removed, but ſoon began to appear well-contrived Habitations, fill'd (in about three or four Years Time) with Artificers and Merchants, who accuſtomed themſelves to Trade and Navigation. The Rivers afforded them Plenty of their Finny Race ; which, being taken, dry'd and harden'd, were call'd *Stock-Fiſh*, and became their principal Commodity. In thoſe Days, it was much more uſeful, and People leſs accuſtom'd to Flesh, than at Preſent. By this, and their Exemption from Taxes, they not only obtain'd immenſe Treaſure ; but had, in Exchange, the luxurious Dainties of the Eaſt, and what was neceſſary from other foreign Parts of the World, brought into their ſafe Harbour, by lofty Ships of the greateſt Burden. Thus the Inhabitants increaſing in Riches, and (in Conſequence thereof) the Place well fortify'd, where it requir'd, with Walls, Towers, and Bulwarks ; it ſoon eclips'd the Glory of the other Towns near it ; ſuch as *Barton, Beverley, Grimsby, Headon, Patrington,* and *Ravenſrod :* which by Degrees, ſunk to that Condition, very little different from what we may now behold them.

The chief Trade.

The Town fortified.

WHO was the firſt Warden, or Bailiff, or what Number in Succeſſion were of them, is not eaſily, if at all, to be found ; but in the Year 1301, RICHARD OYSEL, or SYSSEL, was in the Office of the former ; and ROBERT *de* BARTON, ſupply'd that of the latter. About this Time, RICHARD *de* MAREWELL, one of the King's Gentlemen of the Bed Chamber, who had conſtantly attended his Royal Maſter, ſo gloriouſly ſignaliz'd himſelf by his Valour againſt the *Scots,* and thro' it ſo much won the King's Affections ; that, as a Reward, the Monarch granted him the Cuſtoms of * Peerage for the weighing of Lead, and † Tronage for that of Wool, which were about 6*l.* per *Annum,* no doubt, a great Sum in thoſe Days.

The firſt Warden, or Bayliff, unknown to us, at preſent.

Or Valet.

** An Impoſition for the Maintenance of a Sea Peer.*

† Cuſtom or Toll.

THO'

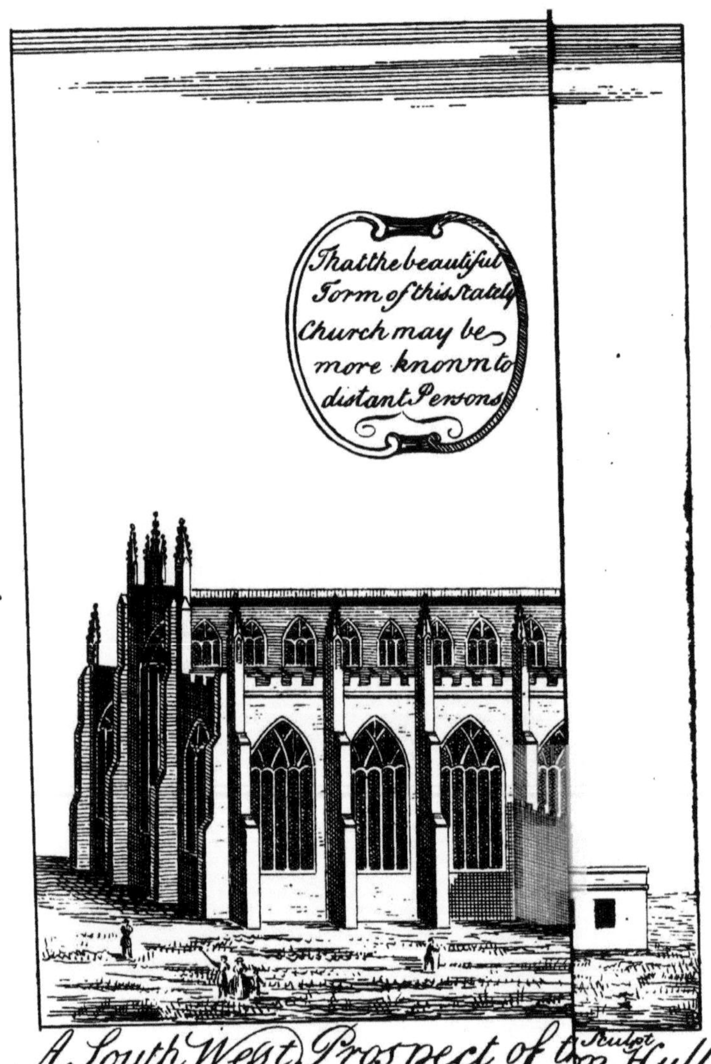

A South West Prospect of [...] in Hull

THO' the Town was happily brought to ſome Perfection, yet were there no conſiderable Incloſures to
beautify the Country about it, or Highways for
the Conveniency of Paſſengers. But theſe were re-
medy'd by the WARDEN, BAILIFF, and BURGESSES; Reg. $\frac{40}{31}$
who, in 1302, petition'd the King to appoint a Ju-
ry, that ſhould ſettle Roads from hence to the
Neighbouring Towns. A Writ for this Purpoſe
was ſoon granted to the chief Inhabitants, *viz.* Sir
RALPH *de* HENGHAM; WILLIAM *de* CARLETON;
and GALFRID *de* HOTHAM: Who, ſetting about *Roads made*
this neceſſary Buſineſs, ordained Highways to be *about the*
made to *Anlaby, Beverley, Cottingham,* and *Holderneſs,* *Town.*
very probably thoſe that remain to this Time.

WE cannot conclude this Chapter, without taking
Notice of the King's Death, after a triumphant
Reign of above thirty four Years. It happen'd at
Burgh-on-the-Sands, a ſmall Town in *Scotland,* where
he was taken ill with a Dyſentery, or Bloody Flux; *The King's*
and expir'd in the Arms of his Servants, on *Friday* *Death.*
the 7th of *July,* 1307; whoſe Body, being brought
into *England,* was interr'd in the Abbey of *Weſtmin-*
ſter, near the Shrine of King EDWARD *the Confeſſor.*

CHAP. II.

Of the Building of the High-Church, *dedicated to the* EDW. II.
HOLY TRINITY: *With the Monuments, and In-* King.
ſcriptions, at preſent therein, and in the Church-
Yard: Likewiſe thoſe of St. MARY'S, *called the*
Low-Church.

NO doubt, but Divine Service was perform'd,
almoſt from the Beginning of the Town's
Foundation; tho' perhaps in little Chapels of
Wood, or Chambers ſet a-part for that Purpoſe. But
as People began to flouriſh, their Thoughts were A. D.
inſpir'd to raiſe a Building, in which it was more fit- 1312.
ting Reg. $\frac{6}{8}$.

ting to ferve the Divine Architect of the World. The late King, their Benefactor, (who, as recorded, founded a famous Monaftry for *White-Fryers*, in a Place call'd from thence *White-Fryergate*) was some Years ago laid in his Tomb, having the Character of the moft excellent of Princes : For he was tall, proportionable, and beautiful ; of great Courage and Intrepidity ; adorn'd with the moft penetrating Judgment, and comprehenfive Underftanding : Who, had he but liv'd 'till the Foundation of this Structure was laid, would without doubt have been a great

EDW. II. Contributor to the Defign. However, his Son,

Another Royal Benefactor, who was then at YORK. was not in this Refpect wanting in his Royal Beneficence ; whofe Example was follow'd not only by the rich Merchants and Tradefmen of the Town, but alfo by the Gentlemen and Inhabitants round about it. 'Tis pity but every one of them should be immortaliz'd, by a grateful Remembrance. Their Names are buried in Oblivion, ex-

Scale-Lane in HULL, *is called from thefe antient Inhabitants.* cept Mr. JOHN SCALES ; who, dying in the Year when the Building of the Church was begun, bequeath'd 20*l.* to be paid out of his Eftate towards its Erection, and requir'd to be bury'd in the Church-Yard ; and one Mr. WILLIAM SCALES alfo, about the fame Time, bequeath'd his Body to be interr'd within the Church itself.

A. D. 1317. Reg. $\frac{10}{11}$

A new Charter granted in the Year 1321. Reg. $\frac{14}{15}$

SOME Years after, the Streets were well paved, (with the Stones, as some write, that were brought in the Ships as Ballaft) both for Beauty and Conveniency ; when the King, hearing of the Town's wonderful Improvements, granted a Charter, which empower'd the rich Inhabitants, for the future, to build their Houfes of Lyme and Stone ; to erect ftrong Caftles and Towers ; to make a Wall, as defign'd by his Royal Predeceffor ; with a Moat for greater Security, as well as to part their Limits from thofe of their Neighbours, in like manner as the *Saxons* of old were wont to do in *England,* by

raifing

raiſing Ramparts, and digging Ditches, at the extremeſt Parts of their Dominions, where there were no Mountains or Rivers to ſerve for Boundaries.

AND when the Church was finiſhed, in the moſt venerable Manner to behold, it continued in great Splendor ; and had ſeveral Chantries founded therein, by Perſons of Eminency, Learning and Piety.

THE *Firſt*, that appears recorded, was founded A. D. by ROBERT *Del* CROSS, formerly Mayor, who left 1383. eight Meſſuages in *Hull*, for the Benefit of the Town ; beſides Eſtates, in other Places, bequeath'd to the Vicar of HOLY TRINITY's, his two Chaplains, and twelve Prieſts of the Choir, for performing Divine Service, in praying for departed Souls : To which Purpoſe, he alſo endow'd another Chantry, in the Conventual Church of MEAUX-ABBEY, and dy'd in the Year 1408.

THERE were *Two* Chantries more founded by 1414. Mr. JOHN GREGG, Merchant, (Mayor in 1416.) one dedicated to St. LAURENCE, the other to St. MARY ; which he endow'd with the annual Rents of ſix or ſeven Meſſuages in *Hull*. He alſo founded the Hoſpital, known by his Name, within the Poſtern- *GREG'S* Gate, then call'd *Old-Church-Lane ;* and built Houſes Hoſpital. for Habitations to the Prieſts, (who officiated in HOLY TRINITY's) near the Weſt End of the Church, which retains the Name of *Prieſts-Row* to this Day.

BUT, here, a ſmall Digreſſion muſt be made from the Chantries, on Account of the Church itſelf, becauſe of ſome Alteration that happen'd in the Service this Year. The *Feaſt Day,* (or *the ſame* annually *Churches* in Memory of THAT, on which the Church ſoon after *Wake-Days* its Erection had been conſecrated) called the *Wake,* *altered.* was held on the 10th of *March,* and St. *Mary's* the 8th. Theſe, frequently, fell in *Lent ;* a Time more fit for Faſting. Upon which, the Worſhipful JOHN BEDFORD, Mayor, with others, petition'd the Archbiſhop of *York*, JOHN KEMPE, (a Prelate, who be-

c

came

came Lord Chancellor, Bishop-Cardinal of St. *Balbinæ*, afterwards of St. *Rufinæ*, and at last translated to *Canterbury*) " That he would be pleas'd, they " should be *Both* celebrated the *Sunday* following " St. *Thomas a Becket.*" To which the good Archbishop confented ; and the Anniverfary Celebrations continued 'till the Reign of King JAMES the Firft. As to the Martyrdom of St. *Thomas a Becket*, the Murder was committed on *Tuefday, Jan.* 4, 1130 ; but the Day of his Translation was Yearly kept on the 7th of *July*.

ANOTHER intervening Digreffion is this. It was a Cuftom (and is obferv'd in/ many Countries to this Day) decently to plant Rows of Trees in the Church-Yards, under whofe flourishing Shade, both before, and after Divine Service, the People might refresh their Souls by Contemplation. But if this be unreafonable to suppofe, it cannot however be deny'd, but that thofe Trees, with their thick Branches, were of great Defence to Places of Worship, from the Fury and Rage of Storms and Tempefts. Such were planted in this Church-Yard. The Vicar fent this Year for *Robert Teftney* and *Richard Wright*, Hewers of Wood, whom he order'd to cut down one of the largeft, and moft ornamental, for Reafons beft known to himfelf. They had scarce obey'd his Command, before the Mayor heard of it ; and, sending for them, committed both to Prifon, for daring to commit such an Action, without Advice and Confent of the Bench and Church-Wardens. And, on the next Hall-Day, sending for the Vicar, told him, *That, by the Conftitutions of the Church, neither he, his Predeceffors, or any other Perfon, had Power to deftroy what was placed there for the Prefervation of that venerable Building.* The juft Authority, with which he spoke, and indeed the Reafonablenefs of the whole Court thus exerting themfelves, for the Good of the Church, so melted the tender Heart of the
Gentleman,

A. D.
1452.

Why Trees
are planted
in Church-
Yards.

1462.

The Right
Worshipful
JOHN
BARKER.

Gentleman, that he moft humbly crav'd their Pardon. Nor were they unwilling to grant it, but alfo difmift the Prifoners, on Condition, That the Vicar would, at his own Expence, plant Six Trees, in the Church-Yard, for that One he had order'd to be cut down. All which the good Prieft chearfully confented to ; and no doubt but it was perform'd accordingly.

THE famous Bishop of *Worcefter,* and Lord Chancellor, JOHN ALCOCK, who was a Native of *Beverley,* founded, in *Hull,* a noble Free-School, to inftruct the Children both in Latin and Greek. About eight Years after, he order'd a little Chapel to be built on the South Side of this Church, where two Altars were erected ; one in Honour of the SAVIOUR of the World, and the other dedicated to St. JOHN the Evangelift. The Chantor, or Prieft of this perpetual Chantry, was to pray for the Soul of King EDWARD IV. that of the said Bishop's, thofe of his † Parents, and of every Chriftian. He was alfo bound, by the Foundation, freely to teach in the aforesaid Grammar-School : For all which, he was to have Ten Pounds Yearly, paid out of Tenements in *Lincolnshire* and *Hull:* Befides, he was allow'd forty Shillings more, to pay to the Clerk of the Church, for teaching the Children to fing ; and three Pounds to be diftributed, Yearly, to twelve of the beft Scholars, (five Shillings each) provided the Revenues would extend to allow it.

A. D. 1476.

1484. *Two Years after he was made Bishop of* Ely. *He was the Founder of* JESUS Coll. *in* CAMBRIDGE. † *They were interr'd in* HULL.

JOHN RIPLINGHAM, D.D. Prefident of *Beverley* College, founded another Chantry ; wherein two Priefts (the laft of whom were LAURENCE ALLAN, and WILLIAM PARKINS) were daily to officiate : One of those had Yearly 5*l.* 8*s.* the other 5*l.* The former, as usual, (on the Day of this pious Benefactor's Death) paid to the Poor 15*s.* 6*d.* the other 4*s.* 2*d.* Yearly. The Doctor erected befides an Hospital in *Vicar-Lane,* for twenty poor People. This, and

1517.

He built Fish Shambles for the Ufe of the Town.

and the Chantry, he endow'd with the Rents of eighteen Tenements, and four Gardens, within the Town : The Hospital continu'd for a long Time, 'till, at length, it was converted to another Use.

Three Chantries in HULL *belonged to* Gisburne *Priory.*

BESIDES the Chantries aforesaid, others were dedicated to the HOLY TRINITY, St. JOHN BAPTIST, St. JAMES, St. ANNE, and St. CHRISTOPHER, &c. Three of these belong'd to the Prior and Convent of St. *Mary's, Gisburn,* (or rather *Gisborough*) in the North Riding of *Yorkshire.* Which Priory, of Regular Canons of the Order of St. *Augustine,* was (thro' Advice of *Calixtus* II. Bishop of *Rome,* and *Thurstan,* Archbishop of *York*) founded *Anno* 1128, after it had taken 9 Years in building, at the Expence of a noble Knight, of *Skelton* Castle, in the same Riding, that accompany'd the Conqueror from *Normandy,* named ROBERT BRUS, *Bruse,* or *Bruce ;* who,

The Founder of that once splendent Building.

giving the Valley of *Anandale,* in *Scotland,* to his youngest Son, called by his Name ; from his Loins descended ROBERT and DAVID, the 97th and 98th Kings of the *Scots ;* who, as their Historians tell us, reigned from the Year of our LORD 1306 to 1352, at which Time JOHN BALIOL their 99th King succeeded to the Throne. WILLIAM, who was crown'd

Benefactors to it.

King of *Scotland, Anno* 1165 ; PETER and ROBERT BRUCE ; RALPH CLARE ; and RICHARD, Bishop of *Durham ;* these were great Benefactors to the Priory above-mention'd. All which, tho' it may seem a Digression, yet is delightful History, and redounds to the Honour of Holy Trinity Church in HULL, when some of the Chantries in it belong'd to such a distinguished Monastry in former Ages.

A. D. 1522.

The Church interdicted.

THE Church having been put under an Interdict, the Windows and Doors were clos'd with Briars and Thorns ; the Pavement turn'd up ; and the Bells (once hallow'd, by Baptism, as tho' their Sounds should drive evil Spirits afar) so curb'd, or perhaps taken away, that there was no Tolling
for

for Prayers, or at the Soul's Departure from the Body : No Worship perform'd within the Walls ; neither Chriftian Burial allow'd therein, or even the Church Yard ; and every Perfon lay under an *Anathema*, who prefum'd to enter the Place ! But no Reafon is affign'd for this severe Sentence ; tho' it may be rightly judg'd, that it was for a Sermon preach'd therein, againft the Romish Religion ; becaufe, some Years after, (a Time, when Editions of the *New-Teftament*, were sent over by Tindal, and others, from *Antwerp*, with many more Books againft Popery) the Vicar of *North-Cave* was forc'd, in this Town, to make publick Recantation of what he had deliver'd from the Pulpit ; and both upon a *Sunday*, and on a *Market-Day*, was oblig'd to walk round the Church in his Shirt only ; his Arms, Legs, and Feet being quite bare ; and, befides, to carry a large Faggot, as tho' he deferv'd Burning for what was then look'd upon to be his great and most capital Offence.

Penance performed by the Vicar of North-Cave.

In the Time of King Edward VI. this Church (with St. Mary's ; as also, Dr. Riplingham's, and Mr. Gregg's Hospitals, with the Charter-House) was refounded ; tho' it never could recover those Revenues which Henry VIII. had given away. In this Reign too, when Images were order'd to be taken from Churches, such of them here as represented the Saints to whom the Chantries had been dedicated, were broke in Pieces ; the Histories of their Actions, painted on the Walls, wash'd over to deface them ; and, inftead of *Legenda Aurea*, which contain'd the Lives and Miracles of Romish Saints, a Common-Prayer Book was introduc'd, by the firft Reformers ; (Doctors in Divinity, as * Cranmer, Cox, Goodrick, Harris, Redman, † Ridley, Robinson, Skip, Taylor, and Thirlby) wrote in such a Style, that was not only thought to be the most eloquent ; but, by the Parliament, concluded to be done with the

A.D. 1547. *The Rood refembling Chrift on the Crofs, with other Images, pulled down.*

* *Archbifhop of* Canterbury. † *Bifhop of* London. *Both Martyrs, at* Oxford. *This Anno* 1555, *and* Cranmer *the Year following.*

the Affiftance of the Holy Spirit ; and confequently establish'd, with their unanimous Confent, over the whole Kingdom.

THE Prelates having, it seems, in the Beginning of the Reign of King HENRY VIII. made Complaint, that the Performance of their high Office (as it should be) lay heavy upon their Shoulders, and that Suffragan Bishops would be a great Comfort, and Eafement ; the King, at their Request, placed Twenty Six of them in several noted Towns. Among thefe, *Kingfton*-upon-*Hull* was one. Thofe Perfons, of that under Stamp of Epifcopal Dignity, who prefided here, lived in *Hull-Street*, where they had a stately Palace, mostly built of Free-Stone, adorn'd with Church-Windows, Gates, and Towers.

A. D. 1557.

AND, at the latter End of Queen MARY'S Reign, when many severe Commiffions were iffu'd against the Protestants, one was directed to the Bishop of this Place. There could not be many more, because the Reformation soon follow'd the Death of that Princefs ; and very probable, that ROBERT PURSGLOVE might be that commiffion'd Person ; whose Epitaph was lately taken Notice of, by an induftrious modern Writer. That Bishop, who dy'd *May* 2, 1579, was bury'd in the Church of † *Tidefwell ;* a Town suppos'd to be call'd so from a Well in *Peake-Forreft*, which us'd to ebb and flow, in just Tides, for the Space of an Hour. His Tomb is in the Chantry, and on it the Portraiture of him in Brass, as tho' in his *Pontificalia*, with an Epitaph, much in this Strain.

† *In* Darby- shire.

Under this Stone, a Corpfe is laid, sometime a Man of Fame,
  In Tidefwell he was bozn and bzed ; Robert Purfglove his Name ;
Brought up, by Parents tender Care, and Masters learned Rules ;
'Till, afterwazds, his Uncle near, fent him to beft of Schools.
He, William Bradshaw, London's Fame, in Paul's the Youth did place ;
In gentle fort did him maintain, full three times three Years space :
Then fent unto an Abbey fair, by William Giffard founded,
Who Bifhop was of Winchefter, and in good Works abounded :
'Twas call'd Saint Mary Overis, in Southwark, near the Thames,
  For Canons Regular, their Blifs, to feek by holy Flames :

They taught much more the learned Youth, who was to Oxford ſent,
In Corpus Chriſti, wheʒe to Truth, his Mind was freely bent:
Four Years he in that College ſtay'd, in Learning moſt renown'd;
To Gisburn ſent, he there diſplay'd, that Knowledge which was crown'd.
For he was plac'd in Prior's Stall, and govern'd o'er the reſt;
Bishop of HULL he was withall, by Heav'n ſupremely bleſt:
Archdeacon too of Nottingham, Provoſt of Rotherham,
(A College once of noble Fame) and of York Suffragan:
Two Grammar Schools he did erect, an Hospital ordain'd;
For Youth he never would neglect, and Old Folks he maintain'd.
O Tidefwell fair, and Gisbrough Towns! mouʒn and lament ye may,
Since he that lov'd you dear, is gone, and but a Lump of Clay:
But yet, tho' dead, he ſeems to ſpeak, Come, Mortal, · come and ſee;
And think, tho' I'm a Corpſe to Day, to Morrow you may be!
Death's cruel Dart has laid him low, yet can't ſuppreſs his fame:
Immoʒtal is the happy Soul, and laſting is his Name.
Chriſt's more to him than Life on Earth, a bleſt Exchange is giv'n,
From pieʒcing Gʒief to raptuʒous Miʒth, fʒom this vain world to Heav'n.
For true it is, the State of Man, is brittle like the Glaſs,
Whoſe Time is deem'd but as a Span, and quick away will paſs.

IN the Year 1622, it was deſign'd that an Organ
should be set up over the Door leading to the Chancel; where, in former Times, there had been one
placed.   The Archbishop of *York*, wrote to the
Mayor and Vicar for that Purpose; but the Deſign
dropt, thro' Jealouſies and Fears that were incident
in those Days.

BUT, at this Time, the Church wants nothing
that is neceſſary, or ornamental.   The Represen- *A fine*
tation of the Last Supper (of our Bleſſed SAVIOUR, *Altar Piece.*
with his APOSTLES) is finely pourtray'd, as a modern
Author tells us, by Monſieur PERMENTIER:
Another writes, "That on the South Side of the
" Choir, is a neat Library, made such from a Place, *The Church*
" where formerly had been a Chapel."   Many, *Library.*
who · were eminent Inhabitants, lie bury'd in this
Church: But as the King of Terrors makes no Dis-
tinction amongst the Race of Humankind, and it
is expected an Historian should omit nothing of
this Nature, because of so tender a Concern to the
meanest Person who has placed the least Memorial;

Epitaphs, &c. eafily found. rial; so every Infcription, both herein, and the Church-Yard, is exhibited with as much Care, as poffible. This will preferve their Remembrance, from the Injury of Time, to their living Friends; for whom, to make them more eafy to be known, they are compil'd in an alphabetical Manner.

EPITAPHS, *and* INSCRIPTIONS, *in the Church.*

A.

J Uxta hanc columnam, cuftodiendum deponitur collapfum, il-luftris Animæ Domicilium, viz. NICHOLAI ANDERSON; *hujus olim Ecclefiæ, per viginti feptem Annos, Vicarii. Qui ob fummam Doctrinam, Morum Sanctitatem, ob Inviolatam, in Ecclefiam Matrem, Pietatem, & Gravitatem circa res facras Apoftolicam, fingularemque tum Prudentiam, tum Humanitatem, cui ob immotam Animi conftantiam, tam minis quam Blanditiis Populi cedere nefcientem; quodcunque aliud magnum & venerabile in confummatiffimo Paftore requiri folet, fummo apud omnes in Pretio erat. Exceptis (qui optimo cuivis obmurmurant) Fanaticis. Horum Splendore Virtutum, Mandati fibi Gregis ad Æternam Vitam Viam præmonftravit: poftquam Vitam mediocriter non Longævam, non mediocriter beneficam, impleverat; multum defideratus occubuit.*

WHICH IS THUS TRANSLATED.

NEAR this Pillar is laid up safe the ruinous Tabernacle of Mr. NICHOLAS ANDERSON, formerly Vicar of this Church for the Space of twenty seven Years: Who, for his confummate Learning, Sanctity of Life, inviolable Attachment to our holy Mother the Church; for his Apoftolical Gravity in all Minifterial Offices; for his fingular Prudence and Humanity; and, above all, for his unshaken Stedfaftnefs of Refolution, that knew not how to yield or give Way either to the Threatnings or Flatteries of the People; and what ever elfe was required as great and venerable in the moft

accom-

accomplish'd Paftor ; made him highly efteem'd by all virtuous Perfons ; except only thofe who differ from our Communion. The Brightnefs of all his fingular Virtues shewed the Flock committed to his Charge the true Way to Eternal Happinefs : Who, after he had spent a Life, not of a great Length, and yet in that Time very ufeful to the World, died much lamented.

Mr. ANDERSON's Latin Infcription is in the Chancel.

North of the Altar, is this following.

HERE lies in Peace HUGH ARMING, Draper, and once Mayor of *Kingfton-upon-Hull*, who departed this Life, in the Faith of Chrift, the 25th of *June*, 1606.

B.

Near the Veftry Door, on the South Wall of the Choir, is the following Infcription.

HAUD procul hinc jacet GEORGIUS BAKER, *Miles,*

Pater
Avus } GEO. BAKER, *Armig.*
Proavus

Qui poftquam multa pro Rege, pro Patria fecijfet tulijfetq ;
Præcipue in propugnando fortiter Novo-Caftro,
Contra Scotos *tunc Rebelles.*
Hic tandem indigno et meritis fuis dijfipari fato concejfit,
4to Augufti *Anno* 1667.
At non pajfus eft Deus tantam virtutem penitus latere :
Obfcure obiit, honorifice tamen fepultus,
Funus ejus profequentibus
Militum Tribuno, totaq ; Cohorte Militari,
Memorabili Honoris Pietatifq ; Exemplo,
Tandem cum per quadraginta plus minus Annos neglectus jacuijfet,
Nepos ejus THOMAS BAKER, *S.T.B. Sancti* Johannis Cantab.
Non tam Virtutis quam adverfæ Fortunæ Hæres,
Avi Charijfimi indignæ fortis mifertus,
Hoc ei Monumentum mærens lubens pofuit.
Anno 1710.   WHICH

D

WHICH IS THUS RENDER'D.

NOT far from this Place lies interr'd GEORGE BAKER, Knight ; the Father (Grandfather, and Great Grandfather) of *George Baker*, Esq. Who, after he had done and suffer'd much for his King and Country, especially for gallantly defending *Newcaſtle* againſt the rebellious *Scots*, at laſt submitted to an unequal Fate, unworthy his great Deſerts, the 4th of *Auguſt*, 1667. But GOD would not suffer so great Virtue to lie conceal'd : Tho' he dy'd obſcurely, he was bury'd honourably ; the Colonel of the Militia, and the whole Train-Band, attending his Funeral, as a memorable Example of Valour and Loyalty. At last, having lain buried unobserved more than forty Years, his Nephew THOMAS BAKER, Batchelor in Divinity, of St. *John's* College, in *Cambridge*, the Heir, not more of his Virtues, as of his adverſe Fortunes, pitying the unhappy Fate of his dear Grandfather, out of his great Affection, cauſed this Funeral Monument to be erected, in the Year 1710.

On a South Pillar, near the Steeple, is the following.

NEAR this Place lieth interr'd the Body of Mrs. GRACE, the Wife of Mr. JOHN BARKER, of this Town, Mariner, who departed this Life, *March* 30, 1718. in the 40th Year of her Age. She was a loving, prudent, virtuous Wife ; a dutiful Daughter, indulgent Mother, a kind Friend, and obliging to all. She had 3 Sons, and 6 Daughters. Her youngeſt Son had not been many Days in this Life, before she exchang'd it for a better. This Inſcription is by her sorrowful Husband, dedicated to her Memory, that, tho' dead, she may yet live in the Minds of thoſe that survive her.

In the South Isle, the Weſt End.

JOHN BARCLATE, Pewterer, dy'd in the Year 1710. *And in the Chancel, North of the Altar, is this.*

HERE lieth the Body of the Worshipful HENRY BARNARD, twice Mayor of this Town, who departed this Life the 4th of *Auguſt*, 1661. And alſo the Body of WILLIAM BARNARD, Esq ; his Grandſon, second Son of Sir *Edward Barnard*, Kt. who died the 28th Day of *January*, 1718, aged 47 Years.

In

In the South Part of the Choir.

HERE lieth the Body of Mrs. MARY BAYNE, who departed this Life the 25th Day of *November*, 1728. in the 67th Year of her Age.

In the South Isle of the Chancel.

HERE lieth interr'd the Body of MICHAEL BEILBY, of this Town, Mercer, who departed this Life the 26th of *September, Anno Dom.* 1707. aged 48 Years. Here alfo lieth the Body of WILLIAM BEILBY, his Son, who died the 14th of *November*, ·1707. aged 6 Months.

In the South Isle, at the Weft End of the Church.

NICHOLAS BEWICKE, Woollen-Draper, dy'd *Oct.* 2, 1680. He lived piously, and died peaceably, had eleven Children, fix of whom are buried befide him.

In the South Isle, at the Weft End of the Church.

HERE lies the Body of Alderman SAMUEL BOISE, twice Mayor, who dy'd *February* 13, 1729. *Ætat.* 79. and ELIZABETH his Wife, who dy'd *April* 12, 1725.

On a Hatchment, upon a South Pillar, is the following Infcription: Alfo a Memorial over her Grave.

NEAR hereunto lieth the Body of ELIZABETH BLOUNT, the Wife of *Francis Blount,* of this Town, Alderman, by whom he had 4 Sons, *William, Charles, Francis,* and *John* ; and 4 Daughters, *Anne, Alathea, Anne* and *Mary.* She was firft-born to *Thomas Bacon* of *Wharram-Grainge,* Gent. She departed this Life the 28th Day of *March,* in the 43rd Year of her Age, 1687. *In the South Isle of the Chancel.*

HERE lieth interred the Body of Mr. THOMAS BROADLEY, of this Town, Merchant, who married *Agnes,* Daughter of *Robert Carlisle,* Alderman, by whom he had Iffue one Son, and one Daughter. He died the 12th of *Sept.* 1724. *Æt.* 64.

In the South of the Chancel, on the Ground, the Effigies in Brafs of an Alderman (and his Lady) with this.

Hic RICARDE jaces BYLT, pluris plene favoris,
  Aldermannus eras, Mercator & istius Urbis,
Peste cadens. † Ense Necis obrute luce secunda,
Anno Milleno C. quater. Semel. I. recitato.

---

† *Nec nimio rigida post ftrati Morte jacebant.* LUCR.

THUS

THUS RENDER'D.

HERE, O RICHARD BYLT, thou lieſt bury'd, (formerly an Alderman, and a Merchant of good Reputation) who dy'd, in two Days Time, by the Peſtilence, in the Year 1401.

At the Feet of the Lady's Effigies, alſo on the Ground.

**Terra clauſe taces, nuper Poſſeſſor Honoris,
Dilecta steteras, generoſa eras, quia-tuta:
Octobris Menſe migrans ad Regna jucunda,
Et quinquageno; una sine fine bibas.**

THAT IS,

THE Earth, being clos'd upon thee, thou art in ſilent Reſt, who lately enjoy'd deſerved Honour, and was belov'd, for thy generous Diſpoſition, proceeding from an upright Heart. This Gentlewoman died in the Month of *October*, in the Fiftieth Year of her Age ; and is now gone into the Regions of Bliſs : Where, may she live happy for ever.

Or, if you pleaſe, take theſe Rhimes.

for the *GENTLEMAN.*

LO ! *RICHARD BYLT*, in Peace is here laid down,
Once Alderman, and Merchant, of this Town :
But two Days Sickneſs ſtopt his vital Breath ;
DEATH'S conq'ring Sword brought him unto his Death.
'Twas paſt the Year (of JESUS CHRIST, behold)
One Thouſand, and One Hundred, four Times told.

for the *LADY.*

LATE in great Fame, and lovely to behold,
Lies here, a Lady's Corpſe, within the Mold !
Heaven's Gifts and Graces crown'd her happy Life ;
The sweetest Maiden, and moſt tender Wife :
October's Month her dying Eyes did cloſe,
When juſt unto her Fifti'th Year she roſe.
O may her Soul, (lamented Shade !) remain
In Heav'n with his, and all th' Angelick Train.

C.

At the Weft End, near the Organ.

An Epitaph upon the Death of Mr. JOHN CARLETON, Master and Mariner ; lost in his Long-Boat, 18th of *November*, 1674. *Ætatis* 21. Son to *William Carleton*, Merchant, Sheriff, *Anno* 1668.

HERE refts his mortal Part asleep again,
 Who was once faved nodding in the Main ;
But caft the fecond Time on † THETIS' *Lap,*
Ah ! Providence fent none to hand him back.
The curled Billows wept to fee him lie,
Divefted of his IMMORTALITY !
Then fomed his Remains above the Deep,
And now his Duft does with his Father's sleep ;
Waiting Awaking, when all Tempefts ceafe,
And toffed Bodies land in perfect Peace. ‡

UPON THE SAME STONE IS THE FOLLOWING.

NOW refts, in his eldest Son's Urn, that divine Philofopher WILLIAM CARLETON, Gentleman, whofe great Wifdom and Learning made him ufeful and defirable. He lived, and died like a Christian, *April* 17, 1705. in the 84th Year of his Age.

Buried in the Great Isle, Weft End.

MRS. DINAH CARLETON, who departed this Life, *March* 13, in the Year of our LORD, 1690.

In the South Isle, at the Weft End.

HERE lieth the Body of Mr. EDWARD CARLETON, who departed this Life in the true Faith of CHRIST, by

---

† Daughter of NEREUS, (a God of the Sea, Son of OCEANUS and TETHYS) Mother of ACHILLES. *Homer* mentions her in the 18th and 19th Books of *Iliad* ; Where that Prince of Poets tells us, the Manner how THETIS obtain'd from VULCAN a Suit of complete impenetrable Armour, adorn'd with the moft curious Devices, for the Ufe of her beautiful and valiant Son, in which he became invulnerable, whilft he was revenging the lamented Death of his dear PATROCLUS, slain by the renowned HECTOR, upon feveral of the Royal Auxiliaries to King PRIAM, many of the *Trojans*, and laftly on that Hero himfelf.

‡ I remember to have read, in a Church-Yard, belonging to a Sea-Port, a pretty Epitaph, over a Sailor, concluding with thefe Lines.
Altho' Death's Anchors ftrong prevail,
 And link us with the Fleet :
Yet, once again, we muft fet Sail,
 Our Admiral CHRIST *to meet.*

whofe

whofe Example he pioufly forgave his Enemies : He was generous, brave, juft, and charitable, willing to affift all in Diftrefs, ever true to his Friend and Promife, tho' to the Hazard of his Life : He liv'd belov'd, and died lamented the 3rd Day of *Auguft*, 1704. Aged 33 Years.

QUicquid DINÆ *Uxoris* Johannis Monckton *Filiæ* GULIELMI CARLETON *et* DINÆ *Uxoris ejus Terrenum fuit in Terram (nullo non lugente) rediit* 15 *Die Augufti* 1731, *Ætatis Anno* 66.

   J. Monckton, *Arm. (fupra nominatus) hujus Villæ Major,* obiit 22 *Sept.* 1733.   *THAT IS,*
WHATEVER was mortal of DINAH, Wife of *John Monckton*, Daughter of *William* CARLETON, and his Wife *Dinah*, return'd to Earth, (lamented by all) the 15th Day of *Auguft*, 1731. in the 66th Year of her Age.

John Monckton, above-named, Mayor of this Town, dy'd the 22d of *September*, 1733.

In the South Isle of the Chancel.

INTERR'D here the Body of ROBERT CARLISLE, twice Mayor of *Kingfton-upon-Hull*, who departed this Life the 17th of *January*, 1707. the 65th Year of his Age. Alfo the Body of his Wife ESTHER. She departed this Life, *February* 13, 1696. the 40th Year of her Age.

North of the Altar, with his Effigy, in Brafs.

HERE lieth in Peace, CHRISTOPHER CHAPMAN, Draper, once Mayor of *Kingfton-upon-Hull*, who died, in the Faith of CHRIST, the 11th Day of *December*, 1615.

In the Chancel.

HERE refteth JAMES CLARKSON, thrice Mayor of *Kingfton-upon-Hull*, Merchant-Adventurer, who died the 17th Day of *Nov. Anno Dom.* 1585. in the true Faith of JESUS CHRIST.

Note, *There are two antient Effigies of a Perfon of Quality, and his Lady, that lie North in the Chancel.*

In the South Isle of the Chancel.

HERE lieth the Body of DOROTHY CLIFFE, Wife of Mr. *Stephen Cliffe*, of this Town, Mercer, Daughter of Alderman *Lambert*, Merchant, who departed this Life the 10th of *June*, 1722. And alfo ANNE their Daughter, who died an Infant.   *In*

In the South Ifle, at the Weft End.

IN this Vault reft the Remains of ANNE, Wife of Alderman JOHN COLLINGS, who departed this Life the 26th of *June*, 1723. *Ætatis fuæ* 39. ALSO here lieth the Body of Alderman JOHN COLLINGS, above-named, thrice Mayor of this Town, who died the 13th Day of *November*, 1733. in the 60th Year of his Age.

Near it are thefe.

MR. JOHN COLLINGS, Merchant, dy'd *June* 15, 1705. and MARY his Wife, *Jan.* 1709.

HERE lies interr'd the Body of Mr. JOHN CORNWALL, Merchant, who departed this Life, in the Faith of CHRIST, the 20th of *October*, 1714. He marry'd *Mary*, the Daughter of Alderman *Hydes*, by whom he had one Son, and one Daughter, who are alfo here interr'd. *Ætatis fuæ* 35.

HERE lieth the Body of *ELEANOR, (Wife of Mr. † *George Crowle*, Merchant, and Alderman) who dy'd *Anno* 1662.

ANNE, Wife of JOHN CROWTHER, Draper, dy'd the 4th (and interr'd the 6th) of *February*, 1650.

❖❖❖❖❖❖❖❖❖❖❖❖❖❖❖❖❖❖❖❖❖❖❖❖❖

D.

In the South Ifle of the Chancel.

HERE lieth the Body of THOMAS DALTON, thrice Mayor of *Kingfton-upon-Hull*, Merchant of the Staple, and Venturer, who died the 4th Day of *June*, A.D. 1590. in the Faith of CHRIST, and in Hope of the Refurrection to Life Eternal.

In the Chancel.

HERE lieth the Body of the Worshipful FRANCIS DEWICK, Merchant-Adventurer, once Mayor of *Kingfton-upon-Hull*, who departed this Life the 2d of *May*, 1663. And alfo MARGARET his Wife, who departed this Life the 15th of *February*, 1661.
A

---

* That pious Gentlewoman was a Benefactrefs to the curious modern Library.
† He erected an Hofpital, and set up this remarkable Infcription.

Da dum Tempus habes, tibi propria Manus Hæres ;
Auferet hoc nemo, quod dabis ipfe Deo.   G. C. 1661. E. C.

THUS REN- } Give whilft you've Time, and ufe a gen'rous Hand :
  DER'D   } What's giv'n to Heav'n, no Mortal can demand.

A Copartment, North Weſt in the Church.

NEar this Place lieth the Body of the Worshipful HUM-PHREY DUNCALF, Alderman, Mayor of this Incorporation, *Anno Dom.* 1668, Woollen Draper. He departed this Life, in the true Faith of CHRIST, the 22d of *Octob.* 1683. *Ætat. ſuæ* 64. Alſo ANNE, his Wife, the Daughter of Alderman *William Popple.* She died, in the Faith of CHRIST, the 25th Day of *November,* 1691.

E.

'South Weſt, near the Church Door, is a Copartment, *with the following Inſcription.*

WIthin the Porch, adjoining to this Church, is interr'd the Body of the Worshipful * JOSEPH ELLIS, who dy'd the 19th of *Auguſt, A.D.* 1683. being then Mayor of this Town, [*Alſo in* 1682.] aged 48 Years. *Mors eſt ultima Linea Rerum.*

F.

In the Great Isle of the Chancel.

HEre lieth the Body of Mr. JOSEPH FERNLEY, Merchant, who married *Mary,* the Daughter of Mr. *John Shepheard,* by whom he had one Daughter, the preſent Wife of *Nathaniel* Rogers, Eſquire. His second Wife was SARAH, the Daughter of Alderman *Henry Maiſter,* who bore him 5 Children ; two of which, one Son, and one Daughter, survived him.

---

* *That Gentleman placed four Widows in an Hoſpital, which he had built in* Salt-Houſe-Lane : *The Management of which, by his Laſt Will, he left to the Corporation. In it, he only deſired, That Mrs.* JANE, *his Spouſe, (join'd with Mr.* RICHARD, *his Brother, Execut. and both oblig'd to keep it in good Repair during their Lives) should upon any Vacancy, have Power to place therein the Perſon she thought fit to nominate. The Gentlewoman was afterwards marry'd to Mr.* SUGDEN *of Beverley ; whom she piously perſuaded generously to depoſite Sixty Pounds in the Hands of the Mayor and Aldermen of* Hull, *so that the Intereſt of that Sum, Three Pounds Yearly, might purchaſe Coals for the Uſe of the said poor Widows : Which, being preſented accordingly, was accepted, for that Purpoſe, by the Worshipful Magiſtrates.*

He

He exchanged this Life for a better, the 5th of *September,* *Anno Dom.* 1725. *Ætatis* 76.

The following lies North of the Altar.

HERE lieth the Body of the Worshipful THOMAS FERRES, Maſter and Mariner, once Mayor of this Town, who departed this Life, in the true Faith of CHRIST, *Anno Dom.* 1631. † *Quod ſum, fueris.*

Within the Altar Rails.

INTERRED within this Vault is the Body of Mrs. MARY FOXLEY, Wife of Mr. *William Foxley,* Alderman, and sometime Major of this Incorporation, who departed this Life the 28th Day of *January,* 1673. being the 68th Year of her Age.

In the Broad Isle of the Choir.

HERE reſteth the Body of the Worshipful WILLIAM FOXLEY, Alderman, and twice Mayor of this Town, who departed this Life, the 24th Day of *September,* 1680. aged 71 Years.

Near the South Wall, at the Weſt End, is a rais'd Tomb,
of Black Marble, with this Inſcription.

HERE lieth the Body of the Worshipful JOSEPH FIELD, twice Mayor of this Town, and Merchant-Adventurer, who departed this Life, in the true Faith of CHRIST.

Here is a Field ſown, that at length muſt sprout,
And 'gainſt the rip'ning Harveſt's Time break out ;
When to that Husband it a Crop shall yield,
Who firſt did dreſs, and till this now ſown Field :
Yet e're this Field you ſee this Crop can give,
The Seed firſt dies, that it again may live.

Anno Dom. Decemb. 1627. Ætat. 63.
Sit Deus Amicus.
Sanctis, vel in Sepulchris, Spes eſt.

A Copartment on the South Wall, the Weſt End.

NEAR this Place is interr'd the Body of the Worshipful JOHN FIELD, Merchant, late Alderman, and ſometime Mayor of *Kingſton-upon-Hull ;* and SARAH his Wife, by whom

---

† In the Cathedral of *Norwich,* dedicated to the Holy Trinity, is the Figure of a Skeleton, with theſe exhortatory Lines.

(All you that do this Place paſs by,
Remember Death, whilſt viewing me :
As you are now, ſo once was I ;
And as I am, ſo shall you be.

E

he

he had 8 Sons, and 6 Daughters. She departed this Life the 30th of *January*, 1685. and he the 26th of *October*, 1689. after they had been married 27 Years. Both Lovers of GOD, and the Church of *England;* in the Faith and Communion of which they lived and died, and do here reſt in Hope of a joyful Reſurrection. *Vivit poſt Funera Virtus.*

In the South Isle of the Chancel.

HERE lieth interr'd the Body of the Worſhipful JOHN FORCET, Grocer, who departed this Life the 30th of *February*, 1685. in the 64th Year of his Age, he being then Mayor of this Corporation. And ELIZABETH, his Wife, who dy'd the 10th of *February*, 1699.

Weſt End of the Church.

HERE lieth interr'd the Body of the Worſhipful GEORGE FROGAT, Merchant, and Alderman of this Town, who departed, in the true Faith of CHRIST, the 29th Day of *October*, 1683. in the 52d Year of his Age.

G.

GILEAD GOCHE, Gent. died 1679. DOROTHEA, Wife of Mr. *Nathaniel Goche*, departed this Life *Anno* 1700.

On a Copartment, inward Pillar, North, W. End.

LIETH interr'd on the Weſt Side of the Font, GILEAD GOCHE, Gent. and ANNE his Wife, with ELIZABETH the Daughter of *Nathaniel Goche;* and DOROTHEA his Wife, eldeſt Daughter of *William Grimſton*, Eſq ; and DOROTHEA NORCLIFFE. Departed the 20th of *July, Anno* 1700.

South Isle, at the W. End.

IN this Vault lieth the Body of Mr. ROBERT GRAY, Son of Alderman *Richard Gray*, who departed this Life *Auguſt* the 26th, *A.D.* 1724. aged 54 Years. Alſo the Body of his Siſter JANE, Widow of Mr. *Richard ·Wait*, Merchant, of this Town. She departed this Life the 26th of *Auguſt*, 1730. Aged 63.

Copartment, on the South Wall, at the W. End.

NEAR this Place is interr'd the Worſhipful Alderman RICHARD GRAY, Merchant, twice Mayor of this Corporation, an able Man, ſuch as fear'd GOD, a Man of Truth,

hating

hating Covetousness, the 18th of *November*, in the 96th Year of his Age, *A. D.* 1727.

❋❋❋❋❋❋❋❋❋❋❋❋❋❋❋❋❋❋❋❋❋❋❋❋

H.

WILLIAM and LEONARD HUDSON, 1621. *Buried in the South Isle, at the West End.*

North of the Altar.

HERE lieth the Body of Mr. HUNT, Surveyor of His Majesty's Customs at *Boston;* who dy'd at *Lincoln, April* 28, 1678; and, by his own Appointment, here interr'd.

❋❋❋❋❋❋❋❋❋❋❋❋❋❋❋❋❋❋❋❋❋❋❋❋

I.

Beneath the Steeple.

HERE lieth the Body of THOMAS JOHNSON, Merchant, twice Mayor of *Hull;* and of JULIANA, his Wife. She departed this Life, the 19th of *August*, 1676. He died the 13th of *June*, 1700. being the 70th Year of his Age; and also the Body of ANNE their Daughter, who died the 24th of *October*, 1689.

In the South Isle of the Chancel.

HERE lieth the Body of Mrs. ELIZABETH JOHNSON, Daughter of *Edward Nelthorpe* of *Barton* in *Lincolnshire*, Esq; Wife and Relict of Alderman *John Rogers;* then of Alderman *Thomas Johnson* of this Town. By the former she had 3 Sons, and 3 Daughters. She dy'd the 23d of *June*, 1707. in the true Faith of CHRIST, *Ætatis suæ* 63.

In the Great Cross Isle.

HERE lieth the Body of the Worshipful ANTHONY IVESON, Alderman, Mayor in 1691. [*His Mayoralty begun* 1690.] Died aged 63, *April* 25, 1697. *Mors Lucrum Sanctis.* Also *Anthony Iveson*, his eldest Son, who dy'd *Octob.* 25, 1700. aged 28. Here also lieth ANNE, the Wife of the above said Alderman, Daughter of *Lancellot Roper*, late Alderman of this Town, who dy'd the 5th of *January*, 1722. Aged 68.

❋❋❋❋❋❋❋❋❋❋❋❋❋❋❋❋❋❋❋❋❋❋❋❋

K.   *Under the Steeple.*

HERE are interr'd the Bodies of Mr. MARK KIRKBY, of this Town, Merchant; and JANE, his Wife. She died the 16th of *June*, 1686. aged 35. And he, *Octob.* 22d, 1718.

aged

aged 80. Alſo their Daughter, MARY, Wife of Mr. *Richard Sykes*, who died *April* the 4th, 1714. aged 32. And their eldeſt Son Mr. RICHARD KIRKBY, who dy'd *October* 11, 1719. aged 40. And their Son **Mr.** CHRISTOPHER.

And on a Pillar, N. of the Great Tower, are the following Inſcriptions of him and his Family.

NIGH this Monument are interr'd the Bodies of Mr. MARK KIRKBY, of this Town, Merchant; and JANE, his Wife, (Daughter of *Chriſtopher Richardſon*, Alderman, and twice Mayor) by whom he had 10 Children: Four died young: The reſt were *Dinah, Richard,* and *Chriſtopher; Mary, Mark,* and *Iſabel:* MARY dy'd before him: The other 5 furviv'd both. He was an affectionate Husband, a kind Father, a prudent Œconomiſt, fincere in promiſing, and punctual in performing. She dy'd *June* 16, 1686, aged 35. He *October* the 22d, 1718, aged 80.

> The ſweet Remembrance of the Juſt,
> Shall flouriſh when he sleeps in Duſt.

Vita Juſti Via Cæli.

ALso nigh this Place lies their Daughter MARY, (late Wife of Mr. *Richard Sykes)* who dy'd *April* 4, 1714. *Ætat.* 32. and their eldeſt Son RICHARD, who dy'd *October* 11, 1719. *Ætat.* 40.

North of the Altar.

UNDER this Stone lieth the Body of Mr. JOHN KING, of the Town of *Kingſton-upon-Hull,* Merchant, who died the 17th Day of *May,* 1678, and in the 23rd Year of his Age.

L.

A Copartment on a Pillar, at the W. End, in the Church, as alſo much the same Words on his Grave Stone.

NEAR this Place lieth the Remains of Alderman ANTHONY LAMBERT, ſometimes Mayor of this Corporation, who took to Wife *Anne* the Daughter of Mr. *George Saltmarsh,* of this Town, and by her had 8 Sons, and 5 Daughters. And after he had lived 58 Years piously towards GOD, faithfully towards his Friend, and uſeful in his Stations to all, he departed this Life, the 28th of *May,* 1688. much lamented.

HERE lieth interr'd the Body of ANNE, Wife of *Anthony Lambert*, Alderman, 1667, with whom he was married 29 Years, and 5 Months, and had by her 8 Sons, and 5 Daughters; and, after a prudent and pious Pilgrimage, departed this frail Life in the true Faith of Chrift, *Aug.* 21, 1684. aged 49 Years, waiting for the Refurrection of the Juft.

Near them are bury'd fome of the Family, viz.

HERE lieth the Body of ANTHONY LAMBERT, Jun. and eldeft Son of the Worfhipful *Anthony Lambert*, Alderman, who was married to *Elizabeth*, Daughter to the Worfhipful *William Skinner*, Alderman, by whom he had one Son. He departed, in the true Chriftian Faith, the 5th of *October*, 1684. *Ætat.* 27 Years, 8 Months.

GEORGE LAMBERT, fecond Son of the Worfhipful *Anthony Lambert*, Alderman, dy'd in the Faith of Chrift, *July* 29, 1684. aged 23.

DOROTHY, the Daughter of *Anthony Lambert*, Alderman, dy'd *June* 4, 1667.

HERE lieth the Body of ANNE, Daughter of Mr. *Henry Lambert*, Merchant, who died the 2d Day of *Sept.* 1690.

In the South Isle of the Chancel.

HERE sleepeth in Hope NICHOLAS LINDLEY, Merchant-Adventurer, once Mayor of this Town, who departed in the Faith of CHRIST, the 12th of *July*, 1624.

In and about the Great Isle of the Chancel.

HERE refteth in Peace JOHN LISTER the Elder, Merchant, twice Mayor of this Town, who departed this Life, in the true Faith of CHRIST, the 19th of *January*, A. D. 1616.

HERE lieth the Body of the, Right Worfhipful * Sir JOHN LISTER, Knight, twice Mayor of this Town, who died, being Burgefs of Parliament, *Dec.* 23, *A. D.* 1640.

Oppofite the South Porch of the Church is an Hofpital, upon the outward Wall of which is this Infcription.

* " An Hofpital, for Six Men and Six Women, by Sir JOHN LISTER, " Knight, twice Mayor; and alfo the Reader's Houfe adjoining to it, " and endow'd it with Lands, to the Value of Six Hundred a Year. He refided in the *High-Street*, and had a beautiful fronted Houfe (with other convenient Buildings) wherein he nobly treated King CHARLES the Firft.

HERE lieth the Body of Lady ELIZABETH LISTER, Wife to Sir *John Lifter*, Knight, deceafed, by whom she had 16 Children. She dy'd the 2d of *December, Anno Dom.* 1656, in the 68th Year of her Age.

HERE lieth the Body of SAMUEL LISTER, who died *May* 1, 1645. *He is bury'd North of the Altar.*

On a Hatchment, near the Altar.

NEAR this Pillar lieth the Body of HUGH LISTER, Efq ; Juftice of Peace in the Eaft-Riding, 4th Son to the Right Worfhipful *John Lifter*, Knight. He took to Wife *Jane*, the Daughter and Heir to the Worfhipful *Barnard Smith*, twice Mayor of this Town, by whom he had Iffue 4 Sons and two Daughters, who all, except one, do yet remain hopeful Reprieves to the Memory of him : *Qui bonis omnibus flebilis occidit, Anno Chrifti* 1666, *Oct.* 9. *Ætat.* 48.

M.

Upon the South Wall of the Chancel, is this.

NEAR this Monument are interr'd the Bodies of WILLIAM MAISTER, Efq ; Merchant of this Town, and of LUCY, his Wife, Daughter of Alderman *John Rogers.* They were mutually happy in a ftrict conjugal Affection, and gave Life to 5 Children, all now living, viz. *Henry, Elizabeth, William, John* and *Nathaniel.* She liv'd as much belov'd, as known ; and dy'd as much lamented, the 4th of *July*, 1704. He, having ferv'd his Country, and this Corporation 7 fucceffive Parliaments with a difinterefted Fidelity, left this Life the 27th of *October*, 1716. His Friends knew his Merit too well, not to mourn for the Lofs of fo great and good a Patriot. May this Monument convey his Memory to Pofterity, and fhew a grateful Senfe his Relations have of the Honour done him by this Loyal Corporation.

On an inward S. Pillar, at the W. End. [And very near the fame Words are on the Grave-Stone, in the Great Isle.]

NEAR this Monument are interr'd the Bodies of Mr. HENRY MAISTER, and ANNE his Wife, Daughter of Mr. *William Raikes.* They had Iffue 9 Sons and 2 Daughters, 7 of
which

which ſurvived them.   He was twice Mayor of this Town, and Deputy Governour to the *Hamburg-Eaſtland* Companies. He died 5th of *April*, 1699. aged 67.   She died *Dec.* 14, 1685. aged 48.   *Hodie nobis cras vobis.*

MARY MASON, Wife of the Vicar, interred *December* 26, 1725. *Buried in the Great Isle of the Chancel.*

ROBERT MASON, dy'd *October* 10, 1727.   *He lies buried within the Rails of the Altar.*

North of the Altar is this, over Mrs. Matſon.

HERE lieth the Body of Mrs. MARY MATSON, Daughter of Mr. *John Matſon*, of *Dover*, Merchant, and *Mary* his Wife, and only Siſter of *Margaret*, the Wife of Mr. *James Houſeman*, of this Town, who died the 25th of *July*, *A.D.* 1688.

NEAR the W. End of the Church lieth buried the Body of JOHN MAUGHAN, who dy'd *A.D.* 1622.

✺✺✺✺✺✺✺✺✺✺✺✺✺✺✺✺✺✺✺✺✺✺✺✺✺✺

N.   *In the South Isle, at the Weſt End.*

ROBERT NETTLETON, Alderman, ſometime Mayor of this Town, interr'd *May* 8, 1706. had 13 Children by *Lydia* his Wife, 7 of which were bury'd in his Grave.   She was Daughter of Mr. *James Blaydes*, and *Anne* his Wife, Daughter to the Reverend * *Andrew Marvell*, and Siſter to † *Andrew Marvell*, Esq ; who about twenty Years ſerved this Town as Member of Parliament.

✺✺✺✺✺✺✺✺✺✺✺✺✺✺✺✺✺✺✺✺✺✺✺✺✺✺

P.   *Within the Chancel.*

HERE lieth the Body of WALTER PECKE, Merchant-Adventurer, who departed this Life in the true Faith of CHRIST, the 8th of *July*, 1598.

In the Great Isle, at the Weſt End.

HERE lieth the Body of Mrs. SUSANNAH PERROTT, Wife of Alderman ANDREW PERROTT, and Daughter of Al-

---

* Mr. EACHARD calls him, The famous *Calviniſtical* Miniſter of *Hull.* p. 960.
† Having had an Academical Education in *Trinity-College*, *Cambridge*, he underſtood *Latin* extremely well, and was an Aſſiſtant to Mr. JOHN MILTON, OLIVER's Secretary.   After the Reſtoration, he was elected Member of Parliament, and ſo continued 'till his Death ; which, it ſeems likely, prevented ſome Troubles that might have come upon him, for his Satyrical Writings againſt both the Church and Crown. *ibid.*

derman *Anthony Lambert.* She departed this Life the 13th Day of *July,* 1716. *Ætat. fuæ* 44.

In the South Isle, at the W. End.

JOHN PEARSON, once Sheriff, twice Warden of the * Trinity-Houfe, died *November* 24, 1666. He had 6 Sons, and 6 Daughters. His Wife *Elizabeth* was Wife to Alderman *Ripley,* who was twice Mayor of *Hull.*

R.

In the South Isle of the Choir.

HERE lieth the Body of THOMAS RAIKES, Alderman, and Merchant, † thrice Mayor of this Town, who departed this Life, the 8th of *Auguft,* 1662.

In the Great Isle, at the Weft End.

HERE lie the Remains of WILLIAM RAIKES, Mafter and Mariner, who exchanged this Life for a better, the 26th Day of *January,* 1668.

HERE is interr'd MARGARET, the Wife of ROBERT RAIKES, Grocer, and eldeft Daughter to Alderman *John Kaye,* Merchant, who departed this Life the 16th of *June, A.D.* 1674.

---

* *This Houfe had its Beginning from a generous Contribution, in order to fupport diftreffed Sailors, and Mariners Widows, of the Town : But a Patent from the Crown being obtain'd, many fuch Perfons, from other Places, have enjoy'd here this happy Benefit. Twelve Elder Brothers, with Six Affiftants, have the Management of it; whofe Determinations, (which relate between Mafters and their Seamen) and Opinions in Tryals at Law, concerning Tranfactions on the Ocean, are very much regarded. From thefe, are chofen annually Two Wardens ; at whofe Election, they alfo join, with their Votes, thofe of the young Brethren : And out of the latter, Two Stewards are likewife appointed. The Place (which has a decent Chapel belonging to it) is the Property of a Society of Merchants, who have richly endow'd it. Herein, below Stairs, are Thirty pretty Chambers, for as many poor Women, where they find comfortable Relief. Above, are Two Noble Rooms : One, for the Brethren to confult their Affairs ; the Other, is the Place wherein are made Sails for large Ships, or leffer Veffels. In the latter, near the Ceiling, hangs a Canoe, or little Boat, cover'd with Skins ; A Groenlander is reprefented in Effigy fitting therein, with his Lower Parts below Deck : A Pair of Oars in his Right Hand ; and a Javelin or Dart (wherewith 'tis thought he wounded the more ftubborn Fish) in his Left. On his Head feems a fort of Trencher Cap ; and a Bag of Skins lay by him, either to feed what he caught of the Finny Race, or elfe to contain a certain Oyl, wherewith he used to entice them. He had alfo with him a large Jaw Bone of a mighty Whale. Captain ANDREW BARKER took him upon the Sea, (in his Boat with all thefe Implements, ftill preferv'd, except the natural Body, for which the Effigy is fubftituted) in the Year 1613. But fo ill did this feeming fon of NEPTUNE brook his Captivity, that, refufing to eat what was kindly offered him, he died in Three Days Time.*

† Two of the Years, fucceffively, he kept in that Office, being upheld by the Parliament, tho' it was a direct Violation of the Laws, and contrary to the Conftitutions of *Kingfton-upon-Hull.*

The following Inscriptions are N. of the Altar.

HERE lieth the Body of the Worshipful † JOHN RAMSDEN, twice Mayor of this Town, and Merchant-Adventurer, who departed, in the true Faith of CHRIST, *Anno* 1637. *Mors omnibus communis.*

---

† In the Year 1635, the Plague, (which had visited the Inhabitants of many other Sea-Ports) begun to rage in this Town, and in Time took away the Life of that Magistrate. No wise Precaution was able to prevent the Contagion. People fled into the Country. The Gates were soon order'd to be shut up. A strict Guard was placed, Day and Night, in order to prevent any more from going out, or coming in; and the Watchmen were only allowed to receive Provisions, which soon became very dear, and were timorously thrust in, at Places made fit for the Purpose. No Societies were suffer'd to meet. The Churches and Schools clos'd up: Scarce any Body walk'd the Streets, (except those who cry'd out *for the Dead!*) where Grass grew between the Stones of the Pavement, as a very melancholy Scene; and all seem'd bury'd in a profound Silence. In Time of LENT, his Grace, *RICHARD NEIL*, Lord Archbishop of *York*, was apply'd to, for Licenfe, that, upon this Occasion, the Inhabitants might eat Flesh. The good Archbishop told the Petitioners, *He could not conceive what Authority he had to grant it: But in all Cases of extreme Necessity, as in Weakness, or Sickness, especially in such a deplorable State as theirs was; the Ministers might, on Certificates from the Physicians, grant such a reasonable Liberty, during the Holy Season: Therefore,* added the pious Prelate, *let the like Method be taken: And I earnestly beseech the Almighty God of Heaven and Earth, to heal, preserve, and strengthen, both the Bodies and Souls of our Afflicted Brethren.* This condescending Advice being taken, had good Effect for some Time: But, alas! in 1638, the Sickness increasing by the Intemperature of the Air, which seem'd to be in a Sort of Stagnation, without the least comfortable Gale or Breeze; the Markets were cry'd down: To supply which Want, and further their Relief, the Justices, of the neighbouring Places, were oblig'd to send in Carts both Provisions and Necessaries to the Side of the Garrison; where they were bought, (by a few of the Town's Inhabitants, deputed on that Account) and after sent in Sledges to the Town's Cross, to be dispos'd of, at the most reasonable Prices. But as all Trade and Mercantile Affairs seem'd as it were under a gloomy Shade, or rather might be deem'd as quite extinct; so the wretched Consequences appear'd, in the deplorable Circumstances of above Two Thousand Persons; who, from opulent Fortunes, were now become the piteous Objects of Christian Charity! Others, that could afford it, were heavily assessed, Weekly, both in Town, and in the Country, to support the Afflicted; besides, to maintain the Attendants of the Visited, whilst they were living in languishing Misery; and to reward those, who took Care to bury the Dead. The Number that perish'd were about 2730 Persons, excluding those who fled, or died of other Distempers, which almost doubled the Number. This Pestilence continued, 'till about the 16th of *June*, 1639, when it pleas'd GOD to cease: And it was near the Middle of the Visitation that Mr. *Ramsden* became a Victim to it, amongst others. He was a Gentleman of great Erudition, remarkable Piety, and universal Esteem. His Corpse was carry'd, by visited Persons, into the Church: And tho' the Rev. Mr. ANDREW MARVELL had the Epithet *facetious*, apply'd to him by several Writers: Yet, to his Praise be it spoken, it was He, that ventur'd, in that imminent Danger, not only to give him Christian Burial, unus'd some Time before; but also, from the Pulpit, deliver'd, to the mournful weeping Congregation, a most excellent Funeral Sermon, (afterwards printed) in such pathetick, moving Oratory, that both prepar'd and comforted their Hearts, chearfully to bear whatever might happen to them, in their lamentable Condition.

Over the Vault, in which the Alderman, and his Lady, are laid.

IN this Vault lieth the Body of the Worſhipful † WILLIAM RAMSDEN, ſometime Deputy to the Right Worſhipful Company of Merchant-Adventurers of *England*, Alderman, and Mayor of this Town twice, a Member of Parliament, for the ſame Corporation, in the Honourable HOUSE of COMMONS. He departed this Life, in the true Faith of CHRIST, the 2d Day of *September*, 1680. in the 63d Year of his Age, waiting the Morning of the Reſurrection.

Engraved on the ſame Stone.

IN this Vault lieth interr'd the Body of Mrs. ANNE RAMSDEN, (Wife to the Worſhipful *William Ramſden*, Esq ; Alderman of this Town) Daughter to the Worſhipful *Thomas Boynton*, of *Roucliff*, Esq ; She departed this Life, in the true Faith of CHRIST, the 23d Day of *April*, 1667.

Near the S. Church-Yard Door.

HERE lieth the Body of the Worſhipful * CHRISTOPHER RICHARDSON, Alderman, and twice Mayor of *Kingſton-upon-Hull*, who dy'd *Feb.* 12, 1701.

---

† That Gentleman, ſome Time before his Death, had a great Deſire to lay down his Gown, so that he might spend the Remainder of his Days, in a happy Retirement, from publick Buſineſs. To obtain which, (in *May*, 1678.) he beſought the BENCH to accept of an Hundred Pounds, the Interest thereof to be apply'd for the Uſe of the Poor ; on Condition, that he might be diſmiſſed from the Office of an Alderman. But the Court requiring Time 'till next Hall-Day, the Mayor then told him, *That as they were all very ſenſible of his being a ſerviceable, good and honourable Perſon ; ſo they were not in the leaſt willing to part with ſo excellent a Magistrate :* And therefore as earnestly requested, *That he would be pleas'd to relinquish his Desire.* After some reasonable Solicitations to him, for that Purpoſe, he was contented to remain in his uſual eminent Station. And tho' the Money offer'd by him seem'd thereby lost to the Poor ; yet his Goodneſs was such, that, (as I found recorded in St. *Mary's* Church, with the Beneficence of Alderman *Popple*, who allow'd Fourteen Pence Worth of Bread to be distributed to them every Lord's Day) he charitably gave Two Shillings, Weekly, to be laid out, the same Way, for the Relief of thoſe, whose Neceſſities requir'd the like Aſſistance.

* In the Year 1678, he desired to be discharged from the Office of an Alderman : And tho' his Request was at first deny'd ; yet he continu'd so earnestly preſſing, that, submitting to any Fine the Court should please to lay upon him for their kind Condeſcension, they withdrew ; and, among themselves, propos'd Three Sums, in the like Caſes, to be paid by such Aldermen, who requested to be discharged for the future : When it was agreed, That either Fifty, Seventy-Five, or One Hundred Pounds, should be the Fine ; and to be voted for, according to Discretion. But the middlemost Sum was allotted for this Gentleman to pay, whereby he obtained an entire Dismiſſion.

Within

Within the Altar Rails.

HERE lieth the Body of the Worfhipful EDWARD RICHARDSON, and once Mayor of this Town, who departed in the true Faith of CHRIST.

South of the Altar.

HERE lieth the Body of Alderman JOHN ROGERS, Merchant, and once Mayor of *Hull*, who married *Elizabeth*, Daughter of *Edward Nelthrop* of *Barton*, Esq ; and departed this Life *February* the 14th, 1680. [*Mayor in* 1652.]

Alfo South of the Altar are the following.

HERE lieth the Body of Mrs. LUCY ROGERS, Daughter to Mr. *Lancellot Roper*, Alderman, and twice Mayor of *Kingfton-upon-Hull*, late Wife to Mr. *John Rogers*, of the fame Town, Merchant, by whom fhe had 17 Children, with whom fhe lived a pious Life 37 Years, and died in the Faith of CHRIST, *February* 15, *Anno Ætatis* 58, *& Salutis* 1665.

HERE lieth the Body of Mr. JOHN ROGERS, who departed this Life, *Dec.* 27, 1723.

In the South Isle of the Chancel.

HERE lieth the Body of Mr. JOHN ROGERS, who departed this Life, *June* 1, 1728.

HERE lieth the Body of Mr. LANCELLOT ROPER, Son of Alderman *Roper*, of *Kingfton-upon-Hull*, who married AGNES the Daughter of Mr. *George Crowle*, Merchant, and Alderman of this Town, by whom he had Iffue one Son, named *Lancellot.* He dy'd the 30th Day of *December*, 1686. in the 29th Year of his Age.

S.   *North of the Altar, are the two following.*

HERE refteth in Peace SAMUEL SALTONSTALL, Esq ; who departed this Life, in the true Faith of CHRIST, the 8th Day of *January*, A.D. 1612.

HERE refteth the Body of JEREMIAH SMYTH, Efq ; Grandfon of Sir *Jeremiah Smyth*, Admiral. He married *Mary*, the Daughter of Mr. *William Skinner*, of this Town. He died the 2d of *September*, 1714. in the 37th Year of his Age.

HERE lieth interr'd the Body of LEONARD SCOTT, who departed this Life the 18th of *December*, 1680. in the 67th Year of his Age. *Buried in the Broad Isle of the Choir.*

In

In the Middle Isle, the Place of Preaching, on a Brafs Plate.

HERE lieth the Body of Mrs. DOROTHY SHAW, (late the dear Wife of Mr. *John Shaw*, Preacher of the Gofpel in this Church) who was here interr'd *December* 12, 1657. waiting for the Morning of the Refurrection of the Juft.

HERE lieth the Body of MICHAEL SHAWTER, who departed this Life the 17th of *February*, 1729. aged 45 Years.

Within the Altar Rails.

HERE lieth interr'd the Body of Alderman † WILLIAM SKINNER, who died at *Peckham*, near *London ;* and was, by his own Appointment, brought hither, and laid near his Wife, *Mary*, the Daughter of Mr. *John Hayes*, late of *London*, Grocer. By her he had 4 Sons, and 7 Daughters. He died *September* the 19th, in the Three and Fiftieth Year of his Age, 1680.

And North of the Altar, is this.

NEAR this Place lieth interr'd the Body of WILLIAM SKINNER, late Alderman, and formerly Mayor of this Town, who had 3 Wives, *Jane* and two *Maries.* By the firft *Mary* he had 4 Sons ; *William*, two *Johns*, and *Thomas ;* 6 Daughters, *Mary, Jane, Lydia, Elizabeth, Ellinor*, and *Sarah*. He died in the 53d Year of his Age, the 19th of *Sept.* 1680.

In the Great Isle of the Chancel.

IN this Vault lieth interr'd the Body of Mrs. MARY SKINNER, Wife of Mr. *William Skinner*, of this Town, Alderman, fometime Mayor, by whom fhe had 4 Sons, and 7 Daughters.

---

† He left such a competent Legacy, That Eight Dozen of Bread (to hold which, there is a convenient Place made in the Church) should for ever be diftributed to the Poor, the first Sunday of every Month. Other Benefactions, I perceiv'd, for their Ufe, are mention'd on a Table, affix'd to a Pillar, (in the Place, where Prayers and Preaching are perform'd) whereon may be read the following Words :

" 1. FRancis Porter bequeathed 40s. to the Poor for Bread, "(An. 1716.) on the Feaft of St. JOHN the Evan- " gelift Yearly.   2. *Mary Harrifon*, his Daughter-in-Law, " left 20l. the Intereft of which for the Diftribution of " Bread for ever, at the Difcretion of the Church-Wardens. " 3. *John Horfeman* (1704.) left 40 Shillings for ever. " 4. Mr. *Francis Smith* (1689.) gave 18d. *per* Week for ever."

Daughters.   She reſigned this Life, for a better, the 13th Day of *April, A.D.* 1674. and of her Age the 42d.

MR. TRISTRAM SUGAR, Woollen-Draper, dy'd *April* 9, 1686. *Anno Ætat.* 39.

✠✠✠✠✠✠✠✠✠✠✠✠✠✠✠✠✠✠✠✠✠✠✠✠✠✠✠✠✠✠

T.   *In the South Isle of the Chancel.*

JAcet hic depoſitum BENJAMINIS TAYLOR in hoc Oppido Profeſſoris Medicinæ, qui obiit Decembris die x°. Ætatis Anno Æræ Chriſtianæ MDCLXXIX.

Near the South Door.

IN this Vault lieth interr'd the Body of THOMAS TOMLIN, Draper, Son of *Marmaduke Tomlin,* of *Riby,* in the County of *Lincoln,* Gentleman, who departed this Life the 12th Day of *February,* 1696. in the 45th Year of his Age, and reſts in Hope of a joyful Reſurrection.   He married *Sarah,* one of the Daughters of *John Batty* of *Warneſworth,* in the Weſt Riding of the County of *York,* Esq ; who order'd this Monument of her Love and Respect to the Memory of her dear deceaſed Husband.

JOSEPH THWINGE, Draper, who dy'd the 23rd of *November,* 1636.   *Buried near the Weſt End.*

JOSEPH TOWERSON; dy'd *A. D.* 1683.   *Lies buried in the South Isle, at the Weſt End.*

✠✠✠✠✠✠✠✠✠✠✠✠✠✠✠✠✠✠✠✠✠✠✠✠✠✠✠✠✠✠

V.

HERE lieth the Body of Mr. CHARLES VAUX, after he had served Clerk of the Corporation 33 Years, and died the 10th of *December,* 1680. in the 69th Year of his Age.

✠✠✠✠✠✠✠✠✠✠✠✠✠✠✠✠✠✠✠✠✠✠✠✠✠✠✠✠✠✠

W.   *In the South Isle of the Chancel.*

HERE reſteth in Peace LEONARD WISTON, Merchant-Adventurer, and once Mayor, who departed this Life, in the Faith of CHRIST, the 20th of *February,* 1598.

On a Pillar in the North Isle, near the Altar.

P. M. MARIÆ WILKINSON Uxoris optimæ 22 *Feb.* 1711. defunctæ, mærens ponit, & fungitur inani munere *Johannes Wilkinſon* Prælector. THUS RENDER'D. *John Wilkinson,* Lecturer, in Sorrow, hath placed this to the ſacred Memory of his dear Wife MARY WILKINSON, who dy'd *Feb.* 22, 1711.

Near the West End.

ROGER WATTS, Mariner, departed this Life, in the Year of our LORD, 1652.

In the South Isle of the Chancel.

HERE lieth the Body of RICHARD WOOD, Woollen-Draper, sometime Mayor of this Town, who departed this Life, in the Faith of CHRIST, the 16th of *December, Anno Domini* 1662. *Ætatis* 63.   [*Mayor in* 1653.]

In the South Wall of the Choir, is the Bust of a venerable Person, with this remarkable Inscription.

QUisquis es (Viator) siste, atque hunc intuere mortuum, quem vivum satius tibi imitari erit Scientiæ multiplicis, profundi Judicii, Vitæ Probitatis, Industriæ indefessæ, Charitatis comitatis, Pietatis Exemplar singulare THOMAM WHINCOP. Eximium DEI Servum, charissimum Theologum, omnium Bonorum Memoriâ & Amore dignum. Qui opt°. max°. (cui plusquam 74 Annos) servivit integerrimi Viri, sapientissimi Civis, vigilantissimi Pastoris Officij fatagens (Annorum tandem famæque gratæ satur) Deo Animam reddidit, Corporisque Resurrectionem præstolatur : Atque etiamnum mortuus vivit. Tantum est, vade Lector, sua Merces est, Creatoris Gloria, Exemplum Tuum.

WHICH IS THUS RENDER'D.

Stop, Traveller, whoever thou art, and look upon him, now dead, who, when alive, it was more useful for thee to imitate : Mr. THOMAS WHINCOP : *An eminent Example of great Learning, sound Judgment, Probity of Life, indefatigable Industry, Charity, Humanity and Piety, A faithful Servant of G O D, an excellent Divine, and one that worthily merited the Love and Remembrance of all good Men : Who, after he had served the Most High, above the Space of Seventy Four Years, diligently executing the Offices of an honest Man, a prudent Citizen, and a vigilant Pastor ; at last, being full of Years and Honour, he resigned his Soul to the Almighty, waiting for the Resurrection of the Body : Who, tho' now dead, yet liveth. All that remains, Go, Reader ! As G O D's Glory is now his Reward, so his Example thine.*

AFTER

AFTER THE LATIN, BEFORE-MENTION'D, IS THIS.

HEREUNDER refts in Peace the Body of Mr. THO-
MAS WHINCOP, born at * *Linton* upon *Wharfe*, in *Yorkshire;*
brought up for the Space of ten Years at the Univerfity of
Cambridge, in *Trinity-College*, whereof he was a Member ; afterwards Preacher at *Beverley* in the *Minfter* about 16 Years ;
then Mafter of Charter-Houfe Hofpital ; and Preacher of
HULL, in this Church, 25 Years.   He dy'd *Sept.* 7, 1624.
in the 75th Year of his Age, belov'd, and bemoan'd, of all.
He left, behind him, *Elizabeth* his Wife, born at *Pockling-
ton;* and, by her, three Sons : *Samuel*, Fellow of St. *John's;*
Thomas, and *John*, both Fellows of *Trinity-College*, in *Cam-
bridge;* and all, fucceffively, domeftick Chaplains to the
Right Honourable WILLIAM, Earl of *Salisbury :*   And two
Daughters ; *Mary*, firft married to Mr. *Leonard Hudfon*, of this
Town ; after to Mr. *William Chantrell*, Rector of *Walking-
ton :* And *Thomafine*, firft married to Mr. *William Smeaton*, of
Hull; after to Mr. *John Vaus*, of *York ;* all bleft in fuch
a Father.

THUS, I hope, after laborious Toil, I have given every In-
    fcription and Epitaph *Within* the Church : At leaft, that
    I have, inadvertently, pafs'd by very few. I will only
    mention, before I proceed to the *Out-Side*, what was omit-
    ted before : That the melodious Organ, (which firft was
    begun to be ufed on *Sunday, March* 2, 1712.) was promo-
    ted principally thro' the Care, Goodnefs and Generofity
    of Mr. NATHANIEL ROGERS, and Mr. JOHN COLLINGS :
    For which, methinks, as they ought to be had in lafting
    Remembrance ; fo, in Regard to their Virtue, I have
    exhibited this humble Memorial.

---

* 'Tis in the Deanery of *Craven*. Not far from hence is *Burnfall* Rectory,
two Medieties, *(as* Linton *is)* in the Patronage of Sir WILLIAM CRAVEN, Bart.
and Mr. ALCOCK. In the Church, which is dedicated to St. *Wilfrid*, I perceived
about the Year 1725, two Pulpits, with a Reading-Desk to each ; which belong to two Ministers, who perform Divine Service alternately.

INSCRIPTIONS

INSCRIPTIONS *in the* ✝ Church-Yard:

Alphabetically digested : Firſt, *In the Choir-Yard :* And, Secondly, *On the South Side of the venerable Building :* *With a few, at the Weſt End, here intermix'd ; but mention'd accordingly, to diſtinguish them from the reſt.*

I. *Epitaphs in the* Yard *of the* CHOIR.

B.

HERE lieth the Body of RICHARD BARKER, who died the 29th Day of *April*, 1714.

HERE lieth interr'd the Body of Mrs. CLARE BAMBROUGH, of this Town, who departed this Life the 5th Day of September, *Anno Dom.* 1684.

✝ In the Year 1385, RICHARD *de Ravenſer*, Archdeacon of *Lincoln*, erected, on the North Side of this Church-Yard, an Hoſpital, for poor People, of both Sexes, 12 in Number. Its Endowment was 9*l.* 2*s.* 6*d.* Yearly, that afforded an Half-Penny a Day to each of them ; which, tho' ſeeming very little now, yet went far in those Days. About the ſame time, he founded a Chantry, in the Chapel of St. ANNE, which join'd to the Church ; where Prayers were to be ſaid for the Souls of King *Edward* III. Queen *Philippa*, *Iſabel* her Mother, and King *Richard ;* as also for his own Soul, and those of all the Faithful departed.

NIGH this Place is interr'd the Body of WILLIAM BEWLEY, of this Town, Wine-Cooper, who departed this Life the 18th of *November. Ætatis* 63, *Anno Salutis,* 1678.

NEAR this Place lieth the Body of ANNE, Widow of *Robert* BINCKS, late Elder Brother of the *Trinity-Houſe,* who departed this Life the 18th Day of *February,* 1730.

HERE lieth the Body of Mrs. ELIZABETH BOULTON, who died *October* the 17th, 1678. Here alſo is interr'd Mrs. BARBARA PELL, her Mother, who died *Auguſt* 1, 1694. Here alſo lieth the Body of Mr. ROBERT PELL, A. M. who was 39 Years Maſter of this School, and died *A. D.* 1716, aged 72 Years. He was an affectionate Husband, a tender Father ; and his School had his utmoſt Care.

C.

HERE lieth the Body of Mr. JAMES CHAMBERS, Maſter and Mariner, who departed this Life the 18th of *December,* 1700. Here alſo lieth the Body of JAMES, Son of Mr. *James Chambers,* who departed this Life, *March* the 10th, *Anno* 1714, in the 25th Year of his Age. Here lieth the Body of JUDITH, Daughter of Mr. *James Chambers,* who departed this Life, *November* 19th, *Anno* 1716, in the 18th Year of her Age. Here lieth the Body of ELIZABETH, Wife of Mr. *William Scaman,* Maſter and Mariner, and Daughter of Mr. *James Chambers,* who departed this Life, *March* the 7th, *Anno* 1726, in the 32d Year of her Age.

HERE lieth interr'd the Body of Mr. THOMAS CLARK, of *Kingſton-upon-Hull,* Merchant, who departed this Life the 30th Day of *November,* 1695. in the 41ſt Year of his Age. And alſo of DOROTHY his Daughter, who died *October* 15, 1695. aged 3 Years. Likewiſe of FRANCES his Daughter, who died the 5th of *November,* 1710. in the 18th Year of her Age. *Spe Beatæ Reſurrectionis.* Here alſo lieth interr'd the Body of Mrs. DOROTHY CLARK, Widow and Relict of the above-named Mr. THOMAS CLARK, who departed this Life the 22d Day of *March,* 1713, in the 44th Year of her Age ; and reſts in Hope of a joyful Reſurrection.

D. JAQUES

D.

JAQUES DEWIT, departed this Life, in the Year of our LORD, 1717. Aged 77 Years.

G.

ROBERTUS GANTON, M. P. *Hic conditur Vir magnæ Probitatis et Induſtriæ, multarum Scientiarum peritus, et Rei Medicæ peritiſſimus. Obiit* 19. *Martij* 1697. *Anno Ætatis ſuæ* 38. THAT IS, *Robert Ganton,* Profeſſor of Phyſick, is here interr'd: A Man of great Probity and Induſtry, skilful in the Sciences, and chiefly in what belong'd to his Practice. He dy'd *March* 19, 1697. in the Year of his Age 38. Here alſo lieth the Body of Mrs. SUSANNAH GANTON, Daughter to Mr. *Robert Fairbarn,* of *Heddon,* Alderman, ſometime Merchant - Adventurer of *Hull,* and Wife to Mr. *Robert Ganton :* By whom ſhe had ſeven Children, and departed this Life the 22d of *February,* 1696, in the 42d Year of her Age.

H.

HERE reſteth the Body of WILLIAM HARROW, Maſter and Mariner, who departed this Life the 8th of *September,* 1638.

MICHAEL HARRISON, Woollen-Draper, buried *May* 6, 1689. ANNE his Wife, *April* 24, 1713.

L.

HERE lieth the Body of Mr. ROBERT LAMBERT, Draper, who died *October* the 2d, in the Faith of CHRIST, 1668. He was Sheriff of this Town. [*In* 1660.]

HERE lieth ELIZABETH, the Wife of *John* LAMPSON, interr'd here the 2d of *May,* 1709.

HERE lieth the Body of Mr. JOHN LEAMAN, of this Town, Maſter and Mariner, who died the 25th Day of *Auguſt,* 1717. *Ætatis ſuæ* 56.

M.

HERE lies the Body of ROBERT MEADLEY, who died the 26th of *June,* 1696. aged 63 Years ; and his two Sons,

and

and one Daughter. STEPHEN, aged 10 Weeks; THOMAS, aged 6 Years; SUSANNA, one Year, and Month. Here alfo lies the Body of WILLIAM, Son of *Robert* MEADLEY, Mafter and Mariner, who died *June* 23, 1705. aged 32, and his Son THOMAS, interr'd with him, died *June* 25, aged 4 Years. And his Daughter SUSANNA died *March* 28, aged 6 Months, a Week, and 4 Days. Here lies the Body of SUSANNA, Wife of *Robert* MEADLEY, who departed this Life *Auguft* 15, 1707, aged 73 Years.

HERE lieth the Body of THOMAS MOXON, Merchant, who departed this Life *March* the 7th, *Anno Dom.* 1673. his Age being 47 Years. And alfo ANNE his Wife, who departed this Life, *July* the 8th, *Anno Dom.* 1675.

R.

HERE lieth interr'd the Body of ARTHUR READHEAD, Son of *Robert Readhead*, late of *Colby*, in *Lincolnshire*, Gentleman, who departed this Life *January* the 19th, 1715. in the 56th Year of his Age.

HERE lieth interr'd the Body of Captain WILLIAM RIPLEY, who departed this Life *September* the 23d, 1680. aged 56. And ELIZABETH, his Wife, who died, *A. D.* 1708.

HERE lieth the Body of GEORGE ROBSON, Mafter and Mariner, who died the 7th of *December*, 1701.

S.

HERE lieth the Body of MICHAEL SHAWTER, who departed this Life the 17th of *February*, 1729. aged 45 Years.

HERE lieth the Body of Mr. WILLIAM SKINNER, eldeft Son of Alderman *William Skinner*, of this Town. He married *Mary*, the Daughter of *Timothy Fulthrop*, of *Tunftal*, in the Bifhoprick of *Durham*, Efq; by whom he had one Son, and Five Daughters: He died the 17th of *July*, Anno 1724. *Ætatis* 70.

HERE lieth the Body of Mr. JOSEPH SUTTON, who departed this Life in the 32d Year of his Age, the 24th of *Auguft* 1712. Here lieth alfo THOMAS the Son of Mr. *Jofeph* SUTTON, who died in the firft Year of his Age, the 5th of *February*, 1710.   HERE

HERE lieth interr'd MARY, the Wife of *George* SWALLLOW, who exchanged this mortal Life, for an immortal one, *December* the 16th, 1728. in the 21ft Year of her Age.

T.

HERE lieth interr'd the Body of ELIZABETH TAYLOR, Widow of Doctor TAYLOR, and Daughter of *Hugh Lifter*, of this Town, Efquire ; who departed this Life the 21ft of *June*, 1714, aged 61 Years.

HERE lieth the Body of ROBERT THORP, who departed this Life the 2d Day of *March*, 1710. in the 68th Year of his Age.

HERE lieth interr'd the Body of Mr. SAMUEL THOMPSON, of this Town, Wine-Cooper, who departed this Life the 15th of *April*, 1717. aged 48 Years.

W.

HERE lieth interr'd the Body of Mrs. MARY WALLIS, Wife of Mr. *Towers Wallis*, of this Town, Merchant, and Daughter to Alderman *Richard Gray*. She departed this Life, in the true Faith of CHRIST, the 15th of *March*, 1695. *Anno Ætatis* 32.

HERE lieth the Body of RICHARD WATSON, who departed this Life the 27th of *June*, 1718. Alfo of HANNAH his Wife, who departed this Life the 16th of *July*, 1715.

HERE lieth interr'd the Body of Mr. JOEL WINSPEARE, of this Town, Merchant, who departed this Life the 21ft Day of *December*, 1681. in the 30th Year of his Age.

II. *Infcriptions on the South Side of the Church.*
B.

HERE lieth the Body of JANE, the Wife of *Francis* BENSON, Mafon, and Daughter of *Richard Roebuck*, Mafon, who died *February* 11, 1720. aged 36 Years.

HERE lieth the Body of RICHARD BRITTAIN, who departed the 5th of *December*, 1728. aged 53 Years.

HERE lieth the Body of ANNE, the Wife of *John* BULLARD, who departed this Life the 22d of *November*, 1730. aged 58 Years.

C. HERE

C.

HEre lieth the Body of LAURENCE CLARK, of this Town, Plummer, who departed this Life the 10th of *December*, 1726. aged 64 Years. Here alſo lieth the Body of LAURENCE CLARK, Plummer, Son of *Laurence Clark*, who departed this Life the 22d of *September*, 1727. *Ætatis ſuæ* 29.

HEre lieth the Body of THOMAS COOK, Pipe-Maker, who died the 7th of *February*, 1720. aged 64.

HEre lieth interr'd the Body of Mr. *John Criſpin*, Maſter and Mariner, who departed this Life, in the true Faith of CHRIST, the 3d Day of *October*, 1679. in the Year of his Wardenſhip for the *Trinity-Houſe*, and in the 45th Year of his Age.

HEre lieth ELIZABETH, (the Daughter of *John* CRISPIN, Maſter and Mariner,) who departed this Life *December* 31, 1669. being Five Years of Age.

HEre lieth the Body of Mr. WILLIAM CROWLE, of this Town, Merchant, who departed this Life the 8th of *Auguſt* 1730. and in the 70th Year of his Age; Son of Alderman *George Crowle*, who was a great Benefactor to this Town. *This Gentleman lies buried near the Side of the Church.*

D.

HEre lies the Body of Mr. GEORGE DICKINSON, Maſter and Mariner, five times Warden of *Trinity-Houſe*, who departed this Life the 4th of *June*, 1698. in the 80th Year of his Age.

NEar this Place is interr'd ROBERT DICKINSON, who died *September* 4, 1680. aged 37. Alſo SUSANNA his Wife, who died the 27th of *February*, 1726. aged 77. ELIZABETH, their Daughter, died the 6th of *April*, 1726. aged 46. JANE, their Daughter, the 13th of *March*, 1714. aged 40. *Thomas Wakefield*, her Husband, died the 26th of *March*, 1718. aged 54. Alſo *John Campſall*, who died the 10th of *October*, 1722. aged 61 Years.

HEre lieth the Body of THOMAS DIXON, who died the 13th of *December*, 1726. in the 29th Year of his Age.

E.

HEre lie the Bodies of HENRY ETHRINGTON, and JANE his Wife. He departed this Life the 4th of *January;* and entered the Ninetieth Year of his Age, *Anno Domini* 1716.

F.

HEre lie the Bodies of RICHARD and ELIZABETH FOSTER, who died in *December*, 1721 ; his Age 30, her Age 25 Years. *Some Lines might have been written of this Pair, as now are over the Grave of Mr.* FRANCIS HUNTRODES, *and* MARY *his Wife, interr'd (in the Year 1680.) near the Choir Door of St.* MARY's *Church,*

Church, Whitby. (*) *Their Birth and Age make, indeed, some Difference: But in the Death of this Couple, (as yet but young, when one Month determin'd their Fate!) they scarcely seem'd divided.*

(*) *Husband, and Wife that did Twelve Children bear,*
Dy'd the same Day, alike both aged were.
'Bout Eighty Years they liv'd, five Hours did part
(Ev'n on the Marriage-Day) *each tender Heart.*
So fit a Match, surely, could never be:
Both, in their Lives, and in their Deaths, agree.

On which Lines, tho' an ingenious Gentleman has paraphras'd, I will not venture to use his Words, but rather something in Imitation.

WAS ever Pair more happily combin'd?
   Or ever *Fortune* seem'd so much divine?
One scarce had Life, the other Heav'n defign'd
   To grant a Being, both in Love to shine.

Thro' rolling Years they past: And when that Death
   Took One, the Other felt his cruel Dart:
Both in one Day, perhaps, one Hour, lost Breath;
   And, as they liv'd, together, they depart!

Could

CAptain WILLIAM FRUGILL, died the 21ſt Day of
April, 1656. [A Sword is carved, with theſe Lines.]
What Sir, they ſay, 'tis ſure: True Men of War,
Of Valour, Art, and Faith, compoſed are.
If Indian, German, Engliſh *Wars yield Fame,*
Read then a Man of War, in Engliſh Name.

G.

HIc jacet JOHANNES GORWOOD, *cum duobus filiis*, (SAMUELE
et JOANNE) *qui obiit* Dec. 16. Anno Dom. 1719. *Ætat. ſuæ*
46. *Jacet hic quoque Uxor prædicti* Joannis. *Ob.* 13. *Septemb.*
A. S. 1728. *Ætat.* 44. [Buried at the Weſt End.]

HEre is interr'd the Body of LYDIA, the Wife of Mr. *John*
GRAVES, Merchant, who departed this Life, *Feb.* 14. 1672.

H.

HEre lieth the Body of ROBERT HALL, late of this Town,
Taylor. *Obiit* 9 *July.* 1719. *Ætatis* 63.

HEre lieth the Body of Mr. THOMAS HARRISON, Writing-
Maſter: Who, after a Life of great Piety, and much Uſeful-
neſs in his Profeſſion, did, with great Satisfaction, reſign up his
Soul into the Hands of his Redeemer, the 9th Day of *December*,
in the Year of our LORD 1715. and of his Age 84.

HEre lieth the Body of Mr. DAVID HESSLEWOOD, Maſter and
Mariner, and Warden of the *Trinity-Houſe*, who died the 25th
of *July*, 1717. aged 58 Years. Alſo MARGARET, his Wife, who
died the 20th of *November*, 1719. aged 49 Years: And JOHN,
their eldeſt Son, died the 31ſt of *December*, 1707. aged 19 Years.

I.

JOhn JOHNSON, died *November* the 5th, in the Fourteenth Year
of his Age, *Anno Dom.* 1712.

L. HERE

Could ever Marriage more conſummate prove?
   Or imitate the moſt harmonious Strings;
Which joining Arts had mov'd, in trueſt Love,
   As when *Orphæus* plays, *Hymenæus* ſings?

But ſtill conjoin'd, melodiouſly, to raiſe,
   Their tuneful Voices, far above the Spheres;
Now both together ſing th' Almighty's Praiſe;
   Whilſt HE, JEHOVAH! pleaſing ſits, and hears.

Thus Birth, and Wedlock, Trouble, Joy, and Death,
   Alternate ſway'd, to Everlaſting Life:
New Joys, in Heav'n, exchang'd for Cares, on Earth:
   Was ever ſuch an happy Man and Wife?

L.

HErE lieth the Body of ELIZABETH LANGDALE, Widow, who died the 27th of *November*, 1718.

HErE lieth MARY, the Daughter of *Nicholas* LINTEY, and Wife of *Samuel Crispin*. She died the 20th of *September*, 1659.

M.

HErE is interr'd WILLIAM MARSINGALE, *March* 3, 1704. aged 58. Nigh this Place MARY, his Wife, *May* 2, 1708. aged 39. Here alfo WILLIAM, their Son, *December* 6, 1723. aged 26. A Deacon truly qualified, *holding the Myftery of the Faith in a pure Confcience*, I. Tim. iii. 9.

HErE lies the Body of ANNE, the Daughter of *Thomas* MARTIN, who died in *May*, 1705; and JAMES, the Son of *Thomas* MARTIN, who died in *July*, 1705.

HErE lieth the Body of GEORGE MATTHEWS, and SARAH, his Wife. She died the 6th of *May*, 1717. *Ætat.* 62. And he died *Octob.* 31. 1717. *Ætat.* 63. And alfo 8 Children, *viz.* SARAH *Roebuck*, late Wife of *John Roebuck*, Free-Mafon. She dy'd the 27th of *December*, 1708. And CHARLES MATTHEWS, Freeman, and Apothecary, of this Town. He died the 26th of *May*, 1715. *Ætat.* 25. The other 6 died in their Infancy.

HErE is interr'd the Body of WILLIAM MOORE, Cordwainer. He died the 14th of *December*, 1714. aged 70. He was the third Son of Mr. *John Moor*, Woollen-Draper.

P.

HErE lieth interr'd the Body of FRANCIS PORTER, of this Town, Innholder, who departed this Life the 28th Day of *September*, *Anno* 1712. in the 72d Year of his Age.

HErE lieth the Body of JOHN PURVER, Son of Mr. *John Purver*, who departed this Life, in the true Faith of CHRIST, on the 8th of *November*, 1702. aged 31 Years. Here alfo lieth the Body of Mrs. ANNE PURVER, late Wife of Mr. *John Purver*, Sheriff of this Town, in the Year, 1705: By whom he had 7 Sons, and 4 Daughters. She departed this Life, in the true Chriftian Faith, the 7th Day of *April*, 1710. in the 71ft Year of her Age. Here alfo lieth interr'd the Body of JOHN PURVER, Gentleman, and Sheriff of this Town, who departed this Life, in the true Faith of CHRIST, the 4th Day of *October*, 1714. in the 72d Year of his Age: He married ELEANOR, his fecond dearly beloved Wife, by whom he had one Son, named *John Purver*. [Buried at W. End.]

R.

HErE lie the Bodies of ANDREW RAYNER, (who departed this Life the 26th of *February*, 1718. in the 85th Year of his Age)

Age) and MARY, his Wife, who died the 6th of *November*, 1719. in the 83d Year of her Age.

HERE lieth the Body of THOMAS ROBERTS, who departed this Life the 27th of *March*, 1727. aged 33 Years.

H E R E lieth interr'd the Body of Mr. WILLIAM ROBINSON, ſometime Sheriff of this Town, who departed this Life the 8th of *December*. Here also interred the Body of Mrs. ELIZA-BETH ROBINSON, late Wife of Mr. *William Robinson*, of this Town, Master and Mariner, and Daughter of the above-named Mr. WILLIAM ROBINSON, who departed this Life the 25th of *May*, 1717. aged 56 Years. And also the Body of Mrs. FRANCES, their Daughter, who died the 5th of *Feb.* 1707. [*Buried at W. End.*]

S.

HERE lieth the Body of REBECCA, the Daughter of Mr. *Robert* SANDERSON, Woollen-Draper ; who married REBECCA, the Daughter of the Worshipful Alderman *Bloom*, 1665.

HERE lieth buried the Body of JAMES SCOLES, Merchant-Adventurer, who departed this Life the 10th of *Nov. A.D.* 1633.

WITHIN this Vault lieth interr'd the Body of the Worshipful Alderman JOHN SOMERSCALES, Merchant, who was twice Mayor of this Town. He departed this Life the 18th Day of *February*, 1732. aged 79. He married *Martha*, the Daughter of Mr. *John Watson*, late of this Town, by whom he had four Sons, and four Daughters. Two of his Sons lie interr'd here. [*Near the West Door.*]

HERE lieth interr'd the Body of ROBERT STANDIGE, who departed this Life *April* 12, in the Year of our LORD, 1677.

JOHN SHORT, of this Town, Wine-Cooper, departed this Life *Feb.* the 26th, *Ætatis* 61, *Anno Salutis* 1717.

HERE lies the Body of HENRY SHORT, Distiller, who died the 24th of *June*, 1733. aged 37. Also the Bodies of HENRY and MARY, two of his Children. Likewise the Bodies of JOHN SHORT the Father (and JOHN SHORT the Brother) of the said *Henry Short*.

THIS in Memory of JOHN STORM, Parish-Clerk 41 Years, excellent in his Way, buried here the 24th of *May*, 1727. aged 74 Years. *He lies on the South Side of the Church Porch.*

HERE lieth the Body of Mr. LEONARD STORY, late Officer of His Majesty's Customs in this Town. He departed this Life the 26th Day of *August*, 1719, in the 70th Year of his Age : Who, after he had survived ELIZABETH, his belovèd Wife, (who died the first of *September*, 1702, in the 58th Year of her Age) was interr'd in the same Grave.

H

W. Here

W.

HERE lies the Body of FRANCIS WATSON, of this Town, Wine-Cooper, who departed this Life the 17th Day of *December*, 1706. in the 70th Year of his Age.

HERE lieth interr'd the Body of DANIEL W HITAKER, who departed this Life *September* 23, *A. Dom.* 1724. aged 55 Years. Alſo four Children: SARAH, SUSANNA, DANIEL and ISAAC.

HERE lieth the Body of THOMAS WOOD, who died *January* the 16th, *A.D.* 1717. aged 79 Years.

HERE lies the Body of Mr. SAMUEL WOOD, who died *August* the 25th, *A.D.* 1730. aged 57 Years.

HERE lieth the Body of Mr. STEPHEN WOOD, who died the 5th of *March*, 1718. aged 48 Years.

Y.

HERE lieth the Body of MARGARET, the Wife of *Robert* YOUNG, who died the 26th Day of *December, Anno Domini* 1715. *Ætatis ſuæ* 64.

Of the CHURCH dedicated to St. MARY, called the Low-Church.

FROM what Manuscripts, or other Accounts I have perus'd, I find this Church to have been built much about the same time as the other, promoted by several of the same Contributors: That it has been a much larger Edifice than at present; and probably there might have been Chantries therein. King *Henry* VIII. us'd it as his Chapel Royal: But the Steeple offending him, because it was opposite the Place where he reſided, he order'd it to be pull'd down; in which Condition the Church continued for a long time, 'till the Inhabitants erected a new one (in which are 3 Bells) at their own Expence. Underneath a Mayor lies buried, upon whoſe Grave-Stone is the following Inſcription.

HERE lieth interr'd the Body of WILLIAM MOULD, *late Merchant, and Alderman of* Hull, *who was twice Mayor of the ſame Town. He departed this Life,* Feb. 26. A.D. 1721. *in the 66th Year of his Age.*

Near this, is another Inſcription, *viz.*

HERE lieth the Body of THOMAS SCAMAN *Maſter and Mariner, who died the 14th of* December, 1712. aged 65.

Round a handſome Font near the foregoing : *Peter Madock,
John Fawſett*, Church-Wardens. A new Clock was put up, 1716.
James Wilkinſon, and *Benjamin Blaydes*, Jun. Church-Wardens.

But, to proceed in the Church. On a painted Board, near the
Pulpit, are the Emblems of *Mercy* and *Juſtice:* Between which, is
ſupported an *Harrow ;* a *Crown* at the Top ; a *Cap* and *Flower-de-
Lis* on each Side. Beſides, are theſe Lines.

> "MERCY and JUSTICE, ſet in pious Station,
>   "Have ever been the ſure Props of a Nation :
> "They uphold Kings ; and Crowns they do ſupport ;
> "Nor is there, againſt Sin, a ſurer Fort :
> "An Emblem of true Regiment is this ;
> "Which, who obſerves, shall never rule amiſs."

Vivat Rex, & floreat Grex. 1660.

The INSCRIPTIONS, and EPITAPHS, are as follow.

B.

HERE lieth interr'd the Body of Mr. MICHAEL BEILBY, of
this Town, Merchant, who dy'd *Octob.* 3, 1705, aged 81.
Alſo PHILADELPHIA BEILBY, late Wife of Mr. *Jonathan Beilby,*
of *Hull*, Merchant, Daughter to *Francis Moore*, Alderman,
thrice Mayor of *Cheſterfield*, buried on the South Side of this
Stone, *Aug.* 6, 1706. aged 43 Years. And on the Weſt Side
lieth PHILADELPHIA, their Daughter, who dy'd the 24th
of *October*, 1710. aged 14 Years. [*Buried in the S. Iſle.*]

AT the Foot of this lies, in Hope of a Bleſſed Reſurrection, the Bodies of JONATHAN BEILBY, Merchant, and
PHILADELPHIA, his Wife ; by whom he had 7 Sons, and
5 Daughters : The former departed this Life the 27th of
October, 1711. in the 54th Year of his Age : The latter
died the 3d of *Auguſt*, 1706. in the 43d Year of her Age.
This Inſcription is near the South Wall.

D.

HERE lieth the Body of the Worſhipful WILLIAM DOBSON,
Merchant-Adventurer, twice Mayor of this Town, who
departed this Life the 20th Day of *October*, 1666. And of
SYBIL, his Wife, who departed this Life the 19th Day of
Auguſt, 1668. *And affix'd to the Wall, (near which he lies bu-
ried, in the North Isle) is a Buſt, under which is this Inſcription.*

IN

IN Memoriam hujus Emporij, bis ad Clavum fedit Præ-
fectus Purpurâ cæterifque Imperii Insignibus donatus;
* Sceptro, Gladioque præcurforibus famulatus eft. Juftitiæ,
& Miferecordiæ Patronum dixeris, an Vindicem? Qui re-
gendo par erat. Cedant Arma Loci, Gladium, Sceptrumque
Colorque. GULIELMUS DOBSON Cæli pretiosus Emptor,
congeftans ubicunque Opes, colligens, dedit, distribuit:
Gemmâ ut fibi lucraret Cælum pretiofius omni. Audi
tria Verba; totidem gratus, pius, fidelis, hofpitalis;
Deum, Regem, Vicinum, colendo, amando, fublevando.
Tali fatellitio ftipatus, hujus Vitæ Laudem meruit. Quid
potuit majus, quid non fperabimus ultrâ, fuge quærere.

WHICH IS THUS RENDER'D.

*IN Memory of the Mayor of this Corporation, who was twice in
that Office, adorn'd in Purple, bearing, as Enfigns of Magiftracy, a Mace, and Sword. It's difficult to fay, whether he
(who had Abilities fit for his Station) was a greater Patron of
Juftice, or fevere Revenger of any Breach made upon it? Let the
Bearings, or Arms, of the Town, or any other Accomplishments
whatever, be of no Account, when laid in the Balance to his fuperior Virtues.* WILLIAM DOBSON, *defirous of Happinefs, whatever Riches he attain'd to, he generously gave, and diftributed to
pious Ufes, in order to purchafe Heaven, far more precious than
any Earthly Treafures. Hear his Character in three (or more)
Words: He was devout, loyal, hofpitable; having a fincere Love
for God, the King, and his Country: Being adorn'd with these
great Virtues, he was well fpoken of in this World; and there is
no Reason to doubt of his Happinefs in the other.*

WILLIAM DOBSON, *Jun.*, departed this Life, *March* 21,
1655. [*Lies buried near his honourable Parents.*]

---

* As to the *Mace*, it is an Emblem of Royal Authority. And King *Henry* VI.
in the Year 1440, (when he confirm'd the old Charters, making it a Corporation Town, which, with its Precincts, should be as a County of itself) ordered,
That, for the future, every Mayor *should have the* Sword (*as well as* Cap of Maintenance) *borne before him on all publick Occafions, in the Name of the King, or his Succeffors: And also that* He, *with the* Aldermen, *should wear Scarlet Gowns, (lined
with Furrs, like the Judges,) with Hoods over their Necks and Shoulders, in the
fame Form, and as great Magnificence, as Those Eminent Perfons, in that high Dignity, were ufually adorn'd with, in the City of* LONDON.

E. HERE

E.

HERE lieth the Body of ELIZABETH EYRES, Daughter of *Matthew Anlaby*, Efq; who departed this Life in *April* 1717. *Ætat.* 39. [*Buried in the South Isle.*] *Her Sifter* MARY *lies interred in* Beverley *Minfter. See my Second Volume of feveral parts of the County,* Page 86.

H.

On the South Wall is a Brafs Plate affix'd, (over a Pew, near the Pulpit) on which are the Effigies of a Man, his two Wives, with thefe Words, and in much the like Characters.

Here lyeth John Harpson, Scherman, and Alderman of this Town; Alys and Agnes his Wyfes; Thomas, John and Wyllim his Sons; whyche John decessed the ix. Day of December, in the Year of our Lord M——. I think he dy'd in 1545 ; but will not be certain, becaufe the Date feem'd to me almoft obliterated. This Gentleman (who was defcended from the antient Family of the HARRISONS of *Yokefleet,* that removed hither in the Reign of *Henry* VII.) was Mayor, *Anno* 1537. The firft Hofpital in the Nation, after the Reformation, was, by Order of his Grandfon, (who was likewife Mayor, in the Year 1548) erected in *Chapel-Lane,* near this Church : To maintain the Poor of which, he endow'd it with Ten Shillings a Week.

HERE lieth the Body of BRIDGET, Wife of *James* HEBLETHWAITE, of *Norton,* Efq; by whom fhe had one Son, and 5 Daughters. She departed this Life the 13th of *June,* 1720. aged 42.

HERE lieth the Body of ROBERT HOLLIS, Efq; Recorder, Benefactor to this Church, who dy'd *Sept.* 4, 1697.

HERE lieth the Body of WILLIAM HUDPETH, Merchant-Adventurer, who dy'd *Auguft,* 21, 1613. [*In S. Isle.*]

L.

Within the Rails of the Altar.

HERE lie the Remains of the Reverend Mr. NATHANIEL LAMB, A.M. Minifter of this Parifh 18 Years, who died the 21ft of *May,* 1702. in the 66th Year of his Age. Also the Body of his Son MICHAEL LAMB, who died the 10th of *July,* 1693. in the 15th Year of his Age.

M. *QUI*

M.

Q U I Pedem huc infers
Æternitatis Contemplator,
Imprudens ne calces eruditos Cineres,
Aftas ad Tumulum CAROLI MOSS, *M. D.*
Viris, Linguarum, Artium, Rerum peritiffimus :
At præter cætera, in Theoria Medicinæ egregie doctus,
In Praxi nulli fecundus.

Quod ad privatas Laudes,
Pectoris fuit omnino aperti, candidi,
Honefto incocti, Humanitate conditi,
Benevolentia referti, eaque in · Amicos
Amiciffima, officiociffima.

Vidua mærens
Hoc Marmor, leve Pignus Amoris,
Poni curavit.

(*) *Obiit* Januarii 17º.
Anno { *Salutis* 1731.
{ *Ætatis* 47.

P.

HERE lieth the Body of Mr. RICHARD PEARSON, of *Ryal,* in *Holdernefs,* who departed this Life *Auguft* 2, 1695.

S.

HERE lieth the Body of SARAH, Wife of WILLIAM SKOOP-HOME, of *Theddlethorpe, Lincolnshire,* Gentleman, who dy'd the 14th of *Auguft,* 1714. aged 63. [*Buried in the North Isle.*]

(*) *This Gentleman lies buried in the Middle (or Broad) Isle of the Church, at the East End. By Miftake, his Epitaph was inferted, in the* Second Volume of Antiquities *Pag.* 87, *where the Church of* St. Mary, *in Beverley, is treated of. The following Lines are a Paraphrafe of what is contained in the Infcription.*

YOU, who come here to meditate
  Upon the Soul's eternal State,
Take Care: You're near the Dr's Urn,
Simply you may his Ashes fpurn,
But treat his Mem'ry not with Scorn.
He was a Man of brighteft Parts;
Knew Languages, the World, and Arts;
But tho' all did in him combine,
In Physick, chiefly he did shine.

So tender, fo fincere his Soul,
That none, *who knew,* but must condole.
Each *Friend,* to whom he seem'd a *Brother*
'Tis fit should grieve with one another;
Since his Benevolence oft' chear'd,
As if for them he only car'd.

This Marble Stone, his mournful Dear,
In Token of her Love, plac'd here.

HERE

HEre refteth in Peace Mr. THOMAS SWAN, Merchant-Adventurer, Mayor of this Town ; who departed, to the Mercy of GOD, the 20th of *January*, 1629. *This Gentleman lies buried within the Rails of the Altar ; whose Effigy, with that of his Lady, are neatly placed on the Stone.*

T.

HERE lieth the Body of the Worfhipful THOMAS THACKRAY, twice Mayor of this Town, and Merchant-Adventurer, who departed in the true Faith of CHRIST, 1630. *Quod fum, fueris.* [*He lies buried within the Altar Rails, over whom is his Effigy, with thofe of his Wife, and Children.*]

Interred in the South Isle.

MRs. MARY THOMAS, dy'd in 1696. Mr. EDWARD THOMPSON, dy'd the fame Year, aged 77.

Buried on the South Side of the Altar.

HERE lieth the Body of the Worshipful Alderman ROBERT TRIPPET, of this Town, Merchant, twice Mayor of this Town, who was married to Mrs. *Mary Wilberforce*, (Daughter of the Worfhipful Alderman *Wilberforce*, formerly Lord-Mayor of *York*) by whom he had 9 Sons, and 5 Daughters, ten whereof lie intomb'd near to this Vault. He departed this Life the 19th of *November*, in the Year of our LORD 1707, and in the 69th Year of his Age.

—————————————————————— *ultima femper*
Expectanda Dies Homini, dicique beatus
Ante obitum nemo, fupremaque funera debet. (†)

HERE alfo lieth the Body of Mrs. MARY TRIPPET, Wife of Alderman *Trippet*, who died *Jan.* 30, 1722, aged 67. Alfo EDWARD, their Son, died the 25th of *July*, 1717. aged 27.

The following Inscription is on a South Pillar.

NEar this Place lieth the Body of the Worfhipful PHILIP WILKINSON, Efq ; twice Mayor of this Town. He had two Wives : The firft was ESTHER, the Daughter of
Arthur

———————————————————————

(†) *Thus render'd.* " Every one of us should be in continual Expectation of our laft " Change : For there is no perfect Felicity in this Life ; and Death only is the "happy Meffenger to conduct our Souls to Immortality."

Arthur * *Ingram*, of *Nottingly*, Efq; by whom he had 11 Children, only two of which furvive him : She died the 28th of *December*, 1683. and lies also interr'd near this Place. The Second was ANNE, the Daughter of Mr. *Thomas Kitching-man*, of *Carlton*, who furvives him : By her he had three Children, all which he furviv'd : He departed this Life, for a better, the 18th of *March*, 1716. in the Seventieth Year of his Age.

* A Knight, of that Name, was one of the Benefactors to the Cathedral of *York*, [See the *Hift.* Pag. 61.] The Family, as I was inform'd, had a Seat, or large Hall, on the Weft Side of the River *Fofs*, two Miles from *York*, near *Huntington*, (deriv'd from *Hunting-Town*, fuppos'd to have been a Receptacle for the Huntfmen, who were formerly employ'd to deftroy the ravenous wild Boars in the Forest of *Gautres)* and nigher the Church, dedicated to St. *Margaret;* in which, 'tis fuppos'd, one of thofe Baronets lies interr'd. The Coat of Arms, once engrav'd on Brafs, is torn off the Grave-Stone : And the Church, which is covered with Lead, feems very antient, with an Iron Crofs at the Eaft End : In the Church-Yard feems to have been another of Stone ; only that Part, on the Top, which form'd it into a Crofs, is broken off. To this Place, is a pleasant Caufey, which leads from the Town to a little Bridge over the faid River. The Parfonage-House is entirely demolish'd : Half of *Earfwick*, and half of *Tolthorp*, belong to *Huntington*; the other Parts appertain to the Parish of *Strenshall.*

In

*In the Church-Yard are Grave Stones placed over the
following perfons.*

THE Reverend Mr. DANIEL ACLAM, A.M. of *Sidney-Suffex*
College, *Cambridge*, Son of Alderman *Aclam*, who departed
this Life, in the Year of our LORD, 1683. THOMAS BELL,
1716. ELIZABETH, his Wife, 1728. GEORGE BELL, 1723.
MARY BEWLEY, 1717. THOMAS JOHNSON, Mayor. JOHN
LILLEY, Chyrurgeon, *Jan.* 1691. WILLIAM PALLISTER,
Mariner, 1727. JOHN ROBINSON. EDWARD THOMPSON, 1676.
NATHAN TODD, 1712. SUSANNA WATSON, 1706. GEORGE
WESTERDALE, 1720. His Wife, 1727. MARY (and JANE)
WILKINSON, 1726.

Conclufion of the Epitaphs and Infcriptions at Hull.

IN my Return, from *Hull, Anno* 1731, I took Notice of St. *Mary's* Church,
at *CAVE;* wherein, on the North Side, near the Chancel, is an antient
Effigy of Sir *George Metham*, Kt. in complete Armour; and that of his Lady is
laid befide him. Near the Altar, is this Infcription: "Here lieth interr'd the
"Body of GEORGE METHAM, Efq; and KATHERINE, his Wife: She died the
"13th of *Auguft*, and He the 11th of *October*, 1672." Within the Rails of the
Altar, is this: "Under this Stone lie two Grandsons of GEORGE METHAM,
"of *North Cave*, Efq; by *Barbary*, his Daughter, Wife to *Hugh Montgomery*, of
"*Hotham*, Efq; *viz.* CÆCIL PHILIP died 23d of *April*, 1719, Nine Months old:
"And WRAY, the 26th of *December*, 1721, about the fame Age." And upon
a Brafs Plate, opposite the Altar: "Here lieth the Body of FRANCIS METHAM,
"Gent. youngeft Son of *George Metham*, of *North Cave*, Efq; who departed this
"Life *March* the 2d, 1701. And of *Margaret*, his Wife, fecond Daughter of
"*William Pearfon*, of *Stokesley*, Efq; who departed this Life, *Aug.* 17. 1725."
This only is in the South Isle: "Here lieth the Body of Mr. RICHARD BALEY, late of
"*Hotham*, in this Parish, who departed this Life the 24th day of *June, Anno Dom.*
"1694. *Ætat. fuæ* 60. *Mors omnibus communis.*"

AND here I beg Leave to conclude (what I have painfully
collected, and would not have loft; or, what feems much
like it, long hidden from the World) with an Infcription
written by the late Rev. Dr. CHARLES BLAKE, (formerly
Minifter of the Church of *S. Sepulchre*, LONDON; Prebendary
of *Stillington*, and Sub-Dean of *York*) which he defign'd as a
pious exhortatory Epitaph; and that eminent Character, given
of him by his Friends after his Death: All which are now to
be read, in the *Latin* Tongue, in fair Characters, (which here,
with the Original, is render'd into *English*) on the Sides of
a beautiful and lofty Monument, contriv'd by a late inge-

I

nious

nious † Architect, (placed over his Grave, or Vault, made of Brick, within the Earth) in the Church-Yard, near the East Window, which gives Light to the Table of the Altar.

On the South Side of the Monument.

THUS RENDER'D.

Huic Marmori subjacent
Rudera Domicilii Terreni,
Cujus olim
Potius Hospes sui, quam Incola,
Carolus Blake,
Hujusce Ecclesiæ Parochialis Rector,
Utinam sane haud prorsus indignus!
Qualis hodie mortuus existo,
Talis semper sui etiam in vivis,
Vermis et non Homo.
O mi Deus,
Da mihi precor, ut dormiam in Christo;
Donec cum omnibus Sanctis Angelis,
Veniet in sua Gloria Judex
Vivorum, simul ac Mortuorum Æquissimus.
In isto Die,
Domine, Deus Misericordiæ,
Miserere mei, miserrimi Peccatoris!
Siste parumper,
Benevole pariter, ac Pie Viator,
Dum Precibus Verbum predictis amplius addas,
Amen.
Hic recubare juvat, quod, Lethi *Nocte peracta,*
Æternæ Vitæ Aurora fulgente, resurgam.
Etiam mortuus loquitur Carolus Blake.

Under this Marble lie the Ruins of my earthly Tabernacle: In which I was rather a Sojourner, than an Inhabitant, Charles Blake Rector of this Parish Church, I wish I might not say, an unworthy one! What I am now dead, such I always was when alive, A Worm, and no Man. Grant, O my GOD, I beseech Thee, that I may sleep in CHRIST, 'till the just Judge of Quick and Dead shall come in his own Glory, accompany'd with all his holy Angels. In that Day, O Lord, thou God of Mercy, have Compassion on me, a miserable Sinner!

Thou courteous and pious Passenger, stop a little while; only to add one Word to these my Prayers, *viz.* AMEN.

I choose to lay my Bones in this Place; that, when the Night of Death is past, I may then rise early in the Morning of the Resurrection to Eternal Life, *Charles Blake,* tho' dead, even now speaketh.

Hic de se Vir modestus,
Parum æquus sui Æstimator,
Quis autem erat, quidque de eo sentiebant Amici,
Aversum latus te docebit.

This modest humble Gentleman, that had such low and mean Opinion of himself, and his own Merits: Yet how worthy a Man he

was, and what his friends thought of him, the opposite Table will further inform you.

At the East End of the Sepulchre.

THAT IS:

N.B. *In Cæmeterio juxta Viam tritam,*
sepeliri volo, peto, atque exopto.

N.B. In the Church-Yard, near the High Road, 'tis my Will; I request;

yes, 'tis my earnest Desire, my Body may be buried.

On

---

† He lies interr'd in S. *Olave's* Church-Yard, *York,* near the venerable Ruins of St. *Mary's* Abbey, with this Inscription, on a rais'd Tomb Stone. *Hic jacet* Dan. Harvey, *Stirpe Gallus, idemq; probus Sculptor, Architectus etiam peritus. Ingenio acer, integer Amicitiæ; Quam sibi; citius, aliis beneficus. Abi Viator, sequi reminiscere. Obiit, undecimo Die Decembris, A.D.* 1733. *Ætatis* 50.

𝔒𝔫 𝔱𝔥𝔢 𝔑𝔬𝔯𝔱𝔥 𝔖𝔦𝔡𝔢 𝔬𝔣 𝔱𝔥𝔢 𝔐𝔬𝔫𝔲𝔪𝔢𝔫𝔱.   THUS TRANSLATED.

CAROLUS BLAKE, S. T. P.
Natus est Readingi Bercherienſis, *Oct. xxxi.*
M DC LXIV. Parentibus, ut in tali Municipio,
Primariis : In Scholæ Publica Mercatorum Sciſſorum
Londini *institutus, pro more electus est in Collegium*
Sancti Johannis Baptiſtæ Oxonij : *ubi bonis Litteris*
se totum dedidit. Linguarum peritus, præsertim
Antiquarum, optimos Authores in Manibus semper
habuit : Poesia tentavit, non infeliciter : In omni
genere Philosophiæ versuius, illam tamen excoluit
præcipue, quæ pertinet ad Mores : Theologiæ vero
(utpote quæ Studiorum Finis) maxime omnium studio-
sissimus, cætera non tanti Faciens, nisi cum rerum
Divinarum Scientiâ conjuncta. His Artibus eximij
Nominis inter Academicos evasit, magnus Ingenij,
magnus Doctrinæ laudibus, major Amore Pietatis.

CHARLES BLAKE, Doctor of Divinity, was born at *Reading* in *Berkshire, October,* 31, 1664. of Parents of the firſt Rank in that Corporation ; educated at Merchant-Taylors School, *London;* and according to its Cuſtom, was elected a Member of St. *John's* College, in *Oxford,* where he ſo diligently apply'd himſelf to his Studies, that he became well skill'd in the learned Languages, especially thoſe of the Antient Fathers; ever made use of the choicest Authors. In Poetry he became no mean Proficient ; well skill'd in all the Parts of Philoſophy, eſpecially in that Branch which leads to Morality : But chiefly inclin'd to the Study of Divinity, (as being the End of all Studies) not regarding other Sciences, but when accompany'd with the Knowledge of Things Divine. By theſe Endowments, he gain'd a great Character amongst his Contemporaries; who admir'd him for his ready Wit, his great Learning, but most of all for his Love of Piety.

Inter hæc Academicâ Studia nata est Amicitia,
quæ vera illi intercessit cum Excellenti Domino
GULIELMO DAWES, *Baronetto. Cui Primum*
Ceſtrienſi *Episcopo, Diende* Eborum *Archiepiscopo*
Facto, Sacris fuit a Domesticis ; atque hæc illi Vita
dulcissima, cum ab ejus latere nunquam discederet. In
tanto tamque benevolo Patrocinio Beneficia & Dignitates
adeo non quæsivit, ut nonnulla recusaverit oblata, alia
etiam possessa ultro resignaverit. Siqua retinuit, id
Factum est obsequio Patroni, qui indignum putabat, si
talis tantusque Vir a se inhonoratus videretur. Vixit
charus, jucundus Amicis ; nemini is, nemo illi Inimicus,
Podagræ Doloribus Complures Annos Cruciatus, tandem
Confectus, obiit Nov. *xxii. M DCC XXX.*

During his Studies in the University, he contracted an intimate friendship with the Hon. Sir WILLIAM DAWES, Baronet : To whom, being first Bishop of *Chester,* afterwards Archbishop of *York,* he was Domestick Chaplain. This way of Life was ſo pleaſing to him, that he never left him, but became his constant Companion. Under ſo noble and generous a Patron, he ſo little ſought after either Honours or Preferments, that
ſeveral, that were offered, he refuſed; others, he was poſseſs'd of, he generously refign'd; and thoſe he kept, he did it to oblige his Patron, who thought it unjust that ſo great and worthy a Man should want all due Honour and Regard. He lived dear and delightful to his Friends: An Enemy to no Body; and none an Enemy to him. He was afflicted with the Gout for many Years; and being worn out, at last he died, the 22nd of *November,* 1730.

Cum defecissent Propinquitate Sanguinis Conjuncti,
Hæredes instituit bene Merentes Amicos,
Qui Monumentum Hoc poni fecerunt.

His Relations that were nearest a-kin to him by Blood, being dead, he appointed those of his Friends,
that most deſerved his Favour, to be his Heirs : Who erected this Monument to his Memory.
Of

Of the MONASTERIES *and other* Religious Houses, *in* Kingſton-upon-HULL : *With an account of their Benefactors : but more eſpecially of the Family of* De la POLE, *ſome of whom came at laſt to be of Royal Blood.*

CHAP. III.

AMONG the ſeveral Orders of the Church of *Rome*, THIS, we are told, had its Riſe from a miraculous Occaſion. A learned Man, named BRUNO, who ſtudy'd Philoſophy at *Paris*, attending the Funeral of his Friend, reputed to have been a good Liver; whilſt the Service was performing in the Church, the Corpſe is ſaid to have rais'd itſelf on the Bier, and utter theſe Words : *By the juſt Vengeance of the Almighty, I am accus'd :* Then it laid down, and again aroſe, ſaying, *The Judgment of the Moſt High is againſt me :* And moving in like manner the third time, declar'd the tremendous Sentence given againſt him : *By the Juſtice of God,* ſaid he, *I am condemn'd !* All preſent were exceedingly ſurpriz'd, eſpecially BRUNO, who, with 6 Companions, went to the Deſert of *Chartreuſe,* in *Dauphine,* where founded a Monaſtery, under the moſt rigorous Conſtitutions. Their Cuſtom was, To wear a Hair Cloth next their Skin ; a white Caſſock, with a Cloak over it ; and a Hood, to cover the Head. They were enjoin'd to Silence ; and not to go out, without Leave from their Superior. Straw was their Bed, coarſe Skins their Pillows, and Covering ; but, to keep themſelves clean, and free from Idleneſs, they were allow'd Needles, Thread, Sciſſures, Combs, Pens, Ink, and Tools of various Sorts. At Meals their Eyes were to be fix'd on the Food, their Hands upon the Table, their Attention on the Lecturer, and their Hearts on the Almighty. Of this Order were thoſe in the Monaſtery of *Mount-Grace,* near *Cleveland,* dedicated to St. NICHOLAS and the B. Virgin MARY,

founded

founded by THOMAS HOLLAND, Duke of *Surrey*, Earl of *Kent*, and Lord *Wake*. But, before I proceed to That, erected by the famous MICHAEL *de la* POLE ; it will be very proper here, to give fome Account of the Rife of the Family of that Name.

ABOUT the Year of CHRIST, 1330. there was a flourifhing Town, call'd *Ravenfrod*, or *Ravenfpurn*, fituated near the mouth of *Humber ;* where Trade had been carry'd on fuccefsfully for a long Series of Time. Herein dwelt a moft skilful rich Merchant, called WILLIAM *de la* *POLE, (the 2d Son of a Knight of that Name) who marry'd KATHERINE, the Daughter of Sir JOHN NORWICH, Kt. by whom he had 3 Children : MICHAEL, MARGARET, and EDMUND. His Paternal Coat of Arms, which was *Azure, a Fefs Or. between Three Leopards Heads*, he laid afide, to bear *Azure 2 Barrs Wavee Argent*, as a Sign of his Maritime Employment. When *Kingfton-upon-Hull* began to rife in Splendour, he removed thither : Where King EDWARD III. *Anno* 1332. being the 6th Year of his Reign, (having proclaimed War againft the *Scots)* coming, with his Nobles, to take a View of its Strength and Magnitude ; He, and all his Attendants, were received and entertained by WILLIAM *de la* POLE with the greateft magnificence. The Monarch, being extremely pleased, every Way, changed the Government of the Place, fo as to be ruled by a Mayor, (with 4 Bailiffs) to be annually elected ; and then knighted this loyal † Merchant, whom he appointed to be the firft of that Worfhipful Order.

THE *French* having, fome time after, affifted the *Scots* againft the King of *England ;* he therefore, in juft Revenge, was refolved to fight, and conquer them, even in their own Country. To which Purpofe, *Anno* 1338, the 12th of his Reign, he fail'd with his gallant Army into *Flanders ;* and arriving at *Antwerp*, vaft Throngs came to meet, (as even did the Emperor afterwards at *Cologn*) and pay their Refpects to his Majefty. Amongft the reft, was Sir WILLIAM *de la* POLE, where he had been managing his Traffick ; who not only generoufly lent and fupply'd the King with what large Sums he had about him, which were feveral thoufands of Pounds ; but even befides mortgaged his Eftate for his Royal Mafter's Ufe. Such attracting Behaviour, and unfpeakable Loyalty, fo charm'd the King, that he made him Knight Banneret in the Field ; gave him Letters Patents of deferved Renown ; and fettled on him, and his Heirs, to the Value of 500 Marks, annually, from Lands and Rents in *Kingfton-upon-Hull*, and other Places. *Moreover*, faid the
King,

* *Hift. of the* De la Poles.

---

† His Houfe was in the *High-Street*, (then open to the Haven) having great Staiths, Ware-Houfes, and all other neceffary Conveniences.

King, *if it pleafes the Almighty that I shall prove succefsful, I will make thofe Five Hundred a Thoufand Marks a Year, to be continued for ever.* The Monarch, becoming profperous, and returning home, was as good as his word : For foon after, fending for Sir *William*, he made him firft Gentleman of his Bed-Chamber, then Lord of the Seigniory of *Holdernefs*, befides giving him other Places of Honour and Profit; 'till, at laft, he was advanc'd to be Chief-Baron of the *Exchequer*, and enjoy'd what Happinefs he could poffibly hope for.

AND now his chief Study was to fhow his Gratitude to Heaven, by whofe divine Providence he was fo remarkably bleft. He there-

* *Sir* William *begins to found a Religious House.*

fore, obtaining Licence from King *Edward*, began to erect a ftately *Building, to the Honour of GOD, near the Town. But dying, before it was half perfected, about the Year 1356, he left the finifhing of it to his Son MICHAEL; who, as plainly appears, was a great Benefactor to this Town: For foon after, on the 6th of *Auguft*, in the Year aforefaid, the 30th of the fame King's Reign, he procured a Charter, empowering him, and his Heirs, for ever, to fend Juftices to *Kingfton-upon-Hull*, in order to try, acquit or condemn, the Prifoners committed on fundry Occafions. And continuing the Building as then incomplete, he finifh'd it, in the Year

‡ *Sir* Michael *his Son finishes the* Charter-Houfe.

‡ 1377, the 1ft of the Reign of King *Richard* II. The Charter is dated *Feb.* 18. the Year after, witneffed by a Mayor of *Hull*, with others: Upon which Account, and as it mightily tends to open the Hiftory of the *De la Poles*, as well as to defcribe the antient Situation of the Monaftery, the following Translation from Sir *William Dugdale's Monafticon Anglicanum*, Pag. 966, *&c.* muft furely be very acceptable to the Reader.

*T*O all the Faithful of CHRIST, *who shall either fee or hear thefe Letters.* Michael de la Pole, *Knight, Lord of* Wingfield, *everlafting greeting in our Lord. Whilft we continually revolve in our Mind, how our moft dear Father and Lord* William de la Pole, *Knight, (now deceafed) whilft he lived, by the Infpiration of the Holy Spirit, firft founded an Hofpital for the Poor : and afterwards, out of greater Devotion, altering this, his Purpofe, was refolved to erect, at* KINGSTON-upon-HULL, *a certain Religious Houfe of Nuns, or Poor Sifters Minoreffes Regular, of the Order of St.* CLARE, *for the Enlargement and Honour of the Church of* England, *and to the Intent that he might make* CHRIST *his Heir: And feeing our faid Father left this World, when he had not yet compleated what he intended to have endow'd; and having, before his Death, moft ftrictly*
charg'd

charg'd us, that we should take such Order concerning the said Building, as might tend to its greater Security, and better promote the Ends of Piety, according to our own Will and Discretion: We being heartily and sollicitously desirous to accomplish, effectually, his devout Intention, by making wholesome Provision for the better Government and stronger Defence of the said House: KNOW YE, therefore, That, for the Honour of GOD, and his most glorious Mother the Virgin MARY; of the blessed Archangel St. MICHAEL, all of that Celestial Order, with Angels, and holy Spirits; of the blessed THOMAS *the Martyr late Archbishop of* Canterbury, *and all the Saints of the Almighty Being: For the spiritual Affection which we have and bear to the most devout Religion of the Order of* Carthusians, *according to the License and Authority of our most dread Sovereign Lord* EDWARD, *late King of* England, *the Third (of that Name) after the Conquest, now deceased, and of Others, whose Consent was necessary to be obtain'd in this Affair: We* found, *and* erect, *in one of our Messuages, without the Walls of the said Town of* KINGSTON-upon-HULL, *a certain Religious House to continue for ever. And in the Room of the said Nuns, or Sisters, (which are not yet appointed for that Place) let there be Thirteen Monks of the aforesaid* Carthusian *Order; one of which to be called and elected Prior: And, according to the Rule of his Order, have a Regimen over Others; by whom, we believe, their Rules will be kept more safely, and with more Vigilance and Devotion, than by Women, thro' all Probability, in the aforesaid House: Which, from this Time, we will, order, constitute, and ordain, by these our Letters, shall be called,* The Religious House of St *MICHAEL* of the CARTHUSIAN Order. *And by the Assent of the Greater Prior of the* Carthusians *in the* Savoy, *who is Principal of the Order of the aforesaid House, from whence also the said Order took its Original; we appoint Master* WALTER de KELE, *Prior of the Monks of the aforesaid Monastery. We give also, and grant, by Licence and Authority of the most noble Prince, and our Sovereign Lord* RICHARD, *now the illustrious King of* England, *and of Others, whom it concerneth; and by these we confirm, to the aforesaid Prior and Monks, the said Messuage, with the Appurtenances, containing 7 Acres of Land, which formerly was a a Parcel of the Manor of* Myton, *call'd* La Maison Dieu, *and which from this Time we will should be called the House of St.* Michael *of the Order of* Carthusians *of* KINGSTON-upon-HULL, *as heretofore; together with a certain Chapel, built on the said Messuage; and all other Buildings standing thereupon, with all Appurtenances whatsoever, as it is situated, within a certain Pitfall of Dame* Katherine de la Pole, *our most dear Mother towards the West; and a certain*
Hospital,

Hofpital of ours, now called La Maifon Dieu, *facing the Eaft, and a Trench of our aforefaid Mother towards the South; and the Land, formerly belonging to* ROGER SWERDE, *towards the North. And alfo the Advowfon of the Church of* Fofton, *to be poffefs'd and enjoy'd by himfelf, and his Succeffors: To wit, the faid Meffuage, with a Chapel, Edifices, and aforesaid Appurtenances, as an Habitation for them; together with free and fufficient Ingrefs and Egrefs to the faid Meffuage and Advowfon, as an Endowment to the aforefaid Prior and Monks, and their Successors, by due and accuftom'd Service to the Chief Lords of the Fees, for ever. We grant therefore, by the Licenfe and Authority aforefaid, that the Manor of* Sculcotes, *with its Appurtenances, and* 10 *Meffuages,* 2 *Caracutes of Land,* 100 *Acres of Pasture, and* 10 *Marks of the Income of the Lands, with the Appurtenances, in* Bifhop-Burton, *and* Sutton *in* Holdernefs, *which* THOMAS RAYNARD, *Clerk, holds for Term of Life, after the Demife of* JOHN de NEVILL, *Kt. (and which, after the Death of the faid* THOMAS, *are to remain to Us, and our Heirs) after the Deceafe of the faid* THOMAS, *should continue to the aforefaid Prior and Monks, together with the faid Meffuage and Advowfon, given and affign'd to him as abovefaid by us, and the aforefaid Church appropriated by us for ever, for the Time to come.*

Alfo that the faid Prior and Monks, by Vertue of the faid Licenfe and Authority aforefaid, the faid Meffuage, and its Appurtenances, with a Paffage, for going out, and entering therein, with the Advowfon aforefaid, shall receive them, as they are given and affign'd by us; and appropriate the faid Church, and it, so appropriated, keep to their own proper Ufe; and the aforefaid Manor, Meffuages, Land, Pafture, and Profits, with Appurtenances, shall remain to them, as above, after the Death of the faid THOMAS; *and may enter thereupon, and keep to themfelves, and their Succeffors aforesaid, by Services due and accuftomed, of the Chief Lord of the Fee, for ever.*

We will, therefore, and ordain, that the said Prior and Monks, and their Succeffors, do especially recommend in their Church-Service, Prayers, and other Divine Offices, the State of our Sovereign Lord King RICHARD *aforesaid, and of Us; and our noble Lady und Mother* KATHARINE, *and* KATHARINE *our moft dear Consort;* Mafter * EDMUND *our Brother;* MICHAEL *our Son and Heir;*
and

---

* He was Governour of *Calais:* But proved fo unkind a Brother, that when this very MICHAEL, who became Earl of *Suffolk,* was obliged (after his Royal Mafter's Forces were defeated by thofe of fome of the Lords) to fly to him, in *France, Anno* 1387, for Shelter, in his Diftrefs; he not only refus'd to grant
his

*and all our Children and Heirs. And in like manner to pray for
the Happiness of the venerable Father* Alexander *Archbishop of*
York, John de † **Nevill** *Lord of* Raby, *and Lord* Richard le
Scrop, *whilst living: And when we are all departed this Life,
let them offer (and cause to be offered) Prayers for our Souls ; especially, and perpetually, for That of our Sovereign Lord* EDWARD
aforesaid, and likewise of our most dear Father ; for the Souls of
Thomas *and* Walter, *our Brothers, Knights ;* Blanch, *our Sister,
late Wife of the said Lord* Richard le **Scrop;** *for the Souls of*
Ralph de **Nevill** *the Father and* Alice *the Mother of the said*
John ; *for That of* Matilda, *formerly Wife of the aforesaid*
John ; *for all our Benefactors, and of our Father's, for whom we
are bound to pray, and for the Souls of all the Faithful departed.
And We, the aforesaid* Michael *and our Heirs, the said Messuage,
Chapel, and Edifices, with all the Appurtenances, in the said Town
of ** **Kingston,** *the said Advowson, and aforesaid Manor, Messuages, Land, Pasture, and Profits, with the Appurtenances, to remain with them as above, with what shall accrue ; We will warrant and defend, against all Persons, to the aforesaid Prior and
Monks, and their Successors, for ever. In Testimony of which
Thing, we have set our Seal to these Presents. Witnessed by
the aforesaid* Richard le **Scrop,** *then Chancellor of* ENGLAND ;
Thomas *de* **Sutton,** Gerard *de* **Aflete,** Walter　Fauconberge,
and Robert *de* **Wilton,** *Knights ;* Richard *de* **Ferribie,** *then Mayor
of the said Town of* KINGSTON-upon-HULL ; Robert *de* **Selby,**
Walter *de* **Frost,** *and others of the same Town. Given at*
Kingston-upon-Hull, *the* 18th *Day of* February, *in the Year
of our* LORD, 1378, *in the Second Year of the Reign of our
Sovereign Lord King* RICHARD *aforesaid.*

---

his Protection, but seiz'd and deliver'd him up to the Lord *Beauchamp*, who
commanded in the Town, by whom he was sent Prisoner into *England*, where
he was soon at Liberty by the King, for whose Cause it was, that he was thus
obliged another Time to depart the Realm, and die in a Foreign Country.

† From the *NEVIL*'s Family sprung the Venerable Archbishop *USHER :*
One of whose Ancestors having been Usher to King *John*, occasion'd that Favourite to change his Original Name for that of his Office.

* In After-Times, a great Benefactor to both the Churches, in *Hull*, bequeath'd
his Mansion-House, (in which was a great Hall open to the Roof, with old Pictures tolerably well painted on Wood) to these *Carthusians*. 'Twas built in the
High-Street, opposite *Bishop-Lane*, which afterwards became the Property of the
Hildyards. On several Parts of it were Escutcheons Arg. 3 Battle-Axes, Or. with
the Mark of a Merchant: But the Name of the first Owner is unknown.
Much the like Arms are borne by *John Hall*, of *Bradford*, in *Wiltshire*, Esq.

AFTER this, in *March, Anno* 1383, Sir *Michael* was made Lord Chancellor by King *Richard* II. being the 6th of his Reign. The Year following the Knight founded and endow'd an † Hospital, with a ‡ Chapel over-against it, for the Use of poor People: And over-against the West-End of St. *Mary's* Church, in a Place, antiently called *Market-Gate*, he erected a stately Palace. The magnificent Gate-House, made of Brick, was supported by great Timber, having two Chambers, and cover'd with Tyle: Thro' this first Passage, and an Entry 20 Foot broad, and 100 long, was a spacious Tower, built of Brick and Stone, 3 Stories high, cover'd with Lead, in which were Chambers 18 Foot Square: From hence was a Court-Yard, the Space of half an Acre, paved with large Stones: About which were 17 Chambers (7 below Stairs, and 10 above) having Chimnies and Jacks in them, as those had in the aforesaid Tower. On one Side was

A Description of a famous Palace, afterwards called, The Duke of Suffolk's.

---

† It was pull'd down in the Civil Wars, but rebuilt after the Restoration: When the Arms of the *De la Poles*, having been found amongst the Ruins, was placed over the Door, with this Inscription.

Deo & *Pauperibus posuit Dom.* MICHAEL de la POLE, *A.D.* 1384.

THUS PARAPHRAS'D, *in Regard to the Memory of Sir* WILLIAM.

IN Thirteen Hundred Eighty Four,
  This House was built, for needy Poor,

By famous *Michael de la Pole*,
Of Spirit, like his Father's Soul :
Who finish'd what that Knight begun,
And gave to GOD, when he had done.

‡ This too had the same Fate ; But being rebuilt upon the old Foundation, there was placed, over the Entrance, the following Inscription.

Hoc Sacellum Deo & *Pauperibus posuit Dom* MICHAEL de la POLE, *Anno Dom.* 1384. *quod ingruente Bello Civili dirutum, An.* 1643. *tandem auctius instauratum fuit Anno* 1673. Richardo Kitson, *S. T. B. Rectore Domus Dei super* Hull.

ON WHICH I THUS PARAPHRASE.

THen, mindful they should *God* adore,
  He built this Chapel for those Poor,
'Twas ruin'd (piteous Sight to see !)
In Sixteen Hundred Forty Three,
When Churches desecrate were laid,
As if Religion was decay'd.

But rolling Years its Head has rais'd,
Where *Christ* is taught, *Jehovah* prais'd.
O may Six Hundred Seventy Three,
An happy Year, remember'd be ;
When *Richard Kitson*, (good Divine !)
A Rector of *GOD's House*, did shine.

And a new Hospital having been built, near this Chapel, (for the better Reception of the Poor, which the other was not well able to contain, along with the Master and his Family) there is this Inscription over the Entrance.

Deo & *Pauperibus posuit* MICHAEL de la POLE. *Hæc omnes reparata Domus perduret in Annos.* W. Ainsworth, *Rector, A.D.* 1663.

THUS ENLARG'D.

ERected too, by *Pole's* Command,
  A gracious Monument to stand,
For Sanctuary to the Poor,
Who here may live, and *Heav'n* implore :

Its humble Pile let nothing sever ;
Since now repair'd, may't last for ever !
May Sixteen Hundred Sixty Three,   ⎞
And Rev'rend *Ainsworth*, always be ⎬
Blest in a happy Memory !   ⎠

was a great Hall, to dine in, built of the like Materials, 60 Foot long, and 40 broad. At the Weft End, was a large Chamber, 60 in Length, and 20 in Breadth, with two adjoining Rooms, which had the fame Conveniences ; and at the Eaft, were Pantries, &c. with Lodgings over them: Beyond which, was a great Kitchen, 20 Foot Square, leaded at the Top; with a Larder, and Scullery, cover'd with Tyle. North of the Hall, ftood a beautiful * *Chapel*, I fuppofe, dedicated to St. *Michael* the Archangel, 28 Foot long, and 15 broad, built of fine Brick and Stone, which was cover'd with Lead : And, North of the Court, was an Entrance into a greater Area than the Yard aforefaid, which contained a whole Acre of Land, ufefully ornamented with a Fifh-Pond, and Dove-Cote, all ftrongly wall'd about. Weft of this, in like manner furrounded, there was a beautiful Field, containing 2 Acres Pafture. Before the Great Hall Window, was a moft charming *Flower-Garden*, contrived with wonderful Curiofity, in the Space of an Acre of Ground, enclofed by a fair Wall: Adjoining to which, was the Kitchen-Garden, in ⅓ of that Compafs, which had in it another Dove-Cote. South of the aforefaid Hall, or Dining-Room, was a Court, the Extent of a Rood, about which were erected Houfes for Baking, Brewing, . Wafhing, and all other Conveniences whatever.

To this Grandeur rofe the Palace erected by Sir MICHAEL ; to which, no doubt, but fome of thefe Parts had been added by his Succeffors : But, befides what has been mention'd of his Performances, he erected three fumptuous Houfes, with ftately Towers : Two of which were in the Town ; and the Third, which yielded a beautiful Profpect, ftood on the pleafant Bank of *Hull* River.

As he appears to have been a Perfon of remarkable Generofity, I am little inclin'd to believe the Reflections againft him, wrote by

an

---

* The Chapel, and Garden, were call'd, *The King's* ; probably from their Confifcation, at various Times. In the Year 1538, a Survey was taken of this magnificent Building : Two Years afterwards, *Henry* VIII. (vifiting the Town) beautify'd, repair'd, and enlarg'd it. Not many Years after, he granted the whole Buildings, with all belonging, to Sir *Henry Gate*, and Dame *Lucy* his Wife, for what Services they had done him : From them it came, in Queen *Elizabeth's* Reign, to the *Hildyard's* of *Wynfted*, who rented it for a Great Mart : But King *Charles* I. hired it, at 50*l.* yearly, for a Magazine, which he had provided. *Henry Hildyard*, Efq. fold it, *Anno* 1648, to the Mayor and Aldermen : And it was bought of them, in the Year 1661, by *Henry Hildyard*, of *Eaft Horfeley*, in the County of *Surrey*, Efq ; by whom it was fold to other Perfons : Who, pulling down the whole, converted it into feveral Habitations, fuch as we may behold at this Day. In what Parifh the old Manor lay, was once a Subject of Contention. A Story is told, of a strange Decifion, that a Perfon, called *John of the Bowling Green*, in *Henry* VIIIth's Time, who lived within the Manor, bury'd a beloved Dog of his in the Low-Church-Yard, for which he was feverely punifh'd. From hence, it was concluded, the Manor was (and, if so, confequently the new Buildings must have been) within that Parish.

an envious Poet ; and lefs, to make Obfervations on fuch Times, when Minifters are hated for being faithful to their Sovereigns, which indeed feem'd to have been his Cafe. But however he was vilify'd by many, he was belov'd by his King ; who, the 9th Year of his Reign, 1385, created him Earl of *Suffolk*, in Right of his Wife ELI-ZABETH, eldeft Daughter to Sir* JOHN WINGFIELD, who married ELIZABETH, Daughter and Heir to GILBERT GLANVILLE, Earl of *Suffolk.* After receiving this Dignity, he earneftly requefted, that he might be freed from his Chancellorfhip, which was granted. He prevail'd with the King to enlarge the Charter of *Kingfton-upon-Hull*, with many other Priviledges ; one of which was, the promoting of a good Harbour. But fo unfortunate was this Great Man, that he was openly accufed, in the Year 1386. The Objection againft him, was, That he had defrauded the King of his annual Rents ; in particular 4000 Marks Yearly of the Cuftoms in *Hull.* Notwithftanding which, being much in Favour with his

The Fall and Death of this great Bene-factor.

Prince, he was fet at Liberty : But, in 1388, the Parliament, who then were called *Unmerciful*, impeach'd him, with others, of 𝕳igh-𝕿reafon; whofe Eftate therefore being feiz'd upon, he was obliged a fecond Time to fly to *France ;* where, no doubt, but he avoided the Hands of his unprotecting and unnatural Brother ; and travelling to *Paris* for Shelter, he died, the Year after, in that great City.

THO' the End of this Favourite might be accounted unhappy ; yet feveral Defcendents from him were more unfortunate, but in different Degrees remarkable for Adverfity, Profperity and Glory.

** Continuation of the Family of* De la Pole.

For* *Michael de la Pole*, the valiant Earl of *Suffolk*, was slain at the Siege of *Harfleur, Anno* 1415. His eldeft Son foon after loft his Life at the famous Battle of *Agincourt ;* two younger fell in thofe Wars ; and a devout Perfon, (who was in Holy Orders) dy'd about that Time, as appears by the following Infcription on his Grave-Stone, in the Collegiate Church of WINGFIELD. *Here lieth the Body of Mafter* John de la Pole, (*Son of* MICHAEL de la POLE, *formerly Earl of* Suffolk) *Batchellor of Laws, Canon of the Cathedral Church of* † York, *and the Collegiate Church of*

† He was made Prebendary of *Wiftow*, 1380.

Beverley, *who died the Twenty Third Day of the Month of* February, 1415. *in the Fourth Year of King* HENRY *the Fifth.* But a Perfon of great Fame, was *William de la Pole*, Brother to thofe before-named illuftrious Warriors, slain in Battle. For he too, fays

an

an Hiftorian, warr'd in *France* 44 Years without Intermiffion, in 17 of which he never faw his Country.   When a Knight, being taken Prifoner, his Ranfom coft him 20000 Pounds.   On his Father's Death, he became Earl of *Suffolk*. In 1444, he was created a Marquefs ; and Duke, 1448.   Two Years after, he was impeach'd for being inftrumental towards the Death of *Humphrey*, Duke of *Glocefter*, interr'd at St. *Albans ;* his confenting to the yielding up *Anjou* and *Main ;* and for his being too familiar with Queen *Margaret*, Wife to *Henry* VI.   But the King, not really believing the Accufations, took him again into Favour: Yet foon after, to pacify the People, he banifh'd the Duke for 5 Years :   Who, embarking for *France*, was met by an *English* Ship (belonging to the Duke of *Exeter*, Conftable of the Tower) called the *Nicholas* : The Captain of which brought him into *Dover* Road, and order'd his Head to be cut off, on the Side of a Cock-Boat, *May* 2, 1450.   His Body, being left a while as a miferable Spectacle on the Sands, was taken up by the Care of his forrowful Chaplain, and interr'd at *Wingfield* in *Suffolk ;* tho' some write he was bury'd in the *Charter-Houfe*, near *Hull ;* but truly I know not with what Certainty.

THIS great tho' unfortunate Perfon had Iffue *John de la Pole*, Duke of *Suffolk*, who married *Elizabeth*, Sifter to King *Edward* the IVth; by whom he had Iffue *John de la Pole*, Earl of *Lincoln*. The laft therefore fprung from Royal Blood, of the Houfe of *York*. But his Hopes being blafted by the Death of his Uncle *Richard* III. (who had declar'd him his Succeffor in Cafe he should die without Children) and King *Henry* the VIIth's fudden Acceffion to the Throne ; the Earl was as little pleafed with that Prince, as he was with this Nobleman : Who, therefore, fiding with the Enemies of *Henry*, fled into *Flanders*, *Anno* 1486.   Soon after he sailed to *Ireland ;* where he joined Forces with *Perkin Lambert*, and tranfported them into *England*.   At *Stoke*, near *Nottingham*, they encounter'd with Part of the King's Army ; againft whom they were unfuccefsful : For here the Earl, with one *Martin Swerde*, a valiant Captain, (whom I take to have defcended from a Perfon of that Name, the Owner of some Lands, mention'd in the foregoing Charter of the *Carthufian* Monaftery, near *Hull)* and many others, fell in the Place of Battle, which happen'd in the Year, 1487.

THE Brother of this Earl was *Edmund* Earl of *Suffolk ;* a Perfon very unfortunate, as being of the Royal Blood, which made him take greater Liberty: Having kill'd a Man in a cruel Manner ; tho' the King pardon'd him, yet he was obliged firft to receive publick Condemnation.   This was such a Mortification to his Pride, that he went into Flanders, in 1502 : But the Duchefs *Margaret* his Aunt, giving him no great Countenance to oppofe
King

King *Henry* VII. he returned, and was the same Year reconciled to him. But in 1504, he fled a second Time, and took along with him his *Brother Richard.* This so provok'd the King, that he attach'd *William de la Pole* his Brother, with other illuſtrious Perſons, either belonging, or affeᴄted, to the Houſe of *York.* And finding the Earl out of his Reach, as being in the Caſtle of *Namur,* under the Proteᴄtion of the King of *Spain,* he got from the Pope a dreadful Excommunication, which was proclaimed in *England.* His Eſtates being forfeited, amongſt the reſt, were theſe in and near *Kingſton-upon-Hull:* The Great Manor-Hall, with its contiguous Edifices, and Gardens : One Hundred Meſſuages, 1000 Acres of common Land, with 200 of Meadow and Paſture : One of theſe had belonging to it 100 Acres, beſides 200 of Paſture, call'd *Tupcotes.* With this was seiz'd the famous Manor itſelf, along with *Myton,* and conſequently all the Liberties, Priviledges, Preſentations, Goods, Chattels, Debts, *&c.* including the Advowſon of the Hoſpital, and Patronage of the Priory.   But the King, commiſerating his Lady, granted the Ducheſs a noble Subſiſtence, which ſhe enjoy'd to her Death.   But it very ſtrangely happen'd, that HENRY at length made her Huſband Priſoner : For the Arch-Duke *Philip,* who became King of *Spain,* being with his Spouſe driven by a Tempeſt into *England,* HENRY obtain'd of him the Deliverance of the Earl into his Hands, provided his Life *was but ſpared.*   Accordingly *Edmund de la Pole,* being deliver'd up, *Anno* 1507, was committed to the * *Tower.*   Here I may date the

<table>
<tr><td>* A Period of the Honour of the Family, relating to Kingſton, &c.</td><td>End of his Grandeur : For the King, lying on his Death-Bed, in 1509, imitated David's Advice to Solomon, concerning Joab : He order'd his Son, who ſucceeded him, by the remarkable</td></tr>
</table>

Name of HENRY *the Eighth,* to make an End of this noble Priſoner : Who, accordingly, after a long Detention, commanded his Head to be ſevered from his Body, in the Year, 1513.

AND thus a Period was put to the Glory of the *De la Poles,* Rulers of *Suffolk,* whoſe higheſt Title of *Duke* was, *Anno* 1514, conferr'd on * CHARLES BRANDON, Viſcount *Lisle,* who, in 1527,

marry'd

---

* He died, *Anno* 1549, and was buried at *Windſor.*   His Son, by a ſecond Wife, became Duke of *Suffolk;* who, in the Year 1551, departed this Life of the *Sweating Sickneſs;* his Death being follow'd, in two Days Time, by that of his Brother, and Succeſſor.   The Earl of *Warwick,* afterwards Duke of *Northumberland,* who was Miniſter of State to *Edward* VI. cauſed *Henry Grey,* Marqueſs of *Northampton,* to be created Duke of *Suffolk,* ſoon after.   He was eſpous'd to *Frances Brandon,* (Daughter to *Charles Brandon,* the firſt above-mention'd Duke of *Suffolk,* of that Name, by *Mary,* Siſter to *Henry* VIII. as related) the Mother of

the

marry'd *Henry* the VIIIth's Sifter, MARY, who was the Widow of *Lewis* XII. King of *France.*

I INTEND not to proceed much further about the *De la Poles ;* only to remark, that fome of the Branches of that Family were in fome meafure confpicuous : For *Richard de la Pole*, the very Year of his Brother's Death, became in the *French* Intereft, and commanded 6000 Men for the Relief of *Terouenne* in *Artois*, againft King *Henry* VIII. who befieg'd, and took it, but a very little while after.   The other, I wou'd mention, was *Henry Pole* Lord *Montague*, who, with Sir *Edward Nevill*, was committed to the Tower, in 1521, for concealing what the noble and eloquent *Edward*, Duke of *Buckingham*, had faid in relation to his having a Right to the Crown, *in Cafe the King died without Iffue ; and if fo, he would punish Cardinal* Wolfey *according to his Deferts;* for which he was condemn'd before the Duke of *Suffolk*, and accordingly beheaded. But *Henry Pole*, the Lord before-mention'd, was fet at Liberty ; and afterwards created Earl of *Wiltshire.*

WHETHER the famous Cardinal *Pole* was a Branch or no, I'll not determine ; but refume the Subject of Religious Houfes, and efpe-. cially draw This to a Conclufion ; the Rife and Profperity of which, have occafioned, in Refpect to the Memory of its Benefactors, fo long, but fo remarkable a Digreffion, fill'd with the moft affecting Tranf-actions, enough to convince us of the Vanity of all fublunary Glory.

AT the Diffolution, in 1536, when the leffer Monafteries were given to *Henry* VIII. the famous * *Charter-Houfe*, near *Hull*, of whofe Foundation fo much has been faid, and valu'd at a confiderable Sum, was reckon'd one of that Number : The Lands, which belong'd

---

the Lady *Jane Grey.* As to this latter Duke, tho' he had been pardon'd after his acting against Queen *Mary*, in having contributed to place his Daughter upon the Throne ; yet, his promoting a Confpiracy occafion'd his Child's Death fooner than was imagin'd ; becaufe it was thought the Queen would have pardon'd her, in Confideration of her Youth, and Obedience to her Father. But foon after *Wyat's* Rebellion, the beautiful Lady *Jane Grey*, with her Husband *Guilford Dudley*, younger Son to the Duke of *Northumberland*, were beheaded *Feb.* 12, 1554. In which Year the Duke's Sentence was confirm'd, and he executed.   In 1561, one *Arthur Pole* confpir'd against Queen *Elizabeth :*. But tho' he was pardon'd, yet *Catherine Grey*, own Sifter to the late unfortunate Lady *Jane*, was fent to the Tower, for privately marrying the Earl of *Hertford.*   She died in Confinement, having a Right to the Crown ; which, it was thought, occafioned the Severity of the Queen, who was exceeding jealous of her Dignity.   Thus the Duchefs, *Frances Brandon*, her Mother, was left in great Calamity, having feen the Deftruction almoft of her Family ;   who, for her Security, was oblig'd to marry one *Adrian Stokes*, a private Gentleman, and died in the Year 1563. Secretary *Cecil* was thought to have been a great Friend to the Houfe of *Suffolk*. But I forbear any further Enquiries on this Head.

* The Arms of *De la Pole*, were in the Churches Painted Windows, and in Stone, as well as their having been in the Charter-Houfe.

long'd to it, were given to Laymen ; its ftately Building pull'd down ; and the Stones, with other Materials, sold to thofe Perfons, who pleas'd to buy them: What happen'd the Year before, might seem to foretell this : The Priories of *Merton* and *Hornby*, both in *Yorkshire*, were then surrender'd : And now *Ferreby* Priory was ruin'd, valu'd at 91*l. per Annum*, which was founded by an Earl of *Cumberland;* and that of *Haltemprife*, eftimated yearly at 178*l.* founded, for the Order of St. *Auguftine*, by the Lord WAKE of *Lydel*, and THOMAS HOLLAND Earl of *Kent.* This Suppreffion, throughout *England*, occafion'd 1500 Religious Perfons to be turn'd into an inclement World, whereby many were pin'd and ftarv'd, who had been well defcended from Families of Antiquity, Honour, and Reputation.

AND yet, about 2 Years after, the King, to pleafe the People for a while, and ftop their Infurrections, (of which was a remark- able one in the Northern Parts, headed by a Gentleman named *Ask)* 'till he could better obtain his Ends, refounded this Monaftery, (with 27 others) tho' under the fevereft Rules imaginable. But when he obtain'd that full Power he wifh'd for, in getting the larger Houfes at his Difpofal, then this Place fuffer'd a fecond Diffolution. For when the Parliament 1545, had given them all to his unprof- perous Avarice, then too fell the great College, or Prebendary, in *Hull*, that was founded by WALTER SKIRLAW ; with all the Gilds, and Chanteries, about 30 in Number. But King *Edward* VI. upon Complaint of the Decay of Religion and Learning, re- founded this Place once more, to fatisfy a general Importunity.

THUS, having, in the firft Chapter, written of the Priory, foun- ded by King *Edward* the Firft ; treated, in this, of the Charter- Houfe, in which I have but juft now hinted of the famous Bifhop *Skirlaw's* Foundation, *Anno* 1400; I proceed to mention another Edifice, which has been of antient Fame, and fingularly remarkable.

THIS Friery was founded, in the Year 1331, by a moft devout Knight, *dedicated to St. *Auguftine*, for Black Monks, or Hermits, of that Order : It was fo great a Build- ing, that it took up half the Place, which
* GALFRID de Ho- from thence was called *Monk-Gate*, or *Street.* THAM *founds a Mo-* The back Parts extended even to the Mar- *naftry, to the Honour* ket-Place, where thofe Priefts had a ftately *of* GOD, *&c.* Chapel, which had Right of Sepulture, as appear'd, by having Human Bones found therein. This Friery was adorn'd with fpacious Courts, curious Gardens, and pleafant Fountains. About 3 Years after the finifhing of it, Sir *Richard*, Son and Heir of the Founder, took upon him, and obliged his

Succeffors,

Successors, to pay the Fee-Farm Rent Yearly to the King, provided the Priests would pray for the Souls of him, his dear Wife *Avicia*, and their Pofterity.   About 5 Years after, the Mayor and Commonalty made fuch another Agreement, on Account of the Meffuages which thefe Monks poffeffed, (in *Hull-Street*, and *Market-Gate*) for the Benefit of their pious Petitions.   At which ·Time, *John de* * *Wetwang* beftowed on them feveral others, with good Tenements. This Monaftery was pull'd down at the Suppreffion ; and only now appear fome Remains of the old Wall, that are become a Part of the Town's-Hall.

AN Hofpital was founded, about the Year 1400, by a very great and pious *Merchant, who was thrice Mayor of *Hull*, built in a Lane, called afterwards by his Name.   Having finifhed it, a little before his Death, he gave, for its Endowment, the Rents of 6 Messuages and Tenements, in the Town. The Poor, in it, thus fupported by his Beneficence, were, like thofe of other Foundations, obliged to pray for the Soul of him, that of his Consort, and thofe of all Chriftians.   But a Period was put both to the Building, and their Prayers, in the Reign of *Edw.* VI.

**SIMON de GRIMSBY founds a large Hospital.*

THE next remarkable Obfervation, is of †GILDS : As, That of *Corpus Chrifti*, which ftood not far from the afore-mention'd *Augustinian* Friery, adorn'd with a fair Hall, Chapel, and several Meffuages belonging to it : The Gild of *St. Barbara*, (which contain'd 4 Tenements, and a large Chapel) in *Salt-House Lane* ; both Thefe were ruin'd by *Henry* the VIIIth : And a very antient Gild, built in a Lane, near the ‡Low Church Yard, was diffolv'd by *Edw.* VI

---

* One *Richard Wetwang*, Rector of S. *Dennis's* Church, in *Walmgate, York*, caufed the East Window to be enlarged, and whole Choir to be covered with Lead.

† These Gilds, Houfes, &c. were begg'd and bought by *John Thornton, William Ray, Roger Gaiton, William Wilfon*, and *Luke Thurfcrofs*. This last purchas'd a Meffuage, in *Chapel-Lane*, (that belong'd to the Convent of *Watton*, or *Wet Town*, founded by *Euftace Fitz John*, for the *Gilbertine* Order) which he sold to one Mr. *Smith*, Mafter of a Veffel.   The Suffragan Bishop's Palace, in *Hull-Street*, as mentioned Chap. I. likewife falling into his Hands, he partly demolifh'd the greateft Part, turning it into Shops, and private Buildings : However, he was so good, that, a little before his Death, he bequeath'd thefe converted Buildings, with their annual Profits, to the Charter Houfe Hofpital, for ever.

‡ In this Church was Service perform'd for the Soul of the Worshipful *Robert Holm*, Mayor in 1427, who had built a ftately Market-Cross, covered with a vast Quantity of Lead.   But, in 1462, the Town happening to be in Debt, by general Confent, the Crofs was demolifh'd, and the Lead fold, to pay off the Creditors : Yet, out of a grateful Refpect to the Memory of fo generous a Benefactor, it was decreed, That 13 *s.* 4 *d.* should, by the Chamberlain, be annually paid for a Funeral *Dirge*, to be fung (when the Bell-Man had proclaim'd his Name) by Twelve Priefts, with a Clerk attending upon them ; at which Time there should be Wax-Candles burning about the Grave ; and the Bells order'd to be rung on the fame Day, the more to honour their refpectful Solemnity.

which, in Queen *Elizabeth's* Time, came to Mr. *Luke Thurscross,* who gave it to the * Merchant Taylors Company. Thefe Gilds, after the Reformation, were defam'd for having been Structures of Superftition, and Places where the State then thought that Confpiracies were, or might be, form'd againft them : And Tradition informs us, there were two Sorts of Gilds, *viz.* Religious, and Civil: The former, for fettling Matters fpiritual; the latter, temporal: The firft confifted of both Clergy and Laity, whofe Intent was to fee Religion, and the Rules of the Church perform'd more ftrictly ; for which End, they contributed to erect a Chapel, and Hall, wherewith to pray and keep an *Agapæ*, or Love-Feaft, by which Revenues accrued to them, as tho' they might be reckoned a kind of Lay-Monafteries. But thofe Gilds, that were purely for particular Trades, were managed by the Profeffors of fuch Occupations, who often built Hofpitals to maintain their Poor. The learned *Selden* extends further, by what he has written : GILDARUM *Nomine continentur non folum minores Fraternitates & Sodalitia, sed ipfæ etiam Civitatum Communitates.* THAT IS, *By the Name of* Gilds, *are not only inluded the leffer Fraternities and Sodalities, but also Societies of Cities.* And this appears by the *Guild Halls*, where Courts of Seffions are kept up ; and higher Judicial Proceedings duly adminifter'd, for the Benefit of Subjects, in thefe our Days.

SEVERAL Religious Houfes were befide in this Town, as well as other extenfive † *Buildings:* But the Suppreffion, and Time, having, as it were, abolifh'd the old Worfhip, and brought both Sorts almoft to a Period, there is no finding a direct Certainty of their former State : However, thefe mention'd, may, in fome meafure, fet forth the Grandeur of HULL ; which, I prefume, will be fufficient to fatisfy the Curiofity of any reafonable Enquirer.

---

* In the Hall, of the like Company, at *York*, the following Words are painted on the Glafs of a large Window, by H. GYLES. *CONCORDIA PARVÆ CRESCUNT RES. This Company had been dignified, in the Year* 1679, *by having in the Fraternity Eight Kings, Eleven Dukes, Thirty Earls, and Forty Four Lords.* Happening to perufe an old Historian, I find 7 of those Monarchs were as follow: King *Richard* II. *Hen.* IVth, Vth, and VIth ; *Edward* IV. *Richard* III. and *Henry* VIIth, who gave them the Title of *Merchant Taylors, Anno* 1503.

† Of other Buildings, fuch as Manfion-Houfes, *&c.* there have been feveral: As, Sir *Humphrey Stafford's* Houfe, in *Hull Street*, whofe Arms were *Or. a Chev. G. quartered with G. 2 Feffes Arg. in Chief, a Mullet of the Second:* Which Building was given, by the Family of SCALES, to the Corporation, *Anno* 1556. Over the Enterance of which was the Cloth-Hall.——The *Merchants-Exchange*, in the same Street, built in 1621, repair'd and adorn'd 1673 ; over which is the Custom-House ; of late years enlarg'd, fash'd, and ornamented : Behind the whole, is a large Ware-Houfe, founded upon great Piles of Timber.——An antient House, was not far from hence, which, by its curious Windows, carved Wood, adorn'd with the Head of Angels, Cherubims and Seraphims, feem'd to have belong'd to some Religious Society.——*Club Hall*, (over against which was another old Edifice) and *Charity Hall*, (where poor Children were formerly us'd to work) in the *Market-Place*.——No doubt but there were several others.

AND now I will conclude this Chapter, with what iffues from the aforefaid Religious Foundations; from whence for the moft part the following *Wards* derive their Names. To thefe Six Divifions, the Town was, as it were, canton'd out (upon their Petition, which was granted by King *Henry* VI. *Anno* 1443.) into little Territories, which had Barrs, and Gates, that were shut up every Night: And each Divifion was govern'd by two refiding Aldermen, who heard Complaints; and had two Conftables to obey their Orders, in feizing the Delinquents, and bringing them to Juftice. And there was formerly a particular Prifon, in one of the antient Turrets of the old Wall, near the *Ropery,* called *Cold and Unquoth,* into which Offenders were committed by them or their Succeffors. Thefe *Wards* with their firft Settlement, are as follow.

I. *HUMBER* WARD. [1] This included *Black-Fryer-Gate,* from *Rotten Herring Staith* to *Finkhill Street,*and the *Butchery.*

II. *AUSTIN* WARD. [2] From the aforefaid *Staith,* to, (and with) *Grimsby Lane,* and down, behind the Church, to the *Butchery,* with *Myton-Gate,* and the *Lanes* appertaining thereto.

III. *TRINITY* WARD. [3] From *Grimsby-Lane,* to *White-Fryer-Gate:* Including the Chambers which belong'd to the Priefts; the E. W. and N. Sides of the Church-Yard, with *Old-Church Lane.*

IV. *WHITE-FRYERS* WARD. [4] This included *Scale-Lane,* to *White-Fryer-Gate;* and, from the End of the faid Lane, to *Bishop-Lane;* with *Denton-Lane,* and *Low-Gate,* included.

V. St. *MARY'S* WARD. [5] From *Bishop-Lane* to *Hornsey-Staith,* to the W. by *Clitherhouse* Garth, leading by *Low-Gate* to *Denton-Lane.*

VI. *NORTH* WARD. [6] From the End of the faid *Staith* to the W. End of *Clitherhouse* Garth, containing all thofe Parts lying Northward, which were within the Liberties of the Town.

---

[1] THOMAS DAY, and THOMAS DICKINSON, were the Aldermen; *Thomas Cooper,* and *John Titlat,* Conftables.——[2] ROBERT AWNSWELL, and RICHARD HANSON, Aldermen; *John Forrest, Francis Duck,* Conftables.——[3] RALPH HORN, JOHN SCALES, Aldermen; *William Hewitt, Jonathan Hall,* Conftables.—— [4] JOHN BEDFORD, JOHN STEETON, Aldermen; *Thomas Hackfter, John Burton,* Conftables. The Hospital in *White Fryers-Gate,* fo called becaufe the Order of *Carmelites* therein wore white Garments, was founded in the Year 1338, thro' the Benefaction of King *Edward* III. *Richard de la Pole,* and Sir *Robert Outred,* by whofe Munificence it became very famous.——[5] ROBERT HOLM, JOHN AWNWICKE, Aldermen; *John Danes, William Clitheroe,* Conftables.——[6] No others are mention'd.

CHAP.

CHAP. IV.

An Account of the Streets, Lanes, *&c. that are in* KINGSTON-upon-HULL.

Firſt. THE *High* (or HULL) *Street*, called, from the latter Name, in Antient Writings, as having been built on the Side of that River ; which, as before obſerv'd, was fronting the Water, in manner of a large *Key :* It reaches from the *North-Gate*, to the *South-End*, where there is a beautiful Proſpect of the Haven. From the ſaid *High-Street*, five Lanes iſſue towards the River ; which I ſhall mention as preparatory to the Plan, at the End of this Deſcription ; that ſets it forth in a more plain and intelligent Manner, by *Words* and *Letters.*

A. * *Salt - House - Lane,* in which, it is thought, Salt was formerly made. — B. *Chapel - Lane* Staith. — C. *Bishop - Lane* Staith. — D. *Scale-Lane* Staith. — E. *Church-Lane* Staith. —
F. Rotten

---

* Mr. ROBERT RATCLIFF, founded an Hoſpital in this Lane, about the Year 1570, bequeathing Two Tenements therein, with a Paſture, to feed one Cow, in the Kirk-Field of *Drypool,* for the Support of ſuch poor People, who were to be placed therein, at the Diſcretion of the Mayors of *Hull.*

RIVER
R
HUMBER
THE
ROPERY
FRYER G.
Blanket R.
Myton G.
G
K
N
a
b

F. *Rotten-End* Staith.——G. *Horse* Staith.——On the other Side of *High-Street*, terminate moſt of theſe Lanes : As, 1. Over-against *Salter-House* Staith Lane, is either the Continuance of that very Lane, or a particular Place called *Salter-Lane*, which has its Ending near unto the Beginning of *Lowgate*.   2. Againſt *Chapel* Staith Lane, ends *Chapel-Lane*, leading (by St. *Mary's* Church) into *Low-Gate*.   3. † *Bishops-Lane*, croſs the *High-Street*, fronts the *Staith* Lane of that Name.—4. *Scale-Lane* faces *That* of the *Staith*, in like manner. —5. *Church-Lane* the same, which leads to the Market-Place.— 6. *Rotten-End* Staith is partly towards *Black-Fryer-Gate*.— 7. *Horse* Staith is near to the *South-End*, facing the *Humber*, and almoſt oppoſite a Tower of the *Garrison*, on the East Side of the River, (built *Anno* 1681, and well ſtored with Ordnance) mark'd with Three *Aſteriſms*, thus * * * to denote the Form of its Situation, (where there are diſtinct Houſes for the Officers, with convenient Apartments for the common Soldiers, who have an Engine to convert Salt Water into Freſh, beſides there is a South Block-House in this Citadel) and the *New Cut* for the Water to flow near it, both for its greater Ornament and ſtronger Defence.

Second. The *Low-Gate*, which leads from the End of *Salt-House-Lane* to a large Opening, antiently called *High-Gate*, but now better known, for its never-ending Commodities, by the Name of the *Market-Place*. Near which is the *High-Church*, or that dedicated to the Holy Trinity, of which I have already treated ; the Eaſt Part, or glorious Window of it particularly, caſts a venerable Figure this Way.   But, to explain

---

† Before the Reformation, it belong'd to the Archbiſhops of *York*; and, thro' them, came to the Suffragans. But being taken from the latter in King EDWARD VIth's Time, that young Prince granted, in the laſt Year of his Reign, by Letters Patents, Twenty Three Meſſuages, Cottages, Houſes, and Tenements, to CHRISTO-PHER EASTOFT, of *Ellicar*, Esq ; and to THOMAS DOWMAN, of *Pocklington*, Gentleman. But ſome how, or other, Queen MARY I, getting them into her Hands, ſold them to HENRY THURSCROSS, Mayor of *Hull*, who obtain'd Letters Patents from the Queen, that they should appertain to him, and his Heirs, for ever.

explain the Plan, according to the Alphabet, the next *Letter*, I. denotes ROBINSON'S *Row.*——K. The *South-End.*—— L. St. *Mary's,* (in * *Chapel-Lane* aforefaid) called the Low-Church: The Patronage of which, perhaps, might antiently have belong'd to the before-mention'd Monastery of *Carthufian*

---

* In this Lane, Mr. *Harrison* founded an Hofpital, as shall be mention'd hereafter. But the famous Mr. *William Gee,* Merchant and Alderman, having likewife erected another, about the Year 1600, his Will, being very remarkable, it would be a Crime, (nay, even almost a Sin) if I should here omit the Substance of it. —WHEREAS, *in the Scriptures, the Great God has willed, by the Prophet, to fay to* Hezekiah, *to make his Will, and to put Things in order, for that he must die; fo I do now pray, and humbly beseech the Great God, to confound and deftroy all thofe* MEN, LAWYERS, *and Others whosoever, to the* 𝕯𝖊𝖛𝖎𝖑, *in the* 𝕻𝖎𝖙 𝖔𝖋 𝕳𝖊𝖑𝖑, *which do, or shall do, or take upon them to alter this my Will, Amen: Good Lord, Amen! I bequeath for Privy Tythes forgotten, Twenty Shillings. To my Son* William Gee, *Two Thousand Pounds. My Son* Walter, *Two Hundred Pounds, &c. To Twelve Poor Men, and as many Poor Women, at my Burial, Ten Pounds; to each of these, One Shilling a-piece; Bread, Cheefe, and Drink; alfo a Mourning Gown. To my Executors, One Hundred and Fifty Pounds, to be bestowed on Land, for the which shall be yearly given to the Poor People in* Hull, *for ever, Six Pounds, Thirteen Shillings, and Four Pence, at the Time and Day of the Year that I depart forth of this mortal World; for which they shall give Thanks and Honour to God, the moft Holy and Bleffed Lord, that openeth the Heart of Man to give fome of His Riches to the needy Souls remaining in the World; for which I praife his great Goodnefs that fent it me, and give moft hearty Thanks, Glory and Praife, with my very Heart and Soul.—— Five Shillings a-piece to all my God-Sons and God-Daughters; Two Pounds, Thirteen Shillings, and Four Pence, to my Neighbours of the fame Street, to be chearful with, and give Thanks to my good God.——Six Hundred Pounds, to Trinity Church, to be put out at five per Cent. Four Pounds yearly (of the fame) to be expended on the said Church; and the reft, on St.* Mary's.——*To the Town's Chamber, Twenty Pounds. To them more, One Hundred and Sixty Pounds; the Intereft of which, Mr. Mayor, and his Brethren, shall yearly lay out for Corn for the poor People: And if they do not, nor will do the fame, that then the City of* York *shall have the Money, and do it for their Poor. Also, in the name of* Jesus Christ, *my*

thuſian Monks ; but is now in the Gift of *Ellerker Bradshaw*, Esq ; and under the Juriſdiction of the Deanery of *Harthill.*—— M. *Billingsgate,* which is nigh the *Ropery.*——N. A Clew, which lets in the Water, at the *New-Cut,* when it is full Tide.——O. *Beverley* Gate. —— P. *Myton* Gate. —— Q. The *Dolphin,* by which the Ships ſail in, and out. —— R. Low-Water Mark in *Humber.* —— S. The *North-Gate.*——T. The Fish-Shambles. —— V. GRIMSBY-*Lane* ; which is between *Church-Lane* and *Black-Fryer-Gate,* when you enter into it from the *High-Street :* From hence you may go either to the *Market-Cross ;* or, by other Ways, which are called *Dirty Alleys,* be led to the *Fish-Shambles.* —— W. *Little-Lane,* that leads from *Black-Fryer-Gate* towards the *Ropery.*—— X. The Land of *Green-Ginger.*—Y. The *Dirty Alleys,* before-mention'd. —— *Heſſel* Gate, now clos'd up, as uſeleſs. —— a. *The* Butchery. — b. *Finkhill-Street.* — * The *Sugar-Houſe,* built in 1731, 74 Foot high, with 138 Windows, 79 Foot in Length, and 46 in Breadth. The Reader may perceive
other

my Saviour, I bequeath, and give to the Town's Chamber, the Mai-ſon Dieu, and House, that I built in Chapel-Lane, *for the Poor, by God's Permiſſion, with the Four Tenements adjoining, and two Houſes more, in the ſame Lane : That Ten poor old ſingle Women dwell in the ſaid Houſe, and that they, and their Succeſſors, have Four Pence a Week paid them. Likewiſe I give and bequeath to the School of* Hull, *erected by me, two Houſes in the Butchery for ever, &c.*——ALL *which Premiſſes,* (as we are aſſured by a Gentle-man of great Veracity) *his Son,* William Gee, *of* Bishop-Burton, *in the County of* York, *Eſq; and* Mary, *his Spouſe, did, by Deed, confirm, ſettle and convey to* Joshua Field, Anthony Cole, John Lister, Marmaduke Haddlesey, Thomas Thackray, *the Reverend* Thomas Whincop, *and* Thomas Fowberry, *School-Master, their Heirs, and Aſſigns, for ever : That they, and their Succeſſors, should pay out of thoſe Rents in* Chapel-Lane, *Weekly, to Ten poor People, in the Maiſon-Dieu aforeſaid, Four Pence each, for ever; And to pay, out of the two Meſſuages in the Butchery, to the Schoolmaſter of* Hull, *Six Pounds, Yearly, for ever, at* Lady-Day *and* Michaelmas : *Provided, that if the ſaid Premiſſes are not performed; that then it shall be lawful to, and for, the ſaid* William Gee, *Eſq; his Son and Heirs, to re-enter on the said Meſſuages and Tenements.*

·other Places, beſide thoſe ſpecified in the Alphabet, mention'd more fully in the Plan.

Third. SILVER-*Street :* With Lanes, Alleys, *&c.* As, *Bowl-Alley* ; *White-Fryer-Gate ; Trinity-Houſe-Lane,* not far from *Priests* or *Canon-Row* ; *Church-Lane,* or *Side,* in antient Writings, called *New-Kirk-Lane,* in order to distinguish it from *That* prior to it, then well known by the Name of the *Old,* as it is now for. that of *Postern-Gate.* On the South Side of the Church is *Vicar-Lane,* which leads to *Myton-Gate;* and from this laſt, you go, thro' *Finkhill Street,* to *Blanket-Row.* Other Places are *Fish-Street,* near *Robinson's-Row ; Dagger-Lane, Sewer-Lane, &c.* The Form of their Situation is more easily ſeen, and underſtood by the Plan, as I mention'd before, to which I now entirely refer the reader.

CHAP. V.

Containing ſome few Incidents from the Foundation of the Churches, 'till the Time when the first MAYOR *of* Kingſton-upon-Hull *was elected in the Year* 1332.

I CONCLUDED the Firſt Chapter with the Riſe of the Church, in the Year 1312; which, with several Religious Buildings, have produced Three Others, of conſiderable Length, and Variety : It is now neceſſary to uſe a Retroſpection, as near as poſſible, to that Time, from which I was obliged to digreſs ; and relate thoſe Tranſactions, preceding the Dignity of that high Office, diſcharged by ſo many excellent Magiſtrates, with Probity, Juſtice and Honour : Which, after a little Space, I ſhall proceed to mention, with as much Care, and Exactness, as poſſible I can.

IN the Year 1316, *Robert* de **Sandal** was Warden : He founded the *Ferry* from *Hull* to *Barton,* now ſo univerſally known ; the Profits of which he gave the Town. The Grant was dated at *Lincoln, August* 28. Every ſingle Perſon was to pay an Half-Penny : If an Horſeman, One Penny ; and every Cart, with 2 Horſes, Two-Pence. Two Days after which Grant, the King ſet out a Proclamation, *That no*
Goods

Goods should be fold in the Haven of the Town, before they were brought to Land.

Anno 1317, Sir ROBERT HASTINGS, Knight, was made Warden, (*John Sutton* and *Peter Mold* being then Bayliffs) by Letters Patents, for fome fingular and valorous Exploits againft the *Scots ;* for which he had befide granted him the Fee-Farm Rents of this Town, *Myton* and *Tupcotes*, to the Value of 70*l. per Annum.* Nor was he undeferving ; for, two Years after, he waited upon the King, then at *York*, and obtain'd the Grant for a Toll on Corn, Cattle, Fifh, Allom, Copperas, *&c.* that were expos'd for Sale in the Town : By which prudent Management, he procur'd a handfomer Pavement to be made ; the Stones of which, it is thought, were brought from *Spurn - Head*, where there are great Plenty. The Town had been formerly made a Staple ; but Wool, and its Felts, not turning to Advantage, prov'd rather a Detriment to it. But, however, the Inhabitants grew opulent, without that Way of Dealing. In 1322, they petition'd the King for Licenfe to fortify the Town with a Ditch ; to raife near it a ftrong Stone Wall, whereon Towers might be erected ; and to build their Houfes of Lyme and Stone, a much more durable and fafer Way, than that of Wood. When the condefcending Prince had granted this, they befought him further, *That a Toll might be rais'd of a Penny in the Pound for all Goods brought in, and carried out, for the Space of three Years ; and that the Produce of it might be apply'd for that Purpofe.* The Monarch confenting alfo to this Petition, the Town foon became enabled to attain what was fo ardently defired. And towards the End of the Reign of King *Edward* II. the Office of a Warden was changed to That of a Bayliff.

I CANNOT conclude this little Chapter, without deploring the Miferies of that unfortunate Prince, who denied nothing that was for the Happinefs of the Town : To make Room for his Son, he was depofed in the Year 1327, occafioned by fome feeming Defects in Government, but more through the violent Difpofition of his Queen : A Woman of fuch a cruel Temper, as not only to deny the Comforts of Life to her Royal Husband ; but alfo to prevent the young Monarch

M

from

from vifiting his diftreffed Father in Prifon : Who was igno-miniously hurry'd from one Caftle to another ; difguifed, in-fulted, tormented ; 'till, at laft, (by the Bifhop of *Hereford*'s wickedly ambiguous Line, EDWARDUM *occidere nolite timere bonum eft*, which both encourag'd the Murder, and left Room to excufe himfelf) an End was put to his Life, *Sept.* 22, that very Year, by thrufting a red-hot Iron through a ductile Pipe into his Bowels and Body, fo that no Mark might be found upon him.   Thus fell this unhappy Prince, not fo much fit for this vain World, as he was for an immortal State ; the Meek-nefs of whofe Behaviour having occafion'd him to be look'd upon as a Saint : His Body now lies interr'd under a fair Monument, which has his Effigy upon it, of Alabafter, in the Cathedral Church, at *Glocefter*.

EDWARD III. a victorious King, proved a very great Be-nefactor to this Town.   In 1328, he marry'd (at *York)* the youngeft Daughter of the Earl of *Hainalt,* named *Philippa,* who became the happy Mother *(Anno* 1331.) of a Royal In-fant, afterwards a moft renowned Warriour, known by the Title of *The Black Prince ;* whofe Brother dying in a Mona-ftery at *York,* his Effigy is to be feen in that Cathedral.

AND now I come to the memorable Year 1332, when the King (vifiting *Hull,* as related in the Third Chapter) being nobly entertained by that great Merchant *William de la Pole,* not only knighted him, but at the fame Time made him the firft Mayor of this important Town. This was HE that founded the Charter-Houfe aforefaid, which his Son *Michael* finifh'd, and endow'd (including the Chapel, and Hofpital, which moreover he had erected, for Thirty Poor People) with the Value of 260*l.* a Year.

IT is, to me, fome Matter of Concern, that the conftant Suc-ceffion of Mayors was not exactly recorded ; or, if it was, that the Account fhould be loft for near 50 Years. To further, perhaps, the Difcovery of it ; at leaft, to prevent the like Complaint in fucceeding Ages ; my Bufinefs fhall be, in the following Chapters, to reconcile, as well as I am able, the various Manufcripts, carefully perus'd by me for this Pur-pofe : And, with what Improvements I have made herein, humbly fubmit the whole to my Reader's Judgment.

CHAP. VI.

An Account of the MAYORS, *from the Year* 1332, *'till* 1439, *when* Sheriffs *were appointed : With what remarkable Accidents happened, relating to* HULL.

A.D. **S**IR WILLIAM *de la* POLE, called by the King
1332   *Mercator Dilectus Noster.* Firſt Mayor.
1333 *Sir* WILLIAM, 2d Year, was Mayor alſo : The
    Bayliffs, *Stephen* de *Begholm,* and *John* de *Bedford*
1334 We do not find him again mention'd, till
1335 *Sir* WILLIAM, 3d Time Mayor. The Figures
    1, 2, 3, 4, *&c.* shall be the Method, after the
    Name, to denote how many Times ſuch Perſon
    has (or thoſe of the ſame Name, probably Sons,
    &c. have) been Mayor of the Town. *William* de
    Birkin, and *Walter* de **Cavernieur,** Bayliffs.

1336 ❋ 1338 ❋ 1340 ❋ 1342 ❋ 1344 ❋ 1346 ❋
1337 ❋ 1339 ❋ 1341 ❋ 1343 ❋ 1345 ❋ 1347 ❋ 1348
1349 See the *Agreement,* in the Note below. *(a)*
1350 ❋ 1351 ❋ 1352 ❋ 1353 ❋ 1354 ❋ 1355

(a) THIS Year an Agreement was made between *Hull* and *Scarborough,* to which was affix'd both the Corporation Seals, *That they, and theirs, should hereafter be mutually exempted, in each Place, from all Manner of Tolls, Pontage, Murage, Cuſtoms,* &c. The
            Town

1356 ROBERT *del* CROSS. *The Conſtitutions of* Hull, *in his Time, were written in the* French *Tongue.*

1357 ❖ 1360 ❖ 1363 ❖ 1366 ❖ 1369 ❖ 1372 ❖ 1375
1358 ❖ 1361 ❖ 1364 ❖ 1367 ❖ 1370 ❖ 1373 ❖ 1376 *(b)*
1359 ❖ 1362 ❖ 1365 ❖ 1368 ❖ 1371 ❖ 1374 ❖ 1377

Town ſupply'd the King, for his Expedition to *France*, with 16 gallant Ships, mann'd with 466 Mariners ; and *Scarborough* only one Ship, with 16 Sailors : But what might the latter now do, was the Prince to require an Aid, that Way, from his Sea-Port Towns? There happening to be a great Tyde, the Banks of *Humber*, between *Sculcotes* and *Hull* were broken down ; Meadows and Paſtures lay under Water; Cattle and Sheep were ſuddenly drowned, with abundance of People ! Whereupon a Petition was ſent to the King, to commiſſion ſome Gentlemen to examine into the Cauſe of the Defects of the Bank, as well as that of the Inundation, by which ſuch like terrible Misfortunes might be prevented: Accordingly their Requeſt was granted, and the following Perſons were impowered for this Purpoſe. *William* de **Skipwith**, *Richard* de **Ravenſer**, Provoſt of the Collegiate Church of *Beverley*, *John* de **Bothby**, *John* de **Bentley**, and *Thomas* de **Egmonton** ; who took Care to act therein accordingly.

(b) This Year, the Mayor and Burgeſſes of *Hull*, made great Complaint unto the King, That their Town, being ſituated upon the Coaſt of the great River *Humber*, and built upon a Salt Soil, ſo that they had no freſh Water, nor could they procure any, but ſuch as was brought daily in Boats out of *Lincolnſhire*, to their great Expence, Trouble, and Damage : Whilſt Neighbouring Towns in *Yorkſhire*, as *Heſſel, Anlaby, Cottingham*, and Others, had combin'd together, and abſolutely refus'd to let them have any of their Freſh Streams ; by which Means, this Town would in a ſhort Time, be totally ruined, unleſs his Majeſty would be pleas'd to direct ſome Way, or other, how this great Want might be ſupply'd. Upon which the King immediately iſſued out a Commiſſion to *Michael de la Pole, Roger de Filthorp, Gerard de Uſlete, Gilbert de Salwen*, and *Peter de Grimsby*, Knights : Who, meeting for that Purpoſe, order'd and decreed, by the Power granted them, That a large Canal ſhould be immediately cut, from *Anlaby* Spring on the North Side of the King's High-Road ; that it ſhould be 40 Foot broad, in order to convey the freſh Water thither ; and that ſevere Puniſhment ſhould be inflicted on thoſe, who durſt offer to hinder the Work, and prevent ſo neceſſary a Supply. But when the

Inhabitants

1378 Richard *de* Ferraby, *or* fferibie. *(c)*

Inhabitants of the aforefaid Towns were alarm'd at thefe Proceedings, they bitterly complain'd to his Majefty, That the making of fuch a Canal would be the total Ruin of their Lands and Effects ; that, at *Heffel*, there was a famous Ferry over to *Barton ;* that if the frefh Water fhould be turn'd out of the Haven, it would foon be warp'd up, to the incredible Damage of the King, and Town itfelf: " Whofe People, *faid they*, complain without a Caufe ? Have " they not a large deep River, called by the Town's Name, which " runneth into the Haven, clofe by the Side of *Kingston* itself, with " Water, frefh and fufficient to fupply it, if it was even as large as " the City of *London ?*" Upon thefe Arguments, there was another Commiffion iffued forth; and a Jury being impanell'd, they were called after this Manner: *John Pothow, Thomas le Moyne* and *John Fugill* of *Heffel, Robert de Swanland, John Atwell, John le Gard, Robert de Watfonhoufe, John de Hoton, John Alanfon, William Fitling, John Robinson,* and *John de Skirlaw.* These Men proved, by their Oaths, what was before reprefented. But in the Midft of thefe Contentions, the renowned King EDWARD III. departed out of this mortal Life, and was fucceeded by RICHARD II.

(c) It plainly appears, that he was Mayor this year, as having been a Witnefs to the Charter of the famous *Carthufian* Monaftery. [*Richardo de* fferibie, *tunc Majore dictæ Villæ de* Kingfton *fuper* Hull. *Vid.* DUGD. Pag. 968.] The *Scots*, and *French*, were Enemies to *England* about this Time: The firft entering on our Borders, and the fecond, having a Naval Force, coming upon our Sea-Coafts, burnt and deftroy'd where ever they could obtain a Power. The King therefore fent to *Hull*, to have the Town put into a Pofture of Defence. The long happy Reign of his Predeceffor had render'd their Walls and Ditches ufelefs ; but now the Cafe being alter'd, the young King commanded them to be repair'd, at the Expence of the Inhabitants, and thofe who had Eftates in the Town. But, after all, wanting a Caftle for its greater Defence, Sir *Thomas de Sutton*, Kt. fold to *Robert Del Crofs, Walter de Froft, Robert de Selby, Thomas de Waltham, Walter de Dymlington, Thomas de Malton*, and their Heirs, as Magiftrates of *Hull*, a Piece of Land on the Eaft Side of the River, on the Banks of *Drypool*, which was North of the Key: As alfo fome Land, containing 10 Ells broad, and 100 long, upon the Key; the whole about 100 Ells facing the Eaft, and as many towards the North. To this Deed, JOHN CONSTABLE, of *Halsham*, then Sheriff of *Yorkshire ;* ROBERT *de* Wilton, JOHN *de* St. Quintin, Knights, and others, were Witneffes.

1379 (For thefe 2 Years, it is not unlikely, the Office
1380 (might have been fupply'd by the fame Mayor.
1381 Thomas *de* Waltham. *He was a Knight Baronet, and Secondary Baron* [*d.*]
1382 Walter Dimlington, *or* Dymbleton, 1.

(d) A great Conteft happened between this Mayor and the Archbifhop of *York.* The Cafe was thus: The Lord *Sayer*, as before-mention'd, had a great Intereft in the Haven, which from him was called *Sayer-Cryke*, having feveral Priviledges, as the firft tafting, and buying Wines, *&c.* before the Magiftrates had fuch Permiffion. That Nobleman, a little before his Death, bequeath'd this Power to the Archbifhop of the Province, and his Succeffors, which they enjoy'd for many Years. But, in Progrefs of Time, the Governours of the Town, claiming the fame Priviledges, upon Refufal of the Archbifhop, feveral troublefome Law-Suits commenced between them. *Alexander Nevill* being now Archbifhop, and perfonally contending the Matter, with Sir *Thomas de Waltham ;* the Mayor was fo provok'd, that, without much Ceremony, he fnatch'd the Crofier out of the Prelate's Hand. Each of them having their Attendants, a Scuffle enfu'd ; but, as I find, the Archbifhop's Party had the worft of it ; feveral of them being wounded by the Crofs, (valu'd at 40*l.*) which the Knight ufed in a ftrange furious Manner. Complaint being made to the King, the Mayor, with *John Arnold* and *Thomas Green* his Bayliffs, alfo *Lawrence de Frothingham, Richard de Hornfey*, and feveral others, were fummoned to *Weftminfter*, at *Trinity-Term*, to anfwer for what they had done. How this Affair was concluded, does not appear ; but I fuppofe it was amicably decided : For on the 4th of *July*, the Haven of the Town was granted to this Extent, that it fhould reach from *Sculcotes*, to the Middle Stream of *Humber.* About which Time, the King renewed the Old Charters, with new Priviledges ; in particular, he gave them the Profits belonging to him, or his Succeffors, from Markets, Fairs, *&c.* upon this Condition, that they fhould pay Seventy Pounds, Yearly, into the *Exchequer :* And that, from their Burgeffes, four Bailiffs fhould be annually elected : For which, the Town was fo exceeding grateful, as moft loyally to take their Monarch's Part in his Troubles, occafioned thro' the *French, Scots*, and his own rebellious Subjects: They raifed him Soldiers, and procured Ships, for his Service : Which the King remembering, when the Storms of his Enemies were abated, he affur'd the Inhabitants of *Hull*, That neither he, or his Succeffors, would ever mortmain

any

1383 Robert Del Crofs. *He dy'd* 1408.
1384 John Dimlington.
1385†Robert *de* Selby, or **Selbie.**   † The Lord *John Holland,* this Year, in a Quarrel, near *York,* kill'd the eldest Son of the Earl of *Strafford,* for which he was forc'd to fly for Sanctuary to *Beverley* Minster.
1386 Thomas *de* Waltham, 2
1387 John Birkin, *or* Berkin, 1
1388 Walter Dimlington, 2
1389 John *de* Colthorpe. [*e.*]
1390 Simon *de* Grimsby, 1
1391 Robert Baffet.
1392 Peter Steeler, *or* Stiler. [*f*]   Buried in the High-Church, and over him this Inscription, *Hic jacet* Petrus Steeler, *quondam Major hujus Villæ, qui obiit* 20 *Junii,* 1396.

any Lands to their Detriment : And that they fhould have a Common-Seal, to confift of two Parts ; the upper of which to be depofited in the Hands of a Clerk, for that Purpofe, appointed by him, or any fucceeding Sovereign.

[*e*] He lies interr'd in St. *Mary's* Church, and had over him and his Confort this Infcription : **Hic jacet** JOHANNES *de* Colthorpe, **quondam Major Ville De** Kingfton *fuper* Hull; **et** ALICIA **Uxor ejus : Quorum Animabus propitietur Deus. Amen.** In this Mayor's Time, the great Weigh-Houfe, before-mention'd, was built over part of the Haven, founded deep into the Earth underneath with large Piles of Timber, and crofs Beams above, over which the Structure was raifed.

[*f*] In the Spring Time, near a thoufand Perfons, belonging to *Cottingham, Woolferton, Anlaby,* and other neighbouring Towns, being offended, that the Inhabitants of *Hull,* had, by cutting the Earth, drawn fome frefh Water from them ; they bound themfelves, with a terrible Oath, to ftand by one another whilft they were able to fhed their laft Drops of Blood.   Then, having ordain'd the moft ruftical Leaders, they appear'd in the like Sort of Arms, ranfacking Houfes, and abufing fuch Owners, who would not as madly confederate with them. Soon did they lay Siege to *Hull,* vowing the utter Deftruction of it.   Being ftrangely poetically given too, they made fuch infipid Rhimes, to encourage the Seditious, as indeed would difhonour the Flights of Antiquity, fhould fuch ridiculous Stuff be publickly fet forth. The Canals, which had been made at a vaft Expence, they quickly fill'd up, almoft as they had been before. But tho' by thefe Means they had spitefully deprived the Town of frefh flowing Streams, and ftopt Provifions that were fent to the valiant Inhabitants ; yet thefe ill-advifed Wretches found themfelves too

much

1393 John Liverſedge, 1
1394 *John Berkin, 2   * *Queen* ANNE *died this Year.*
1395 William Terry, 1   *She firſt taught the* English *Ladies how to ride on Side Saddles.*
1396 Simon *de* Grimsby, 2   *J. Liverſedge.*
1397 John Liverſedge, 2   *John Birkin.*
1398 Thomas *de* Waltham, 3   *Will. Terry.*
1399 John Tutbury, 1 [*g*]   *S.* de *Grimsby.*

much deluded, and withal too impotent, to prevail againſt them·
Upon which, withdrawing to *Cottingham;* and afterwards, through
Fear, diſperſing ; ſome fled quite away ; others, taken, and ſent to
York, were executed ; and about 30 obtain'd Pardon, upon their Pe-
nitence, and faithful Promiſe, never to attempt the like again.

[*g*] When HENRY Duke of *Lancaſter,* after his Baniſhment,
landed at *Ravenſpurn* this Year, and was join'd by the Lords *Willoughby, Roſs, Beaumont,* with Numbers of Gentry, *&c.* this good
Mayor, as ſoon as he heard of it, order'd the Gates to be ſhut up,
and the Burgeſſes to appear under Arms. The Duke and his Aſ-
ſociates, ſoon after, demanding Enterance, received this Anſwer
from the worſhipful Magiſtrate : *My Lord ! when I enter'd upon
my office, I was ſworn to be true to my Sovereign, who indeed has been
a Royal Benefactor to us : No Conſideration therefore ſhall ſeperate
me from that firm Allegiance, which I owe to my Prince, but Death
itſelf : And, whilſt I live, nothing, except my King's expreſs Command, ſhall prevail with me to deliver up this important Town.*
Upon this reſolute Anſwer, which even Enemies could not but
applaud, the Duke, and all his Attendants, quickly withdrew, and
march'd to *Doncaſter,* where they were joined by Numbers : Soon
after which, the unfortunate King, returning from *Ireland,* was by
ſubtle Contrivance, deliver'd up, and ſent to the Tower. And this
Year the Merchants of *Wiſmer, Roſtock,* &c. falling upon the *Engliſh* Ships, ſailing near *Norway,* the aforeſaid Mayor was depriv'd
of 5 Pieces of Wax, 400 and ½ of Werk ; *Terry,* and Oſmunds, a
Laſt of each ; 30 Pieces of Woollen Broad-Cloths, 1000 and ½ of
narrow. They took likewiſe, of Mr. *Wiſdom's* Property, ſuch Quan-
tities of Oyl, Wax, Werk, *&c.* as were eſtimated at 300*l.* Two
Cakes of Wax, which belong'd to Mr. *Wiltpund* 13*l.* With ſuch
like Merchandize, from Mr. *Richard Horne,* as were reckon'd at
50*l.* Complaint of theſe Seizures being made to the King, Sir
William Sturmy, Kt. was ſent to demand Reparation for the Da-
mages ; and accordingly obtain'd a full Reſtitution.

KING

KING *HENRY* IV. *Sept.* 29. 1399.

1400	SIMON *de* Grimsby, 3 [*h*]	[.*.] *J. Liverfege*
1401	John Liverfedge, 3 [*i*]	*T. Waltham*

[*h*] On the 14th of *February*, 1⁴⁰⁰⁄₀₈. King RICHARD II. (who had been depofed fome Months before) was cruelly murder'd in *Pontefract* Caftle: The Charter of *Hull* was renew'd and confirm'd on the 4th of *November*. The Town ftood firm to the Intereft of the new King, when they found his Predeceffor was no more.

[.*.] Several Manufcripts, I have reduced into two Sorts, which I thought would be moft conducive to my Purpofe: So that where the Readers find the Mayors twice mention'd, *&c.* on each Side of the Columns of the Page, it fhows, that, as there is a Difparity, I leave it to their Judgment: But ftill, the Series of Time is preferv'd, tho' the Names of thefe Magiftrates feem to be difplac'd, without an Infallibility could be conferr'd on one Side: Which I think is not very material; tho', in this Cafe, 'tis abfolutely neceffary I fhould exhibit the different Accounts. Thefe Incongruities are but in few Places; in the greater Part the Manufcripts are coherent, efpecially in the later Centuries.

[*i*] The Inhabitants of *Hull* having reprefented to the new Monarch, the vaft Expences they were at, in defending the Town from the Inundations of an Incroaching Sea; yet fuch was their Misfortune, thro' the Want of frefh Water, that they were obliged to fend into *Lincolnshire* for it, at fo great a Price, as occafioned many to leave the Place, which in Time might produce an utter Deftruction to it: The King therefore commiffion'd *John Scroop, Henry* (and *Robert) Percy, Peter Burton, William Gafcoign, John Routh, Robert Hilton*, and *John Hotham*, Knights; with *William Loddington, Hugh Arden, Robert* (and *Richard) Turwit*, Efqrs. to confult Methods, in order to procure frefh Streams, to fatisfy their Defire. Accordingly, being met at *Sculcotes*, they propos'd, without Damage to any Perfon, That a Sewer might be cut, from the noted JULIAN Well, in the Fields of *Anlaby*, 12 Feet in Breadth, to the *Would-Carr-Dyke;* from thence to *Hull:* And, in like Manner, from the Well of *Daringham*, and Spring of *Haltemprife;* near

N

which

1402 William Terry, *or* Cherry, 2. [*k*] *Rich. Kirkbie*
1403 John Humbleton. *Sim. Grimsby*
1404 John Fittling, 1. *J. Liverfedge*
1405 John Fittling, 2. [*King at* York.] *J. Liverfedge*
1406 Simon *de* Grimsby, 4. *J. Humbleton*
1407 Robert Shacklefs. *J. Fittlinge*
1408 John Tutbury, 2. *J. Fittlinge*
1409 John Wallas, 1. *Sim. Grimsby*
1410 Simon Bedall. *Rob. Shackells*
1411 J. Wallas, 2 *Charter renew'd* Dec. 20. *John Tutbury*

KING *HENRY V. March* 20.

1412 JOHN Bedford, 1. [*l*] *John Wallas*
1413 John Tutbury, 3. *Simon Bedall*

which, was a famous Monaftery. Thefe Commiffioners met after-wards at *Headon,* and *Hull,* where they fully obtain'd the feeming Confent of all Parties, upon the Oaths of *John de Anlaby,* and fe-veral others, before the King's Juftices, affign'd for that Purpofe.

[*k*] Tho', the laft Year, all feem'd to be satisfy'd ; yet, in this, when the Work was begun, the Labourers were prevented, and abufed, thro' the Fury of *Nicholas Wright;* William *Aislabie* and *Brown;* John *Cope, Robinfon, Wood, Swine,* and *Sharp,* of *Bay-nard-Caftle,* with other riotous Perfons. They acted like their mif-chievous Predeceffors, in filling up the Canal, and ftriving to ren-der the late good Defign impracticable. But, being taken, and imprifon'd at *Hull,* they were oblig'd to implore for Mercy, pro-mife Satisfaction, walk with uncovered Heads, and bare Feet, once every Year, with Wax Tapers in their Hands, to be offer'd up in the Chancel of the Great Church ; yield up their Weapons, and give fufficient Security for their good Behaviour : And upon any further Trefpafs, each of them was to pay 5*l.* to the Vicar ; 10*l.* to the Chamberlain for Reparation of the Walls ; and 40*l.* a piece, fhould they ever attempt to get this Sentence abolifh'd, to which they had fubmitted. Notwithftanding thefe Severities, feveral other malicious Perfons, in the Night Time, continued to fpoil the Works, and pollute the Streams.

[*l*] Such was the inveterate Rancour of the Inhabitants of the a-forefaid Towns, by letting falt Water, and throwing ftinking Carrion,

into

1414 J. Bedford, 2 [*m*] ⎰ *Charter confirm'd* ⎱ *John Wallas*
1415 Tho. Marshall, 1 ⎱   Dec. 10.   ⎰ *Jno. Bedford*
1416 John Gregg, *Founder of an* Hofpital *John Tutbury*

into the Canals, which now were finifh'd; that ftimulated the Magiftrates of *Hull*, this Year, to befeech *Alexander* V. Bifhop of *Rome*, to thunder out his Excommunication againft them: But the Pontiff recommending the Cafe to FRANCIS, Cardinal of the Holy Crofs at *Jerufalem;* ANTHONY, of *Sufanna;* and JOHN of St. *Peter ad Vincula;* thefe merciful Fathers, inftead of denouncing Curfes, fent (after long and due Confideration) an exhortatory Writing, fealed and figned by Pope JOHN XXI. in the firft Year of his Pontificate, dated at *Rome*, the 20th of *July*.   In it was reprefented, *The Account every one muft make at the tremendous Day of Judgment; and confequently what miferable Sinners thofe malicious Perfons muft appear, who, by the Suggeftions of Satan, should endeavour to ruin the Inhabitants of fo large a Town: That there was yet a Time for Repentance, which might be accepted, upon the Forbearance of the Guilty from fuch deteftable Crimes, fo directly oppofite to the Will of Heaven, which would difpenfe its Bleffings to all Mankind: To follow fuch divine Philanthropy, every Perfon should rather contribute to a general Advantage, tho' perhaps fome way difcordant to their Intereft, than prevent thofe defired fresh flowing Streams, to their neceffitous Neighbours: And therefore, the paft Offenders, by ufing their Endeavours, for redreffing thofe Grievances, which themfelves had occafion'd; and others, who generously contributed to promote the Publick Welfare and Happinefs; should not only obtain Pardon for their various Sins and Offences; but alfo be entitled to the Protection of* St. PETER, *St.* PAUL, *with all the Hoft of Heaven, both here, and hereafter.* This Inftrument, tho' procur'd at a hurtful Expence, yet produc'd fuperior Benefit: For all Attempts of deftroying the Canals, or poyfoning the Waters, ceafed from this Time: The People were overpowerfully charm'd with innocent Mildnefs, and foft Reprehenfion; which, perhaps, they never would have been, had feverer Methods been ufed to enforce them.

[*m*] The King, having, on the 18th of *March*, written, from *Kenelworth*, to the Mayor and Burgeffes of the Town, demanding their Affiftance, (amongft others) in procuring Shipping, to withftand thofe of *France, Scotland*, and fuch Powers that affifted them; a Letter was directed to the King's Uncle, HENRY BEAUFORD, Bifhop of *Winchefter*, Lord Chancellor, (afterwards Cardinal) dated the 28th of the fame Month. In it, they defired his Lordfhip to inform his Majefty, *That, having difcours'd the Owners of feveral*
gallant

1417 John Fittling, 3.	*John Bedford*
1418 Thomas Marshall, 2.	*MSS.* agree
1419 Robert Holm, 1.	*John Gregge,* Buried in Trinity Church.
1420 John Bedford, 3.	*John Fittling*
1421 Francis Hewit.	*Tho. Marshall*

KING *HENRY* VI. *August* 31.

1422 JAMES Spead.	*Robert Holme*
1423 J Thomas Marshall, 3.	*John Bedford*
1424 John Grimsby, 1.	*Francis Hewit*
1425 John Tutbury, 4.	*James Speed*
1426 Thomas Wells.	*Tho. Marshall*
1427 Robert Holm, 2.	*John Grimsby*
1428 John Bedford, 4.	*James Speed*
1429 Robert Kirton, 1.	*Francis Hewit*
1430 Ralph Horn, 1. [*n*]	*Tho. Marshall*
1431 John Grimsby, 2.	*The King crown'd at* PARIS
1432 John Tutbury, 5.	*Returns to* ENGLAND *in* Feb.
1433 Thomas Wallas,	*Terrible Struggles in* France
1434 Robert Holm, 3.	NORMANDY *in Rebellion*
1435 [*o*] John Bedford, 5.	*The Regent dy'd at* Paris

gallant Veſſels, together with the Town's Inhabitants, they were unanimously resolved to ſupply his Majeſty with what he wanted, ſo that he took upon him to manage, and provide Sustenance for his willing Naval Forces, that should be ready, at Command.

[*n*] In his Mayoralty, the Town's Charter was confirmed by Act of Parliament.

[*o*] Orders were made either in this Year, or when he was Mayor before, "That neither Markets, or Traffick, ſhould be kept "or dealt with on a *Sunday,* (except, according to antient Cu- "ſtom, from *Lammas* to *Michaelmas*) on Penalty of 6s. 8d. to the "Seller, and ⅓ of that sum to the Buyer: No Cooks to dreſs Meat, "except for Strangers; and that too, before 11 a Clock: No "Vintners or Ale-Sellers to vend their Liquors, under the aforeſaid "Penalties: One Shilling and Eight Pence being allow'd to the In- "former; provided he acted out of pure Zeal, and not thro' ſel- "fiſh Intereſt, or malicious Inclination." [*p*] The

1436 Robert Kirton, 2. 1437 Ralph Horn, 2.
1438 Ralph Holmes.

The King (as his Royal Father had done, about the 3d Year of his Reign) confirm'd the Election of a Mayor ; but chang'd the Affiftance of 4 Bayliffs, to that of 12 Aldermen, elected from the Burgeffes, (as mentioned, except *Hugh Clitheroe* and *John Hanfon*, in Pag. 81. where the Wards are faid to be divided) and authorized, by their Dignity, as Juftices of the Peace. This was in the 17th Year of his Reign ; when he order'd, that the Aldermen (out of whom a MAYOR was Yearly to be chofen, and not to rule fo often, as had been us'd in the Time of Bayliffs) fhould be adorn'd in Scarlet, as I mention'd in a Note under the Epitaph of the Worfhipful *William Dobfon.* Moreover, he granted them a Sheriff ; who, much in the like Manner, was to wear a Scarlet Gown. When the firft of that Dignity, (a rich Merchant) was chofen the fame Year, (entering upon his Office the Day after *Trinity-Sunday*, which he held 'till *Michaelmas)* it was ordain'd, by the Mayor and Aldermen, that he fhould have 2 Serjeants to attend him ; and all, in thefe Stations, to be annually elected : I fhall therefore, in the next Chapter, add the Names of the Sheriffs to Thofe of the Mayors, as many as could be gather'd, 'till we come to what Tradition has exhibited, of other Perfons, who ferved as Chamberlains ; tho' fuch had been for feveral Years, before the Gentlemen to be hereafter mention'd.

CHAP. VII.

A Continuation of the MAYORS, *and Beginning of the* Sheriffs, *'till the Year of* CHRIST, 1561.

A.D.	MAYORS.	SHERIFFS.
1439	JOHN Awnwicke.	JOhn Spenfer, or Spen-
1440	[*p*] Thomas Day.	cer. Richard Hanfon.

[*p*] The King, being charm'd with the Town's Loyalty, confirm'd, on the 10th of *May*, their old Charters ; granted them a perpetual Succeffion ; and capacitated them to implead, in any of
his

1441 Hugh Clitheroe, 1 [q] *Robert Awnſwell*
1442 Ralph Horn, 3   *John Garton*
1443 John Bedford, 6 [r] *Wil. Proƈtor* or *Jn. Proƈter*
1444 Thomas Dickinſon   *Nicholas Ellis*
1445 John Handſon *Jn. Dares, Dacres,* or *Danes*
1446 Hugh Clitheroe, 2 *Thomas Farley,* or *Turbey*

his Courts, before the Judges : But, what was more, he order'd, That the Town, with the Precinƈts thereof, ſhould be a COUNTY of itſelf; excluded from (or the Power of any Juſtice in) *Yorkshire:* That the Mayor ſhould be the King's Eſcheator, to ſee what Forfeitures, or Lands (thro' want of Heirs) fell to his Majeſty; the Sheriff to be an Aſſiſtant; and both to have ſuch Power, that was uſed in any other Part of the Realm : That no Burgeſs was to be try'd before him, or his Succeſſors, for Crimes committed *within the Town;* but ſhould anſwer before the Mayor and Sheriff : And if the Caſe could not be well terminated, for want of ſome Point of Law to be diſcuſs'd, then it was to be referr'd to the Judge of Aſſize.   The King alſo granted, That the Sword ſhould be carried ereƈt before the Mayor : Who, with the Aldermen, ordain'd, That no Sheriff ſhould walk abroad, (eſpecially to Church, Hall, or Market) without having his Mace borne before him, on Pain of forfeiting Forty Shillings for every ſuch Negleƈt. Mr. *Richard Hanſon,* and Mr. *William Riplingham,* were Chamberlains this Year.

[*q*] It was ordain'd, this Year, *That no Mayor (during his Mayoralty) should praƈtise as a Butcher, Vintner, Viƈtualler, or Ale-Houſe-Keeper: Neither should he go abroad, as to Church, Market, or on any Concern of the Town, without having the Mace borne before him, under the Penalty of 40s. for every Offence.* The King, having loſt ſeveral Places in *France, Paris* in particular, and alſo in the Dutchy of *Normandy,* ſent a letter, from his Manor of *Shene,* dated *Aug.* 24. to the Mayor and Aldermen of *Hull,* to borrow ſuch Sum of Money, as might contribute to enable him to regain his loſt Territories: Which Requeſt was generouſly comply'd with, by the Corporation.

[*r*] A Charter was granted, *June* 25. for purchaſing to the Value of 100*l per Annum,* in order to defend the Town againſt the Impetuoſity of the Tides. In it, alſo was inſerted : How, and where, the Eleƈtions were to be made : That Two Aldermen ſhould be ſet up as Lights, for the Burgeſſes to chuſe a Mayor : Two Burgeſſes put up, that one might be eleƈted Sheriff : Four, in like Manner, whoſe Names ſhould be given in, from whom two Chamberlains ſhould be appointed : And in Caſe any Mayor departed this Life, or thro' Sickneſs, *&c.* was incapacitated from performing his Office; the reſt of the Aldermen were to nominate Two

1447 John Steeton [∫] *John Northby* or *Notherby*
1448 Hugh Clitheroe, 3 [t] *Richard Bell*, or *Bill*
1449 John Scales, 1   *John Titlat*, or *Hillat*
1450 Richard Hanfon, 1 *Nicholas Stubbs*, or *Stubber*
1451 Simon Burton   *Richard Flinton*
1452 John Spencer, 2   *Thomas Pattrington*
1453 Richard Hanfon, 2 *Edw.*[or *Edm.*] *Coppindale*
1454 Robert Awnfwell   *John Green*, or *Greene*
1455 Nicholas Ellis   *John Swan*, or *Swanne.*
1456 John Scales, 2   *Thomas Eaton*, or *Etton*
1457 Hugh Clitheroe, 4 *Thomas Hawthorpe*

Burgeffes, whereby One of them was to be elected to that high Dignity. This Year the Town was divided into *Wards.*

[∫] About two Years before this, there happening fome Riots in the North, wherein this Town might, thro' fome little Miftake, feem culpable ; the Magiftrates extremely unwilling to incur the King's Difpleafure, humbly befought Pardon, for what Crimes had been committed, thro' Inadvertency, and contrary to their Approbation. The good King readily granted what they ask'd ; except to a few Perfons, unworthy to be nam'd, who had been guilty of the cruel Murder of one Mr. *Christopher Talbot.* And fo well pleaf'd was he with this humble Submiffion, that he confirm'd all their Priviledges, both of the Town, and new-made County ; which had a Coroner to each, with proper Officers ; And granted, that, after the Deceafe of the Duke of *Exeter,* and his Son, they might chufe an Admiral ; whofe Authority, without Interpofition of any other Perfon in that Station, was to extend over the County of *Kingfton* ; *Drypool,* with its Precincts ; and all the River *Humber :* That the Profits fhould be apply'd towards fupporting the Town of *Hull :* That the Mayor, Aldermen, *&c.* fhould have Liberty to command Wells and Springs to be dug for, within their County, and convey the Water, by Leaden Pipes, as they thought expedient. The former Charter was this Year further explain'd, in a new one, relating to Fines ; Forfeitures of Bread, Wine, and Ale ; the Power of punifhing Delinquents, guilty of Extortion, Felony, and other Matters, againft the Laws.

[t] In *September,* the King making a Progrefs to the North, vifited *Beverley,* and this Town : Which, being fill'd with univerfal Joy, and loud Acclamations, at the Sight of their Royal Benefactor, fhew'd an equal Demonftration of their loyal Affection, by entertaining their gracious Monarch, with the greateft Chearfulnefs, Magnificence, and Splendour.   [v] This

1458 Richard Hanſon, 3   *William Eland*
1459 Edmund Coppindale, 2 *Richard Hill*

KING *EDWARD* IV. *March* 4.

1460 **R**Ichard Hanſon, 4 [v] **R**Obert *Saunderſon*
1461   Nicholas Stubbes   *Roger Bushel*
1462 John Barker [w] *John Hadleſey,* or *Haddleſey*

[v] This Year, which began the Reign of EDWARD, is reckon'd the laſt of King HENRY VI. The Differences, between the Houſes of *York* and *Lancaſter,* began to be more apparent, ſince they had three terrible Engagements already : And the fourth was by *Sandal* Caſtle, in Sight of *Wakefield,* where the Duke of *York,* Father to King *Edward* was slain. The ſecond, after this, was the dreadful Fight at *Towton.* But all the Battles fought, between the Adherents of the Two Houſes, are mention'd, in my *Second Volume* of Yorkſhire *Antiquities,* Pag. 140, 141. to which I refer the Reader. As the Loyalty of *Kingſton* was always conſpicuous to their Princes, however unfortunate ; ſo this Year did it more eminently ſhine, when the MAYOR himſelf headed a Company for the Cauſe of his Royal Maſter, then in Affliction : And tho' Fortune crown'd his beloved Party with deſired Succeſs ; yet this valiant Magiſtrate, (who ſpent his deareſt Blood in his Sovereign's Defence) fought with ſuch Courage and Intrepidity, 'till at length he fell down amongſt ſeveral diſtinguiſh'd Heroes, cover'd over with Glory, and Wounds.

HANSON ! *Thy Name, shall, like fresh Roſes, bloom ;*
Pleaſant, be heard, for Ages, yet to come :
As † FLEMING, *Great ; whoſe Life, unſtain'd from Blots,*
Was bravely loſt, amidſt invading Scots.
Now your bright Souls, bleſt with Eternal Springs,
Enjoy your GOD, by fighting for your Kings.

† NICHOLAS FLEMING, Lord-Mayor of *York ;* who, valiantly leading his Citizens, in the Year 1319, againſt the then ravaging *Scots,* was overpower'd by their Numbers, and slain in the Battle of *Myton-upon-Swale.* See in the Hiſtory of *York,* Pag. 177. While Mr. *Hanſon* was living, it was decreed in the Town's Hall, *That, for the future, the Mayor and Aldermen should nominate thoſe Perſons they thought moſt fitting to bear the Office of Head Magiſtrate ; and then refer the Election of one of them to the Burgeſſes.* Such Regulations were made as to other Officers.

[w] He was buried in the High Church, and had over his Grave theſe two Words : *Orate Speculati.*   [x] King

1463 John Green   [*x*]   *John Day*
1464 Nicholas Ellis [*y*]   *Robert Rimington*

[*x*] King HENRY efcaping out of the Tower, to the North, and, thro' Means of his Queen, obtaining Succours from *France*, he entred *Northumberland*, took *Bamborough* Caftle, and proceeded to *Durham*, where he was joined by Numbers. King EDWARD hearing this, raifing an Army, fent thofe Forces againft him, whilft he, unexpected, came this Year to *Barton-upon-Humber*, attended by his Lords and Commanders : When landing at *Hull*, he fecur'd the Town to his Intereft ; tho' the Inhabitants were very much in-clin'd to K. HENRY : But what could any People do, when two Kings reign'd in one Kingdom? "When, *writes an ingenious Hifto-* " *rian*, the White Rofe in every Place was dy'd red with the Blood. " of the Nobility ; and the red Rofe turn'd pale with Horror, to " view the Calamities occafion'd by this Diffention ? " The King *de Facto* march'd to *York*, where he continu'd a while ; and fent the Vifcount *Montague*, with a Party, to fecure the Loyalty of the *Northumbrians*, againft the King *de Jure.* That Nobleman was fuddenly attack'd (on a well-known fpacious Plain called the Levels of *Hexham*) by the Lords *Hungerford, Rofs,* and *Mollins ;* Sir *Ralph Grey,* and Sir *Ralph Percy,* Knights : But *Montague* ftanding their Affault, got the Victory. Whilft Sir *Ralph Percy* was dying in the Field, from which he would not be drove, he comforted himfelf with this pretty Expreffion, *I have fav'd the little Bird in my Bofom :* As much as to fay, he had preferv'd his Oath to King HENRY, from which nothing but Death could fe-perate him. Thus greatly he gave up his Soul ; but the Lords, before-mention'd, with other Perfons of Note, became miferable Captives, and were beheaded in cold Blood. As to the unfortu-nate King HENRY, he was forc'd to retire into *Scotland* for Safety : But the fame Year returning into *England,* in difguis'd Apparel, was difcover'd as he fat at Dinner at *Waddington Hall,* carry'd up to *London,* with his Legs bound under the Horfe's Belly, and committed clofe Prifoner to the Tower.

[*y*] By fome ftrange Caufe, or other, the Haven was this Year almoft ruin'd : The dreadful Confideration of which, oblig'd the Magiftrates and People to obtain a Grant from the King, empower-ing them to lay upon the Mafters of every Foreign Ship, of 100 Tuns, when coming in, or going out, the Sum of Three Shillings and Four Pence, and fo in Proportion the leffer Veffels ; By which Means, they being enabled to get the Port clear'd, it became re-ftor'd to its priftine Condition. This Year was alfo remarkable for King *Edward's* being crown'd at *York,* and that magnificent Ca-thedral's taking Fire by Lightning, or thro' fome other Mifchance.

1465	John Swan, 1	*John Whitfield*
1466	John Day, 1	*William Brompton*
1467	John Dares, *or* Danes,	*William Barton*
1468	Roger Bushell, 1	*Thomas Alcocke*
1469	John Day, 2 [z]	*John Richards*
1470	John Hadlesey	*Robert Marshall*
1471	Robert Bennington	*Robert Alcocke*
1472	John Whitfield [aa]	*Thomas Wood*
1473	William Brompton	*Ralph Langton*
1474	John Swan, 2	*Richard Burdon*
1475	Roger Bushell, 2	*Robert Fisher*
1476	John Richards [bb]	*Robert Scales* [lips
1477	Edmund Coppindale, 3	*Tho. Phelippe,* or *Phil-*
1478	Thomas Alcock [cc]	*Robert Chapman*
1479	Thomas Wood	*Rich. Doughtie* or *Doughty*
1480	Robert Alcock [dd]	*Jas. Thudlington,* or *Thom-*
1481	Ralph Langton	*Robert Flinton* [linson
1482	William Barton	*John Dalton*

❈❈❈❈❈❈❈❈❈❈❈❈❈❈❈❈❈❈❈❈❈❈❈❈❈

King *EDWARD* V. *April* 9.

† King *RICHARD* III. *June* 22.

| 1483 | Thomas Phillips | *Bartholomew Gylliot* |
| 1484 | Richard Burdon | *Thomas Dalton* |

[z] This Mayor (with ALICE, his Wife) was buried in the Chancel of *S. Trinity* Church, *Anno* 1470.

[aa] This Worfhipful Mayor died of the Plague, then raging.

[bb] The Peftilence alfo put a Period to his Life.

[cc] The Plague (which had alternately raged, more or lefs, from 1472, deftroying near 1600 Perfons) ceafed this Year; but not before it had proved the Death of this Worfhipful Magiftrate; and brought his dear Wife and Children to their filent Graves.

[dd] This Mayor was related to *William* ALCOCK, Merchant of *Hull,* whofe Confort was delivered of a Son at *Beverley,* named JOHN; who, in Time, became Bifhop of *Ely,* and prov'd a great Benefactor to *Kingfton,* in founding a School, Chantries, &c.

† Tho' a very wicked King, yet he founded *Middleham* College. The fecond time he was crown'd, was in *York* Minfter, accompany'd by his Queen, where he invefted his Son in the Principality of *Wales.*

[ee] KING *HENRY* VII. *August* 22.

1485	Ralph Langton, 1	*Lawrence Swatoricke*
1486	Robert Chapman, 1	*Jn. Wilson* or *Willison*
1487	John Dalton, 1	*Thomas Wickliffe*
1488	Thos. Etton, *or* Eaton	*Thos. Bridge* or *Bridges*
1489	Thomas Dalton, 1	*Robert Hoole* or *Howle*
1490	Law (*or* Tho) Swatoricke	*Hen. Myndram,* or *Mindram*
1491	Thomas Phillips	*John Spicer* [ff]
1492	Robert Chapman, 2	*Tho. Andrew* or *Andrews*
1493	Thomas Willison	*William Goodknappe*
1494	Ralph Langton, 2 [gg]	*Edwd. Baron,* or *Barron*
1495	John Dalton, 2	*Thomas Cocke* or *Cook*
1496	Henry Mindram, 1	*Edw. Greenley,* or *Greenby*
1497	[hh] Wm. Goodknap	*Thomas Gooseman*
1498	Robt. Hoole *or* Howle	*William Moncketon*
1499	Thomas Dalton, 2	*John Gill*
1500	Thomas Gooseman	*Robert Garner*
1501	Edw. Baron, *or* Barron, 1	*Thomas Wilkinson*
1502	Thomas Cocke	*Thomas Powis*
1503	Robert Garner	*Alexander Wharton*
1504	John Gill	*Robert* or (*Roger*) *Bushell*
1505	Alexander Wharton [ii]	*William Taylor*
1506	Henry Mindram, 2	*John Eland*

[ee] By this King's Conqueſt over RICHARD the Third, in *Boſworth-Field*, (where that Uſurper was slain) and by marrying ELIZABETH, eldeſt Daughter to King EDWARD IV. the Houſes of *York* and *Lancaſter* became happily united.

[ff] This Sheriff lies buried in the South Isle of the Chancel of Holy Trinity Church.

[gg] He died in his Mayoralty; and was interr'd in the Middle of the Chancel, over whom was a Tomb-Stone, which declar'd the Worſhipful JOHN DALTON was his Succeſſor.

[hh] He was an excellent Merchant; and, deſigning to return home, was taken ill at *Calais*, in *France*, where he departed this Life: Upon which another Perſon ſupply'd the Office this Year.

[ii] This Gentleman died at *London*, in Time of his Mayoralty.

[kk] In

1507 Thomas Wilkinſon, 1 *Robert Harriſon*
1508 Rob.(*or* Rog.)Bushell, 1 *Wil. Williamſon, or Williſon*

[*kk*] KING *HENRY* VIII. *April* 22.

1509 EDwd. Barron, 2 EDm. *Riddale*, or *Riſdale*
1510   John Eland, 1   *Geo. Mattiſon*, or *Mad-*
1511 Robert Harriſon *Thos. Huntington*, [*diſon*
1512 Will. Williamſon [*ll*] *John Langton*
1513 Edw. Riddale [*mm*] *Rob. Hapſam*, or *Hampſon*

[*kk*] In the Beginning of his Reign, to pleaſe the People, who had been ſore oppreſſed, in his Father's Time, by thoſe two vile Informers and Proſecutors **Empſon** and **Dudley**, he order'd Informations to be taken againſt them, in all noted Towns. Hither, for that Purpoſe, came the Earl of *Northumberland*, with ſeveral Lords; who (in the *Town's-Hall*) received the Complaints of the Sufferers: Which, with the Grievances of other People, being ſent to *London*. occaſion'd thoſe two wicked Inſtruments deſervedly to ſuffer Death, who had been the miſerable Ruin of many poor Families.

[*ll*] The King, denouncing War againſt the *Scots*, both by Sea and Land, ſent an Inſtrument in Writing to this Town, ſetting forth the Affronts which he had received from the *Gallick* Monarch, who was an Enemy to the *Roman* Emperor elect, which he order'd to be proclaim'd. The *French* King, being alarm'd at the News, prevail'd with *James* IV. of *Scotland*, to break his Truce with the King of *England;* which he did, on Complaint of the *English* Admiral's deſtroying Sir *Andrew Barton;* the valiant *Heron's* killing the *Scots* Warden; with other pretended Matters of Offence. The aforeſaid *Heron* was a Gentleman that lived on the Borders; who, by knowing the *Scottish* Wiles, was a great Help to the *English*, in obtaining the Victory over them the following Year.

[*mm*] Sir *Edward Howard*, Lord High-Admiral of *England*, came this Year, with a numerous Fleet, ſailing up the *Humber*, to this Town; where he took in Numbers of Voluntiers, with Arms, and Proviſions: And, ſome time after, landing at *Newcaſtle*, made haſte, with the Forces, to join the Earl of *Surrey*, Lieutenant of the North, at the famous Battle of *Floddon-Field;* where the *Scots* were routed, their King ſlain, with 12 Earls, 17 Lords, 2 Biſhops, 4 Abbots, and about ten thouſand common Soldiers. This Year one Mr. *Godfrey*, the King's Searcher, was thrown into the Haven, near *Hull;* where, as I ſuppoſe, he periſhed. [*nn*] About

1514 [*nn*] George Mattiſon, 1 *Edmnd. Mattiſon* [*oo*]
1515 Thomas Huntington *John Harriſon*

[*nn*] About this Time, Sir WILLIAM SIDNEY, deſcended from thoſe, of that Name, who came over with King *Henry* II. from *Anjou,* flouriſhed in his Monarch's Favour: For he was one of his Houſhold 'Squires, in the third Year of his Reign, when he accompanied the Lord *Thomas Darcy;* who, with 1500 Archers, was ſent to aſſiſt *Ferdinand,* King of *Spain,* againſt the Moors of *Africa.* That Lord, with him, and moſt of thoſe Bowmen, returned home, after having been richly rewarded by the *Spanish* Monarch. The next Year the King knighted SIDNEY, and made him Captain of a Man of War againſt the *French ;* ſent him afterwards into the North, againſt the *Scots,* where he was a Commander in *Floddon-Field.* To reward this great Captain ſtill further, the King beſtow'd upon him, and his Heirs Male, the Lordſhip of *Myton* and *Tupcotes,* with the Manor, Lands, Appurtenances, *&c.* as have been amply mention'd before, which belong'd to *Edmund de la Pole,* the laſt Earl of *Suffolk,* of that Name, before it became forfeited to the Crown.

[*oo*] A very sharp Scuffle happen'd between Sheriff MATTI-SON, (or MADDISON) and the Prior of *Haltemprise.* The Matter was thus : Tho' the Monaſtry was within the County of *Hull;* yet the Prior aſſerted, That as the Rights of the Church ought not to be invaded; ſo neither had the Sheriff any Power to enter into his Liberties, which included *Wolferton,* a Village alſo in the County aforeſaid. Heretofore Complaints had been made, againſt former Sheriffs, in the *Star-Chamber:* Which Court, by Agreement on both Sides, had referr'd the Matter to the Arbitration of the Abbot of *Meaux ;* Sir *Marmaduke Conſtable;* Sir *Bryan Palms,* Serjeant at Law, Knights ; and *Ralph Rokesby* Eſq ; But, however, this Officer, on the 6th of *October,* going to *Wolferton,* to keep his Turn, according to former Cuſtom ; the Prior arm'd the Monks ; rais'd the Tenants ; ſtopt up the Roads, and Paſſages ; abuſed the Sheriff, and reſiſted his Attendants: Who, not able tamely to bear theſe Provocations, return'd the like inſulting Terms, which quickly was ſucceeded by a cruel Battle. Certainly, it muſt have been a diſmal Sight to behold, on the one Side, both young and old, fat and macerated Monks, arm'd with temporal Weapons, having broken Heads, torn Gowns, intermingl'd with their strange undiſciplin'd Rusticks ; whilst, on the other, an Officer of the Civil Government was making Uſe of the Truncheon of his then impelling Authority, more stimulated by Opposition, and the Fury of his Attendants,

1516 Roger (*or* Rob.) Bushell, 2   *Stephen Clave,* or *Clare.*
1517 John Eland, 2   *Jeffrey Thurfcrofs,* or *Thrif-*
1518 Robert Hapfam   *Robert Parker*   [*crofs*
1519 Edward Mattifon, 1   *Thomas Thompfon*
1520 Thomas Wilkinfon, 2 *William Goodknappe*
1521 John Langton   *William Knowles*
1522 George Mattifon, 2 [*pp*] *Richard Dean*

dants, in their now dreadful Formalities, by fo bloody an Engagement ! For fome Time they fought with alternate Succefs ; 'till, at laft, the Sheriff's Party, obtaining the better, drove the Monks to their Priory ; and then, as if they had been fo many King *Harry's,* threaten'd to pull the Building down about their Ears. Nor is it to be doubted, but they would at least have rifled it, had not the Mayor of *Hull* timely heard of the Skirmish. He therefore, with threefcore Horfe-Men, which he raifed, in a very little Space, posted thither, to prevent further Mifchief. The Prior, who, it feems was the first Agreffor, as to the Infults that were offered, had not Patience to bear the Ignominy of a Defeat ; which he could not remedy, but by a Courfe in Law. To obtain Satisfaction therefore, he fil'd a Bill, in the *Star-Chamber,* against the Sheriff, and his Party ; and indicted them, not only for a Riot, but as Offenders against feveral of the Statutes. Thefe Proceedings occafion'd Suits to commence, that took three Years Time, before they could think of terminating their Differences. At length, both Sides growing cooler, it was left to the Decifion of the Worshipful JOHN ELAND, GEORGE and EDWARD MADDISON, Aldermen of *Hull.* In fine, it was agreed, *That, if thofe of the Monaftry, on their Part, would yield, to the Inhabitants of* Hull, *all Manner of Right they had in the fresh Water Springs of* Anlaby ; *the Mayor and Burgeffes, would, on their Side, give up to them the Royalty of* Willerby *and* Newton, *to enjoy without Moleftation.* To confirm which Agreement, there was an Indenture drawn between them, figned and fealed before fufficient Witneffes : And thus all Animofities, upon this Diffention, ceafed between them for the future.

[*pp*] The King, fending to borrow Money of the Town, for the carrying on his Wars against the *French* and *Scots,* they lent him above 250*l.* which was then accounted a great Sum. The Inhabitants having feiz'd fome Corn, that was to be convey'd to *Scotland,* the King, in a Letter, thank'd them for their Loyalty ; and, upon the fame Subject, wrote to Sir *John Nevill,* at *Cottingham.*

[*qq*]

1523 Thomas Thompfon, 1.　*Thomas Dalton*
1524 John Eland, 3　　　*William Rogers*
1525 William Knowles, 1 *Richd. Meekley,* or *Meekly*
1526 Robert Parker　　*William Swailes,* or *Swale*
1527 Thos. Wilkinfon, 3 [*qq*] *Richd. Swale,* or *Saule*
1528 Edward Mattifon, 2 *John Davy, Day,* or *Daniel*
1529 George Mattifon, 3 *James Johnfon*
1530 Stephen Clare　　*William Robinfon*
1531 Tho. Thompfon, 2 [*rr*] *John Harrifon*
1532 William Rogers, 1　*John Brown*
1533 James Johnfon, 1 *Wm. Catheral,* or *Catterill*
1534 William Knowles, 2　*Hugh Overfall*
1535 Thomas Dalton [*ff*] *Peter Mavis,* or *Macus*
1536 William Rogers [*tt*] *William Clark*

[*qq*] A prodigious Flood happened in his Time, by fo flowing a Tide, that a great Part of the adjacent Country lay under Water. In the Town, it was 5 Foot high ; to the difmal Confufion of the Inhabitants, whofe Goods were incredibly damag'd, that lay in their Low Rooms, and Ware-Houfes.

[*rr*] This Year the Fifh-Garths in *Humber* and *Oufe* were order'd to be pull'd up, (in Confequence of a Petition of the Magiftrates of *York* to the Parliament) for the better Paffage of Ships of Burden, up the River, to that antient City.

[*ff*] The Worfhipful Mayor died this Year, and HENRY THURSCROSS officiated 'till the next fucceeded.

[*tt*] In *ASK's* Infurrection, (after Diffolution of fome Monafteries) ftyl'd, *The Pilgrimage of Grace,* when the main Body was broken at *Doncaster,* Alderman ELAND, Mr. KNOWLES, and fome others, feiz'd upon *HALLUM,* the Captain of one of their Parties in this Town. The King, granting them a Commiffion to try him, with fome of his Affociates, they were condemn'd, and Executed : After which, the above Gentlemen were knighted and rewarded. But yet another Infurrection burft out at *Settrington, Pickering-Lyth, Scarborough,* and other Places, in the North and Eaftern Parts : Sir FRANCIS BIGOT was their Leader. The Earl of *Northumberland,* from his Seat at *Leckenfield,* near *Hull,* fent thither for both Men and Horfe, in order to withftand them. BIGOT, with his Forces, came alfo as haftily to furprize the Town : But Sir RALPH ELLERKIR, and Sir JOHN CONSTABLE, Knights,
who

1537 [*vv*] Jn. Harrison, 2 *Wm. Crifcroffe* or *Goofcroft*

who were Neighbours hard by, raifing what Affiftance they could, threw themfelves therein, fhut up the Gates, and ftood upon their Defence. This made their Enemies, who were juft at their Heels, fo mad, to think they had loft the Start, in fecuring this ftrong Fortrefs, that they revenged themfelves on the Wind-Mills near it, which they fet on Fire ; and then furiously demanded the Delivery of the Town, with the Bodies of the aforefaid *falfe* Knights, as they were then pleas'd to call them : But meeting with an abfolute Denyal, they could do little elfe, except ufing threatening Words ; 'till, hearing the Country was rifing againft them, they rais'd the Siege, and march'd away. Upon their being purfu'd by the Mayor, and his Affiftants, feveral were taken, and committed to Goal. It was not long after, when Sir ROBERT CONSTABLE, and others of his Sentiments, (finding their Strength could not avail to feize *Kingfton*, which is indeed the Key of the Eaftern Parts) betook themfelves to Art and Stratagem : And entering the Town, difguifed like Market-People, yet fecretly arm'd, having befides Eggs, Butter, Chickens, *&c.* they feiz'd the Gates, let in the Remainder of their Followers, and quickly difpers'd themfelves into every Part, neceffary for their Purpofe, before the People were well appriz'd thereof. Then did Sir ROBERT quickly affume to himfelf the Title of *Governour ;* fent Ships into foreign Parts for Forces to affift him ; imprifon'd thofe Perfons (after he had plunder'd them of their Effects) whom he fuspected not to favour his Defigns; and laid up Stores of Provifions, Ammunition, with whatever elfe was neceffary to fupport them againft a Siege. Thus he ftrictly ruled about a Month ; when, to his Mortification, he heard how his Partners in the Country were either slain, difpers'd, or taken. Hereupon he became fo very much difpirited, that a cloudy Melancholly appear'd in his Looks, as a difmal Prefage of that Punifhment, which he was fhortly to undergo ! By how much he was afflicted, in Proportion was the Mayor and Inhabitants encouraged : Who, falling upon the difconfolate Knight, and his unfortunate Adherents, committed them to Prifon, at the fame time fending News thereof to the King ; who return'd an Anfwer, from *Greenwich*, dated *Feb.* 2, 163⅞. by Sir *Ralph Ellerkir*, Jun. *That he had previously commiffion'd the active Duke of* Norfolk *to bring them all to their Tryals for their Rebellion againft him.*

[*vv*] The Judgment of the aforefaid Perfons foon followed ; For Mr. Ask, a Gentleman of *Lincolnshire*, was hang'd in Chains, at *York*, upon a lofty Tower : He, and his Numbers, which had increas'd

1538 [*ww*] John Brown   *James Rogers*
1539 [*xx*] William Catherall   *Henry Dingley*

creas'd to 40000, oblig'd the Archbifhop of *York*, with the old Lord *Darcy*, to accompany them; making them take an Oath, *To reftore the Church, extirpate Hereticks, preferve the Royal Family, and to drive away evil Counfellors from the King.* They furrounded *Skipton*, which was defended againft them by the Earl of *Cumberland ;* and Sir RALPH EVERS held out *Scarborough* Caftle for 20 Days. The unhappy Lord DARCY was beheaded on *Tower Hill*, tho' he was fourfcore Years old: The Lord HUSSEY loft his Head at *Lincoln :* Several of the inferior Captains, with 70 others, were executed, for the laft Infurrection, in divers Parts of *Yorkshire:* And, in *Hull*, many received Sentence of Death, which they fuffer'd accordingly: But Sir *R O B E R T   C O N S T A B L E*, in particular, as having been the Principal Head in the Seizure of the Town, was hang'd in Chains over *Beverley-Gate*, (fo call'd, I fuppofe, becaufe it leads to that beautiful Place) that the Body of this unhappy Knight might ftrike the greater Terror into every one, in Town, or County, who beheld fo difmal and wretched a Spectacle! After this, a Pardon was granted, except to twenty two Perfons; moft of whom were taken, and fuffer'd in one Place, or other. Much about this time, the King and Parliament were petition'd, *That the Fee-Farm Rent* (70 l. per An.) *of this Corporation, should be apply'd to the Expences of his Majesty's Houshold; and that the Town should be difcharged from about* 12 l. *as Part of it, becaufe it proceeded from fuch Lands as were forfeited by* EDMUND de la POLE, *Earl of* Suffolk : *A Sum demanded of (and paid by) the Mayor and Aldermen, to the great Detriment of the Town.* The Magiftrates too, being afraid, left the Corporation-Plate fhould, in thefe troublefome Times, be feiz'd upon, and loft; they very prudently, by Sale, converted the fame into Money, which amounted to feveral Hundreds of Pounds: Which, it is written, was apply'd to bear the Expences of their Members in Parliament; and to repair the Church of the Holy Trinity, for which there was Occafion.

[*w w*] This Year the *Bush-Dyke* was finifhed, which was begun to be caft up the Year before.

[*x x*] Upon the Suppreffion of the greater Monafteries, the pious Bifhops *Latimer, Ridley*, and others, befought the King, this Year, That but two, or even one, of thofe venerable Edifices, might be fuffer'd to remain in each County : " Not for any Kindnefs to " the Monks, *faid they;* but to be Nurferies of Charity, Learn-

1540 [*yy*] Henry Thurfcrofs, 1 *Alexander Stockdale*

"ing, Prayers, and Preaching." Thefe feeming forcible Reafons were ufed in vain to an inflexible Monarch, who would be contented with nothing, except their final Deftruction. His Defigns were rather to erect ftrong Holds of Defence : For about this Time he purchas'd, of Sir *William Sydney*, the forfeited Manors of the Earl of *Suffolk*, and their Appurtenances, (which he had, as before-written, given to this Favourite) with Refolution to ftrengthen, and add Fortifications, to make the Town of *Hull* impregnable.

[*yy*] The King, with his Queen, fet out from *London*, in *Auguft*, for *York*, to meet *James* V. his Nephew, the 106th King of *Scotland*, in order to advife him to act, in the fame Manner he had done, againft the Abbeys, and other Religious Houfes, in that Kingdom. Therefore, proceeding thro' By-Ways, for fear of fome of the enraged People, he came unexpectedly within a few Miles of the Town. When the Mayor was appriz'd of it, he fent the Sheriff, with a numerous Train, to meet his Majefty, at the Boarded-Bridge, near *Newland*, on the Confines of the County. There, paying his Compliments of Welcome, he kifs'd the white Rod, that he carry'd; and delivering it to the King, receiv'd it again from his Hands : Then, mounting his Horfe, rode before the Monarch towards the Town. At *Beverley-Gate*, the Mayor and Aldermen ftood, in their Formalities, to receive their Majefties. At the Sight of the Royal Pair, there were no Words, no Demonftrations wanting, to teftify the moft hearty Welcome. The Mayor, falling upon his Knees, kifs'd, and prefented the Mace; which, being return'd, that Magiftrate carried it, before his Majefty, to the *Manor-Hall;* which was then the Place of Refidence. Here, for three Days, the King, Queen, and Attendants, were fplendidly entertain'd. After which, they fet out for *York;* where they ftay'd a little Time. But no King of *Scotland* appearing; the *Englifh* Monarch left that antient City, on the 29th of *September*. At Night the Royal Vifitants lodg'd at the Earl of *Northumberland's* Seat, at *Leckenfield*. The Inhabitants of *Hull*, little thinking the King was fo near, were affembled the next Morning (in order to elect a new Mayor) in the Town's-Hall; where Mr. *Dalton*, and Mr. *Johnfon*, were fet up for that Purpofe. But they were furpriz'd, when News was brought, that the King would be in Town at Dinner Time. This prevented the Election : The Candidates, with others, went to meet their Majefties; whilft the Mayor in Being was left to pay his Compliments upon their Arrival. The King, upon his Enterance, hearing of the Matter, order'd, the Corporation to meet afrefh; and, that Sir *John Eland* fhould be nominated along with the two Gentlemen aforefaid :

Which,

1541 *Sir* John Eland, *Kt.* 4   *John Thacker*

Which, being done, and his Majefty voting for him, the Knight was immediately elected. Upon this, the King prefented him with his Sword, in Honour to the Corporation ; which Sir *John* received, kneeling, in the moft obfequious Manner: Afterwards, the Day was fpent in Feafts, and Recreations. The next Morning, the King and Nobles, viewing the Town, found no Fault, but that it wanted fufficient Strength to defend it. Hereupon he gave Orders for a Caftle, and two ftrong Block-Houfes, to be erected, with other Fortifications, to environ the Town : Alfo, for his Manor-Hall to be repair'd ; and, that a new Dyke fhould be cut from *Newland* to *Kingfton.* The Pay-Mafter-General of the Works was Mr. *Thomas Allured ;* and the Surveyor Mr. *John Rogers,* who was alfo Comptroller. Thefe Gentlemen were to be affifted by Wardens ; one of whom, (Mr. *Richard Mills*) laid the Foundation-Stone of the Caftle, on the 22d of *February,* 154$\frac{9}{1}$. The Expence of the whole, indeed, the King was folely at himfelf; which amounted to above twenty-three thoufand Pounds. About this Time the North-Gate of the Town was made. After the King (as aforefaid) had given thefe Orders, he, with his Attendants, embark'd ; and fafely were landed in *Barrow* Haven, from whence they proceeded to *Thornton* Monaftery, fituated near the *Humber,* in *Lincolnfhire.* The humble Monks, tho' they were fenfible of the King's fatal Defigns againft them, were not wanting in their Duty : They met, and welcom'd him, his Queen, and Attendants, in a moft folemn Proceffion ; and entertain'd them fplendidly in that very Monaftery, which but a little Time after he oblig'd them to forfake, and commanded the † Edifice itfelf to be laid in Ruins. Upon the King's arrival at *London,* he conftituted Sir *Richard Long* to be Governour of *Hull;* and *Michael Stanhope,* Efq ; his Lieutenant, by an Inftrument, dated *Feb.* 17, 154$\frac{9}{1}$, with Power to levy Forces, when Occafion requir'd : But inform'd the Inhabitants, that none of their Priviledges fhould be abridg'd upon this Occafion ; which was contriv'd for their greater Defence, 'till fuch Time as the aforefaid Buildings and Fortreffes were perfected, when they might better fecure themfelves. Thus he took Care to preferve thofe of the Temporality, for the Prefervation of his Kingdom ; whilft he prov'd an Enemy to the Clergy, thro' their Attachment to the *Roman* See. An Enquiry of his Actions, in this Affair, is now quite out of Date ; any farther, than, to remark, what ftately Buildings have been, from Antiquity, in this Kingdom ; to fome of which, we are obliged for our Cathedral and Collegiate Churches, the pleafant Remains of them, at this very Day.

† That the Reader may be inform'd of thofe large Monafteries, which had Peeral Abbots, that were fummon'd to Parliament ; I have felected the following

ing Accounts, I think, more comprehenfive, and perfect, than I have yet feen in various Authors.———1. St. *Mary's* Abbey, for the Order of *Benedictines*, without the Walls of *York* City, founded by *Alan*, Earl of *Britain*, *Anno.* 1088.——— 2. *Selby*, in *Yorkshire*, for the fame Order, by *William* the Conqueror, 1078.——— 3. *Bardney*, built by King *Ethelred*, in 712, afterwards deftroy'd by the *Danes*. 4. *Croyland*, by *Ethelred*, King of *Mercia*, 726. who erected the Church belonging to it. 5. *Spalding* Priory, alfo *Benedictines*, by *Talboys*, E. of *Angiers*, 1074. 6. *Semplingham*, for the Order of *Gilbertines*, 1131. The preceding four Religious Houfes were in *Lincolnshire*.———7. St. *Peter's*, in the City of *Glocefter*, founded by *Ofric*, King of *Northumberland*, for *Benedictines*, about the End of the 7th Century. 8. *Winchelcumb*, which at firft was a Nunnery, built by King *Offa*, in 787, was afterwards, *An.* 798. converted into a *Benedictine* Monaftery, and enlarg'd by *Kenulph*, King of *Mercia* ; who built the Church, which was dedicated by Archbishop *Wilfrid*, of *Canterbury*, and 13 Bishops, with the greateft Splendour of their Religious Magnificence. 9. *Cirencefter*, founded for the Order of St. *Auguftine*, by King *Henry* I. *Anno* 1133. The 2 foregoing in *Glocefershire*.———10. St. *Alban's*, in *Hartfordshire*, tor *Benedictines*, founded by *Offa*, King of *Mercia*, 795.——— 11. St. *Peter's*, *Weftminfter*, for the fame, by *Seabert*, King of the *Eaft-Saxons*, in 604.———12. St. *Auftin's*, *Canterbury*, by King *Ethelbert*, *Anno* 602.———13. *Glaftonbury*, in *Somersetshire*, firft founded by *Joseph* of *Arimathea ;* afterwards rebuilt by *Inas*, King of the *Eaft-Saxons*, *Anno* 708, and had *Benedictines* therein. ———14. St. *Edmund's Bury*, in *Suffolk*, founded by King *Canute*, 1020.——— 15. St. *Bennet's* de *Hulm*, in *Norfolk*, by the fame named King, *Anno* 1026.——— 16. *Shrewsbury*, in *Shropshire*, by *Roger* Earl of *Montgomery*, and his pious Lady, in the Year 1081.———17. *Evesham*, in *Worcefershire*, by *Egwin*, third Bishop of the City, 700.————18. *Abington*, founded by a virtuous Lady, named *Ciffa*, in 675. And, 19. *Reading*, (both of thefe in *Barkshire)* by King *Henry* I. *Anno* 1126.———20. *Malmsbury*, in *Wiltshire*, much improved by *Maidulphus*, a Philofopher, and Monk, who came from the North of *Ireland*, (tho' some affirm from *Scotland)* about the Year 635.———21. *Peterborough*, in *Northamptonshire*, founded by the converted King of *Mercia*, called *Wulfere*, *Anno* 664, to expiate the barbarous Murder of the Princes, his own Sons, in whofe innocent Blood he had embrued his unnatural Hands, becaufe they had embraced the Faith of CHRIST, whofe Names were *Wulphad* and *Rufine*. The aforefaid 8 Monafteries were all of the *Benedictine* Order. ——— 22. *Thorney*, in *Cambridgeshire*, founded by Bishop *Adelwald* and King *Edgar*, about the Year 973.———23. *Ramfey*, in *Huntingtonshire*, a *Benedictine* Monaftry, to which feveral Kings became Benefactors, was built by Duke *Alwyn*, 969, at the Perfuafion of *Ofwald*, Archbishop of *York*. ———24. *Thornton* Abbey, upon the *Humber*, in *Lincolnshire*, where the King had been fo well entertain'd, founded by *William Grofs*, Earl of *Albemarle*, for *Auguftinian* Monks, taken from *Kirkham* Priory, about the Middle of the 12th Century.———25. *Leicefter-Abbey*, by *Robert Boffe*, Earl of that Town, 1141.——— 26. *Waltham*, in *Effex*, by King *Harold*, 1036. for the Order of St. *Auguftine*.——— 27. St. *John's* in *Colchefter*, by *Eudo*, Butler to *Henry* I. Another writes, that it was founded by a religious Man, named *Eynulphus*, for *Auguftines*.———28. *Beaulieu*, in *Bedfordshire*, by King *John*, 1205, for *Benedictines*.———29. *Tavifock*, for the like Order, in *Devonshire*, built by *Ordgar* (who had a Son of Gigantick Stature) in the Year 981.———30. St. *Peter's*, *Coventry*, in *Warwickshire*, for *Benedictines*, by Earl *Leofrick*, about the Year 1043.———31. *Hide*, in *Hampshire*, for the faid Order, by King *Alured*, (or *Egfrid*,) *Anno* 922.———32. St. *Auftin's* in *Briftol*, for that Saint's Order, erected by King *Henry* I.———33. *Lewes*, in *Suffex*, by *William* de *Warren*, firft Earl of *Surrey*, *Anno* 1078. for the Order of *Clugni*.——— 34. *Battle Abbey*, dedicated to St. *Martin*, alfo in *Suffex*, founded by *William* the Conqueror, 1067.———35. St. *John's* of *Jerufalem*, in the Suburbs of *London*, by *Jordan Brifet*, and his Confort, *Anno* 1100. for Knights Hofpitallers. But,

1543 James Rogers *John Knowles*

But, befides the foregoing, there were other Religious Places, in every County, and particularly in *Yorkshire:* As, the Abbeys, Monafteries, or Priories, of *Whitby, Kirkham, Kirkftall, Rivaux,* &c. confifting of beautiful Churches, Refectories, Offices, Dormitories, Infirmaries, with contiguous Stables; and other neceffary Houfes, for the Entertainment of Strangers, or Pilgrims. The Monks us'd to pray at Midnight, or the Cock-Crowing; 6 o'Clock in the Morning, or *Matutines,* which they call'd the firft Hour; at 9 o'Clock, or the third Hour before Noon; at the fixth Hour, or 12 o'Clock at High Noon: The ninth Hour, or 3 in the Afternoon; the twelfth Hour, or 6 o'Clock in the Evening, when the *Vefpers* began; and at 7 at Night, which was reckon'd to be the firft Hour of the nocturnal Twelve. A certain Author, tho' very ironical againft them, yet owns, that thefe Abbeys were very convenient for the younger Children of the Nobility and Gentry, and confequently the Diffolution a very great Lofs, fince that Provifion was taken away, by the Enjoyment of which, there was lefs Occafion to rack the poor Tenants; and the Abbots were glad to receive thofe juvenile Perfons with little, or nothing; becaufe fo kind a Reception endear'd their Parents to befriend them in Parliament. Their Convents taught *Latin,* to the neighbouring Children, without any Reward: The Nunneries, to read, and work, with fometimes *Latin,* to enable them to underftand the Church-Service: The Monks were Hiftorians; and the Abbots excellent Landlords, who impos'd but eafy Fines on their Tenants, and were remarkable for an univerfal Hofpitality. But whatever Excellencies they feem'd to have been dignify'd with; all could not avert their impending Ruin. What pulling down of Buildings foon follow'd! The Materials were fold; the curious painted Glafs broken to Pieces; Copes, and Surplices, converted to Curtains, and Cufhions; and the Bells melted for other Ufes. Tho' their Mottoes fignify'd Power; as *Funera plango; Fulgura, Fulmina frango; Sabbato pango; excito Lentos; diffipo Ventos; paco Cruentos:* Yet neither their various Significations, or piercing Sounds, foretelling Death, breaking Thunder and Lightning, calling to the Sabbath, exciting the Sleepy, diffipating the Winds, or affwaging the Tyranny of Men, had any Effect at all upon King *Henry;* So far from it, that playing at Dice with Sir *Miles Parteridge,* one Throw loft him the tunable Ring of *Jefus* Bells, (againft One Hundred Pound) not far from St. *Paul's, London.* Nay, he gave a Religious Houfe to a Gentlewoman, who had obliged him with a Mefs of Pottage; or, as fome fay, a Difh of Puddings:

dings:

dings: And thofe Perfons, to whom he beftow'd the Monafteries, fold, for trifling Sums, the choiceft Manufcript Books, adorn'd with curious Boffes and Clasps, to Merchants, Grocers, Sope-Sellers, and other Trades, who ufed them to lap up their Goods. The Church-Lands were efteem'd at, Yearly, to the Value of Fifteen Hundred Thoufand Pounds: And yet, the King became but poor afterwards, thro' his fquandering them away, in the moft profligate Manner, before he could accomplifh his Defigns of founding 18 new Bifhopricks ; and one, in particular, thro' the Invention of Sir *Nicholas Bacon*, to erect a Royal Seminary for Ambaffadors, Statefmen, and Hiftorians ; which would fupply the lofs of the latter, confequent on the Destruction of Abbies ; where, for the most part, was preferv'd a Chronicle of the Times. But I fhall draw towards a Conclufion of this Manner of Difcourfe, by quoting the Words of a *Latin* Poem, (from what was excellently written by Sir *John Denham*, Knight of the Bath, entitled *Cooper's* Hill) infcrib'd to the most Noble *William* Lord *Cavendish*, only Son to the Earl of *Devonshire*.   Herein, defcribing the charming Beauties of Nature, in a Country abounding with Woods, Streams, Dales and Mountains, (as the fublime Author had a little before expatiated on Art, which rais'd the fair and lofty Pinacles and Towers of *Windfor* Castle) he takes Notice of a pleafant Summit, on which had stood a beautiful Chapel, 'till fuch Time as it fhar'd in the Fate of the fubfiding Abbey, both in venerable Ruins! And then he makes his melancholly Reflexion upon thefe lamentable Objects.

Quis vero hæc cernens dubitet quin exterus Hoftis
Terram omnem Ferro fuerit populatus, & Igni?
At poftquam audierit, quod tantis ftragibus Auctor
Nec durus Scytha *fit, gelida nec* Gotthus *ab Arcto,*
Sed Rex indigena, & CHRISTI *de Nomine dictus ;*
Cum nihil interfit, fed folo Nomine diftent
Optima noftra, atque illorum turpiffima Facta ;
Talia cum fuerint Pietatis Vulnera, quid jam
Sacrilega reftare Manu inviolabile credat ?

THUS PARAPHRAS'D.

Who, viewing Thefe ! can doubt the plunder'd Land,
By Sword and Fire, had felt th' Invader's Hand ?
Yet, when th' Enquirer hears, no *Scythian* bold,
Nor harden'd *Goths*, have done, what we behold ;
But, that a Natural, and a CHRISTIAN King,
Could, of himfelf, fuch Defolations bring :   Could

1545 [*zz*] James Johnſon, 2　　*Walter Jobson*

Could be the Author of theſe dread Remains,
Which once adorn'd the Hills, the Groves, or Plains :
When nothing, but a ſpecious Name, appears
Between *His* chief, and filthieſt Deeds of theirs :
What muſt be thought, vile Sacriledge would crave,
When, thro' Devotion, bleeding Wounds he gave,
So deep, as ſent *His Church* near to *Her* Grave.

[*z z*] But the King dy'd the following Year ; and was bury'd at *Windſor,* where he had begun for himſelf a Princely Monument, and founded a College for 13 poor Knights, and two Prieſts. Thus much more may be ſaid of him : That, by a Tyrant Popiſh Monarch, the Kingdom was deliver'd from Subjection to the See of *Rome :* The Conſequence of which, was, That the Bleſſed Goſpel of Peace, Meekneſs, and Love, ſoon after took Place ; and, when it had paſt ſome ſevere and fiery Tryals of Perſecution, triumph'd, in Splendour, as we now behold it : In which happy State, G O D grant it may long continue, amongſt its faithful Profeſſors, who are adorn'd with univerſal Charity, even to the End of the World.

❖❖❖❖❖❖❖❖❖❖❖❖❖❖❖❖❖❖❖❖❖❖❖❖❖❖❖❖

KING *EDWARD* VI. *Jan.* 28.

1546 JOhn Thacker, 1　*JNo.Overſall,*or *Overſale*
1547 J Thos. Dalton, 1　*William Johnſon*
1548 [*aaa*] John Harriſon　*John Thorpe,* or *Thorn*

[*aaa*] Tho' ſo many Hoſpitals had been lately deſtroy'd ; yet this learned and excellent Magiſtrate had the courageous Piety to erect a New One, near the Low-Church, in *Chapel-Lane,* for poor People, as many as Ten Shillings a Week, in common, would maintain. But he order'd, in his Will, dated in 1550, (in which Year he dy'd) That what he left his dear Wife *Elizabeth,* ſhould, after her Deceaſe, be apply'd to their Uſe, for better Maintenance, which was conſiderable, to be paid to them, Weekly, thro' the Care of the Mayor, Burgeſſes, and their Succeſſors, whom he appointed to ſee his Will executed. And indeed he had pretty Eſtates in *Hull ;* as three Meſſuages and Gardens in *High-Street ;* with Lands, Tenements, Meadows, and Paſtures, in the County ; others, at *Eaſtwick,* in *Holderneſs ; Cottingham,* in *Yorkſhire ; Barton,* in *Lincolnſhire ;* and in other Places : All which, at the Lady's Death, were apply'd to his Deſire : And, no doubt, but the Number in the Hoſpital were increaſ'd, in Proportion to the additional Charity.

1549 [*bbb*] Walter Jobſon, 1. *Wm. Angle* or *Angel*
1550 Jn. Overſail, *or* Overſall *Thos.*(or *Robt.*) *Dalton*
1551 [*ccc*] Alexander Stockdaile, 2 *Walter Flinton*
1552 John Thacker, 2   *James Stockdaile*

[*bbb*] This Year the Corporation made a ſtrict Regulation, to prevent what might be remiſs in the Civil Government. They came to a Reſolution, to puniſh Vice, and Immorality, in a more ſevere Manner ; and to correct the paſt Negligences of thoſe who had been, or future Remiſneſs of others who were to be, in Power, for diſhonourable Actions, whilſt in Office. Upon which Account, ſending for Mr. *Jobſon*, Mr. *Johnſon*, and Mr. *Thorpe*, who had been Sheriffs but of late, and had not feaſted ſo ſplendidly as they ought to have done ; nor, as the Charter ordain'd, upon Enterance into their Office, bought, along with their own, Scarlet Gowns, alſo, for their Ladies (the Penalty of which Neglect was decreed to be 20*l.* to be levy'd for the Uſe of the Corporation, and 10*l.* to be apply'd towards the ſettling of the Poor in Charity-Hall) to be ornamented with, on publick Occaſions, during their Husbands Shrievalty ; the Court laid a heavy Fine upon them : And further decreed, that every Sheriff, for the future, ſhould (as they were to do) pay 6*l.* 13*s.* 4*d.* for every ſuch Offence, which ſeem'd to be an Affront upon the Magiſtracy, to whom they were oblig'd to be ſubſervient, purely for the Honour and Dignity of the Town.

[*ccc*] Becauſe the Town of *Hull* had been always loyal to the Anceſtors of the King, and conſequently to him, the young Monarch granted, to the Inhabitants, the entire Manor of the Town ; the 6th Part of That of *Sutton*, in *Holderneſs;* the Manor of *Tupcotes*, with *Myton*, which lately belong'd to Sir *William Sidney;* the Patronage of the Charter-Houſe Hoſpital ; and, in ſhort, all the Juriſdictions, relating to Courts, Eccleſiaſtical, or Civil, in *Kingſton*, and Towns belonging to the County of *Hull.* Nor was his careful Munificence leſs, than that of his Bounty : For he deliver'd, into their Cuſtody, the Caſtle, and Block Houſes, (including the Gardens and Lands within their Circuit) which ſtood on the Side of *Drypool,* in the County of *York.* Thus were they to be abſolute Keepers, independant, without being accountable, of the Profits, to the King, or his Succeſſors : Only, that they were obliged to uphold the Works at their own Expence (except 50*l.* Yearly, which his Majeſty allow'd out of ſome of his Revenues) with ſufficient Ordnance and Ammunition for their Security : And therefore, the King further granted, That, from thenceforth, the Places, whereon they ſtood,
with

QUEEN *MARY* I. *July* 6.

| 1553 | HEnry Thurfcrofs, 2 [ddd] | HUgh Hall |
| 1554 | Tho. Dalton, *Jun.* 1 [eee] | *Wm. Dingley* |

with their Bounds, fhould be no more faid to be within the Limits of *Yorkshire,* but in the Priviledge of *Hull;* whofe Inhabitants fhould have the fame Power, as they had in the Town. To make their Authority yet greater, they might place therein, or difplace, whom they thought convenient. They had alfo given them the Right of Prefentation of the Church-Hofpital, near the Town, to commence after the Death of the Incumbent : Which House they were then to infpect, that the People might not be Sufferers therein ; but live comfortably, according to the pious Intent of the Founder. Yet foon after Commiffioners being fent to examine what Riches, Plate, or Jewels, belong'd to Churches in general ; under their Examination, thofe of *Hull* were again plunder'd to fuch degree, that they had fcarcely remaining a Cloth to cover the Altar in Decency, or a Chalice to hold the Wine, at the Adminiftration of the Bleffed Sacrament ! This Year was taken, at *Haffel* Cliff, a prodigious Fifh, 20 Yards in Length ; which was look'd upon as an unhappy Omen : But I will not, nay, I cannot fay, of the young innocent King's Death ; tho' it was not very long after this, that his precious Soul departed from the World, into the Hands of the Almighty.

[*ddd*] The Inhabitants of *Hull,* having had a long Suit with thofe of *Beverley,* who, as they deny'd to pay for, were prevented from, paffing thro' the Bridge of *Hull,* that had been erected by the Queen's Father, was this Year left to the Decifion of *Robert Conftable,* and *Wright,* of *Hotham,* and *Wellwick ; Anthony Smethby,* of *Brantingham ; Thomas Grimfton,* of *Godmanham,* Efquires ; and *Thomas Dowman,* of *Pocklington,* Gentleman. Each Party was oblig'd, in 200*l.* Bond, to fubmit to thefe Arbitrators : Who gave it againft the former Inhabitants, by allowing the Veffels, belonging to *Beverley,* and all the Towns, joining on the River, to fail freely through the Bridge, with their Mafts upright, if they thought convenient. About this time, feveral of the Reformed Clergy were either forced to quit this Realm, or obliged to live in a private Retirement, from the Duties of their Holy Function.

[*eee*] Sir *W. Knowles,* this Year, prefented the Corporation with a Gold Chain, weighing 4 Ounces, and a half ; upon Condition, that the Mayor fhould wear it every Sunday, Holiday, and on particular Occafions, or elfe to forfeit 40*l.* for every Omiffion. Upon the Hopes of the Queen's being with Child, great Rejoicings were

Q

made

1555 John Thornton [*fff*] *Jas.* (or *Jno.*) *Clarkson*
1556 Walter Jobson, 2 *John* (or *George*) *Shawes,* or
1557 Robert Dalton, 1 *Edward Dalton* (*Shares*

QUEEN *ELIZABETH. Nov.* 17.

1558 A Lex. Stockdaile, 3 L Aw. *Warton,* or *Wharton*
1559 A Jas. Clarkson [*ggg*] L *Franc. Thorp,* or *Thorpe*
1560 Thomas Dalton, 2 *William Gee*

made by the Catholicks in this Town: Their Prieft exerted his Oratory on the Occafion, with the higheft Panegyricks on her Majefty, and her Royal Confort King PHILIP: *Te Deum* was fung in the Chancel of the High Church; to which, and returning from thence, they walk'd, in folemn Proceffion: But their Triumphs were blafted, when News came, that there was no Sign of the Queen's Pregnancy.

[*fff*] The Cloth Hall was let this Year, to Mr. *Thornton,* for one and forty Years, at the Annual Rent of 6*l.* 13*s.* 4*d.* In former Times, it was ufual, that all Cloth fhould be examin'd herein, before it was expos'd to Sale, by Strangers, under the Penalty of 3*s.* 4*d.* for every Neglect: Which cuftom was now renew'd by a frefh Order, to render it more binding.

[*ggg*] One Mr. *Gregory* being chofen Sheriff this Year, upon denying to ftand, a great Confufion fpread over the Town. This, very juftly, mov'd the Magiftrates to complain of him to the Court. The Queen, and her Privy-Council, being much incenfed at his Refufal, order'd him to be fined One Hundred Pounds, disfranchifed, and turned out of the Town: All which was executed accordingly, to the great Difgrace of that obftinate Gentleman.

AND here I conclude this long Chapter, wherein a tolerable Account has been given of the MAYORS and SHERIFFS; but, indeed, very little, or almoft none, of the *Chamberlains;* any farther, than, that their Original fprung from antient Times, not long after the Building of the Town; But now, proceeding, for the greater part, to a regular Succeffion; their Names, alfo, fhall be mention'd, under the next Head, with as much Care, and Exactnefs, as the feveral Accounts, that I fhall carefully perufe, will poffibly enable me to perform. CHAP.

CHAP. VIII.

A Continuation of the MAYORS, SHERIFFS, *together with some Account of the* Chamberlains, *and what Transactions have happen'd, relating to* Kingston-upon-Hull, *until the Year of* CHRIST, 1611.

A. D. MAYORS *and* SHERIFFS.	CHAMBERLAINS.
1561 THomas Allured	RObert Wood
[*hhh*] *John Smith*	Geo. Hewit, *or* Hewet
1562 William Gee, 1	Wil. Williamson, *or* Wilson.
[*iii*] *Rob. Armin,* or *Armyn.*	James (*or* Sam.) Almond.

[*hhh*] The Reader is desired to observe, That, for the future, the Letters, which refer to Notes at the Bottom of the Page, will be under the Figures of each Year, preceding the Sheriff's Name. This Year, therefore, *Anno* 1561, His Grace, THOMAS YOUNG, Archbishop of *York,* coming to visit *Hull,* the 9th Day of *June,* was met, upon his Enterance, by the Mayor and Aldermen, in their Scarlet Robes, attended by the Sheriff, Chamberlains, Burgesses, *&c.* in their several Formalities. That Prelate, being invited to the House of the Head Magistrate, was there splendidly entertain'd. Soon after, having settled Ecclesiastical Affairs, he preach'd an excellent Sermon, and confirmed some thousands of People.

[*iii*] A notorious Impiety was discovered. One *Thomas West,* a Taylor, and *Isabel,* his Wife, being, thro' Idleness, put to their Shifts to live, contriv'd a very wicked Method; the one, to turn a hectoring Bully; the other, a scandalous Prostitute. No sooner had she entic'd each juvenile *Mars* into the Net of her lustful Embraces; but, out comes the valiant Taylor, Sword in Hand, more fierce than a terrible *Vulcan,* threatning either to castrate the Offender, or sheath the dreadful Blade in his tender Heart's Blood; except he paid very dear, considerably above the Market-Price, for his Redemption! This Trade the thriving Couple had carry'd on for some Time; 'till, at length, being discover'd, they were apprehended, and brought to Justice. The man was disfranchis'd; both committed to Prison, where they were kept a Month on Bread and Water; afterwards ignominiously drawn, through the Streets, in a Cart, with a Paper on their Heads, declaring their abominable Actions; and, at last, banish'd out of the Town, never to set Foot therein again, under Pain of more severe Punishment.

[*kkk*] Madam

1563 John Smith	William Smith
John Bir, or *Bever*	John Drake, *or* Brake
1564 R. Gayton, *or* Cayton	Thomas Hog, *or* Hogge
Jn. or *Wil. Parker*, or *Barker*	Wil. Scearth, *or* Seath
1565 Walter Flinton	Tho. Arenston, *or* Arneston
Rob. Naylor, or *Nayler*	Jn. Mattison, *or* Maddison
1566 John Thornton, 1	Hugh Kirlfoot, *or* Kirkfoot
Thomas Dowley	Jn. Hodgson, *or* Hodgden
1567 Robert Dalton, 2	Jⁿ. Fawther *or* Fairweather
Jn. Gregorie, or *Gregory*	Wil. Scholes, *or* Scales
1568 James Clarkson, 2	William Carlisle
[*kkk*] *William Wilson*	Edward Clarke
1569 Thomas Dalton, 3	John Loggan, *or* Logan
[*lll*] *John Rimington*	John Mounsey, *or* Alansy

[*kkk*] Madam KNOWLES, (who became the Spouse of JOHN AILFORD, Esq;) enlarg'd the Golden Chain, (which the Knight, her former Husband, had given, for the Mayor's Use) by adding the Value of Ten Pounds in Angel Gold. That of Three Pounds more was given by Madam THURSCROSS. So that the Whole, which consisted of 317 Links, weighed near 12 Ounces.

[*lll*] An Insurrection broke out in the North. *Nicholas Morton*, a Romish Priest, is said to have been sent, by the Pope, to pronounce the Queen an Heretick; which occasion'd a Writing, That the old English Religion was to be restor'd, for which they had taken up Arms. The Duke of *Norfolk*, and several Catholicks, declaring against it, offer'd their Persons, and Purses, against those Men that begun it; and who now, being increas'd to 4000 Foot, and 6000 Horse, were march'd to *Durham;* in which Cathedral they tore both Common-Prayer-Books, and Bibles. The Heads of these, were the [1] Earls of *Northumberland* and *Westmorland;* the Lords *Edward Dacres* and *Nevill;* with Gentlemen of Note; as [2] *Norton, Tempest, Danby,* and others. But hearing, they were soon to be oppos'd by the Earl of *Suffex*, Lieutenant of the North, whom they thought to have taken Prisoner at *Cawood*, where he resided; that he was to be assisted by the Lord *Scroop*, with Sir *George Bowes;* and that MARY, Queen of *Scots*, for whose Sake they rose, was removed from *Tutbury* to *Coventry;* then they came, in Fury, and besieg'd [3] *Baynard* Castle: Which, after some time surrendering, they thought to have surprized *Kingston-*
upon-

1570 Lawrence Wharton	Luke Thurſcrofs, *or* Thriſ-
William Smith	Chriſtopher May (croſs
1571 Chriſt. Stockdaile	John Frewick, *or* Frowick
[*mmm*] *Jno. Fairweather*	Jn. Whedall, *or* Whelpdail

upon-Hull, thro' the Treachery of one named 𝕾𝖒𝖎𝖙𝖍, who engaged, in the Night Time, to ſet open the Gates. But the Man, being taken, and diſcovering his Intention, the Deſign was timely prevented. After this, the People of the Country ariſing, purſued them into the North ; where ſeveral were taken, and from whence others eſcaped into *Scotland.* Above 60 Men were hang'd, for this Offence, at [4] *Durham.* The Earl of *Weſtmoreland* lived to an old Age ; but in a miſerable Condition, amongſt the *Spaniards,* to whom he fled, being ſupported by them but with a very ſmall Penſion : And at [5] *York,* where ſeveral had been executed, the Earl of *Northumberland* was, on a Scaffold erected at the *Pavement,* beheaded on the 22d of *Auguſt,* 1572. The pale and ghaſtly Head was placed, as a wretched Spectacle of Adverſe Fortune, on a high Pole, upon the Top of *Micklegate* Bar : [From which, about two Years after, much about the Time when a great Earthquake happen'd in *York,* it was ſtolen away] But his Body was interr'd in *Crux* Church, only attended by two of his Men Servants, and three Women. The other Rebellion, that ſoon, in the ſame Year, [*viz.* 1569.] follow'd what has been mention'd, was at *Naworth* Caſtle, belonging (and near) to which was a Town, of that Name, in *Cumberland,* occaſion'd (in order likewiſe to procure the Queen of *Scots* Deliverance) by *Leonard Dacres,* Son to the late Lord of that Name. The Youth very bravely withſtood, for ſome time, the Attacks of the valiant Lord *Hunſdon,* Governour of *Berwick :* But being over-power'd, was obliged to fly into *Flanders ;* and coming to *Lovain,* he made his laſt *Exit,* in miſerable Poverty.

[*mmm*] A diſmal [6] Flood happen'd, on the Night of *All-Souls,* which occaſion'd the like Damage to *Hull,* and indeed to many other Parts, as happened at the laſt mention'd dreadful Inundation, when Merchandize, People, and Cattle, were deſtroy'd.

Explanatory Inferences to the Notes belonging to the Years 1569 *and* 1571.

[1] *Thomas Percy,* and *Charles.*—[2] On the 27th of *May,* 1570. *Thomas* and *Chriſtopher* were drawn from the Tower of *London* to *Tyburn,* and there hang'd, and quarter'd.—[3] It was defended 11 Days, thro' the the Valour of Sir *George Bowes,* and his Brother *Robert.*—[4] The chiefeſt of whom, was an Alderman of the City ; and Mr. *Plumtree,* a Prieſt.—[5] On the 27th of *March,* 1570. *Simon Digby,* of *Askue ; John Fulthorpe,* of *Iſilbeck, Yorkshire,* Eſqrs. *Robert Peneman,* of *Stokesley,* and *Simon Bishop,* Jun. of *Pocklington,* Gentlemen, were hang'd at *Knaveſmire,* their Heads and Quarters placed on the City Gates, and at publick Places in the County.—[6] *Hollingshead* writes, it was the Year before.

[nnn] The

1572 John Smith, 2	Rich. Lodge, *or* Logan
William Scearth	Edw. Priston, *or* Preston
1573 William Gee, 2	*Here I find that no Cham-*
John Hardcaſtle	*berlains are mention'd.*
1574 Wil. Williamſon	Step. Prieſtwood, *or* Preſton
[*nnn*] *Tho. Arnelſon,* or *Arenton*	Leonard Wilſon, *or* Wiſton
1575 Robert Gayton	Jeffery Jeffers, *or* Jefferſon
[*ooo*] *John Logan*	Robert Legard
1576 Jn. Fairweather	Jn. Harryſon, *or* Harriſon
[*ppp*] *Edmund Clarke*	Peter Richardſon

[*nnn*] The Magiſtrates, this Year, by the wholſome Inſtructions of the Archbiſhop of *York*, dated *July* 20, ſet about the Puniſhment of Vice, (occaſion'd thro' the Multitude of Mariners coming to *Hull*) without any Reſpect of Perſons.

[*ooo*] Agreeable to the Deſign, in the former Year, Church-Wardens, and Sideſmen, were appointed, in every Ward; to viſit Ale-Houſes, Streets, and Cloſes; to ſee who were ſinfully ſpending their Time, when they ſhould have been at Church; and to preſent their Names, and Places of Abode.

[*ppp*] The Plague raging beyond Sea, and Quarentine not being well perform'd, it was brought, in ſome degree, by Seamen, to this Town: And that fatal Diſtemper, being chiefly confin'd to *Black-Fryer-Gate*, (where, however, ſcarcely periſh'd one hundred Perſons) it was immur'd, at both Ends, by Order of the Magiſtrates; only two little Doors, with ſmall Porches, for the Watchmen, that none of the Infected might eſcape from thence; and to take in Proviſions, with what was neceſſary, for the Sick, in their deplorable Condition: But GOD, in Mercy, ſtopping the Progreſs of the Contagion, the Town was quickly repleniſh'd, for what People they had loſt.—Soon after, a prodigious Exceſs of Apparel, growing common amongſt the Ladies, the Magiſtrates uſed their Endeavours to prevent it, by engaging the Miniſters to pronounce their Orders, very ſolemnly, in the Churches. But the lovely Females, not much regarding that Doctrine, a more coercive Declaration came forth, which quoted the Words of a Statute, *That whatever Woman wore Velvet in her Apparel, should immediately quit the ſame, or find a light Horſe to ſerve in Battle.* What might be thought of *Mantcens,* had they been uſed in thoſe Days?

[*qqq*] The

1577	John Thornton, 2	William Bray
	[*qqq*] *John Whelpdaile*	Robert Taylor
1578	James Clarkfon, 3	Wil. Robfon, *or* Robertfon
	Edward Wakefield	Chriftopher Wormley
1579	John Gregory	Tho. Emfon, *or* Empfon
	Edward Prefton	Robert Pelton, *or* Dalton
1580	William Smith	John Lynne (sley
	Robert Legard	Greg. Porman, *or* Worm-
1581	Edward Wakefield	Michael Webfter
	Leonard Wifton	William Richardfon
1582	William Gee, 3	Bartholomew Burnet
	[*rrr*] *William Bray*	Peter Crew, *or* Green
1583	John Smith, 3	Anthony Burnfall, *or*
	Robert Taylor	George Davis (Burnfell

[*qqq*] The Archbifhop of *York*, Dr. *Thomas Young*, returning from *London* (where he had been a long time fick) into *Yorkshire ;* the Magiftrates of *Hull* fent his Grace, as a Mark of their Affection, a Prefent of a Butt of Sack.—*Henry Haftings*, Earl of *Huntington*, being Lord Prefident of the North, fent in Cuftody, to this Town, feveral Romifh Priefts, Incendiaries, and Recufants, of their Perfuafion, to be kept under clofe Confinement.—Pyrates were fo common at this time, that fcarce a Merchant Ship could fail in Safety : The Queen then ordering the Lord High Admiral to ufe his Endeavours againft them, he required this Town to fit out two ftout Men of War. Thefe, being gallantly mann'd, took feveral of thofe Robbers, and brought 'em Captives to *Hull.* They were try'd before the Mayor and Aldermen, (to whom the Queen had fent a Commiffion) affifted by the active Lord Prefident aforefaid, Sir *Thomas Gargrave*, Sir *Henry Gates*, together with feveral Gentlemen. The guilty Wretches could plead nothing, to Purpofe, in Defence of their Lives ; and therefore fix of them were condemn'd to be hung in Chains upon the Sea-Coafts, as a Warning to others.

[*rrr*] The Lord WILLOUGHBY, being fent Ambaffador to the King of *Denmark*, embark'd at *Hull*, on the 14th of *July*, attended by the King at Arms, to carry the moft noble Order of the Garter to the Danifh Monarch.—The Archbifhop of *York* fent an Ecclefiaftical Commiffion, dated *July* 7. empowering the Magiftrates more effectually to fupprefs finful Immorality.

[*fff*] Sir

1584 William Wilfon	}	Anthony Cole, *or* Pole
[*fff*] *Robert Dalton*	}	Edward Coke, *or* Cocke
1585 Leonard Wiston	}	John Lister
[*ttt*] *William Richardfon*	}	Lawrence Blacklocke
1586 Luke Thriscroffe	}	George Almonde
John Lynne	}	John Graves
1587 William Bray	}	John Chapman
Richard Read	}	Hugh Arming
1588 Robert Dalton	}	John Yates
Anthony Cole	}	Robert Spencer
1589 John Gregory	}	William Barnard
Edward Cocke	}	Marmaduke Hadlesey
1590 William Smith	}	James Halfey, *or* Halfter
John Lifter	}	Thomas Thackeray
1591 William Richardfon	}	Hugh Graves
John Chapman	}	Mich. Beisbies, *or* Beisley
1592 Edward Wakefield	}	Walter Peck
[*vvv*] *Anthony Burnfell*	}	John Dobson

[*fff*] Sir *Francis Walfingham* was made (this Year) High-Steward of *Hull*, to which he prov'd a kind Benefactor.

[*ttt*] The Lord Prefident fat as Judge of the Criminals: Some, being convicted of Felony, and Burglary, fuffer'd the Law: Yet, what was more remarkable, an old Woman, for fuppofed Witch-craft, was fentenc'd to ftand 4 times in the Pillory, 4 Hours every time, and to fuffer a Year's Imprifonment. But fuch like Accu-fations have been little regarded, fince the Tryal of *Jane Wenham*, at *Hartford*, thro' the eminent Wifdom of the learned Judge, who then fat upon the Bench.—About 800 Perfons, in *Hull*, fign'd an Affociation to ftand by the Queen againft the *Spanish* Armado ; when the Town alfo lent her 600*l*. to be paid out of the Exche-quer, as foon as the Danger was over : Which, indeed, was not long, thro' the Valour of her Naval Forces ; who, bringing intire Confufion amongft the *Spaniards*, made them fly for their Lives.

[*vvv*] On the 26th of *September*, an odd and furprizing Fifh was (by Storms from the South Eaft) driven to Shore on *Drypool*. It was almoft of an Oval Shape, 6 Foot long, 5 broad, and 6 be-tween the extreme Parts of the upper and lower Fins : One of which

was

1593 Anthony Cole	⎱ Chriſtopher Harriſon
[*www*] *Jas. Haddleſey*	⎰ James Caſſon, *or* Caſſion
1594 Robert Taylor	⎱ * Adam Barkdaile (ſon
Marmaduke Haddleſey	⎰ * Geo. Wilſon *or* William-
1595 John Liſter	⎱ † George Chapman
John Graves	⎰ † Hugh Scott
1596 John Chapman	⎱ Barnard Smith
[*xxx*] *Hugh Arming*	⎰ John Priſton, *or* Preſton

was placed on the Back ; and the other on the Belly. 'Twas taken for that which (according to PLINY) is call'd a little Sea Hog; of ſuch Species, as, I think, I have ſeen, very common, in the *Iriſh* Ocean, different in Sizes, according to the Time ſince they were ſpawn'd. This Year the Town, being at great Expence, in fitting out a Man of War, to ſerve the Queen againſt the *Spaniards ;* her Majeſty order'd, that the Inhabitants of *Wakefield, Leeds,* and *Halifax,* who traded hither, ſhould bear a Part ; to which they willingly conſented.

[*www*] The Aldermen granted, to the Mayor in Being, the Priviledge of preſenting a Townsman with his Freedom, during the Time of that Mayoralty : But the Inconvenience of this appearing, a few years after, to be very detrimental ; it was put a Period to, by general Conſent of the Corporation.

* The Chamberlains, with an Aſteriſm preceding their Names, are placed, (according to another Manuſcript) *Anno* 1598.

[*xxx*] Sir THOMAS HENEAGE was made High-Steward of *Hull ;* but, dying this Year, was ſucceeded by Sir ROBERT CECIL, one of the Queen's Privy Council. Her Majeſty gave Authority to the Magiſtrates to make what Laws they pleaſed, for the Government of the Town ; with Power to puniſh ſuch Perſons, who ſhou'd offend againſt them : That two Markets ſhould be held in what Places they thought convenient : That (in Imitation of the Lord-Mayor and Aldermen of *London*) they ſhould be the Protectors of Orphans, by taking into their Cuſtody what was belonging to them, thereby to prevent the Childrens being wrong'd, or afflicted : That they, and their Succeſſors, ſhould hereafter be called the Common-Council : That they ſhould receive the Cuſtoms due for Landing of Goods, that were brought into the River *Humber,* (except what appertained to the Citizens of *York*) by which they might be better enabled to take Care of the Haven, and all other Works, that conduced to the Safety of the Town.

† Thoſe Chamberlains (with this Mark † before them) are ſaid to be in Office, *Anno* 1600. Mr. SMITH, and Mr. PRESTON, 1602.

R

1597 Edward Coke	}	‖ Francis Hodgſon
George Almond		‖ Thomas Mault
1598 John Graves	}	‡ John White
[*yyy*] *William Barnard*		‡ Cuthbert Thompſon
1599 Anthony Burnſall	}	**Robert Morton
[*zzz*] *Robert Spencer*		**Jn. Maugham, *or* Maugh

‖ The Chamberlains with this Mark ‖ are mention'd *Anno* 1608. [*yyy*] New Seats being now made in the High-Church for all Degrees of Mankind in the Town ; they tamely ſubmitted to thoſe Places, which were allotted for them.   But it was not ſo with the Fair Sex : Their Diſputes ran ſo high, that Eccleſiaſtical Commiſſioners were required to regulate the Affair ; which they did to Satisfaction.   On the 12th of *June*, his Grace, the Archbiſhop of *York*, gave the Magiſtrates a Power to correct the Vices of the Poorer Sort, in relation to Drunkenneſs, or Fornication ; and, for thoſe of the Rich, to preſent them to his Chancellor, who ſhould take Care of their Puniſhment, or Reformation.——A very ſtrong Order was made, in the Time of the above Zealous and Worſhipful Mayor, againſt the Stage-Players.   It call'd them, idle People ; the Debauchers of the virtuous Principles of Youth ; and, in ſhort, ſtyl'd thoſe itinerary Gentlemen no better than *Strolling Vagrants* : Therefore Two Shillings and Six-Pence was laid (by the Magiſtrates of *Hull*) as a Fine, upon every Inhabitant, who ſhould reſort to hear them : And the Landlord was to forfeit Twenty Pounds, who let a convenient Place to the Actors, wherein their Comedies or Tragedies were to be diſplay'd.   What a vaſt Alteration between this Year, and future Times !   Where were then the mighty Defenders of the Stage ; ſome of whom have ſince been remarkable, in proving that Vice is thereon corrected, and Virtue adorn'd, in more pathetick full-mouth'd Rhetorick, than the ſoft and eaſy Eloquence of other moving Orators ?   But their further Defence is left to themſelves, who are indeed moſt fit for that Employment.

‡ The Chamberlains, thus mark'd ‡, are ſaid to be ſuch, in 1609.

[*zzz*] The Obſtinancy of Mr. *Gregory*, in refuſing (after he was elected) to ſtand Sheriff, I find, in various Manuſcripts, to be mention'd under this Year, tho' I've follow'd others (I know not, if thro' Miſtake) by inſerting it about the Beginning of the Queen's Reign, which makes me thus caution the Reader :   However, all Accounts agree, that he ſuffered the Indignities mentioned for his Contempt. The Queen had a Suit with the Town, for not upholding the Block-Houſes and Caſtle, built by her Father :   But it dropt by Degrees.

** Theſe Chamberlains are placed (by another MS.) in 1610.

1600 Hugh Armyng, *or* Armin ⎱ *There was a great*
    Joseph Feild, or *Field*   ⎰ *Want of Corn this Year*
1601 Marmaduke Haddlefey ⎱ *E. of* Essex *beheaded, thro'*
[a] *Thomas Thackeray*   ⎰ Nottingham's *Treachery*

✠✠✠✠✠✠✠✠✠✠✠✠✠✠✠✠✠✠✠✠✠✠✠✠

KING *JAMES* I. *March* 24.

1602 William Barnard   ⎱ *Queen* Elizabeth
[b]   Chriftopher Chapman ⎰ *departed this life.*
1603 Jofeph Field, 1 ⎱ *The King, arriving at* York,
    James Caffon ⎰ *was fumptuously treated.*
1604 Tho. Thackeray, 1 ⎱ *Above* 3500 *Perfons dy'd*
    James Watkinfon ⎰ *in that City by the Plague.*
1605 James Caffon   ⎱ *The Gun-Powder Plot was*
    Thomas Swann ⎰ *hatching in this Year.*
1606 George Almond   ⎱ *The faid horrid Plot*
    Rich. Burgeffe, or Burgefs ⎰ *happily difcovered.*
1607 Thomas Swann   ⎱ *The King of* Den-
Nicholas Linsley, or *Hausley* ⎰ mark *came into* England.
1608 Richard Burgefs ⎱ *An Union defign'd betwixt*
    Jno. (or *Joshua*) *Hall* ⎰ England *and* Scotland.
1609 Chriftopher Chapman ⎱ *The* Hollanders *throw*
    Barnard Smith   ⎰ *off the* Spanish *Yoke.*
1610 Jas. Watkinfon, 1 ⎱ *King* HENRY IV. *of* France
    John Prefton   ⎰ *wickedly affaffinated.*

---

[a] The Lord *Burleigh,* with the Lord Prefident of the North, accompany'd by many Knights and Gentlemen, vifiting *Hull,* on the 23d of *Auguft,* dined at the Mayor's Houfe ; and were afterwards diverted with Fire-Works : But, thro' the over-charging an old Cannon, that was brought into the Market-Place, which contain'd many curious Contrivances, to be play'd off by that forcible Element ; it immediately burft in many fmall Pieces, kill'd 4 Men on the Spot, and wounded feveral Perfons.

[b] An Earthquake, being felt over *England,* affected this Town, in a very fenfible Manner.—The King granted a new Charter to the Corporation ; but it coft them 600*l.* Upon which Account, fome of the Town's Lands were obliged to be fold.

CHAP. IX.

A Continuation of the MAYORS, SHERIFFS, *together with some Account of the* Chamberlains, *and what Transactions have happen'd, relating to* Kingston-upon-Hull, *until the Death of King* CHARLES I.

A.D.	MAYORS and SHERIFFS.	CHAMBERLAINS.
1611	James Haddlesey *Edward Richardson*	Joseph Blaides Hugh Foddle
1612	John Lister [c] *Lancelot Roper*	John Woodmansey John Ramsden
1613	Nicholas Linsley, *or* Lynley [d] *Robert Chapman*	Wm. Cawood Martin Jefferson
1614	Joseph Feild, 2 *Thomas* (or *Robert*) *Ferris*	John Burnsall Michael Haddlesey
1615	Barnard Smith, 1 *William Dobson*	Thomas Raikes Thomas Johnson

[c] The Place of High-Steward (late in Possession of the Earl of *Salisbury,* Lord-Treasurer) being vacant ; *Thomas* Lord *Ellesmere,* had that Dignity conferr'd upon him, this Year.

[d] Tho' there had been so much Stir, in former Times, about procuring fresh Water from *Anlaby, Daringham,* &c. yet those Streams, passing thro' the Mote of the Town, were rarely so sweet as they should be, and often polluted. This occasion'd the Magistrates to make Application to *Richard Sharpeigh,* Esq ; who lived at *Westminster; William* * *Maltby,* of London ; and *John* ‖ *Cayer,* of *Neither-Loughton,* in *Lincolnshire,* Gentlemen ; three famous Artists, and Engineers : Who, coming to view the Place, found practicable what they intended ; and therefore took a Piece of Ground, for 100 Years, which (for their Encouragement) they had at a small Annual Rent. On this they erected Water-Works : They had the Liberty also, to lay Pipes in the Streets, so as they did not exceed 10 Yards long, and 1 broad, at a time ; which they were to fill up, before they proceeded further : All this, with whatever should after want Repair, to be at their own Expence ; since the Inhabitants were Yearly, to allow a profitable Compensation, for the Water.

* Or MALTLEY.   ‖ Or CAIER.   [e] The

1616 Edwd. Richardson	George Carlile, *or* Carlisle
[e] *John Ramsden*	James Watkinson
1617 John Prefton	John Barnard
John White	William Haddlefey
1618 John Lifter, *Jun.*	Christopher Freistby
Robert Morton	Joel Gaskin, *or* Gafcoigne
1619 Lancelot Roper, 1	Robert Raikes
[f] *James Watkinfon*	Thomas Moor, *or* Moon
1620 Tho. Ferris, *or* Ferret	William Foxley [phries
Henry Chambers	Joseph (*or* Joshua) Hum-
1621 Joshua (*or* John) *Hall	William Saltmarsh
[g] *Thomas Raikes*	William Popple

[e] The Water-Works were now finifh'd, to the unfpeakable Satisfaction of the whole Town.

[f] The EXCHANGE was begun to be erected, in the *High-Street*, at the Expence of Five Hundred Pounds, given by the Merchants: But the King allow'd a 5th Part, on Condition, to have certain contiguous Rooms, for a Cuftom-Houfe, on a leafe of 50 Years.

* The Worfhipful Mayor (in the Year 1621) removed the Fifh-Shambles, that were formerly built by Dr. RIPLINGHAM.

[g] A Brief, dated *Sept.* 26. was fent (by the Archbishop of *York*) to this Town, for the Relief of *French* Proteftants, who fled to *England*, on Account of Religion; for whom was a Collection of near 150*l.* and fent them accordingly: But foon after appear'd another, of a different Nature, for redeeming thirteen Religious, and to repair an antient Chapel, on Mount *Golgotha*, where our Saviour had fuffer'd, which was built by St. HELEN, a British Princefs: But this was very coldly received by the People; who thought the King was doting in his old Age, upon Account of the Spanish Match: And there were but Five Pounds gathered on this unwelcome Occafion.—Great Jealoufies, being epidemical in thefe Times, were accompany'd by an univerfal Decay of Trade, and Want of Money. As the Privy-Council had fent to feveral Magiftrates, in *England,* to know the Reafons, and how to redrefs thefe Grievances; it fell to Mr. *John Ramfden's* Share, in this Town; who wrote of the fame, in fuch an exquifite Manner, as merited an univerfal Approbation.—The Exchange was finished this Year; and the Town adorned with a New Pavement: To perform which, a Mafter-Workman was fent for to *London*, who performed the fame, in the neateft Manner, to general Satisfaction.

[h] A

1622 John Ramſden   } Nich. Denman, *or* Dewman
[*h*] *Joseph*(or *Josh.*)*Blaides* } Jonas Harwood, *or*
1623 Jas. Watkinson, 2 } Tho. Elsam [Haywood
    Martin Jefferſon } Coniston Wrightington
1624 Thomas Thackeray, 2 } Henry Barnard
    John Barnard   } Alexander Swan

[*h*] A great Law-Suit commenc'd (this Year) between the Inhabitants of *York* and *Hull*, concerning a Cuſtom of *Foreign bought, and Foreign ſold.* That is, (if I underſtand it right) Whatever was offer'd to Sale, or bought, by *Strangers,* reckon'd *ſuch,* who were *not* free of the Town) should be forfeited to the Corporation. It began, thro' a Seizure, made by the latter, of 50 Quarters of Rye, belonging to Mr. *Barker,* a Citizen. The Magiſtrates of *Hull,* in a Petition to the King, pleaded, That the City of *York* had formerly, (*Anno* 157⅘. before the Earl of *Huntington,* Lord Preſident, in the Reign of Q. ELIZABETH, when ſuch another Suit had happen'd) articled with them, amongſt other Things, That they would *never* pretend to ſuperſede *That Antient Cuſtom :* A Cuſtom, which they enjoy'd, by Vertue of their Charters, for enabling them to ſupport the Walls, Banks, and Haven, of the Town ; Works, that were very expenſive : And if this Liberty was taken from them, it might, by impoveriſhing the Place, be a great Impediment of the King's Annual Revenues. The Cauſe being heard, before the Privy-Council, with the moſt cogent Arguments, on both Sides; their Lordships could not find any Reaſon for the Seizure, it being Proviſion ; and that *York* was a principal Member of the Port : But ſince they were both opulent Corporations, they deſired them to be reconciled, by a free and mutual Intercourſe with each other : Therefore the Barley was to be return'd; or Money, to the Value : And the Citizens of *York,* to be at Liberty, to bring, into *Hull,* what Quantity they pleas'd, at their own Adventure; and ſell therein, as formerly accuſtom'd : But not to attempt farther, in any Breach of the Articles, which had been made before the Lord Preſident.— Copper Farthings were invented about this Time : And tho' ſo very uſeful to the Publick ; yet ſeveral Proclamations were iſſued forth, before the People could be brought to utter them.

We are now drawing near a troubleſome Reign, both to King and People : The Recital of which might, ſome way, ſeem to adminiſter Offence, to Parties of different Sentiments, in relation to this important Town, were it not that Regard is to be had (without the leaſt Partiality) to Truth alone ; which I ſhall endeavour to follow, as beſt becomes a faithful Hiſtorian.   [*i*] GEORGE

1625 Thomas Swan   } William Crew
    Cuthbert Thompson } Daniel Smith

✠✠✠✠✠✠✠✠✠✠✠✠✠✠✠✠✠✠✠✠✠✠✠✠✠✠

King *CHARLES* I. *March* 27.

1626 **B**Arnard Smith, 2   } Chriſtopher Chapman
[*i*]   *William Popple* } Samuel Smithſon

[*i*] GEORGE ABBOT, Archbishop of *Canterbury*, became High
Steward of *Hull ;* whoſe Brother, with Sir JOHN LISTER, were
elected Burgeſſes.—The Inhabitants very generously comply'd
with the Firſt Loan, (for which the Lords *Dunbar* and *Clifford*
came hither) and ſent to the King between Three and Four Hundred Pounds ; tho' many, in ſeveral Places of the Kingdom, appear'd to be very much againſt it.—The Diſagreements between
the King (demanding Subſidies of his People, whilſt he vindicated
his great Favourite the Duke of *Buckingham*) and his Parliament,
(unwilling to comply with his Deſires, in Oppoſition to the Advice
of that Nobleman) were now increaſed, by Reaſon, that the King
of *Denmark*, his Majeſty's Uncle, had, with other Powers, taken up
Arms againſt the Emperor.   The King, thinking himſelf oblig'd
to aſſiſt his Uncle, ſent to the Magiſtrates of *Hull*, to provide ſuch
a Number of Ships, that might tranſport near 1400 Men : Which
being done, they ſafely arrived at *Staden*, a very ſtrong Town of
Germany, on the River *Scuvenge*, near the *Elbe*. But all Aſſiſtances
were to little Purpoſe ; for the Danish Monarch, with his Forces,
were defeated, near *Luttern*, *Auguſt* 27. by Count *Tilly*, the Emperor's General, who was a Perſon of great Conduct and Valour. A
Letter was ſent to *Hull*, from his Majeſty, dated *May* 29. requiring
the Inhabitants to fit out Ships againſt Privateers, which very much
infeſted the Coaſts : And that, ſince his own Revenues were inſuf-
ficient to ſupply his neceſſary Occaſions, he deſired them (as may be
ſuppoſed he did others) to grant him 6*d.* on every Chaldron of
Coals, as should be tranſported thither, from *Sunderland* and *Newcaſtle ;* where the ſame Sums were to be collected for what Quanti-
ties were to be ſent over Sea : But this, the King besought them to
do, out of their own free Will. The *General Loan*, which began
this Year, as it was much promoted by ſome, was oppoſed by others;
whilſt Troubles ſeemed to overſpread all *Europe !* The Lieutenants, of all the Counties in *England*, had Orders, to put each Province, and Diſtrict, into a Poſture of Defence ; by training up, for
War, ſufficient Men, who were to diſarm the Recuſahts. *HULL*,
                                               with

1627 Robert Morton	⎱	George Todd
[*k*] *Coniston Wrightington,* †	⎰	George Cartwright
1628 Henry Chambers *	⎱	William Peck
[*l*] *Nicholas Denman*	⎰	John Chambers

with its Share of Soldiers, was to procure, against sudden Warning, 3 Lasts and ¾ of Powder, 3 Tun and ¾ of Match, 3 Tun and ¼ of Lead ; with Pick-Axes, Carts, Carriages, Ammunition, and Provisions: The Beacons too were got ready; and all other Things necessary. *England* seem'd to be surpriz'd at these dreadful Preparations; and could not tell how to judge, whether they had not more Reason to fear the supposed Arbitrary Proceedings of their natural Prince, than the destructive Designs of foreign Enemies.

[*k*] The King, who had been unhappy in his Actions, by assisting the Emperor against *Spain,* was now (thro' the Duke of *Buckingham's* Resentment against the *Gallick* Court, for being frustrated in his private Attempt upon a Lady of sublime Quality, suppos'd to be their Queen ; and because Cardinal *Richlieu* had prevailed with the French King to deny him Admittance in Quality of Ambassador) as unfortunate in proclaiming War against *France.* But other Reasons were, the French King's misemploying 7 English Ships, against the Protestants of the large opulent City of *Rochelle,* which were lent purely to assist him upon the Italian Coasts : On this follow'd a Dismission of the Queen's Attendants, to the great Grief of his Royal Consort. But this War proved very unsuccessful: The Duke of *Buckingham,* instead of relieving the Inhabitants of *Rochelle,* was forc'd to retreat with great Loss : For that Expedition, by Order of the Privy-Council, three Men of War, (each able to bear 200 Tun, and 12 Pieces of Ordnance) had been fitted out by the Inhabitants of *Kingston-upon-Hull :* One of these was lost by the Enemy ; but the others returned in Safety.—Two Great Bulwarks *(An.* 162⅞.*)* were erected : One, at the South-End ; the other, on the Side of the Garrison.

† Mr. *Wrightington,* (or *Wrightleston*) the Sheriff, was fined 3*l.* 6*s.* 8*d.* for not wearing a crimson Gown on the Festival Days, and at other appointed Times : But he refusing to pay the Fine, it was levy'd on him by Distress.

* Mr. *Chambers* was fined, *(An.* 163⁰⁄₁) because he had not follow'd the antient laudable Custom, when he was made Alderman, in preparing a Feast, for the Burgesses of *Hull :* And then it was decreed, That whoever was exalted, to that Dignity, should make a Banquet, (within 40 Days, if at home ; if not, within the same Space of Time after) under the Penalty of Twenty Pounds.—As I am mentioning *Fines,* I must here take Notice of an Omission, in

relation

1629 *Sir* John Lifter, *Kt.* ⎱ Percival Linley
[*m*]   *Robert Raikes* ⎰ Robert Berrier
1630 Lancelot Roper, **2** ⎱ William Linley
[*n*]   *Henry Barnard* ⎰ Peregrine Pelham
1631 John Barnard   ⎱ Rich. Parkins, *or* Perkins
[*o*]   *Alexander Swan* ⎰ Tristram Pearfon

relation to Alderman *Dalton,* who was Mayor in 1588. He was accufed, a while after, for having ingroffed moft of the Mills (about
Town) in his Hands ; taking (inftead of Money, which was cufto-
mary) *Moulter-Corn;* nay, *more* of that, than *he ought to have done;*
and, which aggravated his Offences, had therewith mingled *Plaifter,*
to increafe the Weight : For thefe Things, he was feverely reprehended ; and might have been fin'd, had not he humbly fubmitted
himfelf, craving Pardon, with a Promife, never to commit the like
again, or any thing elfe, that fhould bring him under Difpleafure.

[*l*] Tunnage, and Poundage, being laid upon Merchant-Ships,
(*Anno* 1628, as this Note refers to that Year, in the preceding Page)
it was willingly comply'd with, by the Gentlemen of *Hull.*—
The Duke of *Buckingham* was ftabb'd at *Portfmouth,* by *John
Felton,* (formerly a Lieutenant) on the 23d of *Auguft.*

[*m*] The Lord *Thomas Wentworth,* Earl of *Strafford,* being
Prefident of the North, had fent him (by the Mayor and Aldermen)
feveral valuable Prefents in Silver Plate, and choiceft Wines : And
the like was fent to His Grace, *Samuel Harfnet,* Archbifhop of
York, upon his Advancement to that See.—Baron TRAPP came
this Year (in Mr. *Crew's* Ship) to *Hull,* as Judge of Affize; before
whom a Man was convicted, and received Sentence of Death.

[*n*] A Proclamation was publifh'd againft vile Infinuations, lying and treafonable Speeches.

[*o*] An Order being fent to *Hull,* That the Inhabitants fhould
guard themfelves againft Strangers, and Care might be taken of the
Town ; the Magiftrates order'd, (at the Expence of all within their
Boundaries) the Ditches immediately to be cleanfed, the Walls and
Block-Houfes repaired, and every Article (neceffary for a Warlike
Defence) provided.—Baron TRAVER arriving at *Barton,* in order
to pafs the *Humber,* and hold the Affize at this Town ; two of the
Aldermen were fent in a Ship to conduct the Judge hither ; Three
Guns were fired at his Reception on Board ; five more at his Land-
ing : Three others were let off from the Block-Houfes, and four on
the South End. At the *Horfe-Staith,* the Mayor, Aldermen, She-
riff, and Attendants, received his Lordfhip, in their Formalities :
And then he was conducted in Honour to his Apartment.

S

[*p*] The

1632 Henry Barnard	}	Leonard Barnard
[*p*] *John Chambers*	}	John Swan
1633 Thomas Raikes, 1	}	William Dobfon
[*q*] *Leonard Barnard*	}	Jofeph Thwing
1634 Nicholas Denman	}	Hugh Torton
[*r*] *William Peck*	}	John Peck, *or* Pecket
1635 Martin Jefferfon	}	Richard Hasla, *or* Hasley
Robert Cartwright	}	Robert Drewe
1636 Jofeph Blaides	}	John Rogers
Peregrine Pelham	}	Richard Wood

[*p*] The valiant King of *Sweden* (who had conquer'd the Emperor's General *Tilly*) was slain at the Battle of *Lutzen, Nov.* 6.

[*q*] The Magistrates of *Hull* fent 2 Casks of Sturgeon, with a Butt of Sack, as Prefents, to the Archbifhop of *York :* His Grace returning them two lovely Bucks, a great Feaft was made in the Hall for the Burgeffes.—Sir HUMPHREY DAVENPORT, the Judge of Affize, was fplendidly received.—Upon the Deceafe of Dr. ABBOT, Archbifhop of *Canterbury,* (who died at *Croyden,* the 4th of *Auguft,* aged 71, and interr'd in *Guilford,* where his Monument, on which is the Effigy of him, may now be feen) the Lord *Coventry* Vifcount *Ailesbury* became High-Steward of *Kingfton-upon-Hull.*—The King (being attended by the Earls of *Northumberland, Pembroke, Arundel, Southampton* and *Holland,* the Marquefs of *Hamilton,* Bifhop of *London,* and other dignify'd Perfons) made his Progrefs towards *Scotland.* On the 24th of *May,* arriving at *York,* he dined with the Lord-Mayor, (the Right Hon. *William Allenfon*) whom he was pleafed to knight; conferring the fame Dignity upon *William Belt,* Esq ; then Recorder. The King afterwards afcended to the Top of the Great Steeple of *York* Minfter, taking a View from thence of the Situation of the City, with Part of *Yorkshire.* When he had lain 4 Nights in his Palace, call'd the *Manor,* he proceeded to *Edinborough,* where he was folemnly crown'd ; and held a Parliament for about 8 Days : After five Weeks Stay in *Scotland,* his Majefty returned, by Poft, to the Queen, who then refided at *Greenwich.*

[*r*] Ship-Money was now begun, occafion'd (in a great Meafure) on Account, that the *Dutch* had affum'd a Right to Fifh on the Coafts of *England;* in which they were vindicated by GROTIUS, in a Treatife, call'd *Mare Liberum:* But this was anfwer'd and confuted by that learned Antiquary, Mr. SELDEN, in his *Mare Claufum,* to the Nation's Satisfaction, and his own Fame.

[*S*] A

1637 Jacob (*or* Jas.) Watkinſon	}	William Maiſters
[ſ] *William Crew*	}	Francis Dewick
1638 William Popple	}	Matthew Topham
William Dobſon	}	Robert Ripley
1639 Robert Morton	}	Robert Peaſe, *or* Place
[t] *Richard Parkins*	}	Maccabeus Hollis

[ſ] A Suit was renew'd on the Crown Side (tho' not rigorously proſecuted) for ſupporting the Block Houſes and Caſtle, built by *Henry* VIII. But this ſoon dropt, thro' the King's love to many of the Inhabitants: And the Civil Wars, which demoliſh'd all ſuch Places, put a final End to any Diſputes of that Nature.

[t] The Worſhipful Mayor, Aldermen, and Inhabitants, when they heard the *Scots* were approaching the Borders, put themſelves upon their Guard: Forty Men watch'd daily; they doubled their Number at Night; and every thing prepared, in Caſe a Siege ſhould happen. Sir *Francis Windbanke*, Secretary of State, ſent to the Magiſtrates of *Hull*, by the King's Order, to underſtand the Strength of the Town: The Letter was brought by the Maſter of the King's Armory, Captain *Legg :* Who, viewing the Place, carefully, told them, *It was abſolutely neceſſary to cleanſe the Ditches, repair the Gates, and make Draw-Bridges thereto.* After ſome ſmall Diſputes with the neighbouring Towns, (who endeavour'd to evade their Parts in the common Expence, yet at laſt conſented) all Things were begun to be put in good Order for Defence: And then the Captain, conſidering where to fix a Magazine, the old Manor-Hall was pitch'd upon, and rented of *Henry Hildyard*, Eſq ; as I have before mention'd, in treating of that Edifice. Mr. *Boſwell*, his Majeſty's Reſident in *Holland*, having bought Arms there, (to the Value of 6000*l.*) for the King's Service, ſent them over to *Hull;* where they were landed, and put into the Magazine (which was partly fill'd before) about End of *March.* Theſe conſiſted of the following Inſtruments of War: Three Hundred Head-Pieces; the like Number, each, of Pykes, Corslets and Fire-Locks: Twelve Hundred Muskets, 1500 Belts of Bandaliers ; Shovels, and Spades, 200 each ; with 100 Pick-Axes : Halberts, and Black Bills, 15 each : Six Carriages, each having 4 Wheels, ſhod with Iron : Six Braſs Cannon, 7 Petards : Twenty Five Barrels of Whole Powder ; and of Sifted Powder, 5 : Twenty Four Barrels of Musket-Shot, 410 Cannon-Bullets, and 32 Matches. But from this Store, 18 Waggon-Loads were ordered, from hence, to *Newcaſtle* and *Berwick*, by the Earl of *Newport ;* who, riding Poſt, arrived at *Hull*, on the 4th of
April,

April: On the 11th, the Lord *Conway* came, with 200 Horfe-men, who arm'd themfelves, and convey'd more Ammunition to the Camp. And, towards the End of *April*, the King, with his No-bles, fet out for *London* to *York*, in order to pafs to his Army, in the North, againft the *Scots:* But being perfuaded, firft to take a View of *Hull*, he fent them Word, from that antient City, *That he would vifit them within three Days.* He came accordingly, was met on the Confines of the County by the Sheriff, and fome of the Burgeffes ; and, at *Beverley* Gate, by the Mayor, Aldermen, with the better Sort of Inhabitants, where there were Rails and Carpets to grace the So-lemnity, in their feveral Stations. The Recorder addrefs'd himfelf to the King, in Behalf of the Corporation, to this Effect : *That as they were not fo converfant in fpeaking to Sacred Majefty on Earth, as they were in Prayers to the Throne of Heaven for his Preferua-tion ; they humbly begg'd Pardon, if anything, now to be utter'd, fhould prove unacceptable, fince proceeding from nothing, but want of Knowledge how to exprefs themfelves upon fo happy an Occafion: That the Fulnefs of their Hearts, ftopt up the Paffages of Speech ; and their affectionate Loyalty were better expreffed in Silence, than Words : That the Town might be compared to* SEVILLE, *the moft antient and beautiful City in all* Spain : *Not only ftrongly wall'd, but garrifon'd with Fire : Not dead, or fenfelefs ; but ardent, and awaking : Not only a Place of Store, for military Provifions ; but of Hearts, enflam'd with Zeal for his Majefty's Service : The moft faithful Subjects, careful of thofe Fortifications committed to their Charge by his Royal Predeceffors ; which they would defend purely for his Ufe alone : That they befought the Divine Power, to convert the Thorns of his Travels into Diadems ; that his Battles might be crown'd with Lawrels ; many Years added to a Life, the Bleffing of the prefent Age, (as it would be the Glory of future Generations) and that he might live for ever in an happy Immortality.* When the || Orator had ended his Speech, the King thank'd both him, and the Affembly ; declaring, That the Good of his People lay next to his Heart, whom he would endeavour to preferve from their Enemies. Then the Mayor fell upon his Knees : But being order'd to arife, the King gave him his Hand to kifs : The Magiftrate, then embracing the Mace, prefented it to his Majefty ; telling him, *He lay'd that Emblem of Regal Authority, with the utmoft Humility and Confi-*
dence,

|| *However, this very Man, being afterwards made a Judge, prov'd a bitter Enemy to the King: But this cannot be laid to the Charge of the Corporation, whofe Servant he was, and order'd by them to pronounce their Sentiments, tho' perhaps not then his own.*

dence, at his Majefty's Feet. Which, being accepted, was return'd by the King, faying, *He reftor'd to them all the Priviledges which it fignify'd; and that ufing it to his Honour, would prove their own Felicity.* Then the Keys were prefented, as an Emblem of their Truft in his Majefty; for whofe Service they were ready to venture their Lives and Fortunes. *I wish,* (faid the King, returning the fame with majeftick Sweetnefs) *I never may have Occafion for you to lay either of them at Stake, for my Sake alone : Here, take them again: Exclude the Vicious, but harbour the Innocent : And, for my part, I defire to reign, or live, no longer, than to prove a Comfort to you, and all my faithful People.* The Sword was prefented (and return'd) with much the like Ceremony : And, at laft, the Ribbon, with a Purfe of 100 Guineas; which the King kindly received. Then the Mayor, with low Reverence, taking up the Mace on his Shoulders, went out of the Rails, conducting his Majefty thro' the Streets, which were lined on both Sides by Soldiers ; alfo Train-Bands, neatly habited, at the common Expence of Town and County. The Walls, Banks, with other Matters, would have been repair'd, had there been but Time: However, Things were acted as neat as poffible. His Majefty, being led to the Houfe of Sir JOHN LISTER, was fplendidly entertain'd, and lodg'd. The next Morning he furvey'd the Town ; took Notice of the Great Gates, which Captain LEGG only allow'd for Enterance; and thofe defenfive Works that were preparing by his Order. Then the King, fending the Mayor before him, follow'd to the Garrifon Side, where the Guns were fired at his Approach. Seeing every thing, to his Satisfaction, he returned Thanks to the Magiftrates for their Courtefy : Then, mounting his Horfe, was attended by the Mayor to the Gates; and, by the Aldermen, with the Chief Burgeffes, to the Limits of the County, where they took Leave of his Majefty. That Night the King lodg'd at *Beverley,* the next at *York,* and fome Days after at *Newcaftle ;* From whence, by his Command, the Earl of *Holland* wrote a Letter, dated *July* 29. to the Magiftrates of *Hull,* thanking them, and Captain *Legg,* for their Entertainment of him, and fecuring the Town by all neceffary Preparations of Defence, as he perceiv'd when he was amongft them : And indeed they deferved Praife ; for the Works were finifhed in the Month after.—His Majefty, being advanc'd towards the Borders, the *Scots* fent him fubmiffive Letters, only to gain Time, whilft they increas'd their Forces: And taking Advantage of the inglorious Timidity of the Earl of *Holland;* (whom *Lesley,* their Leader, impos'd upon, by fetting fome of the ordinary Tribe of that Country on the Side of a Hill for Show only, as tho' they never wanted *Multitudes*) as alfo of the Marquefs of *Hamil-*

ton's

1640 John Barnard, 2   } John Ramfden
 [*u*] *Robert Berrier*   } Lionel Buckle

ton's poor Succefs (by fpending his Time with his Mother, and other *Covenanters,* when he fhould have been employ'd in another Manner) they took Courage to write to the Englifh Generals, by whofe Means their Petition coming to his Majefty, the eafy, unfortunate Monarch was brought to a difhonourable Pacification, and obliged to disband the greater Part of his Army.

[*u*] Some of the injur'd King's Soldiers, as yet unbroke, were quarter'd near *Hull,* left a frefh Rupture fhould happen ; as indeed foon after came to pafs, thro' the frefh Infolencies of the *Scots.* To act againft whom, the King fent to *Ireland,* for the Great Lord WENTWORTH, made him Knight of the Garter, and Earl of *Strafford,* in *Yorkshire.* That Nobleman, by Order of the King, fent a Letter, (dated *Aug.* 14.) to fome of the loyal Burgeffes of *Hull,* and Inhabitants of the adjacent Towns, thanking them for their Goodnefs, in paying the Soldiers Quarters thereabouts, which they fhould be honeftly repaid ; as the Earl himfelf now engag'd for, which was afterwards punctually perform'd.—Tho' the King could fcarce obtain any Money from Parliament ; yet, by a generous Subfcription of his loyal Subjects, having made new Preparations, he fent the Earl of *Northumberland,* with an Army, againft the *Scots,* whom he proclaim'd as Rebels. The King came to *York* the 22d of the fame Month : On the 29th, he rode to *Northallerton :* But hearing the *Scots* (who, without Oppofition, had entered, into *England,* the 21ft Inftant ; and, a little while after, routed the Lord CONWAY at *Newburn*) had taken *Newcaftle,* were poffefs'd of *Northumberland* and the Bifhoprick of *Durham,* intending, in a Week's Time, to be at *York;* he thought it convenient to return, and defend that antient City. His Army confifted of almoft 12000 Foot, and 3000 Horfe : And fending, to *Hull,* for thirty large Pieces of Ordnance, with other Inftruments of War, they were fent thither in three Days Time. *Clifton-Ings,* (a fpacious beautiful Plain, near the River Side, fince ufed for Races) the Bifhop's Field, with other convenient Places, were the Theatres of Artillery, and War : Here Tents Cannons, and Bulwarks, were ranged, fix'd, and erected : A Bridge of Boats lay crofs the River ; and every thing in a Condition to engage the Enemy.—On the 6th of *September,* the Earl of *Strafford* fent to the Magiftrates of *Hull,* to defire them to accept of Sir THOMAS GLEMHAM (who commanded a Regiment of Foot) as Governour, only for a while, it being the King's Pleafure : This, at firft, met with Oppofition, becaufe it would fuperfede the Mayor's Autho-

rity,

rity, in that Respect: But finding his Majesty was resolved to go thither in Person; and being assur'd, that the King had only the Safety of the Town nearest his Heart; they accepted Sir *Thomas* in the Quality desired, and accordingly deliver'd him the Keys.— While his Majesty was expecting the *Scots*, who had threaten'd *York;* they were better pleas'd to enjoy the Plenty of *England*, in the North, than to increase their Hostilities: And, indeed, had the Modesty, to send a Petition to the King, without mentioning Particulars: But afterwards thus explain'd themselves: That the Castle of *Edinborough*, and other Forts might be repair'd for their Defence; no Oaths to be impos'd upon 'em, contrary to their national Oath and Covenant: That a Parliament of *England* should meet as soon as possible; and that the Declaration might be revok'd, which called them *Traytors!* Thus, after all their Proceedings, they would willingly stigmatize their Sovereign, in obliging him to esteem them as honest Men. Now could any Prince be more insulted, or unfortunate than his Majesty, under the greatest Necessity, thro' the Distraction of the Times? An insolent corrupted Enemy, who had feperated the Interests of King and People; a mutinous and divided Country; a disheartned, if not, for the greater part, a corrupted Army; a Treasury exhausted in raising and disbanding his first Forces; and no sufficient Time left, to call a Parliament? What could then relieve both him, and his loyal Subjects, labouring under these seeming insuperable Difficulties! Why, an antient Custom was found out, in calling the Peers, to attend the King at *York*. They obey'd the Summons: And his Majesty, in the Hall of the Dean of *York*, (*Sept.* 24.) after a short Speech upon the Occasion, declar'd his Intention of calling a new Parliament. This Court was held 'till the 18th of *October* following: During which Time, the Corporation of *Hull* sent Alderman POPPLE to his Majesty, desiring to receive his Advice, and know his Pleasure; and that Alderman WILLIAM LISTER might attend his Court, to give Notice of what Passed from time to time: And the King received a Present of 4 stately Horses, with rich Capparisons, from the King of *Denmark*. The Beginning of *November*, the Army was disposed into Winter Quarters about the Country, as there seem'd to be a Cessation: And soon after, near the Election of New Members for the *Long Parliament*, follow'd several Projects for altering the Government, or abridging the Regal Power; which added but Fewel to the former Heart-Burnings. The Earl of *Strafford's* Troubles succeeded: The Canons of the Church were condemn'd; the Archbishop of *Canterbury* impeach'd; and the Lord-Keeper *Finch* voted a Traytor.— This Year, the Rev. Mr. ANDREW MARVEL, Lecturer of *Hull,*

failing

1641 Henry Barnard, 2	}	Rob. (*or* Rich.) Robinſon
[*w*] *John Rogers*		Thomas Lawrence
1642 Thomas Raikes, 2	}	William Raikes
[*x*] *Richard Wood*		James Lupton

ſailing over the *Humber,* in Company with Madam SKINNER, of *Thornton-College,* and a young beautiful Couple, who were going to be wedded ; a ſpeedy Fate prevented the deſigned happy Union, thro' a violent Storm, which overſet the Boat, and put a Period to all their Lives; Nor were there any Remains of them, or the Veſſel, ever after found, tho' earneſtly sought for, on diſtant Shores!

[*w*] On the 12th of *May,* the noble Earl of *Strafford* was brought to the Scaffold on *Tower-Hill:* Where ſuch was his comely Deportment, Chriſtian Behaviour, and melting Speeches, that (a few Days after he was beheaded) the Great and Venerable Archbiſhop *Usher* told his Majeſty, (who wept upon the mournful Occaſion) *He had ſeen many Perſons die ; but never perceiv'd ſo white a Soul return to its Maker.*—The King, arriving at *York,* (in his Progreſs to *Scotland,* and finding both Armies ſtanding, he ſent Sir *Jacob Ashley,* and Captain *Legg,* to *Hull,* in order to diſcharge what Forces were therein: The Earl of *Northumberland,* and Lord *Conway,* were preſent, on the Occaſion, which was about the Beginning of *July.* On the 12th, Sir *Thomas Glemham,* the Governour, (being on his Departure for *London*) deliver'd the Charge, which he had been intruſted with, up to the Mayor: Who then plainly found, that the King had no Intention to infringe on his Authority; but purely to defend the Town, by a valiant Captain, expert in the Arts of War. After which, the Inſtruments of Battle, lately carry'd againſt the *Scots,* were brought back, and replac'd in the King's Magazine. His Majeſty, accompany'd by the Prince of *Wales,* the Palſgrave of the *Rhine,* Duke of *Lennox,* Marqueſs of *Hamilton,* and other Lords (in his Journey from *Scotland,* where he had made vaſt Conceſſions, and even preferr'd his very Enemies) reviſited *York,* on the 20th of *November ;* but ſoon ſet out from thence to his Palace at *White-Hall,* where he arrived the 25th of the ſame Month.

[*x*] The Bulwarks, erected about 10 Years before, were now faced with Brick, to a conſiderable Thickneſs, with Port-Holes, which were to be placed towards the Haven, and the River *Humber.*—The Parliament was now riſen to an exceſſive Height of Greatneſs: But thro' their Impeachment of the Bishops, (whom they ſent to the *Tower*) and their Pretences in diſcovering *Secret Plots,* (eſpecially the Cauſe of the Irish Rebellion, begun the laſt Year) which they could not make out to their Reputation ; their Glory
would

would foon have been upon the Decline, had not the King (thro'
the unhappy Advice of the Lord *Digby*, and fome write of the Queen
too) endeavour'd to feize fix of their Members, which gave them
new Advantages.　His Majefty accordingly impeach'd of High
Treafon the Lord *Kimbolton ;* with Sir *Arthur Hafterigg, Pym,
Hampden, Hollis* and *Strode*, five Commoners: Nay, he went himfelf into the Houfe, fat in the Speaker's Chair, and demanded thofe
Members, who were now abfconded.　This occafion'd them to complain of a *Breach of Priviledge !*　By which, in a few Days, thofe
they had corrupted, were fo far alienated from the King, that he
became reduc'd to a low Condition.　The Parliament reprefented
him as Popifhly inclin'd ; and that he had a Defign to cut all their
Throats!　Sir *Henry Vane*, a buftling Secretary, wrote terrible Letters, of fuch like Stuff, to feveral Towns, with an Addition, That the
King defign'd to bring them under a foreign Power.　One of his
Scrolls, dated *Jan.* 13. coming to the Magiftrates of *Hull*, was the
Occafion of their fecuring the Catholicks, and arming the Inhabitants from the King's Magazine, as tho' indeed they had been upon
the Brink of Deftruction.　Notwithftanding fuch Infinuations, three
noted Perfons, Mr. *Cartwright*, Mr. *Dobfon*, and Mr. *Parkins*, ftood
firm to the Intereft of his Majefty : Nor was it to be wonder'd at,
if (as the Parliament thought, whofe 6 Members were, in popular
Triumph, brought back to their Houfe) the King fhould have a
Defign to fecure the Tower of *London, Portfmouth*, and *Hull.* But
they fet about to prevent him in the two former ; and, (having, by
their own Authority, order'd away to the Tower a Part of the aforefaid Magazine) fent one of their Members, Sir *John Hotham*, as Governour, to feize upon the latter.　To this Intent, the Knight, attended by his Son, raifed 3000 Men, and march'd towards it : But
the loyal Mayor prevented their Enterance, by ordering the Bridges
to be drawn up, the Gates fhut, the Cannons charg'd, the Inhabitants to appear in Arms upon the Walls, and threatening to fire at
them, as Enemies, if they did not retire at a diftance.　Upon Sir
John's fending an Account thereof to the Parliament, an Order was
made, for delivering up the Town to him as Governour, under Pain
of High-Treafon.　Thus being furrender'd, a War was begun by
the Commons, who infulted the Bifhops ; and abufed the King himfelf, by inflaming the People againft them.　Hereupon his Majefty,
attended by feveral Nobles, rode towards the Northern Parts : But,
whilft he was upon his Journey, his Enemies fent Expreffes, to the
Magiftrates of the Eaftern Ports, to deny him Enterance : For this
Reafon, 200 Men were ordered to *Scarborough*, 600 to *Tinmouth*,
and 1000 to *Newcaftle. March* the 18th, the King came to *York.*
The 7th of *April* his *Qualify'd* Printers fet up their Preffes in a Houfe

T

(fome

(fome Time after ufed as the King's *Mint*) then belonging to Sir *Henry Jenkins*, in the Minfter Yard.   The 22d, the King fent to *Hull* the Duke of *York*, with the young Elector Palatine, and fome Attendants, among whom were the Earl of *Newport*, Lord *Willough-by*, and Sir *Thomas Glemham*, under Colour to view the Town. It was on a Market-Day, when they entered therein, along with the Country People. The Mayor, at firft, was ignorant of their Coming; but, upon their Appearance in publick, he, accompany'd with Sir *John Hotham*, fplendidly entertain'd 'em, according to their high Rank, both at Dinner and Supper :   And the Governour invited them to dine with him on the Feftival of St. *George*, which was the Day after. The King (refolving to have Poffeffion of a Place, which had lately refufed the Earl of *Newcaftle*, as Governour, commiffion'd by him, when the Parliament had fo ftrangely exerted themfelves ; and who, upon his Landing, being feized as a Criminal, was hur-ry'd before the Mayor, and vilely infulted by Captain * *Hotham*, the Son of Sir *John*) rode from *York*, towards *Hull*, early that Morning, attended by two or three hundred Perfons, fome of them Gentle-men of the County, and the reft his Servants. About 10 o'Clock, Sir *Lewis Dives* was fent before, by the King, to the Governour, (then complementing his Princely Guefts) with a Meffage, *That his Majefty defign'd to dine with him that Day ; for that he was but a few Miles off, attended by fome of the Nobility and Gentry.* Sir *John*, much furpriz'd, retir'd to his Clofet ; where, fending for Alderman *Pelham*, a Member of Parliament, it was immediately agreed, to deny the King Enterance, by fhutting up the Gates, and placing a Guard over the Mayor and Burgeffes. Thus order'd, a Meffage was fent by the Governour to his Majefty, defiring him, *Not to approach the Town ; becaufe he could not, without betraying the Truft repofed in him by the Parliament, fet open the Gates to fo great a Company, with which his Majefty was attended.* But the King, tho' furpriz'd, kept on his Way ; whilft the Meffenger rode with Speed before him, and told the Governour of his Majefty's Approach. Upon which, he order'd the Bridges to be drawn up, the Gates fhut, the Inhabitants

to

---

* He was a great Incendiary : For upon the Earl of *Newcaftle's* Departure, he inftigated the Inhabitants, by ftrange invented Stories of his own : He told them, that the Lord *Dunbar* kept many Horfes, and armed Men, under Ground, in fpacious Vaults, and gloomy Caverns, in order to furprize them, whilft they were afleep ! That Mr. TERWHIT, a Gentleman of *Lincolnfhire*, was to affift them with 300 Men, cover'd over [*like the Ghoft in* HAMLET] with complete Armour of burnifh'd Steel ! That the *Spaniards* were expected, with a mighty Fleet, to aid thofe terrible Champions ! and therefore he thought it neceffary to plunder the Royalifts, while they were fearching for Letters, Caldrons, and Grid-Irons, prepared to ruin and torment them !—By thefe Infinuations, the Train'd Bands were increafed to 800 in Number.

Drawn and Reprinted by M. C. Peck & Son, Hull, from the Original Engraving.

to be confin'd in their Houses 'till Sun-Set, the Cannons charg'd, and the Soldiers to appear in Arms on the Walls. At 11 o'Clock, the King, coming to *Beverley-Gate*, call'd for the Governour, and demanded Enterance. Sir *John* roughly answer'd, *As he was intrusted by the Parliament, he could not grant it:* And yet smoothly, with feigned Loyalty, desired, *That his Actions might not be misinterpreted; for he meant nothing, in this Denyal, but for the Kingdom's Good, and that of his Majesty!* Pray, *said the King*, by what Authority do you thus behave yourself? *By the Order of both Houses of Parliament*, reply'd Sir *John.* Read, or show it, *said his Majesty:* Or mention the Time it was made? But no satisfactory Answer being given, the King ask'd, Whether the Mayor had seen it? *No*, answer'd the Governour, *I scorn he shou'd.* Upon which, the King, calling out to the Mayor, demanded him to give him Enterance: But he, *(now turn'd Dissembler)* fell on his Knees, Tears running down his Cheeks, "My Liege *said he*, how glad should I be "to obey you, were it in my Power: But, alas! both I, and the "Inhabitants are guarded, as well as the Gates; where Soldiers "stand, with drawn Swords, having Orders to take away the Lives "of those Persons, who shall dare attempt to open them." Sir *John* then told his Majesty, *If he pleased to enter with* 12 *Persons, he should be welcome:* But the King said, *No, Sir* John, *They are too little a Number to attend my Person: But suffer only* 30 *to enter with me, and I shall be satisfy'd.* This being deny'd, *Come hither to me, Sir* John, (said his Majesty) *let us confer a little while together: Assure yourself, on the Word of your King, you shall have a safe Return.* But the Governour made a wretched Excuse, why he could not condescend. *Well*, (answer'd his Majesty) *this unparallel'd Action of your's, Sir* John, *will produce a very dismal Consequence: After such an Indignity, I must both proclaim (and proceed against) you, as a Traytor: Your Disobedience, I am afraid, will be the Occasion of many Miseries, and much Bloodshed; which you may prevent, in performing the Duty of a faithful Subject: Therefore think seriously of it; and thereby prevent the Cause of numberless Calamities, which must lie at your Charge!* The Princes, and Nobles, who were within the Town, finding they could not do any Good, went out to his Majesty, at one o'Clock, and had a great Consultation. At 5, the King call'd again to Sir *John*, and offer'd to pardon him for all that was past, if he would but admit him with 20 Attendants; desiring him, to take an Hour's Time, to consider of it: But the Knight still persisting in his Denyal, the King order'd two Heralds to proclaim this pretended Governour a Traytor; and that those, who obey'd him, should be esteem'd guilty of High-Treason.

This

This being perform'd, and his Majesty enraged, he cry'd out, *Fling the Traytor over the Wall, throw the Rebel into the Ditch;* But none regarding thefe Words, the affronted Monarch, and his Retinue, were oblig'd to return to *Beverley* that Night. The next Morning, his Majesty fent a Herald, with 3 Noblemen, to the Governour, with a-full Pardon, upon his Compliance; but in vain: So that the King, riding to *York,* wrote from thence a Letter of Complaint to the Parliament. But they, instead of regarding his Majesty, justify'd the Governour, as a loyal Perfon; afferting, That the King's proclaiming him a Traytor, was a Breach of their Priviledge, oppofite to the Liberty of the Subjeéts, and the Laws of the Land: Therefore declared for the Militia, which they foon fet on foot. Upon the King's obtaining a Guard for his Perfon, by Confent of the Gentlemen of *Yorkshire,* on the 12th of *May;* the Commons voted against it, on the 19th. However, many of both Houfes came to attend his Majesty, (particularly the Lord-Keeper *Littleton*) for which the Parliament incapacitated them, as Members, for the future. On the 13th of *June,* feveral Lords engaged to stand by the King; and, in the fame Month, fome thoufands of men met his Majcsty, near *York,* to whom the King then declared his Intentions: On the other Hand, the Parliament feiz'd the Fleet, which his Majesty thought to have fecur'd. About the latter End of the Month, the Queen, who had been forc'd beyond Sea, fent a little Ship, named the *Providence,* into *Humber,* with 16 Pieces of Cannon, and Store of Ammunition, for the King's Service. With thefe, the Forces, being partly armed, proceeded to befiege *Hull:* They turn'd the Streams of the Canals another Way; and stopt Provifions from coming into the Town. On the 3d of *July,* his Majesty came to *Beverley,* attended by 3000 Foot, and 1000 Horfe: Who, to encourage the Siege, fent fome Soldiers into *Lincolnshire,* to stop the Intercourfe of Provifions to the Befieged; for which Reafon, the King order'd a Fort to be built at *Haffel* Cliff, and another at *Paul,* where Cannons were placed. In the mean while, Sir *John Hotham* order'd a great Part of the Charter-Houfe to be blown up, together with the Houses at *Myton;* becaufe the Royalists fhould never have them in Poffeffion to aét against him: Who, yet, hearing that his Majesty was refolv'd to march with his Army to the Walls of *Hull,* fent three Meffengers, alternately, to befeech him, to defist from fuch an Enterprize, against his faithful Subjeéts, who refolved to continue fo, whilst they had Breath! But, as the King had no particular Notion of his Loyalty; fo he fecur'd each Perfon, who brought the Errand. This fo enflam'd the Knight, that, calling a Council of War, it was agreed, The Sluices fhould be immediately pull'd up; and to

cut

cut the Banks of *Hull* and *Humber*, whereby the Country fhould be laid under Water. This dreadful Performance proved fuch an incredible Damage, that the Parliament, upon Sir *John's* Requeft, promised to repair it, at the Expence of the King's Party. To his prefent Affiftance, they fent him down many Soldiers by Sea, who landed fafe on the 10th of *July*. The next Day, one of their cruizing Men of War took the King's Packet-Boat, in which were Colonel *Ashburnham*, Sir *Edward Stradling*, with others, who were carrying Meffages to the Queen in *Holland:* They were committed to Prifon, and the Letters fent to the Parliament.   The King's long Pinnace, loaden with Cannon and Ammunition for *Lincolnshire*, meeting with Captain *Piggot's* Ship, would not fubmit to be taken ; but fought 'till fhe receiv'd 100 Shot, and then funk to the Bottom. The Captains *Horner*, *Vaughan*, *Newton*, and * others, failing in an open Boat to *Lincolnshire*, were brought Prifoners to *Hull:* From whence the Cannons continually thunder'd from the Walls; which were return'd by the King's Batteries. The Townfmen, failing in their Ardency; Sir *John*, wonderful in Invention, ftimulated them with a new-difcover'd Plot: That the King had hired feveral wicked Men to fet fire to *Hull*, in various Places, near the Middle of a prefixed Night: Then, while the Inhabitants were employ'd in quenching the Flames, the Town was to be ftorm'd ; and every Man, Woman, and Child, to perifh by the Sword! By this Contrivance, their Courage increafed, fo as to venture to fally forth, particularly 500 at one time, under Sir *John Meldrum*, at the latter End of *July ;* and at other times, with fuch Succefs, as to kill, put to Flight, and take Prifoners, many of the Befiegers. The Earl of *Newport*, (whom the King left to carry on the Blockade, whilft he went to engage new Friends in other Parts) was fhot, by a Cannon-Ball, from the Walls, into a Ditch, where he would have perifh'd, had not timely Relief been afforded him. Upon the King's Return to *Beverley*, a Petition was prefented him, from the Parliament, to defire him, to disband his Army, and return amongft 'em. But the King refus'd to hearken to thofe Men, who had raifed an
Army

---

* *Amongft them was the gallant Lord* Digby, *who difcover'd himfelf to Sir* John Hotham, *trufting his Life to the Generofity of the Governour : Which, with Arguments ufed againft the Behaviour of the Parliament, with a Promife of the King's Mercy and Favour, fo prevail'd with the Knight, that he promifed the Delivery of the Town to his Majefty. But one intervening Accident, or another, prevented it ; And it proved of ill Confequence to the Governour, when it came to the Ears of the Parliament.*

Army againſt him, commanded by the Earls of *Eſſex* and *Bedford;* whom he knew to be Enemies both to him, and all his faithful Adherents.   As he found, by Report of the Earl of *Newport,* that it was impoſſible to take *Hull,* for want of Men of War, he order'd the Siege to be rais'd on the 27th of *July,* review'd the Army at *Beverley,* and march'd among them, into *York,* with the Cannon and Ammunition.——Captain *Hotham,* ſoon after, with a ſtrong Party, ravag'd the Royaliſts, in the Country : But upon the well-known *Woulds,* near *Malton,* being attack'd by Sir *Thomas Glemham,* received ſuch a Bruſh, that he was glad to run home, and ſcarcely would venture out of *Hull* for a conſiderable Time after. In *Aug.* the King being at *York,* publiſh'd, on the 12th, a Declaration, *That he deſign'd to ſet up the Royal Standard at* NOTTINGHAM :   And this he did, upon the 22d. The 20th of *September,* he enter'd into *Shrewsbury.*   The Fight at *Powick-Bridge* was three Days after, headed by Prince *Rupert,* to the King's Advantage; who returned to *Shrewsbury,* where his Strength increaſed; and from thence went towards *London.* On the 23d of *October,* was ſought the Battle of *Edghill,* in *Warwickſhire,* where the brave ROBERT BERTIE, Earl of *Lindſey,* received ſo many Wounds, as occaſion'd his Death. Being carry'd out of the Field, he was brought into a little Cottage, and laid upon Straw ! When the Officers of the Parliament Army (by Order of their General, who thought to have ſeen him alſo) came to viſit him, they found him bleeding, in a plentiful Manner ; and yet his Looks were full of Vigour and Sweetneſs! He bid 'em tell the Earl of *Eſſex,* " To caſt himſelf at the King's Feet : And " (*added he*) my approaching Death, as I am apt to think will be " ſoon, does not half ſo much pierce my Heart, as to perceive ſo " many Gentlemen, ſome of you my former Friends and Acquaint- " ance, now engag'd in ſo foul a Rebellion againſt our Sovereign !" The Spectators, both charm'd and confounded, withdrew; and reported his Words to the Commander, he ſent him the beſt Surgeons of the Army, out of Reſpect to his diſtinguiſh'd Merit; But in the opening of his Wounds, this Great and Heroick Nobleman expired.——During theſe Tranſactions, WILLIAM CAVENDISH, Earl of *Newcaſtle,* was ſuccefsful in the North: His Army was more numerous, than the Forces commanded by the Lord *Fairfax.* He made Captain *Hotham* retreat; who pretended to ſtop his Paſſage at *Piercebridge,* beyond the River *Tees.* He march'd afterwards to *York,* which was then put into a Poſture of Defence, under Sir *Thomas Glemham,* Governour, who kindly received him; and to whom he preſented ſome Pieces of Cannon, and Ammunition. He drove Lord *Fairfax* and Captain *Hotham* out of *Tadcaſter;* and took *Brad-*

ford

1643 Thomas Raikes, 3 ⎱   John Rawſon
[*y*] *Robert Ripley*   ⎰   Henry Metcalf

ford by Storm. Thus was he frequently proſperous, but not altogether; elſe he might have gotten Poſſeſſion of *Leeds*, which Sir *Thomas Fairfax*, (Son of the Lord of that Name) after a conſiderable Loſs, did at laſt moſt valiantly obtain. A ſmall Sketch of which Town, with the Inſcriptions in the Churches, the Reader may find, Pag. 17 of my Travels, towards the latter End of the Second Volume of the Antiquities of *Yorkshire*, very faithfully collected.

[*y*] The Mayor, being now on the Parliament's Side, was this Year, alſo, order'd to continue in his Office, by the Governour contrary to antient Charters. To give a further Light into the War, in which this Hiſtory ſeems to be a Principal Part, it is here neceſſary to take Notice, Who were friends, or Enemies, to the King, or Parliament. On the Part of his Majeſty, were Prince RUPERT, his Nephew ; JAMES STUART, Duke of *Richmond ;* WILLIAM SEYMOUR, Marquefs of *Hertford ;* THOMAS WRIOTHESLEY, Earl of *Southampton ;* ROBERT SIDNEY, Earl of *Leiceſter ;* JOHN DIGBY, Earl of *Briſtol ;* the Earl of *Newcaſtle*, as before-mention'd : With the Lord-Keeper *Littleton*, Secretary *Nicholas*, and other Officers of State. For the Parliament, were ALGERNON PIERCY, Earl of *Northumberland ;* WILLIAM CECIL, Earl of *Salisbury ;* ROBERT RICH, Earl of *Warwick ;* HENRY VANE, the Elder ; the valiant CAPEL, Earl of *Eſſex ;* the Lord BROOK, *&c.* On *Jan.* 19. was fought the deſperate Battle of *Leskerd*, or *Bradock-Down ;* where the Victory was won, on the King's Side, under Sir *Ralph Hopton*. The Parliament was now reſolv'd to obtain Revenge : And ſending Word to Sir *John Hotham*, and his Son, at *Hull*, to raiſe Forces, ravage the Country, and ruin the Royaliſts ; they accordingly obey'd the Command, burning and deſtroying all before them ! I take it, that from hence came the Deſtruction of *Cawood* Caſtle ; firſt built, as Tradition informs us, by King *Athelſtan :* The ſad Ruins of which are now to be ſeen, as I have imitated (with the Church, in which that once famous Prelate *Mountain* lies interred) by a ſmall Sketch, (Pag. 61. of the Travels) in my Second Volume of the Antiquities of *Yorkshire :* An Edifice, that once had been a ſtately Palace for the Archbiſhops of the Province, ſituated on the pleaſant Banks of the River *Ouſe*, where the Streams are more clear, by the Proximity of the Tide. Among the allow'd Pranks of Father and Son, one Deſign of their's was to ſeize *Scarborough*, a remarkable and beautiful Town, upon the Sea-Coaſts : To accompliſh which, they ſent two Ships thither, with arm'd Soldiers, provided
with

with 10 Cannon, 4 Barrels of Powder, and 4 of Bullets : ·But Sir *Hugh Cholmley*, Governour of *Scarborough* Castle, (who was once on the Parliament Side ; and, perceiving what they drove at, had return'd to his Allegiance) having private Intelligence thereof, came down by Night, and (consulting with the Magistrates) suffer'd the Vessels to enter peaceably into the Port : Which they had no sooner done, but the Knight, with his Assistants, seiz'd the Men ; and arm'd themselves with what was prepar'd against the Inhabitants ; who also planted the Cannon against the Arrival of Captain *Hotham*, and his Forces. Not long after they came, thinking all the Way, of nothing but Success ; and approaching within Shot, the Artillery and Muskets were discharged, which killed 20 of them : Then, being furiously attack'd, 30 more were taken Prisoners, and the rest put to Flight ; the Captain scouring homewards, amongst them, to tell the pitiful News thereof to his Father. About this time, *Clifford's* Tower, in *York*, was repairing, from its weak and antient Condition, and made habitable for Officers and Soldiers, to withstand a Siege. The Beginning of *February*, Prince *Rupert* took *Cirencester.*   It was not long after, that several Letters were written to Sir *John Hotham*, at *Hull ;* pathetically setting forth, the Innocency of the King, and Tyranny of the Parliament : That his Denyal of Enterance to his Majesty would be the Occasion of a long Civil War ; which it was *yet* in his Power to prevent, and make the Kingdom happy, if he would but deliver the Town into the Hands of his Majesty, who was ready to grant him full Pardon for what was past. These Epistles began to work successfully upon the Governour. On the 19th, the Queen landed on *Bridlington-Key*, attended by several Commanders ; and brought with her Money, Arms, and Ammunition : Here she was visited by Sir *Marmaduke Langdale*, Sir *John Ramsden*, and even by Captain *Hotham ;* who, being sent by his Father, to know what Mercy and Favour he might expect, consulted the Affair with the Earl of *Newcastle*, and was admitted to kiss her Majesty's Hand. Sir *Hugh Cholmley* also waited upon her Majesty ; and deliver'd up *Scarborough* Castle, for the King's Use ; But as, by his late dutiful Behaviour, he seem'd worthy to command that almost impregnable Fortress ; so the Earl of *Newcastle* caus'd him to be re-instated in his Office of Governour. The Queen, staying at *Bridlington* near a Fortnight, waiting for a Guard, (absolutely refusing to be conducted by the Lord *Fairfax*) had like to have lost her Life, by two of the Parliament Ships (which unperceiv'd, in the Night Time, had enter'd the Bay) firing upon the Town, whereby two Bullets fell upon the House where she was, piercing even to the Bottom ; And Her Majesty being forc'd to take Shelter in the Ditch, as she was now and then leaving the Place, the Bullets flew

so

fo very thick, that a Serjeant was slain near her Perfon: And probably they might have ended her Days, had not the Reflux of the
Tide, and the Threatenings of the Dutch Admiral Sir *Martin Van
Trumpe,* who brought the Queen over, reftrained their Fury, and
attended her to *York,* with the Earl of *Montrofs,* (who came Poft
from *Scotland* with 100 Horfe) the Duke of *Richmond,* and others,
where fhe was royally feafted by Sir *Edmund Cooper,* Lord-Mayor.
Her Majefty, having fent the Lady BLAND to *Hull,* to confer with
the Governour, he confented to every Thing propos'd, fign'd Papers, and fent Letters by her to the Queen. The Lady fucceeding
thus far, attempted to win the * Vicar of the High-Church over to
her Party: But the harmlefs Minifter was fo prepoffefs'd on the Side
of the Parliament, that with up-lifted Hands and Eyes, he anfwer'd
the Lady, *How can you think that I should encourage an Army of
Papifts, who, by fighting againft* Them, *oppofe the* PROTESTANT
RELIGION? *'Tis vifible, Madam, that Heaven appears in their
righteous Caufe, by giving Strength to their Arms, and difcovering
the Confpiracies formed againft them!* So much was he deluded on
the one hand, by how much his Zeal might be commended on the
other; even tho' there might be no fuch Danger. There rather
feem'd greater Jeopardy from the King's Enemies among the *Scots;*
who (as the brave Marquefs of *Montrofs* had truly told the Queen)
were ready to join the English Malecontents, to the Subverfion of
the Epifcopal Church, and the late fetled Conftitution of the Land.
The Lady, finding him inflexible, departed; and, going to the
Queen, told her what Succefs fhe had met with from the Governour.
About this Time, the Earl of *Newcaftle,* had obliged Lord *Fairfax*
to retire to *Pontefract.* In the Beginning of *March,* there being fome
Talk of a Pacification, the Corporation fent to Mr. *Pelham,* then
Member of Parliament, to get them included in a general Pardon.
But the Nation was not yet for Unity. On *Sunday,* the 19th, the
Battle of *Hopton-Heath,* near *Stafford* was fought; where the brave
Earl of *Northampton* was slain, who would not (as he had faid) accept of any Quarter from the Hands of fuch notorious Rebels.——
The Queen left *York* on the 6th of *June:* But, before that, fhe had
fent the Lord *Digby* to the Governour of *Hull:* Where we'll leave
them tranfacting Bufinefs, whilft other almoft immediate Actions
are declared.——On the 17th of *June,* Prince *Rupert* was fuccefsful
againft the Earl of *Effex,* whofe very Quarters (near *Thame,* about
10 Miles from *Oxford*) he attack'd, with uncommon Bravery.——The
29th, the Earl of *Newcaftle* routed the Lord *Fairfax's* Forces at *Ad-
derton-Moor:* kill'd 4 or 500 Men; took feveral Pieces of Ordnance,
with many Prifoners; forc'd him, and Sir *Thomas* his Son, to fly to

* The Rev. Mr. WILLIAM STYLES.*Bradford,*

U

Bradford, and then to *Leeds*.   After which, they travell'd towards
Selby: But the Royaliſts, ſtriving to prevent them paſſing the River,
kill'd ſeveral ; obliging the Lord *Fairfax* to fly to *Wreſſel* Caſtle,
and from thence to *Hull.* His Son, being ſeparated from him, was
forced to go to *Carlton* Ferry, *Thorn*, the Devizes of *Hatfield*, and ſo
to *Crowl;* Where, reſting an Hour, and hearing he was purſu'd by
ſome of Colonel *Portington's* Men, he made haſte to get over the
Trent, juſt as they had got to *Anthrop* Ferry : He ſcarce was mounted, when he had like to have been ſeiz'd by another Party from
Gainsborough ; by which Diſaſter, he loſt his Plate, with other valuable Things : But the Sharpneſs of his Spurs, with the Swiftneſs
of the Horſe, brought him ſafe to *Barton ;* from whence he ſail'd to
Hull, much terrify'd, weary'd, and almoſt ſpent with the Loſs of
Blood. His Father was made Governour of this Town not long after : But let us return to ſee how Sir *John Hotham* was prevail'd
upon, by the Arguments of the Lord *Digby*. That gallant Nobleman diſplay'd the unjuſtifiable Actions of the Parliament, in regard both to the King and Realm : *And as to your part, Sir* John,
(ſaid he) *ſee here what is intended for your Deſtruction!* Upon
which, pulling out of his Pocket ſome intercepted Letters from
Fairfax to the Commons, with their Anſwers ; the Knight, who well
knew the Characters, was ſo fully ſatisfy'd, that he treated with him
to deliver up the Town on the 28th of *Auguſt.*—The Parliament,
who had Spies almoſt in every Corner, receiving ſome little Infor-
mation, began to be jealous of Sir *John Hotham's* Deſign. But, to be
more certain, they employ'd one 𝕾𝖆𝖑𝖙𝖒𝖆𝖗𝖘𝖍, his Relation, to make
him a Viſit to *Hull*, as one of their itinerant Preachers ; that thereby, he might pump out the whole Matter. The Deſign ſucceeded :
For that Holderforth, after feigned Salutation, ſeeming to lament,
by crying both againſt the abominable Sins of the Nation, and the
wicked Incroachments of the Parliament, he moved Sir *John* to
give Ear to his Tale ; and, by approving his Diſcourſe, was taken
in the Net, prepared for him. The Teacher, following his Diſcourſe,
wrought upon the Knight, that he became even weak, inſomuch as
to give Hints of the Deſign : Upon this, the other, with feigned Sanctity, promiſed, upon his Salvation, to further the Attempt, ſo he was
but let into the Secret, and would never reveal it to any Mortal living ! This occaſion'd the Opening of every Particular ; which the
other immediately diſpatch'd, by a Meſſenger, to the Parliament ;
who order'd him 2000*l.* for the Diſcovery. And this was Sir *John's*
pious Couſin *Saltmarsh !*—Which ſhould warn every Perſon, in
all Stations of Life, to take great Care how they are *Couzen'd* by
Hypocrites in Religion, when they have the leaſt Reaſon to think,
(but

(but not otherwife) that thofe Men make fuch a Bleffed Calling a Cloak only to their Knavery, purely for Intereft Sake. The Governour, little dreaming of the Treachery of his *trufty* and *well-beloved Kinfman*, foon after (by Command from the Parliament) fent his Son, along with his Troop, to *Nottingham*, to join Forces with Colonel *Cromwell*, and the Lord *Gray:* But many Hours had not paft, after his Arrival; when, about 2 in the Morning, he was fent to Prifon, by fecret Order of thofe Commanders, on Pretence, that he defign'd to betray that Town to the King's Party. The Captain, defperately enflam'd with Anger, fent for his Man *John Kaye*, and folemnly ask'd him, If he would ferve him faithfully, without revealing his Secrets? The Servant readily gave him a Promife; but that not fufficing, the Mafter tender'd him his Oath, faying, He would prefer him for his Fidelity. " Now, *faid the Captain*, repair " to the Queen at *Newark:* Tell her, I am in Prifon; from whence " I am fpeedily to be fent either to the Parliament, or the Earl of " *Effex:* Defire her therefore, to fend Forces to releafe me, as I am " carry'd along: For which I fhall think myfelf not only obliged " to prove her conftant Servant; but will affure her, that I'll do my " Endeavour to obtain, for the King's Service, the Surrender of *Hull*, " *Beverley*, and alfo the City of *Lincoln.*" The Servant went accordingly, and deliver'd his Meffage: The Queen anfwer'd, *She took his Offers very kindly: But*, added fhe, *he might have done fome of thefe things long ago, and prevented his prefent Captivity: And pray, Friend, how may I be affur'd that you are the Captain's Meffenger?* The Man reply'd, "By this Token, that you receiv'd a Letter from " his Father, by him, when you were at *Bridlington.*" *'Tis very true*, faid the Queen; *and I will be as good as my Word, in procuring a Pardon for him, and Sir* John, *with other Favours that I promifed them: Tell him alfo, I shall do my utmoft to releafe him from the Hands of his Enemies.* The Servant return'd with this fatisfactory Anfwer to the Captain: But he foon after, finding an Opportunity to make his Efcape, fled to *Lincoln;* difcourfed with the Lord *Willoughby*, Captain *Purfoye*, and others; and then pofted to *Hull.* Here, acquainting his Father with his Ufage, he fell into a violent Paffion againft the Commons: No better Names, than *Rogues, Rafcals*, and *Anabaptift Dogs*, he gave to *Cromwell*, the Secret Committee and Parliament. This he did, in publick, to outbrave the Matter; and obtain'd a Council of War to be call'd, confifting of Sir *Edward Rhodes*, Sir *Thomas Remington*, Col. *Legard*, Serjeant-Major *Godwich;* with the Captains *Anlaby, Billops*, and *Overton*, &c. who unanimoufly agreed, that *Cromwell* fhould be principally complain'd of, to the Parliament. The Inftrument fet forth, *That the greateft Indignity, which could ever be offer'd to any*
                                                                Perfon,

Perfon, was done to the Governour's Son; and, thro' him, to them, who muft now take Care of their own Safety: That it was very hard to be efteem'd Traytors; by the King, for the fake of others; who fhould endeavour to dig a Pit for them, into which they might happen to fall themfelves: That about 40 Villains fhould break into the Captain's Chamber, rob him of 150 Pounds, take him out of his Bed, imprifon him in the common Gaol for 4 days, not to allow him Liberty to write to his Father, or the Parliament; was, furely, such vile Ufage, that no Age, or Hiftory, could parallel ! And all this done, without any Order from the Generals, by Cromwell, *and another Perfon, thro' a Meffage faid to be brought them from the Secret Committee, by an Anabaptift of* Lincoln, *named* Watfon; *which Story, with them, could not merit Belief.* But the fubtle Commons, inftead of anfwering the Complaint, fent privately to Captain *Mayor,* (who commanded a Man of War, call'd the *Hercules,* then lying in the Haven) with a Letter alfo to Sir *Matthew Boynton,* (Brother-in-Law to Sir *John Hotham*) requiring them, not only to endeavour, to fill the Town with Jealoufies and Fears; but to confult, with the Magiftrates, how to feize the Governour, his Son, with their Adherents, and fend them up as Prifoners to *London.* On this Advice, Reports were quickly fpread, *That Sir* John Hotham *was for delivering up* Hull *to the Royalifts, who were to be affifted by the* Spaniards; *and then to blow it up about their Ears!* Thefe fearful Reprefentations, caus'd the Corporation to fit up all Night, on the 28th of *June,* by Way of Prevention; and confulting how to feize the Governour, his Son, and others, whom they imagin'd to be concern'd with them. The Defign, being form'd, was thus executed. Captain *Mayor,* before Day-Break, fent 100 ftout Men at Arms, to fecure the Garrifon, with the Block-Houfes: This they perform'd, meeting with fmall Refiftance; except from Col. *Legard:* Who, being furrounded, fubmitted, when he found it in vain to contend. Then 1500 Soldiers, and others, on the Parliament's Side, feizing all the Guards, Gates, Cannons, and Magazine, fecur'd Captain *Hotham;* fet a Watch at his Father's Houfe, to prevent his Efcape; and, at 7 o'Clock, fent a Party to feize him. But the Knight, having Notice, slipt out backwards, attended by 6 of his Life-Guards, habited in the fame red Garments, that belong'd to fome of the Attendants of the late unfortunate Earl of *Strafford.* Thus he, who but a little before rul'd as a Tyrant, was now forc'd to fly like a Criminal: Nay, oblig'd to rob a Man of his Horfe, (who, by Chance, paffed by) in order to make his Efcape. He rode thro' the Guards (who as yet had no Orders to apprehend him) at *Beverley*-Gate, where he had deny'd Enterance to his Sovereign; too swift for his Soldiers, to keep him Company, any farther than the End of

the

the Town, where they were taken Prisoners : And those Cannons, which he had placed to keep the Monarch out, were fired after him, by his Pursuers, to take his Life ; which was reserved for a more slow, but severe Vengeance. His Design was to attain his House at *Scarborough*, which he had taken Care to fortify with Men and Ammunition : For this Reason, he turn'd off from *Beverley* Road to *Sculcotes*, and so proceeded to *Wawn* Ferry : But here his Fate seem'd to be determin'd, in having no Vessel ready to receive him, and the Danger too great to swim over.   What to do, he could not well tell ; but, as it were, throwing off all Manner of Concern, he rode to *Beverley :* Where, (alas! for him) News had been sent to Col. *Boynton*, by his Brother Sir *Matthew*, to secure Sir *John*, if he came that Way. The Knight, uncertain of this, rode into the Town, where he beheld 7 or 800 Soldiers in Arms: So, riding up to the first Company, he commanded them to follow him: They did so, as not yet hearing that he was to be apprehended : But, proceeding further, Colonel *Boynton* suddenly took hold of his Horse's Bridle, saying, *Sir* John, *You are my Prisoner, and one that I once very much respected as being my Kinsman : But now I am oblig'd (tho' with the greatest Reluctance) to pass by all tender Respect, upon that Account, and arrest you as a Traytor to the Common-Wealth.* This was another sort of Relation, different from the sly itinerant Teacher : To whom, with a Sigh, the sorrowful Knight reply'd, *Well, Kinsman, since it is your Pleasure it should be so, I must be content to submit !* But, espying an open Lane near him, he suddenly put Spurs to his Horse, disengag'd himself, and gallop'd away as fast as he could : Upon the Colonel's crying out, *Stop him ! Knock the Traytor down !* a Soldier gave him a desperate Blow on the Side of the Head with his Musket; which dismounted him, in a bleeding Condition : And then he was confin'd in that very House, where his insulted Sovereign had taken up his Lodging, after he was deny'd Enterance into *Hull.* All his own Estate, what his Son was possess'd of, and what immense Riches both had plunder'd from the Royalists, became forfeited to the Parliament : They were presently sent (along with Sir *Edward Rhodes*) on Board Captain *Mayor's* Ship; who, quickly hoisting Sail, in a little time arrived at *London*, where we shall at present leave them, particularly the Father and Son, in their melancholly Imprisonment.—Now the Royalists, who as yet knew nothing of these Misfortunes, were marching towards *Beverley*, (possess'd, by the other Party, after the King's Return to *York*) which they thought to have gain'd, as well as *Hull*, according to Agreement with the *Hothams :* But being unexpectedly oppos'd by Col. *Boynton's* Forces, by which they had some kill'd, with many wounded, and ta-

ken

ken Prisoners, they were oblig'd to retire. The Care of *Hull* was now under a Committee, whom the Parliament thankfully approv'd of, confisting of the Mayor; with *Matthew Boynton, Richard Darley, John Bouchier,* and *William Allenson,* Knights; Mr. *Styles,* and *Johnson,* Clergymen ; also the Aldermen *Roper, Denman, John* and *Henry Barnard.* The Earl of *Kingston,* who ruled in *Gainsborough,* wrote to the Corporation of HULL, to turn them on the King's Side; and that, if they pleas'd to admit him as their Governour, he would engage, for them, to procure his Majesty's Pardon and Favour. The Party was too powerful on the one Side, as to admit of any obliging Answer to be sent to this brave Nobleman: Who, resolving to make the Town a Visit, just as he was stepping into a Boat on the *Trent,* he was cowardly shot dead by a Party of his Enemies, who lay in Ambush near the Side of that River.—And now the Corporation of *Hull* sent an Express to the Parliament, desiring, That the Lord *Fairfax,* (who had been in the Town, with Sir *Thomas,* his Son, since their late ill Success, as before-mention'd) might be their Governour, to defend them, by his Valour and Conduct : To which the Commons soon confented ; commanding him also to raise Forces, proportionable to his Care, in the Defence of such an important Fortress. He did so ; and sent his Son with 25 Troops of Horse, and 2000 Foot, to quarter, at *Beverley,* with Colonel *Boynton's* Forces. But they were scarce setled in the Town, when News came, that the Earl of *Newcastle* was marching to attack them with 15000 Horse and Foot. Upon which, Sir *Thomas Fairfax,* calling a Council of War, they judg'd it necessary to quit the Town, because it was no place of Defence. Scarce had they Time to consider this, before the Earl (who was lately made a Marquess) enter'd with his Forces, Sword in Hand: A desperate Fight ensu'd, that quickly strew'd the Ground with dead Bodies, and made the Channels to run with Blood. The Marquess was victorious, killing hundreds of his Enemies, and pursuing the rest almost to the Gates of *Hull:* After which, returning to *Beverley,* he caus'd the Town to be plunder'd ; and sent to *York* all the Goods and Cattle they could find in, and about it. On the 2d of *September,* the Marquess begun the Siege of *Hull,* with an Army of 15000 Horse and Foot. After Midnight, he began to cast up the Out-Works: He cut off the fresh Waters ; and oblig'd the Market-People, instead of supplying the Town with Provisions, to serve his Camp. At Noon, he caused several Batteries to be raised, notwithstanding the incessant Firing of Cannons, from the Walls, to prevent them ; and then return'd the like Furious Usage upon the Town. On the 5th of *September,* another Work (on which 2 Cannons were placed) was erected on the

Banks

Banks of *Hull:* And over that River a Bridge of Boats was laid, for the greater Conveniency of paffing into *Holderneſs.* On the other hand, the Townſmen raiſed an Eminence to oppoſe them, on the Ruins of the famous * *Michael de la Pole's* Charter-Houſe; where they planted a great Braſs Gun, which daily (with Cannons from the Walls and Block-Houſes) were diſcharged on the Earl's Forces. On the 8th of *September*, about 3 in the Morning, the Royaliſts began another Work, near half a Mile of the Walls: But tho' it was daily batter'd down, it was rais'd up every Night; 'till, at laſt, being fi-niſh'd, it was call'd the *King's Fort.* This proved very terrible to the Inhabitants; becauſe, from ſeveral Cannons, placed thereon, red hot Bullets were frequently ſhot into the Town. And now the Governour gave Orders, That a ſtricter Watch ſhould be kept; that what was combuſtible, in every Houſe, ſhould be placed in the lower Parts; and that Veſſels of Water might be laid before every Door: Then he fix'd two large Culverines on the Work, where the Charter-Houſe ſtood: At which Time, as I ſuppoſe, for greater Conveniency, the Chapel was pull'd down, as mention'd, Page 72. He order'd another Fort to be made, at ſome Diſtance, which flank'd the Royaliſts behind the Banks. Here he hung up Bells, to let the Engineers know, when to Fire: And by theſe active Methods, the Royal Fort, being demoliſh'd, a Period was put to their ſending any more dreadful Preſents of red hot Bullets. The 9th of *September*, the Townſmen ventur'd to attack the Royaliſts, at *Anlaby*, with a-bout 400 Horſe and Foot; but were unſucceſsful, being drove back with Slaughter, and the Loſs of ſeveral Priſoners. Four Days after, the Governour, ordering the Sluices to be open'd, the Country was drown'd for about two Miles. This drove the Royaliſts from the Works, except thoſe of the high Banks; which made them pitch upon that of *Daringham*, as being a dry Place, to erect another:

To

---

* In peruſing over antient Hiſtory, I find it recorded, That the unfortunate William *de la* Pole, Duke of *Suffolk*, beheaded at *Dover*, (as I mention'd, while treating of the Family) was really interr'd in the old Chapel of this Place. He had been eſpouſed to Alice, only Daughter of Maſter Thomas Chaucer, (Son to the celebrated Poet of that Sir-Name) by whom the Manor of *Ewelme*, (or *New-Elme*) in *Oxfordshire*, came to his Family. The beautiful Pariſh-Church, on the Top of a pleaſant Hill, was erected at the Expence of him, and his admirable Dutcheſs; beſides a neat Hoſpital at the Weſt End of it, and another at *Dennington* (or *Dunnington*) Caſtle, in *Barkshire;* both which he endow'd with ſeveral Manors. His illuſtrious Lady ſurvived her unhappy Lord about 25 Years; and then was interr'd on the South-Side of the High-Altar, of the aforeſaid Church, in a fair Alabaſter Tomb. On this Monument, her Effigy is plac'd, having a Crown upon the Head; and the Body, as it were, habited in comely Robes, with other Ornaments. Near which is this petitionary Inſcription: *Orate pro Anima Sereniſſimæ Principiſſæ* ALISSIÆ Sulfolchiæ, *hujus Eccleſiæ Patronæ, quæ obiit viginti Die Menſis* Maij, *Anno Domini Milleſimo quadrin-genteſimo ſeptuageſimo quinto. Litera Dominicali* A.

To oppofe which, the Inhabitants rais'd a Battery, not far from the Walls. Whilft both Sides were thus acting againft one another, a ftrange Accident happen'd. One of the Engineers, belonging to the North Block-Houfe, foolifhly entering into the Ammunition-Room, with a lighted Candle, to get fome Carteridges ; a Spark flew amongft the Powder, and blew up half the Building ; by which he, and 4 others, perifh'd. In another Room, there were 12 Barrels of Gun-Powder; which, if the Fire had reach'd, would have ruin'd the whole Pile, kill'd above 300 Men, and done incredible Damage to the Town itfelf. The Marquefs, having received fome flat Bombs from *York*, very indifferent Ufe was made of them, being difcharg'd either fhort, or wide ; wounding chiefly the Earth, in which, at the falling of each, a Hole was made large enough to bury two Horfes. Then the Marquefs, finding he could not prevail in what he had done, fent a Party to the Weft of *Hull.* By which Gate, the Inhabitants foon rais'd a Fort, made other Works in the Fields, and refolutely oppos'd the King's Party. The 22d, a Faft was kept, by Order of the Governour : The 26th, his Son, with 20 Troops, fail'd over *Humber*, to join with Lord *Willoughby*, and Col. *Cromwell ;* who had lately vifited the Lord *Fairfax* at *Hull*, and held a Confultation with him. The 27th, the Royalifts repair'd the Fort at St. *Paul*, and erected another at *Whitgiftin*, in *Lincolnfhire*, to prevent the Town's getting Supplies ; But could not prevail, because the Men of War, belonging to the Parliament, (which protected the Ships that continually brought the Town frefh supplies of every neceffary Thing from *London*) soon batter'd their Forts down ; and, by Affiftance of Land-Forces, speedily demolifh'd them. The Marquefs had a very great Misfortune, at *Cottingham*, on the 29th : For either by Chance, or Treachery, his Magazine was blown up, and many Persons perifhed. The Country, being laid under Water, by the Spring Tides ; the Royalifts were forc'd from their lower Works. The next Day was a Faft in the Town. That Night the King's Party, having rais'd a Work, within Quarter of a Mile on the North Side of *Hull ;* the Inhabitants, inftead of going to Prayers on the *Friday*, as before order'd, were oblig'd to make an Attack, in which they became victorious, seiz'd on their Tools, and demolifh'd the Fort. On the 11th, Captain *Strickland*, with a ftrong Party, was sent, by the Marquefs, at Day-Break, to attack the Town's Battery, on the Weft Jetty, with the Half-Moon ; whilft the King's General, and his Forces, did the like, to other Sides of the Town. They were not discover'd 'till they began to scale the Place ; and then were fir'd upon from the adjoining Half-Moon. The Royalifts wheel'd about : And tho', by the Narrowness of the Enterance, several loft

their

their Lives ; yet, at length, they afcended to the Top, with their valiant Captain, who demanded a Surrender. But fcarce were the Words out of his Mouth, when he was fhot thro' the Heart by one of the Townfmen ; which fo much encourag'd the reft, that, with incredible Fury, they encounter'd his Soldiers ; tho' on their Side, the courageous Captain *Kirby* loft his Life. *Both Parties fuffered extremely ; but that of the King's had very few remaining to carry the difmal News of the Action to their Head Commander ; who began to have but very indifferent Succefs : For tho' he took the Charter-Houfe Battery, one of his Captains was kill'd, with feveral Men ; and he was oblig'd to retire from it, for want of Force to maintain his Conqueft. The fame Day, Sir *Thomas Fairfax*, and others, obtain'd a Victory over the Royalifts at *Horncaftle, Lincolnshire,* (or rather in an open Field near *Winsby*) killing 300 on the Place. Some write, 4 or 500 Men were slain, 8000 taken Prifoners, 30 Colours feiz'd upon, with 1000 Horfes. In this Engagement, fell the brave Sir *George Bowles*, Lieutenant-Colonel *Markham*, Captain *Vernal*, and Sir *Ingram Hopton :* Either the latter, or *Portington*, had like to have slain *Cromwell* in this Battle. The King's chief General was Sir *William* (afterwards Lord) *Widdrington*, who wrote to the Marquefs, before *Hull,* for Affiftance. But he, on this melancholly News, call'd a Council of War, and rais'd the Siege on the 11th (or according to others, the 12th) of *October*, after he had taken Care to prevent Purfuit, by pulling up the Bridges, opening the Canals, and filling the Ways with Water. Some of his Forces he fent into *Lincolnshire*, and march'd with the rest to *York.* The Townfmen, when they found the Royalifts were departed, came out in great Numbers, and levell'd all their Works. Mean while, Sir *Thomas Fairfax* fpread the Terror of his Arms in feveral Places ; as *Scarborough, Burlington*, and *Malton.* The Lord, his Father, was not fo juft as to make the Townfmen any Satisfaction for thofe unreafonable Sums he had rais'd during the Siege ; which he had promifed fhould faithfully be repaid afterwards : Inftead of which, he ruled as a Petty King, 'till fuch Time that *York* was befieged. But I fhall conclude the Tranfactions of this Year, with obferving, what a terrible Shock it was to the Royalifts, and to the King himfelf, that the *Scots* were now making preparations to join the Parliament's Forces in *England.*

---

*In other Parts of the Land, this Year, happen'd thefe Tranfactions. The 5th of *July*, was the Fight of *Lanfdown*, near *Bath*, where the brave Sir *Bevil Greenvil* was slain, on the King's Side, which however got the Field. The 13th was the Battle of *Roundway Down*, where Sir *William Waller* was routed by his Majefty's Forces ; On which Day, the Queen met the King at *Edghill*, and both took up their Refidence at *Oxford*. The 24th, Prince *Rupert* befieged *Briftol*, which furrender'd the 26th. *September* the 20th, *Newborough* Battle was fought, in which fell the brave *Henry Spencer*, Earl of *Sunderland* ; *Robert Dormer*, Earl of *Caernarvon* ; and *Lucius Cary*, the learned *Lord Falkland*.

X

1644   Nicholas Denman   } William Foxley
[*z*]   *John Ramfden*   } William Thompfon

[*z*] Tho' the Royalifts were of late unfuccefsful in *Yorkshire;* yet ftill they were ftrong in other parts of the Realm: So that the Parliament, finding themfelves declining, invited their Bretheren the *Scots* to their Affiftance. It is not my Defign to exhibit what Arguments were ufed to this End, in the Declarations of thofe People. They crofs'd the River *Tweed* at *Berwick*, on the 15th of *January*; and wrote to Sir *Thomas Glemham*, (who was then at *Alnwick*, in *Northumberland*, with feveral of the Gentry) That *they came to prevent the Ruin of the Proteftant Religion, the King's Perfon and Reputation, intended againft them by Papifts and Epifcopalians.* But the Knight in his Anfwer, gave fufficient Reafons to prove, That in thus making War againft their Sovereign, they were acting contrary to the Laws of GOD and Nations. However, the *Scots* reached *Newcaftle*, on the 28th of *February*; and, on the 4th of *March*, enter'd *Sunderland.* About the 23rd, there were fome Skirmifhes near *Hilton*, between them, and the Marquefs of *Newcaftle.* On the 11th of *April*, Col. *Bellafis*, with his Forces, were overcome, at *Selby*, by Sir *Thomas Fairfax*, and his Men; who took the Colonel Prifoner, feveral Officers, 1600 Soldiers, 4 Pieces of Cannon, 2000 Arms, and above 500 Horfe. *York*, being now in Danger, the Marquefs of *Newcaftle* was obliged to march to the City, and defend it. This gave the *Scots*, (who were 20000 in Number) an Opportunity to join their beloved Friends. All the Way, in their March, with uplifted Hands and Eyes, they told the People, *They only came to fave the King from Popery and Deftruction; but that themfelves were far, very far from hurting the leaft Hair in his Majefty's Head!* Yet, with almoft the fame Breath, they revil'd him, as if he had been the moft violent Papift; declared that the Land was accurfed for his Sake; and confequently, that he was meritorious of Death itfelf. True *Scots* indeed, of thofe Times, when the Itch of Treachery had fo corrupted their Blood, as to break out in the Scab of Rebellion! It was on the 1ft of *May*, thofe Legions joined the Earl of *Manchefter*, *Oliver Cromwell*, and others; who foon after laid Siege to the antient City of *York.* The Lord *Fairfax*, hearing this, left *Hull* to the Government of the Mayor, and fome choice Officers; whilft he, with his Son, rode to affift at its Reduction. But the Parliament Generals, having News of Prince *Rupert's* advancing againft them, ingloriously quitted their Undertaking. On *July* the 2d, was fought the Battle of *Marfton-Moor*: Where, for a while, the Royalifts were victorious; but the Scale of Fortune turn'd chiefly at laft in favour of
Cromwell.

MAYOR *and* SHERIFF *of HULL.*　　CHAMBERLAINS.
1645 John Chambers　　　　} Maurice Lincolne
[*aa*] *William Maifters*　　} John Backhoufe

Cromwell. Prince *Rupert* then march'd towards *Chefter* : But the Marquefs of *Newcaftle*, with his two Sons, Sir *Charles Cavendish* his Brother, the Lords *Falconbridge* and *Witherington*, &c. Dr. *Bramhall* Bifhop of *Londonderry*; *William Vavafour*, and *Francis Mackworth*, Knights ; all thefe fled beyond Sea, and fome remain'd 'till the Reftoration. Thus the North was entirely loft to the Royalifts; whofe Enemies laying again Siege to *York*, it was furrender'd to 'em, on the 16th of *July*. The 19th of *October*, the *Scots* ftorm'd *Newcaftle*, which furrender'd on the 27th. On the 1ft of *December*, Sir *John Hotham*, and his Son, were arraign'd in *Guild-Hall, London*, before the Earl of *Manchefter*, and others, appointed their Judges. The Charge againft them, was, *That they had betray'd the Truft, reposed in them by correfponding with the Queen, the Marquefs of* Newcaftle, *and the Lord* Digby, *to deliver up the Town to the Royalifts, under Pretence of exchanging Prifoners* : And this was proved by intercepted Letters, previous Words, and favourable Actions, to the Enemies of the Parliament : In fhort, they were both convicted, and fentenced to be beheaded. The King's Party in the North endured great Extremities this Year. It will not be amifs to infert the Names of thofe Perfons, in and near *Hull*, who fuffer'd Sequeftration of all their Effects. Of the former, were Alderman *James Watkinfon*; with *William Thornton, Edward Dobson, Thomas Swan, Richard Brown, Matthew Topham, John Audley, Robert Cartwright,* and *Finibarn*, Burgeffes ; who had like to have perifh'd thro' meer Want! The latter, *Michael Wharton, Thomas Rufton* and *Brooks*, Knights ; *James Brooks, Michael Martin, Charles Bacon, Robert Hildyard* and *Holdenby, William Percy* and *Ruftan, Thomas Eaftoft* and *Perrot, John Langvile* and *Dalton*, Gentlemen. The Sums of Money, drain'd from thefe Sufferers, were partly to pay the *Scotch* Plunderers : And the Committee appointed for this vile Purpofe, were the Aldermen *Denham, Barnard, Roper, Popple, Peck* and *Chambers*. This Year the Town petition'd the Parliament, to be freed from Affeffments a while, confidering their late great Expence, in withftanding a Siege ; but no notice was taken of their Complaints : So little do defigning Men regard their moft faithful Friends, when once their own finifter Ends are ferv'd.

[*aa*] The laft Day of the paft Year, was defign'd to be the laft that Sir *John Hotham* had to live, according to Sentence by the Court of War, had not the Houfe of Lords fent him a Reprieve

for

for three Days. The Commons, feemingly incens'd, made an Order againſt the Validity of ſuch Reprieves, without they themfelves had a ſhare in granting them: So that the Son, who was order'd to die the Day after his Father, was now (*Jan.* 1. 164⅘.) brought to the ſcaffold a Day before him: Which ſome imagin'd was a concerted Piece of Malice, to prevent his dying a Baronet. The Captain appear'd with great Courage: *And for the ingrateful Parliament,* ſaid he, *who are the principal Authors of Rebellion, by continuing an unjuſt War againſt their injur'd Sovereign and Fellow-Subjects, I have never been guilty of Treaſon to* THEM: In which indeed he concluded rightly; and 'tis hop'd, repented heartily of what he had acted againſt his Majeſty. The Commons enraged, ſent an Order to the Lieutenant of the Tower, not to ſuffer the Father to live out the Time that the Houſe of Lords had allow'd; as tho' they were deſign'd to be the Inſtruments of Divine Vengeance, according to Sir *John's* Words, when he wiſh'd upon his denying the King Enterance at HULL, *That, if he was not a faithful Subject, the Almighty might bring confuſion both on him, and his Poſterity.* And confus'd he now appear'd, attended by his Confeſſor *Hugh Peters*; who was alſo his Spokeſman, by telling the People, *He had reveal'd himself to him, and confeſſed his Offences againſt the Parliament!* ·Thus, leſs gloriouſly than his valiant Son, did he expire the Day after, being the 2d of *January.* On the 10th, the famous Archbiſhop LAUD, was brought to the Block, where he preach'd his Funeral Sermon from *Heb.* xii. 1, 2. *Let us run with Patience the Race that is ſet before us,* &c. and ſuffered with the greateſt Reſignation. His Body was interr'd in the Church of *All-Hallows, Barking;* and over it was ſaid the Office in the Liturgy, notwithſtanding its Aboliſhment by the Parliament, who Inſtituted a Thing call'd 𝕿𝖍𝖊 𝕯𝖎𝖗𝖊𝖈𝖙𝖔𝖗𝖞. In *March,* the Independents, having great Power in the Houſe of Commons, new-modell'd the Army, calling it, that of the Parliament's alone, without naming the King, and diſplaced many of the Commanders; except *Cromwell,* and Sir *Thomas Fairfax,* who was now made General. *June* 14, was the Battle of *Naſeby,* in *Northamptonſhire,* which proved very unfortunate to the King; and very much thro' the Means of the *Scotch* Earl of *Carnwarth,* who catching hold of his Bridle, aſking him, *If he was running to Death in an Inſtant?* prevented him from making an Attack, which might have given a happy Turn to his Succeſs. *Pontefract* Caſtle was taken about this Time. *Bath* was ſurrender'd too, on the 29th of *July,* to the King, who arrived at *Oxford,* the 29th of *Auguſt;* and from thence march'd to *Hereford,* beſieged by the *Scots,* who retired when
they

1646 William Peck	}	John Kay, *or* Ray
[*bb*] *Francis Dewick*	}	Richard Robinſon
1647 William Dobſon	}	Lancelot Roper
[*cc*] *Robert Robinſon*	}	Joseph Hall

they heard of his Approach.   On the other Hand, *Briſtol*, which the King intended to relieve, was ſurrender'd to the Parliament Forces, the 11th of *September.*   Prince *Rupert* was diſcharged by his Majeſty, for his not holding out the City longer.   The King being at *Cheſter*, his Forces were defeated on the 29th at *Routon-Heath*, to his great Mortification, which he perceived from the Walls.—In this Month, the Plague broke out in *Hull;* but by the uſual Care, in ſuch like Caſes, of former Times, it was happily prevented from ſpreading.—The King arrived at *Newark*, about the Beginning of *October;* but was obliged to leave it in *November;* and, after great Perils, got ſafe to *Oxford.*   And now the *Scots* Presbytery was contemn'd by the Independants, and indeed the Parliament were weary of thoſe People in general, which made them wiſh for a Treaty; as the King himſelf deſired about the End of *December.*

[*bb*]   The Beginning of *January, Fairfax* raiſed the Siege of *Plymouth*, and ſoon after took *Dartmouth* by Storm.   On the 14th of *February*, the Lord *Hopton* was routed at *Torrington* by him. On the 5th of *May*, the King (thro' the Negotiation of Monſieur *Montrevil)* truſts himſelf to the *Scotch* Army; and ſoon after ſettled at *Newcaſtle.*   The 24th of June, *Oxford* was ſurrender'd to General *Fairfax.*   The Earl of *Eſſex* dy'd on the 14th of *September.*   On the 12th of *November*, the Town Wall of *Hull*, between *Myton* and Poſtern-Gates, about 50 Yards in Length, fell down into the Ditch, occaſion'd thro' exceſſive Rains that had undermin'd it on the one Side, and the Weight of Earth which preſs'd it down, that lay upon the other: To repair which it coſt about 300*l.*

[*cc*] The Merchants of *Hull* had great Loſſes this Year, through Pyrates and Storms at Sea.   On the 30th of *January*, the *Scotch* Parliament delivered up their King; and left *Newcaſtle* the 11th of *February*, after they had been the greateſt Curſe that ever *England* was afflicted with.   The Lord *Ferdinando Fairfax* dying at *York*, on *March* 13, 164⅚, the Parliament order'd his Son to be Governour; And moreover, that a conſtant Garriſon ſhould be kept therein, at the Nation's Expence, to act againſt the King, Queen, and all the Royaliſts; To whom, if any became afterwards attach'd, and ſhould leave the Place for their Intereſt, they ſhould be

puniſh'd

| 1648 John Ramſden, 2 | } | Richard Vevers |
| [*dd*] *John Kay*, or *Ray* | } | Thomas Cockrill |

puniſh'd with Death, as Enemies, and Deſerters: And, tho' the Town ſtrenuously petition'd againſt ſuch a Burthen; arguing That the Place being little, four or five Families were oblig'd to dwell under one Roof: How inconſiſtent it would be, to have Soldiers live in Houſes with the Wives of abſent Mariners; or, by Marriage, bring an inſupportable Burthen to the Place; That, for the Parliament's Cauſe, Ninety Thouſand Pounds had been already expended; Thirty Thouſand Pounds loſt in Traffick, thro' their being despis'd by Foreigners, for acting with them againſt their unfortunate Sovereign: Beſides, that the Deſtruction of the Walls, the laying the Country under Water, repairing the Fortifications from Time to Time, had impoveriſh'd them to the Value of many Thouſands more; by which, having 300 poor Families, the Garrison would double the Number; and, conſequently, increaſe their Poverty: A Grievance, they would never conſent to, as being contrary to *Magna Charta*, the Petition of Right, and the Liberty of the Subject: — Yet, for all ſuch like ſpecious Pleadings, the arbitrary Commons placed a Garriſon there, as tho' they were far from valuing *Magna Charta*, or any Paper Concern whatever, when they had the Sword in their Hands; which, being drench'd in Blood, could write in more legible coercive Characters. But we'll return to the King, who had been impriſon'd at *Holmby* Houſe in *Northamptoushire*, where he was deny'd his Chaplains. The Independents afterwards took him from the Presbyterians, thro' the Contrivance of *Cromwell*, about the 4th of *June*, by Cornet *Joyce*, a Taylor; who carried him to *Hinchingbrook, Childerley*, and at laſt to *New-Market*. In *Auguſt*, he was fix'd at *Hampton Court*, where he recover'd his Book of Meditations, call'd EIKON BASILIKE, with ſeveral Hiſtorical Writings. In *November*, the King made his eſcape to *Tichfield:* From thence went to *Cariſbrook* Caſtle, in the Isle of *Wight. Cromwell* afterwards, having quell'd the Agitators and Levellers, conſulted at *Windsor* with *Ireton*, about his Majeſty's Death.

[*dd*] The King was made cloſe Priſoner by Colonel *Hammond*, in the ſaid Island, which occaſion'd a ſecond Civil War; but it ended in about five Months Time: Afterwards, he was remov'd to *Hurst* Caſtle, near the Island, and from thence to *Windsor.* Soon after, his Majeſty was brought before the Parliament like a Criminal, as will appear by the moſt unprecedented Treatment he met with, in the following Year.

[ee] The

KING *CHARLES* II. *January* 30.

1649
[*ee*] PEregrine Pelham } JAmes Shepheard
       John Rawson   } J Richard Frank

[*ee*] The Actions of this Year, *as an ingenious Author writes*, were fo dark and hideous, that it cannot be parallel'd in the Annals of any other Monarch's Reign. To bring a King, accountable to None, except the King of Kings *fays another*, to plead for his Life before them, who had formerly fworn Allegiance to him, (and who, as Dr. *South* afferts, ought themfelves to have fuffer'd as the vileft Malefactors) was fuch an audacious Act, that the proudeft of all the *Roman* Pontiffs never attempted, in all their Wanton Freaks of unlimited Power: And all this done to a juft and wife Prince, fprung from Royal Anceftors; learned and valiant; who liv'd like a Saint in a corrupt Age; had broke no Oaths made to his People; and fo merciful to his Enemies, that as the Marquefs of *Worcefter*, told him, *His forgiving Temper might gain him the Kingdom of Heaven, but never secure to him the Realm of* England! CAROLUS *inter Reges, ut Lilium ineer Flores*, writes Sir *Richard Baker*. Thefe Eulogiums, and many more, impartial Hiftorians relate of him: To their particular Accounts of his Tryal, (before the Prefident *Bradshaw*, and other fuch Judges, the Signers of his Death-Warrant, to the Number of 72, among whom, was Alderman *Pelham*, of *Hull*, and Mr. *John Alured*, Member of Parliament for *Headon*) I refer my Readers, for their greater Satisfaction: And, in refpect to the prefent Age, fhall only remark, That I have Charity to believe, there are few, now living, among all Profeffors of the Proteftant Religion, but what look back with Horror of the Action, which brought a Prince, of their own Perfuafion, to fuffer at laft the greateft Afflictions. — His Tryal began on *Saturday* the 20th of *January* 164⅘. In his Impeachment, by *Cook*, he was called Tyrant, and Traytor! His Majefty deny'd their Authority, as being of no Force without him; and by fo doing, became a Civil Martyr, for the People's Liberty: The next Day, being *Sunday*, he fpent it, almoft, in his Devotions. On *Monday*, he was brought again into *Weftminfter-Hall.* *Tuesday* the fame: On *Wednesday*, Witneffes were produced againft him: One was *William Cuthbert*, of *Patrington*, in *Holdernefs*; another, was *John Bennet*, of *Harwood, Yorkshire*, Glover; and about thirty one more, from different Counties. The Fourth and laft Day, tho' his Majefty defired to be heard in the Painted Chamber, yet it was not granted; but Sentence pronounced againft him, as a Murderer, and publick Enemy, on *Saturday* the 27th. He prepar'd
himfelf

himfelf to die ; and defir'd the Affiftance of Dr. *Juxon*, Bifhop of
London, with the Comfort of feeing his Children.   There was
fcarce any Thing, but Sadnefs, that reign'd over the City upon this
Occafion : His Majefty refufed to fubfcribe what his Enemies,
would have him, thereby to enslave the People ; tho' his Life was
offer'd, in Cafe of Condefcenfion. *Holland* interpofed for the King;
but in vain ! For *Cromwell*, and his Officers, feeking GOD, as they
faid, it was refolv'd, that his Majefty muft die.   The King fent Mr.
Herbert, who was Gentleman of his Bed-Chamber, to the Lady
Wheeler, for a Cabinet of fome few Diamonds and Jewels in her
Cuftody, which was all the wealth he had to leave his Children,
the Princefs *Elizabeth*, and Duke of *Glocefter*.   On *Tuefday* the
30th, about Ten, his Majefty was brought forth by Col. *Hacker*,
attended by the Bifhop, and Mr. *Herbert* : He refus'd to eat any
Thing at *White-Hall*, which had been provided for him. Entering
upon the Scaffold, he found it cover'd with Black ; faw two Execu-

tioners, with Frocks and Vizards ; the Block, and Ax ; with Hooks,
and Staples, to draw him to Execution, if he refifted :   But there

* He was bury'd in *York*. See his long Epitaph in my Hiftory, Page 165.

was

was no Occasion. He clear'd himself from beginning the War with the two Houses of Parliament, and hop'd the Lord would in that Case absolve him also : *And yet,* said he, *God forbid I should lay the Blame on them : There is no Necessity. Ill Instruments, between Them, and Me, was the Cause of all this Bloodshed.* He then own'd his Fault, in suffering an unjust Sentence to fall upon the Earl of *Strafford :* For himself, he hop'd, he was become a good Christian : And (pointing to the Bishop) said, *That good Man can bear me Witness, that I have forgiven all the World, and even those who have been the chief Causers of my Death : But this is not all; my Charity must go further : I wish they may repent : I pray God, with St.* STEPHEN, That this be not laid to their Charge : *And not only so, but that they may take the right Way to the Peace of the Kingdom.* After this, he discours'd of what was due to GOD, his Successors, and the People; profess'd his Affection to the Protestant Religion of the Church of *England ;* and then prepar'd to lay down his Royal Head upon the Block. When his Cap was putting on, by the Bishop and Executioner, whilst Tears gush'd from the Eyes of many distant Spectators, the King repeated the Goodness of his Cause, and what a gracious God he had on his Side : The Bishop alluded to a former private Discourse, saying, *There was but one Step more, which tho' turbulent and troublesome, would carry him from Earth to Heaven, from a mortal State, to a glorious Immortality.* The King adjoin'd, *I go from a corruptible, to an incorruptible Crown !* A happy Exchange, *reply'd the Bishop.* The King then gave his GEORGE to the Bishop, and bid him *RE-MEMBER !*—So, turning to the Executioner, after private Ejaculations, he meekly laid down his Neck ; but bid him stay for the Sign. He did so ; and then, stretching forth his Hands, his Head was cut off at one Blow; shown to the astonish'd People; put into his Coffin, cover'd with black Velvet; and so convey'd to *White-Hall.* This was the End of the Royal Martyr, in the 49th Year of his Age, after a Reign of almost twenty four Years : Who, now, dead, was compar'd to *Job, David* and *Solomon,* for Patience, Piety and Wisdom : His Murder was look'd upon as a Crime, of the most horrid Nature, next to that of the Crucifixion of the incarnate Son of GOD : Even his Enemies became afflicted : The Pulpits, fill'd with the most pious Divines of each Persuasion, mutually refounded in Sighs and Lamentations, for the unspeakable Calamities of so unfortunate a Prince ! His Body was carry'd to *Windsor,* and laid in a Vault opposite the 11th Stall, on the Sovereign's Side, where King *Henry* VIII. and his third Wife, Queen *Jane,* were reposited. The Common-Wealth was establish'd, after the King's Death ; his Son proclaim'd

Y

against ;

againſt; the Houſe of Peers, and Regal Government, aboliſh'd; the Duke of *Hamilton*, Earl of *Holland*, and Lord *Capel* executed. **Pontefract* Caſtle held out for the Royaliſts, under the Governour Col. *Morrice*, who had formerly ſurpriz'd it ; (as mention'd Page 10, in the Travels of my Second Volume) but was ſurrender'd on the 24th of *March*.   Several Executions of the King's Party follow'd. *Cromwell* preach'd, cajol'd the Presbyterians, and ſuppreſs'd the Levellers.   In the mean while, the *Scots* invited the young King. *Cromwell*, afterwards, being made Lieutenant of *Ireland*, ſtormed *Drogheda* and *Wexford;* and, with amazing Succeſs, reduc'd moſt of that Kingdom.   The Mayor of *Hull*, **Peregrine Pelham**, mention'd in this Year, was elected the 30th of *September :* And acquainting the Houſe of Commons, of which he was Member, that he was ſent for thither, in order to be ſworn, and enter on his Office ; they, having Occaſion for him, as being one of the **Judges** of the †MARTYR'D KING, ſent an Order for the former Mayor to act as his Deputy :   Which Mr. *Ramſden* did, 'till Mr. *Pelham's* Death, that happen'd in *March* following ; and then the Parliament order'd Mr. *Thomas Raikes*, to govern the Remainder of the Time.   The Commons now defac'd the King's Arms where they could find 'em ; and commanded Charters of Places to be ſurrender'd that ſo they might diſplay the Enſigns and Name of the *Common-Wealth* upon every Occaſion.   They expoſed the King's Fee-Farm Rents to Sale : Thoſe of *Hull*, and its County, amounted annually to 156*l.* 7*s.* 8*d*, out of which was paid 24*l.* 3*s.* 3*d.* to the Reader and Curate of the High and Low Churches, and a Sallary to the School-Maſter : All theſe the Town bought, for which they paid 1467*l.* and generouſly beſtow'd on King CHARLES II. after his Reſtoration.

---

* I have a Proſpect of the Caſtle, the antient Inheritance of the Duke of *Lancaſter*, then a moſt beautiful Structure.   The greateſt Ornament of which, was that call'd the Round-Tower.   There were alſo, the King's, Queen's, Conſtaable's, Swillington's, Treaſurer's, and the Red Towers : Beſides, a noble Magazine, a great Barn, the King's Stable ; the Middle Gate-Houſe, with others to the Eaſt, Weſt and South, which might for their lofty Structure be called Towers alſo.   To this Caſtle, belong'd a beautiful Chapel dedicated to St. *Clement*.   In a Manuſcript, lent me by HENRY FAIRFAX, Esq ; at *Towlſton*, near *Tadcaſter*) a particular Account is given of what Sums were paid to the Workmen for demoliſhing the Edifice, by Order of the Parliament, *March* 27, 1649. and another, in Purſuance of it, the 4th of *April* following.   The total Amount of which, was 1777 *l.* 4*s.* 6*d.*   If ſo much was expended in its Ruin, what immenſe Sums muſt have been ſpent in its Erection !

† Many Verſes were written on the mournful Occaſion of the late King's Death : But theſe, made by the Marqueſs of *Montroſs*, carry, I think, the greateſt Energy.

GReat, Good and Juſt, could I but rate My Grief, and thy too rigid Fate ; I'd weep the World to ſuch a Strain, That it ſhould deluge once again !	But ſince thy Blood demands Supplies, More from *Briareus* Hands, than *Argus* Eyes, I'll ſing thy Obſequies with Trumpet Sounds, And write thy Epitaph in Blood and Wounds.

CHAP. X.

A Continuation of the MAYORS, SHERIFFS, *together with an Account of the* Chamberlains, *and what Tranſactions have happen'd, relating to* Kingſton-upon-Hull, *until the Reſtoration of King* CHARLES *the Second; from thence, to his Death, and Beginning of his unfortunate Brother's Reign.*

A.D. MAYORS and SHERIFFS.	CHAMBERLAINS.
1650 FRancis Dewick	THomas Coats
[*ff*] *Henry Metcalf*	John Blenker
1651 John Kay	James Blaides
[*gg*] *William Raikes*	John Tripp

[*ff*] In this Year was the firſt Appearance of the *Quakers.* The brave Marqueſs of *Montroſs* ſuffer'd Death, at *Edinborough*, on the 21ſt of *May.* The King arriv'd in *Scotland* the 22d of *June;* and was proclaim'd on the 15th of *July.* CROMWELL, returning from *Ireland*, was made General againſt the *Scots.*

[*gg*] The King was crown'd, at *Scone*, by the Marqueſs of *Argyle.* In *Auguſt*, his Majeſty came into *England*, with an Army of 16000 Men: He march'd afterwards into *Lancashire*, and ſetled in *Worceſter*, the 22d. Col. *Lilburn* defeated a Party of the King's, on the 25th, near *Wiggan*, where fell the famous Lord *Withrington*, and others, who aſſiſted the Earl of *Derby*, that was afterward beheaded at *Bolton.* CROMWELL, marching to *Worceſter*, after a ſharp Engagement, obliged the King to fly for his Life. Here Duke *Hamilton* was taken Priſoner, and dy'd of his Wounds. This Victory was ſo great, that *Cromwell* told the Parliament, *It was a Crowning Mercy, the Dimenſions of which were far above his Conceptions.* Some Authors write, with Improvements on the Story, That it was not the King of Heaven had made it ſuch; but the Prince of the infernal Regions, with whom the General contraĉted, in a doleſome Wood, on the 3d of *September*, early in the Morning, ſome Hours before the Battle was fought: When *Lindſey*, one of his Officers, is ſaid to have been a Witneſs; but ſo troubled, that he left the Army, and rode to *Grimſton*, in *Norfolk*, to the Houſe of the Rev. Mr. *Thorowgood*, to whom he related the Affair. The Readers may judge as they pleaſe of this latter Aſſertion: It was with great Difficulty the King eſcap'd, being oblig'd ſoon after to aſcend the Royal-Oak at *Boſcobel-Wood*, in *Shropshire*, (or, ſome ſay, on the

Confines

1652 John Rogers	}	Lancelot Anderſon
[*hh*] *Richard Vevers*	}	John Pearſon
1653 Richard Wood	}	John Harriſon
[*ii*] *Richard Robinſon*	}	Edmund Popple
1654 Bobert Ripley, 1	}	*Capt.* Henry Appleton
[*kk*] *Richard Wilſon*	}	Robert Bloome
1655 William Maiſter	}	Henry Cock
[*ll*] *Chriſt. Richardſon*	}	Richard Lillie
1656 Robert Berrier, 1	}	George Acklam
[*mm*] *William Ramſden*	}	Cuthbert Prieſtwood
1657 William Foxley, 1	}	Philip Wilkinſon
[*nn*] *George Crowle*	}	Charles Vaux

Confines of *Staffordshire*) where he was preſerv'd by the Family of
PENDERELS ; and, after many Dangers, ſafely arrived in *France.*
CROMWELL rode triumphant to *London.* General MONK reduced
Scotland. Lieutenant General IRETON dy'd *November* 26, raving
after Blood, according to the Cruelty of his horrid Diſpoſition.

[*hh*] In this Year happen'd ſeveral deſperate Sea-Engagements
between the *English* and *Dutch ;* but the latter was continually
beaten, and obliged to ſue for Peace.

[*ii*] CROMWELL diſſolv'd the *Long-Parliament* and *Common-
Wealth ;* calling them, in Effect, little better than *Knaves.*   He
call'd his Firſt Parliament, to humour his Deſigns ; to whom he made
a Speech : And theſe Men, being fill'd with Ignorance and Enthu-
ſiaſm, were for removing the Clergy, who *then were*, as they ſaid,
Strangers to the Goſpel! After their Diſſolution, *Cromwell* was made
Protector, ruling as a Monarch ; and united the three Kingdoms.

[*kk*] The Protector called a Second Parliament.

[*ll*] This Parliament too he diſſolv'd the 22d of *January.*
He appointed Major-Generals, as Governours of Provinces : *Lambert* was over *Yorkshire.* He conquer'd the *Spaniards* at Sea, and
took *Jamaica* from them.   Archbiſhop *Usher* dy'd this Year. Orders were renew'd at *Hull*, concerning the Cloth-Hall, which were
made One Hundred Years before.

[*mm*] The Major-Generals were ſuppreſſed, in ſome meaſure.

[*nn*] The Protector was attempted to be made King ; which he
refuſed, tho', it is ſaid, with great Trouble ; and re-aſſumed his former Office, in which he was inaugurated, with as much Pomp, as if
he had been crown'd : Wonderful was his Succeſs afterwards, both
by Land and Sea. To this Great Man, the Corporation of *Hull* petition'd,

1658 William Dobfon, 2	⎫	Ifrael Popple
[*oo*] *Edmund Popple*	⎬	William Shires
1659 William Ramfden	⎫	John Crowther
[*pp*] *John Tripp*	⎬	Simon (*or* Jas.) Siffon
1660 Chrift. Richardfon, 1	⎫	William Blaides
[*qq*] *Robert Lambert*	⎬	William Anderfon

tion'd, *That whereas there were forfaken Wives, and Widows of Soldiers, to the Number of* 200, *with double that Number of Children, then in the Town;* they humbly defired he would grant them an Order, to lay a Duty, on Cloth, and Lead, for their Support: And, further, requefted, *The Allowance of* 400*l. a Year, out of the fequeftered Rectories in* Yorkfhire, *formerly granted to the Minifters of their two Churches, which would be a further Help to their Maintenance.* But Oliver told them, *They muft obtain an Act of Parliament for the firft; and as to the latter, Care should be taken to anfwer their Purpofe.* But the Confequence of this Promife feem'd as if it had never afterwards enter'd into the Protector's Thoughts. Sir *Henry Slingsby* was Prifoner in *Hull,* and afterwards fent to the Tower.

[*oo*] *Cromwell's* old Friends now feem'd to turn his Enemies; and feveral Plots were concerted againft him. Sir Hen. Slingsby, and Dr. Hewet, were beheaded on the 6th of *June:* Others were hang'd, drawn and quarter'd. *Dunkirk* was furrender'd to the *English,* on the 25th. The Protector fell fick in *Auguft;* dy'd the 3d of *September;* and *Richard,* his Son, was proclaim'd.

[*pp*] The Parliament this Year was fufpicious of General *Monk.*

[*qq*] By Order of the Commons, the General pull'd down the Gates of *London:* But excus'd himfelf at *Guild-Hall,* by declaring for a free Parliament. It fat the 25th of *April;* to whom the King's Declaration of a Pardon, with fome Exceptions, and his Letter to the Lords, were read, and accepted, with the greateft Joy. His Majefty was proclaim'd on *Monday,* the 8th of *May.* The News, well confirm'd, reach'd *Hull,* the 16th: Upon which, the Mayor, William Ramsden, Efq; (who held the Office 'till *September,* when Alderman *Richardfon* fucceeded) called a Hall, and imparted the fame to the joyful Inhabitants: When it happen'd, that fome of thofe Men, who had been zealous for the Parliament, feem'd now forward to proclaim the King. Colonel *Charles Fairfax* the Governour, with the Aldermen *Raikes, Barnard,* &c. met the Day following, in their Scarlet Gowns, and beft Apparel. From the Hall, they walk'd in Proceffion to the Market-Place; where a Scaffold being prepar'd, cover'd with red Cloth, they afcended there-

on:

on : When the Mayor, with a loud Voice, proclaim'd his Majefty the Rightful King over the Britifh Realms, and other Dominions : Then the Trumpets refounded, Drums beat, Cannons roar'd, and the Air feem'd to be rent with Acclamations. " The Joy of the " late diftreffed Royalifts, *fays an excellent Author*, broke out with " inconceivable Elafticity ! Tranfports and Ecftacies were emi- " nently confpicuous." A fweet Emulation appear'd amongft the greater Part, who fhould beft exprefs their Gratitude to Heaven ! In the Streets, tho' infinitely crowded, many were feen, on bended Knees, with lift-up Hands, praifing God, they had liv'd to fee this happy Day ! And, at Night, the Windows were illuminated ; the Bells rung ; with all other Demonftrations of an affectionate People. And this, I think, may anticipate an Objection made againft the Town, *That it ought to be ever ftigmatiz'd as a rebellious Place !* An uncharitable, unreafonable Reflection from any Perfon in *England :* Becaufe, the whole Nation might as well lie under the like Calumny ; and indeed the other two Kingdoms, which feem'd to fhare in the Guilt, againft King *Charles* I. thro' an impetuous Torrent of the utmoft Wickednefs, acted under the Cloak of Reli- gion. It was the Strength of *Hull*, that made each Party ftrive to acquire it : And, as a renown'd King was its firft Founder ; fo, 'till then, it continued loyal to diftreffed Princes. Tho' it became a For- trefs againft the Lovers of Monarchy, in a corrupt Age ; yet that Fault did not lie upon the Inhabitants in general ; which appear'd by their Joy for the Reftoration, refembled by their late Grati- tude in regard to the Revolution : And, I truft, this famous Town, will, in future Ages, be as remarkable for Loyalty to their Sove- reigns, as ever they have been thought meritorious of the contrary, lefs by any Crime, than their unhappy Misfortune. On the 24th, the King took Shipping at the *Hague*, and arriv'd at *Dover* the 26th. He came thro' *Canterbury* and *Rochefter ;* and on the 29th, his Birth- Day, made his triumphant Enterance to his Royal Palace at *White- Hall*. On the 8th of *June*, the Aldermen *Rogers, Dewick* and *Wood*, of *Hull*, were turn'd out of Office, by the Mayor, (who was Deputy- Governour, in the Abfence of Lord *Bellafis*) and others of the Cor- poration. Mr. *Shaw*, Lecturer, and Mafter of *God's-Houfe Hofpi- tal*, was difcharg'd on the 13th. Mr. *William Raikes*, being elect- ed an Alderman on the 29th, at firft refufed to ftand, 'till he was fin'd 200*l.* when, thinking better of it, he fubmitted to be fworn and fo fav'd his Money. The Common-Prayer was read under the Mar- ket-Crofs, by the Rev. Mr. *Smith*, furrounded by Multitudes of de- vout People ; which occafion'd an Order for fuch Books to be pro- cur'd for the Churches, that were afterwards kept more Sacred :

The

1661 George Crowle, 1	}	Thomas Coats
[†] *Philip Wilkinſon*	}	Anthony Lambert
1662 Richard Wilſon	}	William Weddell [ton
Henry Cock	}	Tho. Weeton *or* Weigh-
1663 Richard Robinſon	}	William Carleton
[rr] [ſſ] *Humphrey Duncalf*	}	Joſeph Ellis
1664 William Skinner	}	H. Maiſter, *or* Maiſters
[tt] *William Shires*	}	Thomas Houltby
1665 Robert Bloom	}	John Blanchard
[uu] *John Pearſon*	}	Thomas Mowld
1666 Richard Frank	}	Ambroſe Metcalf
[xx] *George Aclam*	}	John Robinſon

The Fonts for Baptiſm were ſet up, as uſual; and the Communion Tables rail'd in, like antient Altars.—[†] The Charter renew'd.

[rr] Upon Petition of the Grand-Jury this Year, there was added 50*l.* to the 26*l.* formerly allow'd to each Mayor, whereby his Office might be kept in greater Splendour.

[ſſ] The Corporation began this Year to ſolemnize his Majeſty's Birth, and Return, by going in their Formalities, to Church, in the Morning; having a Collation, at the Town's Hall, in the Afternoon; to which the former Sheriffs, the preſent Clergy, School-Maſters, and Officers of the Garriſon, were invited; and Liquors given to the Soldiers, and other People.

[tt] The Dukes of *York* and *Buckingham*, with ſeveral Noble-men, coming to viſit *Hull, Auguſt* 16, were met on the Confines of the County, conducted into the Town, lodged by Colonel *Gilby*, Deputy-Governour; and entertain'd by the Mayor and Aldermen.

[uu] The unfortunate Mayor, Mr. Bloom, ſlighting his Election, and taking a Frolick into *Scotland*, was depoſed from his Dignity; and Mr. Robert Ripley choſen in his Room. It was Mr. *Bloom's* great misfortune, as being a Gameſter, to play, at *Edinborough*, with a *Scotch* Man: Who, thinking he was cheated, made no more to do, but (like a blood-thirſty Ruffian) with his Dagger ſtabb'd the unhappy Gentleman to the Heart.—The Town generouſly lending the King a Sum of Money, to aid him in the *Dutch* War; his Majeſty paid them again, ſoon after, when Peace enſu'd.

[xx] The Mayor (Mr. *Frank*) thro' Loſſes at Sea and Land, became ſo very poor; that, in 1680, he petition'd to lay down his Gown: The Court, conſidering his Age, and the Reaſonableneſs of his Requeſt thro' Inability, generouſly diſcharg'd him, without the

leaſt

Year	Mayor	Sheriffs
1667	Anthony Lambert	Edward Hodgſon
[a]	*Thomas Lockwood*	George Frogatt
1668	Humphrey Duncalf	William Robinſon
[b]	*William Carleton*	William Catline
1669	John Tripp	John Harris
	Edward Dobſon	John Baker
1670	George Aclam	Nicholas Dewick
	John Forcett	George Dickinſon
1671	Robert Berrier	John Graves
[c]	*Richard Man*	John Sumerfield
1672	Thomas Johnſon, 1	Richard Gray
	Francis Blunt	Philip Wilkinſon
1673	John Rogers	Robert Carlisle
[d]	*Arthur Saltmarsh*	Triſtram Sugar

leaſt Fine: And, inſpir'd with Charity, they ſent him Ten Pounds for his immediate Relief, 'till they could make better Proviſion for the ſupply of his unfortunate Circumſtances.

[a] Six large Crampus's being taken, by the Fiſhermen of *Barrow* and *Whitten, Lincolnshire,* were ſent to *Hull,* in order to make Oyl: But the Mayor, as Admiral of *Humber,* (where they were kill'd) ſeiz'd the Casks, that contain'd them, for the Town's Uſe.

[b] On the 3d of *January,* dy'd General MONK, Duke of *Albemarle,* who was High-Steward of *Hull:* In which laſt Dignity, he was ſucceeded by the Lord *Bellaſis.* Let us here remember the pious Sir JOHN LISTER, who founded an Hoſpital for poor Men, and Women: The Heirs of the ſaid Knight, with the Mayor and Aldermen, were to have the Management of it: To which, belong'd a Chaplain and Clerk, that Care might be taken of the poor Peoples Souls, as well as Bodies.

[c] The Sheriff's Maid Servant murder'd her Baſtard Child this Year, for which the unhappy Creature ſuffer'd Death in 1673.

[d] The Exchange was very much beautified this Year.—An Examination being order'd to be made about the Fiſh-Garths; the Enquirers met at *Howlden:* And, viſiting *Skelton,* they found two, which had 20 Rooms; the higher 12, and lower 8: One at *Sandholm* Bank, with 28 Rooms; two at *Saltmarsh,* &c. They were order'd to be pull'd up, and Piles placed ſo high, as that, when the Tide was in, the Veſſels might keep clear of them.— Some Complaints were exhibited againſt the Commiſſioners of Wine Licenſes, who ſtrove to engroſs the Sale of that Liquor to them-

felves.

1674 Daniel Hoar	⎱ James Ranfon
[*e*] *Ifrael Popple*	⎰ George Bacchus
1675 William Shires	⎱ Ezekiel Walker
Robert Mafon	⎰ Robert Standige
1676 William Foxley, 2	⎱ William Hayes
[*f*] *Hugh Foddle*	⎰ Matthew Hardy

felves.—Ballaft for Ships was order'd to be dug out of the Haven, under ftrict Penalties ; by which Means, it was render'd more navigable.—An Act of Parliament coming out, incapacitating every Roman Catholick from acting in any Office ; the Lord *Bellafis* was obliged to refign his Places of Governour, and High-Steward of *Hull*, to the Duke of *Monmouth.*

[*e*] This worfhipful Mayor, was (about 4 Years afterwards) turn'd out from being an Alderman ; becaufe he had not took the Sacrament fo folemnly as requir'd; or, if he did, had neglected to have it regifter'd : In his Room, Mr. *John Field* was elected, *Dec.* 9. 1680. As the former Gentleman retir'd to a private Life, I prefume it might have been his Son that was Mayor in 1688.— Mr. *Gilead Goche*, being chofen Sheriff, refufed to ftand ; becaufe fome Obfcurities feem'd to appear in the Charter. I do not perceive that any Fine was laid upon him, feveral Things being then difputable : Which, if (according to Encouragement) I live to publifh another Book relating to *Hull*, fhall be amply treated of, fo far as to be fupplemental to what I have already done. An antient Order, made in King *Henry* the VIIIth's Time, was reviv'd, which related to Chamberlains : Who, being obliged to receive the Town's Rents, and pay the Debts; it fometimes happen'd, that, before the former became due, there was a Demand for the latter ; and, perhaps, they could not be disburfed 'till two or three Years after they were out of Office : To eafe this Grievance, it was decreed, That 100*l.* a-piece, out of the Common-Stock, fhould be freely lent them, upon giving Security. However good was this Defign ; yet Mr. *Ranfon*, when he was elected Chamberlain, refufed to receive the Money, or to obey the Orders of the Bench ; tho' he knew there were feveral By-Laws to inflict Penalties upon him for his Obftinacy ; and by which, no doubt, they diftrain'd upon his Goods, according to Advice, given to the Corporation, by Sir *William Jones*, a celebrated Lawyer, in thofe Days.

[*f*] Some of the Family, of the worfhipful Mayor aforefaid, he bury'd in St. *John's* Church, *Leeds ;* the Infcriptions over whom, the Reader may find, in *Latin*, faithfully inferted, with an exact Translation, in my Second Volume of Antiquities, Pag. 30. in the latter Part of that, concerning *Travels to fome Places in the County.*

1677 Henry Maifter, 1	}	† George Mawſon
[g] *Mark Kirkby*	}	Robert Nettleton
1678 Chriſt. Richardſon, 2	}	William Hydes
[h] *Francis Delacamp*	}	Anthony Caddy
1679 George Crowle, 2	}	Richard Ellis
[i] *Anthony Iveſon*	}	John Chappelow

[g] On the 3d of *December*, an Order was made, *Againſt any Perſon, in Power, who should abſent himſelf, in thoſe Times, when Aſſiſtance was neceſſary to make By-Laws for the Publick Good. Alſo, in Caſe of Refuſal, If an Alderman, being elected Mayor, should deny to execute that high Office, he was to pay* 500l. *If a Burgeſs, choſen Alderman, deny'd to ſtand,* 300l. *For a Sheriff,* 200l. *A Chamberlain,* 50l. Engliſh *Money, to be apply'd to the Uſe of the Corporation. And, in Caſe of intended Reſignation, when the Corporation should not (for want of ſufficient Reaſons) grant ſuch their Deſires ; the Penalty of Ten Pounds was to be laid on thoſe Perſons, for every Offence, who should abſent themſelves from the Hall, after having Notice given for Meeting ; or, appearing, did not perform their Duty, in aſſiſting, to the utmoſt of their Ability, in the Management of the Town's Affairs.*—About this Time, happen'd a Diſpute, concerning the Floods endamaging the *Julian* Well, and Springs of *Daringham.* But this was adjuſted by ſome of the Commiſſioners of Sewers (in the Abſence of Sir *Robert Legard*, a Commiſſioner alſo, who had the Misfortune of a broken Leg) to the Content of the Inhabitants of the neighbouring Towns, and to the Mayor and Aldermen of *Hull.*—† Mr. *George Mawſon*, one of the Chamberlains, might have lived to enjoy a higher Dignity, had not the cruel Uſage he met with, in the Reign of King *James* the Second, prevented it : For being then ſeiz'd upon, by Command of the Governour, he was dragg'd out of his Habitation, convey'd to the Guard-Houſe, and there tied Neck and Heels, for ſuch an unreaſonable Time, that the Blood ſpouted out of his Mouth and Ears ! Thro' the Loſs of which, and ſome Veſſels being broke, he afterwards pin'd, languiſhed, and died !

[h] The Order, in the preceding Year, (concerning the Sums decreed to be paid for Non-Compliance, or Refuſal, at their ſeveral Elections, *&c.*) appeared ſo reaſonable, and agreeeble to a Statute, in King *Henry* VIIIth's Reign ; that, on the 30th of *March*, this Year, it was confirm'd by the Lord-Chancellor *Finch; Richard Rainsforth*, and *Francis North*, Lord-Chief-Juſtices.—The Taylors aroſe againſt the Magiſtrates ; but were ſoon brought to ſubmit.

[i] On *Feb.* 24. *Lemuel Kingdon*, and *William Ramſden*, Eſqrs. were elected Members of Parliament. On the 2d of *May*, JOHN
SHARP,

1680 Simon Siſſon	} Robert Trippet
[†] *Matthew Johnſon*	} Robert Lemon
1681 Robert Maſon	} John Haslewood
[i] *Lionel Buckle*	} Michael Beilby

SHARP, Archbiſhop of St. *Andrew's,* was barbarously murder'd in *Scotland.* Soon after happen'd an Inſurrection, of 1500 Men, who were quelled by the Duke of *Monmouth.* I have heard of a Tragi-Comical Affair, that follow'd, in the Puniſhment of ſome of the Malcontents ; but will not affirm it. *The King's Party, reſolving on Juſtice, brought ſeveral of them to the Gallows : But, at the ſame time inclin'd to Mercy, would fain have ſaved their Lives, provided thoſe deluded Wretches show'd but the leaſt Marks of Repentance ; and, in particular, pray'd for his Majeſty. Yet ſuch was the Obſtinacy of ſome of them, thro' the violent Importunity of their Wives, who would have 'em thought Martyrs, (each crying out, when the Rope was about her Husband's Neck, and faſtened to the Tree,* Jump into Glory, Dear ! Jump into Glory !) *that they throw'd themſelves headlong out of the World indeed. But one good Man, finding his puritannick Dame had over-ſtrain'd herſelf, in ſo often bawling out,* Jump into Glory ! *and, perhaps, conſidering her a ſilly, blind, ungracious Creature, who wanted to be rid of him ; he prudently cry'd out,* Madam, my Place is at your Service : You may e'en jump into Glory yourſelf, and be hang'd ! But, for my part, I lay hold of Royal Clemency ; ſincerely pray, God ſave the King ; and make us all more obedient Subjects, than pretended Martyrs. *Upon this, the poor Man was taken from the Tree ; and ſet at liberty, with the joyful Acclamations of the Friends to Monarchy.—July* the 12th, the Judges *Dolben,* and *Raymond,* came to hold Aſſize, at *Hull.*

[†] About this time, a Diſpute happen'd between the Ferrymen of *Hull,* and thoſe (belonging to the Queen's Ferry) at *Barton.* The latter complain'd, *That the former obſtructed their Landing of Paſſengers, at the Staith, to the Prejudice of his Majeſty, and the Royal Widow :* In which Proſecution, the Council aſſiſted them : But the Mayor and Aldermen, on the other hand, endeavoured to prove, *That their Ferrymen were very uncivilly dealt with, by the Plaintiffs.* As therefore the Difference proceeded from the meer Paſſions of Watermen, it was prevented by the Prudence of the Magiſtrates ; and ſo the Affair ended.

[i] The Mayor was elected Alderman, the preceding Year, on the 25th of *October.* Sir *Michael Warton,* and Sir *William Gee,* were elected Members of Parliament. The King, ſending an En-

gineer

1682 Jofeph Ellis　　　⎱ William Hall
[*k*] *William Robinfon* ⎰ Lionel Ripley

gineer to furvey the Town, and efpecially the Garrifon ; he com-manded a Citadel to be erected within its Boundaries, and regular Fortifications : Which were afterwards founded upon large Piles, the entire Bulks of Trees, drove into the Earth very deep, join'd clofe together, which took up a great Number : The Expence of thefe ftupendous Works coft above One Hundred Thoufand Pounds.

[*k*] The Worfhipful Mayor departed this Life in his Mayoral-ty ; and Mr. ANTHONY LAMBERT, officiated till a new Election. The antient Market-Crofs was pulled down, and a new one erected, at the Expence of near Eight Hundred Pounds.—About this Time, a Suit happen'd, between this Corporation, and that of *Leeds:* Becaufe, the Water-Bailiff, of *Hull,* had diftrain'd, for fome Port-Fees, on the Goods of the latter : Who, to defend themfelves, plead-ed an old Caufe, in Queen *Elizabeth's* Time : When Mr. *Foxley,* Water-Bailiff of *Hull,* and Mr. *Thompfon,* Toll-Gatherer, in *Bever-ley,* were obliged to pay 40*l.* upon fuch another like Occafion : This ended the Difpute.—Another Suit commenc'd betwixt the Corpo-ration, and the * Lead-Merchants of *Darbyshire;* becaufe the latter did not pay Duty for Lead (which help'd towards the Expence of the Haven, *&c.*) in the Common Weigh-Houfe at the King's Great Beam ; but frequently weigh'd the Pigs at private Staiths, and car-ry'd them off in the Night. But tho' many ftrong Arguments were ufed againft the Defendants ; yet they proved infufficient to caft them.—*December* the 22d, the Earl of *Plymouth* came as Gover-nour to *Hull,* in the Duke of *Monmouth's* Room : He was accom-pany'd by the Lord *Windfor,* Sir *John Legard* of *Ganton,* Sir *Wil-loughby Hickman, Thomas Sandys,* Efq ; and feveral Gentlemen. At the Horfe-Staith, the Corporation receiv'd Them in their For-malities : Captain *Copley,* Deputy-Governour, (who had fail'd in the *Humber,* in order to conduct them) regal'd the honourable Compa-ny at his Houfe ; and the next Day they were invited to the Mayor's, at a fplendid Entertainment. After Dinner, they were conducted to the Hall, and fworn Burgeffes. The Earl, making an eloquent Speech, in which he thank'd the Corporation for the kind Reception he met with, moved for two Things. FIRST, *That the Records might be fearch'd, to know what Methods the former Lieutenants had taken, in ordering the Militia ; whereby he might make a more regular Improvement,* SECONDLY, *That the Conventicles, (which he took to be Nurferies of Faction,* &c. *and oppofite to both Divine and Human Laws) might be fupprefs'd.* Some of the Burgeffes,

* One of whom was Mr. TAYLOR of *Waldingwells.*　　　　　hearing

1683 Francis Delacamp, 1 } John Gotherick
[*l*] *William Catline* } Chriftopher Fawthorp
1684 John Field } John Higden
[*m*] *Rich.* (or *Robt.*) *Nettleton* } Samuel Boyfe

hearing the Earl fo bitter againft the Diffenters, inform'd againft the two Meeting-Houfes, then in the Town, whofe Minifters were called Mr. *Ashley,* and Mr. *Charlifs.* Upon which, the Conftables were immediately fent to apprehend them: The former abfconded ; but the latter was taken, fin'd, and committed to* Prifon: Their Hearers (*Michael Beilby, John Graves* and *Robiufon,* &c.) were fharply rebuk'd: And the Earl, when he had view'd the Garrifon, with the Fortifications, (giving neceffary Directions, which kept him about two or three Days) then he departed for *Heddon.*

[*l*] On the 10th of *July,* the Judges (*Jefferies* and *Holloway*) arrived at *Hull:* To whom the Town's Charter was furrender'd.

[*m*] Sir *Edward Barnard* was discharged from being Recorder: The Charters of feveral Cities, and Corporations, having been deliver'd up this Year, in order to have new ones granted, with frefh Advantages ; the Aldermen *Lambert, Siffons, Mafters* and *Mafon,* of HULL, fet out for *London,* on the 27th of *October,* to wait upon the King, with the Hopes of obtaining thefe Amendments. I. *The Election of Mayor out of Two Aldermen: The like Number, in Regard to each Perfon, to be chofe in the feveral other Offices in the Corporation. II. That, in Cafe, either the Days of Election, or Swearing into Office, should happen on a* Sunday, *they might be perform'd the Day after. III. That 3 or 4 of the eldeft Aldermen, should be of the* Quorum *with the Mayor and Recorder. IV. That, in Cafe of Sicknefs to the Mayor, or Sheriff; then the Aldermen, according to Seniority, might fupply their Places, that fo Tryals might not be hinder'd. V. That what King* HENRY VIII. *and King* JAMES I. *had granted, as to the Profits of the Haven,* &c. *might be confirm'd. VI. That, as the Garrifon Side belong'd now to the King; fo the Town might be exempted from the Expence of upholding the Banks, Walls,* &c. All thefe Things, with whatever elfe they ask'd, his Majefty granted ; and fo the Aldermen return'd, with a new Charter, to the incredible Joy of the Town. In *December,* his Majefty requir'd the Names of the moft loyal Inhabitants, to Monarchy, that they might be employ'd in the Magiftracy. All thofe, of the Aldermen, were fent up, except Mr. *Johnfon's:* Who, fince the late Troubles, wifely confidering what might come to pafs, thro' his former Inclination to the late oppofite Government, had gotten a fair legi-

* *Where he was confin'd for half a Year.*   ble

ble Writing, which contain'd the Innocency of his Life, with his Fidelity to the King, and Obedience to the Laws of the Land: And to this, by kind, fubtle Ufage, he obtain'd of his Brethren, at different Times, (as he got them, one by one, into a good Humour) to affix their Names, to his intire Satisfaction. But afterwards he happening to refufe the Signing of fome Warrants, which were levelled againft Diffenters; it fo much affronted the Bench, that they unanimously omitted his Name. Upon which, the Alderman, appealing to the King; his Brethren obtain'd a Hearing, againft him, before his Majefty, and Council: When, fuddenly, Mr. *Johnfon*, pull'd out the Paper, which his Profecutors had fign'd, as an irrefragable Argument againft them.* This *Teftimonium* occafion'd an almoft general Smile: And tho' his Adverfaries pleaded the Infufficiency of it, becaufe not fign'd in the open Hall; yet their private Affent was look'd upon as more valid; their Objection over-rul'd, and ridicul'd: His Majefty therefore took Alderman JOHNSON into Favour; and order'd him to be inferted in the Lift, as a very *Honeft, Worthy, Loyal* and *Ingenious* Perfon.

---

* Much fuch another Piece of Art, or rather (confidering its hafty Invention) more complete, happen'd in *Dublin*; which I fhall mention purely for the Reader's Diverfion. The Rev. Mr. GLANDEE, Rector of St. *Michael's* Church, happening, fome way, or other, to incur the Difpleafure of his Parifhioners, was accufed by them, to the Archbishop, of fome Irregularities, that occafion'd him to be very near his being turn'd out of his Living. This inveterate Ufage from a ftray'd Flock, perhaps to as carelefs a Shepherd, drove the Minifter into fuch an Agony, that he told them, *Since they were refolv'd to deprive him of his Bread, he would rather die in his Pulpit, than be forc'd to return to* Scotland, *where he was born!* To his Church he went; fat, and wept; fometimes, at his Defk; now, in his Pulpit; and then, at the Altar. He continu'd there in the Night; would fuffer none, but himfelf, to officiate the next Day; when he fhow'd all the Tokens of a melancholly Madnefs. At length, feeming to expoftulate with his Parifhioners, he told them, *He was willing to abandon the Place, if they would only give him a tolerable Character, that he might not be defpis'd in his own Country!* They, to get rid of him, promis'd to confent to, and fign, whatever his Heart could wifh for, as to that Point. He therefore caus'd to be wrote, what he pleas'd, according to their Affent; by which he feem'd to be regenerated to a new Creature. They fign'd, and deliver'd the Writing to the Parfon: But he, more wife, inftead of departing to *Scotland*, went with his Teftimonial to his Grace of *Dublin.* "My Lord, *quo' he*, I have been grievoufly "traduc'd in the Spiritual Court, as one unworthy of my Sacred Function, "tho' a faithful Minifter of the Gofpel of our dear Redeemer: But, to ob- "viate the ponderous Accufations of my Enemies; behold here, my gracious "Lord! the Character given me, by the devouteft Perfons of my Parifh.— His Grace, taking the Paper from him, perufing it over, and beholding the Hand-Writing of his Profecutors, held up his Hands, as a Token of his Amazement! And then he afk'd Mr. GLANDEE, What induc'd them to fign fuch an Inftrument? "Truly, my Lord, *quo' he*, tho' they ly'd to your Grace, yet will "not I: They gave it me, that I fhould depart from them: But if they do "not know, when they have got a good Minifter: I have the Senfe to un- "derftand, when I am blefs'd with a beneficent People: And your Grace, "I hope

CHAP. XI.

Continuation of the MAYORS, SHERIFFS, *and* Chamberlains, *down to the Revolution : With what Tranſactions happened thereupon.*

King *JAMES* II. *February* 6.

A. D.	MAYOR *and* SHERIFF.	CHAMBERLAINS.
1685 [*n*]	JOhn Forcet, *or* Forcett Richard Gray	THomas Tomlin William Idell

[*n*] I could not begin the Actions of this King's Reign, without taking Notice of the Character given of his late Royal Brother, by a judicious Pen. * " Now, alas! Death has ſnatch'd from us " our moſt gracious Sovereign, *CHARLES* the Second, Son of " *CHARLES* the Martyr, of Bleſſed Memory ! Royally de- " ſcended, and born to preſerve an eternal Remembrance of *Britain's* Glory. Father of his Country ; an Eſtabliſher of Peace, " and Concord : Magnanimous, when inteſtine Broils, and Civil Diſ- " cord, were very predominant : Patron of Learning ; an Enemy " to jarring Faction, and Strife ; Defender of the Faith ; a conſtant " Lover of Virtue, as well as an Admirer of Piety ; inferior to none " of his Predeceſſors. During the Space of 25 Years, he behav'd " himſelf, as a good and gracious King, to all his loyal Subjects : " At length, he left his terreſtrial Crown, to his Succeſſors, that he " might receive an incorruptible Diadem : And departed this Life " the 6th Day of *February*, in the 37th Year of his Reign, *Anno* " *Domini* 168 4/5."—The new King, being quickly proclaim'd, of his own Accord, ſpoke to his Privy-Council, to this Effect, *That ſince it*

* *Translation from the Latin.*   had

" I hope, will not diſcard me ; becauſe, if I am not a *Paul*, or *Apollos ;* yet, " my Lord, I am your Brother, as a Minister of JESUS CHRIST."——Here the Archbishop [as the King look'd upon Mr. *Johnſon*] perceiving the Gentleman's bright Faculties, under ſuch imminent Danger : " Well, *ſaid he*, Mr. GLAN- " DEE, tho' I am very much afraid, you have been, thro' Infirmity, guilty of " thoſe Immoralities, of which you are accus'd ; yet, for the Sake of your " Wit, and upon your ſincere Promiſe of Repentance, I will endeavour to " ſkreen you from further Proſecution this time."—Hereupon, his Grace, ſend- ing for the Parishioners, and reproaching them for accuſing ſo good a Man, of whom themſelves had ſince given ſo bright a Character, order'd them to beg his Pardon ; never to offend him more : And the affrighted, ſubtle Minister, fulfill'd his Vow to the Archbishop, by afterwards leading a pious, exemplary Life ; which ſkreen'd him, from the Power of his Adverſaries, to his lateſt Breath, when he had little Thoughts of this World to give him any Disturbance.

had pleafed the Almighty to fucceed fo good a Brother, he would endeavour to follow his Example of Tendernefs and Clemency; and, like him, ufe his beft Endeavours to fupport both Church and State, as by Law eftablifh'd; whofe Members, in being Lovers of Monarchy, had prov'd themfelves faithful and obedient Subjects: He knew the Laws were fufficient to make him a happy King. As he fhould not forfake the Rights and Prerogative of his Crown; fo neither would he invade any Man's Property: And fince he had often ventur'd his Life in the Nation's Defence, he would go as far as any Perfon in defending its juft Rights and Liberties. This acceptable Declaration procur'd him, in a little Time, the Name of JAMES the JUST: In *Hull,* the Joy feem'd unfpeakable: The Soldiers difcharged Vollies of Shot; the Cannons were fir'd; with all other Demonftrations. Nor was their Comfort lefs, when, a little after, a New Charter was fent down, to the entire Satisfaction of the Corporation. This occafion'd Mr. FIELD, the Mayor, to be fworn again into the Office, which he had enter'd upon the preceding Year: The Aldermen *Richardfon* and *Lambert* were authorized, for this purpofe, to adminifter to him, the Oath, in the *Act for regulating Corporations;* and to fee him fign the Declaration, which it contain'd, againft the *Solemn League and Covenant.* Thefe being affented to, by the Mayor, (who was alfo Efcheator, Juftice of the Peace, and Admiral) he adminifter'd the fame Oath, *&c.* to the Aldermen *Wilkinfon, Richardfon, Johnfon, Lambert, Siffon, Mafters, Forcet, Carlisle* and *Mafon:* With *Hays* and *Hardy,* (the latter made alfo Coroner with Alderman *Lambert*) who were appointed by his Majefty as their Brethren, and Juftices of the Peace: *Robert Nettleton* was fworn Sheriff; *John Higden,* and *Samuel Boyfe,* Chamberlains. A noble Entertainment, being prepar'd in the Hall, to which the Capital Burgeffes were invited, where the Earl of *Plymouth* honour'd them with his Company; fcarce were ever known greater Mirth and Rejoicing, 'till the Evening; when the Streets and Houfes were adorn'd with Bonefires and Illuminations. But, alas! thefe were fhort-liv'd Joys, when News was brought, *That his Majefty had appear'd publickly at Mafs, the* Sunday *after his being proclaim'd at* London; *and openly declar'd, that the late King dy'd a Roman Catholick.* If he had rul'd with his Brother's Policy, and taken his late Advice, *Not to endeavour the Re-Eftablifhment of* POPERY, he might have been as happy: However, he was crown'd on St. *George's* Day.—In *June,* a Rebellion was rais'd in *Scotland,* by the *Unfortunate* Duke of *Argyle;* who, being taken, was beheaded at *Edinborough.* Another, in *England,* was occafion'd by the Duke of *Monmouth;* who loft his Head, on *Tower-Hill,* the 15th of *July.* Soon after, the King too,

inftead

1686 Philip Wilkinſon	⎫	John Lindall
[*o*] *Richard Ellis*	⎬	John Collings
1687 Robert Carlisle, 1	⎫	Thomas Harriſon
[*p*] *John Blanchard*	⎬	William Cornwall

inſtead of diſplaying his Mercy, ſent Judge *Jefferies* to try the Criminals. At *Wincheſter*, Mrs. *Alice Lisle*, an antient Gentlewoman, (whose Husband was one of King *Charles* the Firſt's Judges) was beheaded for harbouring Mr. *Hicks*, a Non-Conforming Preacher: Twenty Nine ſuffer'd at *Dorcheſter;* 80 in another Place; and near 100 at *Exeter, Taunton* and *Wells.* Colonel KIRK too, with his Soldiers, (call'd *Lambs* in Deriſion) ſhow'd almoſt equal Cruelty with the Judge: Others were executed at *Tyburn*, near *London;* and, indeed, in moſt Parts of the Kingdom. When his Majeſty had reſolv'd to keep ſeveral Popish Officers in his Army, to the great Offence of his Proteſtant Subjects; then, after all the Tryals were over, near the Concluſion of the Year, he publiſh'd a general Pardon; but with ſo many Exceptions, that it might as well have been let alone; for the King obtain'd not the leaſt Thanks for it.—Mr. *Forcet* dying, Alderman *Thomas Johnſon* ſerv'd the Remainder.

[*o*] A new Eccleſiaſtical Commiſſion was erected: The Biſhop of *London*, being order'd to ſuspend Dr. *Sharp;* and, not doing it, ſuffer'd Suſpenſion himſelf. The Rev. Mr. *Samuel Johnſon* was fin'd, impriſon'd, and ſentenc'd to be whipp'd, for writing an *Addreſs to the Proteſtant Soldiers.*—The Judges *Allybone* and *Powell*, coming to hold Aſſize at *Hull;* the Aldermen *Carlisle* and *Hydes* waited upon them, at *Barton;* and conducted 'em thither. But when their Lordſhips were to go to Church, the former order'd the Sheriff and his Officers to attend him to the Romiſh Chapel: They did ſo; but not entering with him, at his Desire, *You deserve that Puniſhment*, ſaid he, *which, aſſure your ſelves, will, in time, fall upon you.* The Earl of *Plymouth*, who was Recorder, as well as Governour, being on his Departure for *London*, ſubſtituted Mr. Serjeant *Millington*, as his Deputy, in the former Office. Sir *Edward Barnard*, who was turn'd out about ſome time before, dy'd this Year: Who is ſaid to have been, * *The Honour of* Kingſton, *the Delight of* Beverley, *and an Ornament of the Law.*

[*p*] The King's Proclamation came out, firſt in *Scotland*, then in *England*, for *Liberty of Conſcience.* Two Suits at Law happen'd about this Time: One was, between the Corporation of *Hull*,
and

---

* KINGSTONIÆ *Decus*, BEVERLACI *Amor, Legis Ornamentum*, &c. See my Second Volume of Antiquities, Pag. 86. in which I have faithfully treated of *Beverley*, where that good Knight lies interr'd, in the Church of St. *Mary.*

| 1688 William Hydes | } | William Crowl |
| [*q*] *Thomas Tomlin* | } | John Bower |

and *Leeds*, concerning Port Duties, which was accommodated: The other, with *Beverley;* becaufe the Water-Bailiff of *Hull* had feized fome of their Firr-Deals: But pleading the Merits of St. *John* the Archbifhop, for whofe fake King *Henry* I. had exempted them from all Tolls and Customs, thro' *England*, they got clear for that time. His Majefty was now addrefs'd, from feveral Places, with the moft flattering Speeches; whilft the Church of *England* feem'd to be in a declining Condition. The Univerfities were proceeded againft; becaufe they refufed to accept of difqualify'd Perfons, as Prefidents, or Governours, contrary to their Statutes.—The Parliament was diffolv'd the 2d of *July;* and Preparations were foon in Hand for a new one.—His Majefty went a Progrefs to feveral Places.

[*q*] The Queen (in *January*) was faid to be great with Child: The King was congratulated upon it, by Addreffes from feveral Parts; but one, from *SCARBOROUGH, excell'd all the others.
The

* That from *Scarborough*, (which I mention, becaufe in *Yorkshire*) was the moft remarkable, to this Effect: " That *York* and *Lancafter* being united, made the " Inheritance of this Empire One; the Conjunction of *England* and *Scotland* made " two Kingdoms One: But his Majefty's Declaration, had made his Subjects Interefts " One: Every Happinefs was succeeded by a greater; every fucceeding Age, ftrove, " as it were, to outvie the former: 'Twas true, the Civil Wars had been renew'd in " the Time of their Anceftors; and the two Kingdoms difunited by an unnatural " Rebellion: But Liberty of Confcience was fo ftrong a Cement, that no Age could " have Power to diffolve it: Its Firmnefs would increafe with its Duration; because " Men would endeavour to propagate that Bleffing, which brings a vifible Reward " along with it: And if the darling Argument prevail'd, they had an Ocular Experi- " ence already of their Profit; for Fathers would not be more ftudious of tranfmitting " a clear Title of their Poffeffions to their Children, than they would be of leaving an " undoubted Inheritance of Trade, Society, and Brotherly Affection. In the first " Place therefore, they thank'd the Almighty, on their Knees, for so gracious a King; " whom, in the next Place, they thanked, for his providing for them, like a true " Father, fo rich a Patrimony of immortal Happinefs: a Portion put out for the Ufe " of Posterity, which in every feven Years, would double and redouble the Principle. " God Almighty, they hop'd and pray'd, would grant him an Heir Mafculine of his " Body; fince he already had given them one of his Mind, by his gracious Declara- " tion; to whose facred Majefty alone, they stood obliged for it. By the Council or " Procurement of none other, it came to pafs; none would they acknowledge, but a " wife and gracious King, could have found it out; none, but a *Catholick* King, was " able to effect it: They hop'd a Parliament would concur to confirm the Bleffing; " which, by its own Succefs, feem'd ratify'd already, and pafs'd in all the Hearts of " his Loyal People: That what there wanted in the Formality of Law, was fupply'd " by the concurring Votes of difinterested Men: That it would fpread, like the Tree " in Holy *Daniel's* Vifion, 'till it over-shadow'd three Nations; wherein the Birds of
the

The Second Declaration, for *Liberty of Conſcience*, being ſet forth ; the King order'd it to be read in Churches, which occaſion'd Debates among the Biſhops, who petition'd againſt it, on the 18th of *May :* For which, being ſummon'd before his Majeſty, they were, for not recanting, ſent to the *Tower.* The 10th of *June*, the Queen was ſaid to have been brought to Bed of a Son. About this time, great Endeavours were uſed to procure ſuch Members of Parliament, who would abrogate the *Penal Laws* and *Teſt.* The King us'd to *Cloſet* the Gentlemen, that they might *ſerve him in his own Way.* The Mayor of *Hull*, ROBERT CARLISLE, Eſq ; was carreſt, for this purpoſe, by his Majeſty, tho' in vain : For the Corporation, who was very dilatory in their Addreſs to his Majeſty, did not ſend it up to the Earl of *Plymouth*, who was to preſent it, 'till the Month of *October :* And then it was in ſo cold a Manner, that they neither thank'd the King for his Declaration, or gave him any Aſſurrance that they would ſend up Members of Parliament to his Approbation. The conſiderate Earl hereupon altering it, with ſome Additions, ſent it back, to the Corporation, to be freſh written, ſign'd, and ſeal'd ; which was comply'd with (tho' in a reluctant Manner) rather than entirely incur his Majeſty's Diſpleaſure. But before the Return of it, the Earl dying ; *Henry* Lord *Dover*, his Son, ſucceeded him, as High-Steward ; and Lord *Langdale*, as Governour, of *Hull :* Therefore, when the corrected Addreſs was ſent to *White-Hall*, it was preſented by Dr. *Thomas Watſon*, Biſhop of St. *David's ;* which was kindly accepted. Soon after, follow'd another Addreſs, from *Hull*, in the Name of the Goldsmiths, and other Burgeſſes ; which was compoſed by Mr. BAKER, a Brazier, call'd in Deriſion, *The Diſſenting Proteſtant Tinker.* But however, he patch'd up his Addreſs ſo well, to the King's Satisfaction, that it

was

" the Air should not only build, but the Beasts of the Forests find Security beneath
" it : That they pray'd, his Majesty might long enjoy the Fruits of ſo happy a Planta-
" tion, ſet by his auſpicious Hands ; which, they hop'd, might be fenc'd about by the
" Care of the preſent Age, and made ſacred to Futurity. And as it was in their
" Power, ſo they promis'd to ſend two Members to ſerve in Parliament, who should
" vote againſt the Test and all Penal Laws, in Matters of Religion. For Laws, *they*
" *aſſerted*, that were begot under a doubtful Title, being bred up in Perſecution, must
" consequently subvert the Fundamental Freedom of Conſcience, which is G O D's
" *Magna Chartæ* to all reasonable Creatures."

I beg Leave to mention here, as a Memorial, That a Printing Office was first ſet up by me in *Scarborough*, about *June* 16, 1734. in a Houſe in Mr. *Bland's* Lane, formerly call'd his *Cliff* ; a most pleasant Situation, leading to the beautiful Sands : And, I hope, G O D willing, ſome time or other, to print the Antiquities of that delightful Town, and Castle, as I hinted in my Second Volume ; for which Purpoſe I have ſince had ſome Manuſcripts ſent me.

was order'd to be printed; and had not the Revolution happen'd, the Man might have been made an Alderman, as well as others. The Address set forth, *That they had seen some Addresses, which thank'd his Majesty for* Such Part *of his most Gracious Declaration for Liberty of Conscience, so far as it was the Interest of their particular Persuasion, which imply'd their Dislike of all others: But They, as in Duty and Allegiance bound to their dread Sovereign, humbly thank'd Him for* THE WHOLE *Declaration; by which he had proclaim'd a Jubilee to all his People, and set the* Oppressed free. *That Almighty* GOD, *who hath said,* * Touch not mine Anointed, and do my Prophets no Harm, *would certainly reward Him for it: That their Thankfulness, for the Freedom enjoy'd through his Majesty's special Favour, should appear by the peaceable Demeanour, and extensive Charity, to all the Professors of* CHRIST, *under whatsoever Denomination. Such they would not fail to demonstrate, whenever his Majesty should be graciously pleas'd to call a Parliament: Then they would heartily endeavour, to elect such Members, as would repeal the Test and Penal Laws, against all Manner of* Dissenters: *And also pass his most* Gracious Declaration for Liberty of Conscience *into a Law as firm as* MAGNA CHARTA. As the King was pleased upon this Account; so was he as much grieved on another: For Sir *Willoughby Hickman,* Kt. Bar. of *Gainsborough,* and *John Ramsden* Esq; Members of the last Parliament, (elected such the 18th of *March,* 1685.) wrote towards the latter End of this Year, 1688, to the Corporation, *That they would gladly serve them in the approaching Convention.* They were accordingly accepted; which, when the King's Party heard, they occasion'd Orders to be sent, to chuse such as his Majesty requir'd, and had reason to hope for, from their late Address. The Lord LANGDALE severely wrote to the remarkable *Robert Carlisle,* Esq; at *Hull,* asserting, How very unhandsomely the Bench dealt with the King, in not giving him an Assurance to elect such as would approve of his Majesty's Declaration, calculated for the Happiness of this distracted Nation: To make therefore the Monarch their Friend, and he capable of serving them, he propofed Sir JOHN BRADSHAW of *Risby* for one; and the other defigned Member he would nominate in a little Time. But this did not avail: The Corporation pleaded their Promife to the former; but however told him, in a Letter, *The Election should be free, according to antient Custom.* When my Lord fhew'd this to the King, it fo enrag'd him, that, to punish the Town, he fent them near 1200 Soldiers, moftly commanded by Popifh Officers, to live therein upon free Quarters. Thefe almoft ruin'd the private Habitations: The Landlords were us'd as Slaves; and, like Dogs, kick'd

* I. CHRON. XVI. 22.

out

out of their Houfes, unlefs they furrender'd their beft Rooms and
Furniture : The Streets were not fafe, in the Night Time, from the
Robberies, committed by thofe military Plunderers ; who, in the
Day, play'd their Pranks openly, in feizing the Goods of the Market
People : The Capital Burgeffes were made Prifoners, in the Guard-
Houfe, upon the leaft Spleen of the Officers ; to which Mr. *Mawfon,*
as I mention'd before, fell a memorable, tho' unfortunate Victim !
The tender Virgins were threaten'd to be deflour'd ; the Wives, with
their Children, to be murder'd : The Magiftrates were alfo in Fear
of their Lives : In the Citadel, the Cannons were pointed at the
Town, ready to fire upon the firft dreadful Signal ; and nothing
feem'd to appear, but Horror and Deftruction ! No Complaints were
regarded by the Officers, who faid, *They muft implicitly obey their*
Commanders : No Relief was granted by the King ; who, inftead
thereof, iffu'd out his *Quo Warranto,* requiring the Town's Charter ;
not allowing fufficient Time for pleading for it : However, upon
cooler Thoughts, the King granted another ; by which he turn'd out
the Mayor, placing Mr. *Hayes* in his Room : Mr. *John Robinfon* and
Yates, (*William Carlton* and *Robert Nettleton*) Aldermen. And
this Charter, unfatisfactory as it was, was feiz'd by Judge *Jefferies ;*
who, calling the Corporation before him in the Hall, abus'd them
as a Parcel of—whatever his foul Throat could bellow out againft
them. The King order'd another Charter in *Auguft,* unmaking the
Mayor he had but a little before made, and placing Mr. *Daniel*
Hoar in his Stead : *John Blanchard,* Sheriff, (who was alfo made an
Alderman) *Thomas Harrifon,* and *William Cornwall,* Chamberlains.
Thus Things were carried confufedly on, 'till the Day of Election ;
when the Corporation chofe Mr. *Delacamp* Mayor : But they had
not proceeded much further, before an Order came from the King,
as the Effect of his Difpenfing Power, *That he would have the for-*
mer continue a Year longer ; to which they were then forc'd to fubmit, becaufe they could not help themfelves. On the 2d of *Octo-*
ber, the Old Charter was difcharged, by the Arrival of a Meffenger
with a New One ; to which Mr. *Hayes,* and thofe formerly advanc'd
with him, were not fworn. The 24th of the fame Month, the Lord
Langdale, being made Recorder, fubftituted *Robert Hollis,* Efq ; as
his Deputy. *Thomas Cooper,* Gentleman, was order'd to be the Town-
Clerk ; but he never came, from *London,* to make his Appearance.
The King, being appriz'd of the Prince of *Orange's* Intention, revok'd his Arbitrary Proceedings, reftor'd the Bifhops, publifh'd a
general Pardon, and order'd (by Proclamation) that all Corporations fhould return to their former State, which he had compell'd
them to forsake. This was proclaim'd, at *Hull,* the 6th of *Novem-*
ber : Upon which unexpected Deliverance, the Magiftrates, looking

a few

a few Years back, when the Charter was surrender'd to Judge *Jefferies*, and Mr. *Delecamp* ejected from his first Mayoralty: And considering, his being lately deny'd; they now resolutely chose him a third time, to his greater Honour: Who acted that Day, as Mayor, after that Mr. *Hoar* had delivered up the Sword and Mace; and the *Mandamus* Aldermen, *Blanchard, Dickenson,* &c. were excluded. Next Morning, he went to the Hall, accompanied by the Aldermen *Richardson, Maisters, Sisson, Mason, Field, Wilkinson, Kirby,* and *Carlisle,* who enjoy'd that Honour in 1683, when he was first elected over them; where they were replaced in their Office; and, to their Number, were newly added the Aldermen *Trippet, Hays, Skinner,* and *Hydes;* the last of which was afterwards chosen Mayor, to act, 'till a new Election, the Year following: So that 1688, seems memorable for so many Changes of eminent Persons in the Civil Government; whose Names are as follow, besides Those, already mention'd, that were regularly elected before these Contingencies.

MAYORS.	SHERIFFS.	*Chamberlains.*
Daniel Hoar	*John Blanchard*	Thomas Harrison
Fr. Delacamp, 2, 3	[1688.]	William Cornwall
William Hydes	*Samuel Boyse*	William Mar
		John Bower

But now, to secure the Town for King JAMES, the Lord *Langdale* rode Post from *London.* He brought with him Proclamations, sign'd by his Majesty, *For watching the Sea Coasts; to burn and destroy all Places, near to which the Enemy should land; to drive the Cattle, and carry every necessary thing away, whereby they might perish for want of Subsistance.* The Prince of *Orange* set Sail with his Fleet (consisting of 655 Ships, in which were near 15000 Horse and Foot) from *Brill,* on the 19th of *October.* 'Twas thought, by steering Northwards, that they design'd for *Humber;* which occasion'd the Lord *Langdale* to prepare for a Siege: But the Prince, tho' drove back by a violent Storm, yet set Sail again on the 1st of *November;* and landed, on the 5th, with his Forces, at *Torbay,* in *Devonshire.* The Bishop of *Exeter,* Dr. LAMPLUGH, when he heard this, posted up to King *James* with the News; whose Loyalty so much endear'd him to his Majesty, that he plac'd him in the Archbishoprick of * *York,* which had been long vacant (design'd, as once thought, for the Romish Bishop LEYBURN, Vicar Apostolical, who had the Year before visited *York* and *Hull*) and from which King *William* would not remove him, because of his Fidelity to his unfortunate Father-in-Law. As to *Hull,* two Parties were in Fear: The Protestants, who sided not with the King, thought they should have their Throats cut by the Soldiers, as they had threaten'd, in

* *In that* HISTORY, *see his Epitaph, Pag.* 107, &c.   Case

Case of the least Resistance ; whilst they, on the other hand, were as much terrify'd with the Thoughts of the Prince of *Orange.* The Catholicks, of the Country, flew from the Rage of the incens'd rural Inhabitants, to the Protection of the Lords *Langdale* and *Montgomery* (the latter being a Colonel) who receiv'd them kindly, as being of their Persuasion.—In this Month were Insurrections in several Places. The Earl of *Danby,* Lords *Fairfax* and *Willoughby,* with other Persons of Quality, made themselves Masters of *York,* and declar'd for a free Parliament : Many, of the Romish Communion, who stood up for the King, under Shelter of the Duke of *Newcastle,* were disarmed : So that the Regiment of that Nobleman march'd to *Hull,* for greater Security, and to strengthen the Popish Soldiers of that important Sea-Port. On the 3d of *December,* they laid a Plot to secure the Protestant Officers, with their Adherents, by changing the Rounds. Lord LANGDALE, that Night, gave out, That Lord *Montgomery* would take the Rounds of Capt. *Copley,* who was a Protestant. This coming to his Ears, by the Adjutant's telling it to Fort-Major *Barrat,* he was so affronted, that he vow'd, *If the Lord* Montgomery *offer'd such an Indignity, he would lay him by the Heels.* But, to prevent any such Design, and be rather beforehand, he discours'd with *Hanmer, Carvill,* and other Protestant Officers, and they consulting with the Magistrates, it was unanimously agreed, to call the Soldiers of their Party to Arms, *&c.* and seize upon the Chief Heads of the Papists. There were but few Words about it : In two Hours Time, the Market-Hill was cover'd with armed Men ; who were spirited up, by hearing they were call'd to defend the King, and Protestant Religion. The Lord *Langdale* knew nothing of it, 'till he was suddenly seiz'd by a Guard, under Captain *Carvill;* who plainly told him, *He was come to secure his Lordship, as being a Roman-Catholick ; and had no Right to govern, according to the Laws of the Land.* The Governour, in Amazement, reply'd : *What, Captain! Is not the King's Dispensing Power to be admitted of?*—No, said the other bluntly. *Why then,* said his Lordship, *I have no more to say at present;* and so was made Prisoner. The Lord *Montgomery* was secur'd by Captain *Fitzherbert ;* and Major *Mahony,* by Fort-Major *Barrat.* The inferiour Catholick Officers, hearing the Soldiers were under Arms ; they ran, for fear of Blame, to their respective Posts, where they were secur'd. Next Morning, one of the Protestant Captains march'd forth, with 100 Men to relieve the Guards ; and seiz'd the Popish Officers, with others of their Persuasion, who little dreamt of what had been transacted in the Night. Thus the Town, Fort and Citadel, being secur'd by Captain *Copley,* he then set the Prisoners at Liberty,

CHAP. XII.

Continuation of the MAYORS, SHERIFFS, *and* Chamberlains, *down to the present Year.*

King WILLIAM III. and Queen MARY II.
February 13, 168$\frac{8}{9}$.

A.D.	MAYOR and SHERIFF.		CHAMBERLAINS.
1689 [r]	R Obert Trippet, 1 *William Idell*	}	W ill. Crowl, *or* Crowle Will. St. Quintin

berty, when he knew it was impoſſible for them, as being diſarm'd, to make the leaſt Efforts againſt the Proteſtants.—Whilſt the Prince was triumphing, thro' his increaſing Numbers, the King's Affairs were in a declining Condition : 'Twas too late to make Amends for the Breaches he had made with his People. In his going to meet the Prince, to engage him, his Noſe, of a ſudden, bled to ſuch a degree, that proved very diſadvantageous by prolonging the Time: Lord *Churchill* (afterwards Duke of *Marlborough*) left him ; whom he had advanc'd to greateſt Honours. Prince *George* of *Denmark,* follow'd: The Princeſs (afterwards Queen ANNE) was oblig'd to live with her Husband, and deſert her Father: His Queen forc'd to fly beyond Sea ; and he himſelf to ſail from his Kingdom, and ſeek Protection in *France,* under the King of that Country. Thus a mighty Prince, who would grant a Toleration in Religion, to every Body, was forc'd away from his Crown and Dignity, for his own Faith; becauſe he would eſtablish 𝕿𝖍𝖆𝖙, which was contrary to the Conſtitution of his Kingdom ; and muſt have proved, in the End, deſtructive to thoſe, for whoſe Sake he ſeemed to plead for ſuch Liberty of Conſcience: A Liberty, which would ſoon have been deny'd, if the Counſel of Father *Petre,* and other Catholicks, had prevail'd, in what they ſo ardently ſought for, to the Ruin of their Prince.

[r] The Firſt of *January,* King *James* arriv'd at *Ambleteuſe,* in *France.*—Sir *John Hotham* was made Governour, on the Second, tho' in his old Age, being a Perſon of whom the Prince well approved ; more fortunate than his Predeceſſors: But he died the 26th of *March* following.—King *William,* having heard of the gallant Behaviour of Captain *Copley,* made him Lieutenant-Governour ; and, perhaps a Colonel, as I find him call'd by ſeveral Writers.—The Tenth of *January, William Gee,* and *John Ramſden* Eſqrs. appear'd at the Convention.—The Twenty Third, Mr. *George*
Bacchus

1690 Anthony Ivefon	}	Joshua Scott, *or* Scot
[*f*] *William Hall*		Edmund Duncalf
1691 Richard Gray, 1	}	Towers Wallis
[*t*] *John Collings*		Henry Lambert
1692 George Bacchus, 1	}	Michael Bielby, *Mercer*
[*u*] *Thomas Harrifon*		James Mould, *or* Mowld
1693 Richard Ellis	}	Daniel Hoare, *or* Hoar
[*w*] *Edmund Duncalf*		Thomas Clark, *Merchant*
1694 Henry Maifter, 2	}	John Thornton
[*x*] *John Lindall*		John Brown
1695 Simon Siffon	}	John Somerfcales
[*y*] *Martin Rafpin*		Jeremiah Shaw

Bacchus was elected Alderman.—The 13th of *March, Charles Os-born*, and *John Ramfden*, Efqrs. were Members of Parliament.—On the 6th of *May*, the Rev. Mr. *Robert Banks* was elected Vicar. Mr. *William Beilby* was chofen Sheriff, before Mr. *William Idell;* but fet afide, becaufe he refufed to take the Oath. *November* the 12th, the *Danes* arrived at *Hull.*—*William St. Quintin*, Efq; one of the Chamberlains, was afterwards created a Baronet, and made a Member of Parliament for the Town.

[*f*] *Nov.* 13. Lieutenant *Franklin* was try'd for killing Captain *Cony.*—Mr. *Hall* was unfortunately slain the Year following, on the 28th of *September ;* and Mr. *John Higden* was chofen in his Room for the Remainder of the Time.

[*t*] On the 24th of *July*, the Lord Chief Juftice *Holt*, and Judge *Turton*, came to *Hull :* The 7th of *Auguft* following, one *Banifter* was executed.

[*u*] On the 23d of *May*, Mr. *Laurence Pearfon* was kill'd.

[*w*] The 30th of *March*, a large Ship, call'd the *Humber*, was launch'd.—The Firft of *April*, a Lieutenant, of Capt. *Heemskirk's* Company, was fhot.—The 24th, Mr. *Watfon*, and fome others, were unfortunately drowned.—A Soldier was fhot on the 23d of *July;* and another fuffer'd the fame Death on the 29th.—Alderman *Johnfon* was indicted for *Barratry*, on the 7th of *Auguft*.

[*x*] Mr. *John Brown*, Chamberlain, died in his Office this Year ; and Mr. *Erafmus Darwin* was elected to ferve the Remainder of the Time. Mr. *Billington's* Houfes were burnt down.—*July* 10, Enfign *Allgood* was slain by Enfign *Bulmer*.—The 20th, the Judges *Traby* and *Turton* came to *Hull*.

[*y*] A Ship, call'd the *Newark*, was launch'd on the 3d of *June*.

One

1696 Robert Mafon	Thomas Broadley
[z] *Towers Wallis*	Thomas Clark, *Druggift*
1697 Robert Nettleton	John Watfon
[a] *John Chapelow*	J. Sothoron, *or* Southern
1698 William Mowld	Andrew Perrot
[b] *John Thornton*	Benjamin Blaydes
1699 *Sir* W. St. Quintin, *Bar.* 1	W. Fenwick, *or* Fennick
William Maifters	John Field
1700 Daniel Hoare	Thomas Scaman
[c] *John Somerscailes,* or *Somerscales*	John Tripfrogett

One *Haynes,* a Soldier, was executed this Year for ftabbing his Companion.—The 23d of *October,* Sir *William St. Quintin,* and *Charles Osborn,* Efq; were Parliament-Men, *&c.*

[z] About this time the Magiftrates were empower'd to erect Houfes of Correction for idle Perfons, as well as Places for honeft poor People to employ themfelves, if of Strength and Ability, that they might obtain a more comfortable subfiftance.

[a] One Mr. *Barnard Tower* was elected Sheriff this Year: Upon which, a Serjeant being order'd to his Habitation, in or near *Leeds,* he promifed to wait upon the Bench; but afterwards fent a Letter from Y O R K, *That he was taken very ill, which prevented him;* So, upon St. *Luke's* Day, after three Proclamations to take Poffeffion of his Office, and he not appearing, the Court fined him Two Hundred Pounds. Next Day, proceeding to a new Election, the Gentleman above-mention'd was both chofen, and fworn.— The King, upon the Town's Recommendation, made *Edward Barnard,* Efq; (Son of Sir *Edward Barnard,* Kt.) Recorder, as his Father once had worthily been, before *Robert Hollis,* Esq; was made a Deputy-Recorder, by the Lord *Langdale.*

[b] Sir *William St. Quintin,* and *Charles Osborn,* Efq; Parliament-Men.—The Poor Children, in the Cloth-Hall, never thriving in paft Times, as was expected, the Magiftrates this Year got an Act, For promoting the Englifh Manufactures; to incorporate, and appoint Truftees to take Care of the fame. To which End, the antient Edifice was to be granted, under the Town's Seal, in order to be pull'd down, and rebuilt more convenient: Which was confented to, on Condition, That if the Good defigned by the Act did not fully take Effect, it might again revert to the Corporation; and that what was done therein, might be bought for the Ufe of the Town and County, *&c.*

[c] Sir *William St. Quintin,* and *William Maifter,* Efq; Members of Parliament. [d] Mr.

| 1701 Philip Wilkinſon | Barnard Wilkinſon |
| [d] *Andrew Perrot* | Jonathan Beilby |

✠✠✠✠✠✠✠✠✠✠✠✠✠✠✠✠✠✠✠✠✠✠

Queen *ANNE, March* 8.

1702 RObert Carlisle	JOnathan Tims
[e] *Benjamin Blaydes*	Ralph Peacock
1703 William Hydes	John Purver
Thomas Clark	Lawrence Robinſon
1704 Samuel Boiſe, 1	William Walker
Benjamin Wade	Joſeph Green
1705 Robert Trippet, 2	Richard Beaumont
[f] *John Purver*	George Green
1706 Richard Gray, 2	John Beatriff
Lawrence Robinſon	John Burril
1707 Eraſmus Darwin	George Dewick
George Green	Richard Sykes
1708 Andrew Perrot	John Collings
[g] *John Beatriff*	John Maddiſon
1709 William † Fenwick, 1	Thomas Scott
[h] *Richard Beaumont*	Leonard Collings
1710 Towers Wallis	Stephen Cliff
Joſeph Green	Philip Wilkinſon
1711 John Somerſcales, 1	Will. Winſpeare, *Jun*
John Maddiſon	William Thomſon
1712 Benjamin Ward	William Coggin
[i] *Philip Wilkinſon*, Jun.	John Wood

[d] Mr. *Wilkinſon* dying (or as a different Manuſcript has it, *was loſt*) Mr. *Thomas Howard*, or *Haworth*, was choſen for the time. The ſame Members of Parliament this Year, as before-mention'd.

[e] *July* 15, the Judges *Powis* and *Blencoe* came to *Hull*.

[f] Mr. *Thomas Peacock* was elected Town-Clerk, in the Room of Mr. *Duncalf.*

[g] The Judges came to *Hull* this Year.—† *Or* Fennick.

[h] The above Mayor was elected in the Room of Mr. *Bacchus*, who became very infirm, after he was choſen a ſecond Time.

[i] The Mayor proclaimed Peace, at the Market-Place, on the 10th of *March*, 1713.

The

1713	John Collings, 1	}	William Mantle
	Thomas Scot	}	Samuel Beilby

KING *GEORGE* I. *August* 1.

1714	WIlliam Mould, 2	}	RObert Carlisle
	William Coggin	}	Chriftopher Bales
1715	*Sir* Wm. St. Quintin, 2	}	Jonathan Beilby
[k]	*John Wood*	}	William Burnell
1716	Leonard Collings, 1	}	John Wright
[l]	*William Winfpear*	}	William Ashmole
1717	William Coggin	}	John Monckton
	Chriftopher Bailes	}	William Wilberfofs
1718	Samuel Boife, 2	}	Jofiah Robinfon
[m]	*William Ashmole*	}	Thomas Ryles

[k] The abovefaid Mayor was made one of the Privy-Council. The Sheriff, dying in his Office, Mr. *William Thomfon* was elected for the Time. On *Tuefday, Feb.* 1. this Year, was a violent Storm, which blew down Pinacles from St. *Mary's* Church. The Day after, Mr. *Maifter* was chofen Member of Parliament, along with Sir *William St. Quintin.*—A raging Fire happen'd on *Monday,* the 11th of *July,* which held for above a Day and Night, upon which Account fome Houfes were blown up : The Lofs, fuftain'd hereby, was reckon'd to exceed 20000 Pounds.—The 3d of *December,* the Rev. Mr. *Charles Mace* was chofen Vicar of Holy Trinity Church. This Gentleman's * Father dy'd in the Pulpit : For as he was preaching in *York* Caftle to the condemn'd Prifoners, (who were to be executed the Day following) one of them was fo harden'd, as openly to interrupt, and even defy him, in that Part of the Difcourfe, that hinted at his † Crime : Which unparalell'd Audacity fo deeply pierc'd the tender Minifter to the Heart, (whofe melting Oratory was pathetically employ'd in moving the unhappy Wretches to repent of their crying Sins, whereby to obtain Divine Mercy) that he inftantly fainted away, dropt down, and departed this Life, to the great Sorrow of all thofe Perfons, who were Witneffes of his Holy Life, and innocent Converfation.

[l] Mr. *Maifter* died, and Mr. *Rogers* was elected Parliament Man.

[m] A violent Storm happen'd on the 14th of *February,* which blew down two Pinacles of Holy Trinity Church.—In this Mayor's Time, the North-Bridge was built.

* It was about the Year 1711, when the Rev. Mr. *Charles Mace,* Sen, thus departed this Life.

† The Criminal had barbaroufly murder'd a Clergyman, who was his Wife's Uncle; and bury'd him in a Field, where he was found by the Scratching of his own Dog : Yet the Wretch received the Sacrament as a Token of his Innocency ; faid that Mr. Mace's Death was a Judgment upon him for fuppofing him guilty ; and did not confefs till the Moment he was going to be turn'd off the Ladder.

1719 Jonathan Beilby	}	Thomas Bridges
John Mockton		William Watts
1720 Erafmus Darwin, 2	}	James Wallis
Jofiah Robinfon		Ric.*or*Wm.Williamfon
1721 Andrew Perrot, 2	}	George Healey
[*n*] *Thomas Bridges*		Triftram Carlisle
1722 William Wilberfofs	}	Samuel Watfon
[*o*] *Wm. Mantle,* or *Mantel*		William Cornwell
1723 George Green	}	William Ivefon
*George Healah,*or *Healey*		John Farwin
1724 William Ashmole	}	Henry Maifter
[*p*] *John Wright*		John Rogers
1725 John Somerfcales,2	}	Jof.Lafenby,*or*Lafonby
Triftram Carlisle		John Froggett
1726 John Collings, 2	}	Wil. Mowld, *or* Mould
[*q*] *Thomas Ryles*		Theophilus Somerfcales .

✿✿✿✿✿✿✿✿✿✿✿✿✿✿✿✿✿✿✿✿✿✿✿✿✿✿✿✿✿

KING *GEORGE* II. *June* 11.

1727 William Fenwick,2	}	THomas Haworth
[*r*] *Jofeph Lafenby*		Thomas Twisleton

[*n*] In this Mayoralty (172½) the Town-Dyke was dreffed.

[*o*] On the 7th of *April,* Sir *William St. Quintin,* Bart. and Mr. *Rogers,* were chofen Parliament-Men.—The Mayor, abovemention'd, (*William Wilberforce,* or *Wilberfofs,* Efq;) was elected Alderman on *Wednefday* the 25th of *April,* in Mr. *Perrot's* Mayoralty; on which Day, Mr. *William Mafon* was chofen Vicar of Holy Trinity Church.—The Sheriff dy'd in his Office, and was fucceeded by Mr. *William Williamfon.*

[*p*] Qn *Jan.* the 23d, Mr. *George Crowle* was elected Member of Parliament, in the Room of Sir *William St. Quintin,* deceafed.

[*q*] The *Friendly Society* was begun in *Auguft* this Year.

[*r*] The new Bells, in St. *Mary's* Steeple, were firft rung in *April,* having been hung up but a little while before.—The 18th of *June,* the King was proclaim'd at *Hull.*—*Auguft* the 3d, the Lord *Micklethwaite,*and Mr.*George Crowle,*were elected Members of Parliament.—About this time, a new Set of Bells were hung in the High Church Steeple, which were rung on the 17th.—There was

a great

1728	Thomas Scot	}	Henry Lee
[ʃ]	*John Froggett*	}	John Wood
1729	Leonard Collings, 2	}	John Porter
[t]	*Henry Maiſter*	}	Chriſ. Hearel, *or* Heron
1730	Richard Williamſon	}	Benjamin Ward
[u]	*James Melles,* or *Milns*	}	James Roe
1731	Samuel Watson	}	Joseph Pease
[w]	*William Mowld*	}	Lancelot Iveson
1732	John Monckton	}	Peter Thornton
[x]	*Chriſ. Hearel,*or *Heron*	}	George Woodhouse

a great Scarcity this Year: Even Beans were ſold, in the Weſt-Riding, at 40*s.* a Quarter ; and Corn would have been miſerably dear, had not his Majeſty, in Commiſeration to his poorer Subjects, been ſo gracious, as to take off the Duty of foreign Grain : Hereupon, in our Diſtreſs, we were ſupply'd with Ship-Loads, from *Italy, Flanders, Poland,* and other diſtant Parts, to the unſpeakable Comfort of many Houſe-Keepers, who might have been undone, without the King's kind Condeſcenſion, thus to relieve them in Time of their great Neceſſities.

[ʃ] *Myton-Gate* Bridge was entirely built this Year.

[t] In this Mayoralty, *Beverley-Gate* was entirely finiſhed.— On the 17th of *July,* Baron *Hall,* and Juſtice *Page,* came to *Hull;* before whom one *Partrick* was condemn'd for ſtealing ſeveral Pieces of Plate, which belong'd to Mr. *Mowld :* But he made his Eſcape : Since that Time, (about the Year 1732.) a moſt miſerable Wretch was executed, for ſtabbing his tender Wife in the Breaſt with a ſharp Knife, of which Wound ſhe ſoon after died.

[u] The *Sailors Society* was held, I think, about this Time.

[w] The RELIGIOUS SOCIETY, being begun, it occaſion'd ſome Diſputes, about their often receiving the Holy Sacrament : But the Controverſy ſoon ended in a peaceable Manner, thro' the Endeavours, as was said, of a Gentleman, who went under the Name of *Philanthropos.* This Society is eminent for its Religious Zeal ; and eſpecially, its well-order'd Charity, in reſpect to poor Peoples Children, for whoſe Education they take particular Care.—The Wall at the South End was erected this Year.

[x] The above Worſhipful Mayor departed this Life the 20th of *September,* the Year following : Alderman *John Collings* was therefore ſworn to ſerve the few remaining Days 'till the next Election ; (the Day after *Michaelmas,* when Sheriffs, Chamberlains, *&c.* are accuſtom'd to be choſen, tho' not ſworn 'till the Festival of St. *Luke,* the 18th of *October*) by which Means, that Gentleman became a third time Mayor of *Hull,* to his great Honour and Reputation.

1733 Joseph Lasenby	} James Shaw
[*y*] *James Bee*	} J. Haweth, *or* Haworth
1734 William Mould	} Andrew Perrot
[*z*] *John Ferron*	} David Field

[*y*] Mr. *William Hudson* was Warden to the Burgesses Society.

[*z*] A *Sociable Assembly* was held, Mr. *Joseph Berry*, Warden.

As we are now in this Mayoralty, the following Account of what was found about *March* 24, 173⅘, (by a young Damsel, Daughter to a Smith, near the *Roman* Wall in *Northumberland*, hard by a little purling Stream) will, I hope, not be unacceptable, as it is a valuable Relique of Antiquity. The Description is thus. *It is a Piece of Silver, now the Property of Mr.* COOK, *Goldsmith in* Newcastle-on-Tyne, *who bought, and highly esteems it) fashioned like a Tea-Board, 20 inches long, and 15 broad, weighing about 148 Ounces. 'Tis hollow'd about the Depth of an Inch; the Brim flat, an Inch and Quarter in Breadth; flower'd with a Vine full of Grapes, and other Curious Devices. The Figure of* Apollo *is on the right Side of the Plate: A Bow in his Left Hand, and a Physical Herb in his Right, under a Canopy, borne by 2 Pillars of the* Corinthian *Order: Near his left Leg a Tyre, or Girdle; under that an Heliotrope, being an Herb, which is said to turn round, or follow the Course of the Sun; at his Feet a* Python: *This last, was a monsterous Serpent produced by the Earth after* Deucalion's *Flood, which* Apollo *slew with his Arrows, and was thereupon called* Pythius, *in Honour of which the* Pythian *Games were instituted. Near the Right Hand Pillar, is another: but made after a different Manner, with a* Sun *for its Capital. Against this, a Priestess, looking at* Apollo, *sits upon a Tripod, or Three-footed Stool: Beneath her Feet is an Altar, near to which a Stag lies upon his Back. Nigh the Priestess, is a beautiful Woman, with her Head unveil'd, having a Wand, with a Ball on the Top, in her left Hand. Near her, is the Figure of the Goddess* Minerva, *with a Helmet upon her Head; in her left Hand a Spear, pointing with her Right to a suppos'd Huntsman, on the other Side of a large Tree. The Figure of the Head of* Medusa, *one of the* Gorgons, (*who is said to have turn'd the People near the* Tritonian *Lake into Stones, for which she was decollated by* Perseus, *Son of* Jupiter *and* Danae) *was on the Breast of the Goddess; under whose Feet was an Altar, and near it a Wolf looking up to a Man, who has an Arrow in his Right Hand, with a Bow in his Left. In a Corner, beneath him, is the Figure of a Rock, with an Urn in the Middle, which seems to flow with Waters. All these Similitudes are rais'd large, with a just Symmetry of Cast-Work, without any Sign of being engraven:*

On

*On the Back indeed ſeem a few Scratches of a Punch, or Chiſſel:
The Three firſt are,* I. P. X ; *but the reſt are unintelligible. Under
the Middle of it (before the Smith broke it off) was a low Frame,
which had been all of a Piece, about 7 Inches long, 4 broad, 1 and ½
deep : All which may exerciſe the Curioſity of the moſt occult Perſons, who are well learned in the Roman Antiquities.*

But, to return to *Kingſton-upon-Hull.*—As to memorable Perſons born therein, (tho' *Scarborough* claims too the Honour of his
Nativity) one was Sir JOHN LAWSON ; who, from mean Parentage,
and a poor Sea-Lad, was advanc'd to be an Admiral, and obtain'd
the Honour of Knighthood. He gloriously ſignaliz'd himſelf at
Sea, againſt the *Dutch,* about the Middle of the laſt Century. I
have the Copy of his Letter, written in a very religious Style, from
on Board a large Ship, called, *The* GEORGE, to the Honourable
LUKE ROBINSON, Eſq; Member of Parliament, whoſe Seat was
at *Pickering-Lyth, Yorkshire.* This valiant Admiral was ever
faithful to his Truſt ; contributed to the Reſtoration, when it was
in his Power lawfully to do it; and forc'd the *Algerines* to make
an honourable Peace with the Chriſtians: But at length he was
slain, in the Year 1665, by a Shot in the Leg from a *Dutch* Man of
War.—Another Perſon of Note, born here, was Dr. THOMAS
JOHNSON, a great Phyſician, slain at *Bâſinghouſe,* fighting for King
Charles the Firſt, on whom this Epitaph was written.

Hic JOHNSONE, *jaces : ſed ſi Mors cederet Herbis
Arte fugata tua cederet illa tuis.*

THUS PARAPHRAS'D.

JOHNSON ! (O learned Doctor !) here Thou'rt laid
   In Death's cold Arms, to whom all muſt ſubmit ;
But if that Death had Phyſick's Art obey'd,
   Thou would'ſt eſcape, by overcoming it.
The King of Terrors muſt have fall'n to Thee,
   Who now has plac'd thy Soul in happy State,
Where Thou ſhalt live (when *He* no more *shall be*)
   A glorious Saint, beyond the Power of Fate.

Several other eminent Perſons have been born in this Town :
Which has given the Title of Earl to ROBERT PIERPOINT, of
Holme, (whoſe valiant Family came in with the Conqueror) Viſcount *Newark,* created ſuch the 25th of *July,* 1628. King *Charles*
the Firſt us'd to call him, *The good Earl of* KINGSTON. He is
ſaid to have been taken Priſoner at *Gainsborough ;* and slain by
ſome of his own Friends, upon the *Humber,* who thought to reſcue
him, as he was on his Paſſage to *Hull,* in order to be more ſecurely
con-

confin'd ; tho' his Death, with the Circumftances of it, are differently related, from others, in Pag. 156. of this Book. His Son and
Succeffor, *Henry*, was made Marquefs of *Dorchefter, Anno* 1645,
which Title dy'd with him, in 1680, as having no Heirs : But the
Earldom went to *Robert* PIERPOINT, Son of *Robert*, Son of *William*
of *Thowersby*, fecond Son of Earl *Robert* ; who departing this Life
unmarried, was fucceeded by his Brother *William, A. D.* 1690.
And he dying without Iffue, the Succeffion pafs'd to *Evelin*, his
Brother, who became Marquefs of *Dorchefter*, Duke of *Kingfton*,
and not long fince was made Lord Privy-Seal.

An ACCOUNT *of the* Plate, *with other Things, that* *belong to the* CORPORATION *of* Kingfton-upon-Hull.

C H A I N S, &c.

THE Mayor's Gold Chain,
given by Sir WILLIAM
KNOWLES, Knight.
The Gold Chain, worn by the
Mayorefs, the Gift of Mr. *Gee.*
Four Silver Chains for the
Waits.
A Large Sackbut.

S W O R D S, &c.

A Large One, and a leffer :
With a *Cap of Mainte-*
nance, for the Sword-Bearer.

M A C E S, &c.

ONE Large, and Gilt.
Another of a Leffer Size.
Two fmall Silver Ones.
A Mace, made of Wood, but
tipt with Silver, for the Ufe
of the Water-Bailiff.
A *Wood-Oar*, for the Admi-
ralty-Office.

S E A L S.

A Silver One, kept by the
MAYOR.
A Seal, call'd, *The Corporation*
Seal, made of Copper.

A Seal for paffing Fines.
Another for Statute Merchants
A Stone-Seal, being the Gift of
Mr. *Robert Stockdale.*

B A D G E S, &c.

TWO Brafs Ones for the
Beadles.
A Badge for the Mafter of the
Houfe of Correction.
Two Bells for the Bellman.

C A N D L E S T I C K S, &c.

TWO Large Candlefticks,
2 Snuffers, and a Cradle, given by Alderman *Skinner.*

B O X E S.

A Silver Tobacco-Box, given
by Mr. *Vaux's* Executors.
A Silver Sugar-Box, given by
Alderman *Jofeph Ellis.*

L A D L E S, &c.

A Silver One, bought by the
Town.
Another Silver Ladle, given by
Mr. *William Cook*, who was
Cook to the Corporation.
A Bafon, and Ure.

PLATES,

PLATES, SPOONS, &c.

TWO Silver Plates.
   A Silver Spoon, given by Alderman *Joseph Ellis.*
Others, called, *The Twelve Apostles Spoons,* the Gift of Mr. *Smeaton.*
A Silver Salt.

BOWLS.

A Silver Bowl, the Gift of Mr. *John Dobbins.*
A Large Gilt One, with a Cover.
One, for Beer, that was given by Mr. *Thurscrofs.*
Another Bowl, which was the Gift of Mr. *George Painter.*

FLAGGONS.

TWO handsome Ones, made of Silver, were given by Mr. *John Lister.*

TANKARDS.

A Silver Tankard, given by Alderman *Crowle.*
Two Large Silver Ones, were given by Alderman *Dobson.*
Mr. *Robert Hog,* the Town's Cook, made the Corporation a Present of another large Silver Tankard.

CUPS, &c.

ONE called, *The Chalice Cup,* which has a Cover.
Another Silver Cup, and Cover, presented as a Sheriff's Fine, by Mr. *Johnson,* who became an Alderman, *&c.*
A gilt Cup, and Cover, given by Alderman *Crowle,* in his second Mayoralty.
A Silver Goblet, the Gift of Mr. *Smeaton.*

But here, with Reverence, I come to exemplify the Gratitude of *Hull,* to the immortal Memory of King *William* III. by the following plain, but comprehensive Inscription, under the Equestrian Statue, (made by Mr. *Scheemaker,* and set up *Nov.* 3. 1734.) on the Side of the Pedestal, which is lately rail'd about.

THIS

STATUE

Was erected in the Year
MDCC XXX IV.
To the Memory of
King WILLIAM III.
Our Great

DELIVERER.

Another Inscription, but not set up.

Memoriæ GULIELMI *tertii Regis*
Hæc Statua fuit erecta A.D. 1734.
Si quæris quare hic posita ;
Abi :
Sin ex ipsa Visu reliqua novisti
Sisle parumper :
Et illud Britanniæ *Numen*
Grata Mente venerare.

THUS RENDER'D.

"This Statue was erected to the Memory of King *William* the "Third, in the Year, 1734. If you make Enquiry, why it was
placed

E. Geldard sculp:

" placed here, go your Ways ; But if you have a Mind to know
" every Particular from its Sight, ftay a while, and gratefully pay
" Homage to the Deity of *Great-Britain*."

AND here, one may reflect on the Modefty, with which both
thefe Infcriptions have been written : That, while the glorious Memory of King *William* is juftly commemorated, (fince by Him along
with the Right of his Queen, we are oblig'd for the prefent Succeffion) no viperous Reflections are thrown upon his unfortunate,
mifguided Father-in-Law, King *James ;* for whofe Imprifonment
he would not confent, but fuffer'd him to efcape. Contrary Ufage
did he receive from fome Sectaries ; who, having enjoy'd their full
Liberty of Confcience, and when *their Turns were once ferv'd*, thro'
his Endeavours, which render'd him befotted and defpicable ; inftead of generous Pity to him, who always commiferated them,
openly and *ungratefully* befpatter'd his Royal Character, whilft in his
great, tho' deferved Diftrefs ; when, feemingly, for their Sake, he bore
upon him almoft the Indignation of three flourifhing Kingdoms.
But the Corporation has wifely avoided all bitter Reproaches, (by
cafting as it were the downy Veil of Silence over the great Deme-
rits of that unfortunate Prince) as well thro' kind Refpect to the Memory of his Royal Son-in-Law, whofe Statue they have gratefully
erected, as in a dutiful Regard for Regal Dignity : Well knowing
we have a MONARCH upon the Throne, under whofe gracious Influence we may be very happy, if we pleafe to lay afide all fenfelefs,
noify Diftinctions, which are nothing but meer empty Sounds ; and
fincerely unite to make the Government eafy to His Sacred Perfon,
happy for the Royal Family, and comfortable to us all in general.

THUS, with almoft inconceivable Induftry, (as any *ingenuous*
and *fenfible* Perfon may confider) have I brought this Hiftory to
the Eighth Year of His prefent Majefty's Reign : And, to conclude
my laft Chapter, let this be an univerfal Prayer, That the Town
of *Kingfton-upon-Hull*, with its lateft Inhabitants, may continue in
rifing Splendour ; 'till the Laft Great Coming of JESUS CHRIST,
only Son to the *King of Kings !* When Time will foon after ceafe
to be any more ; and every Place, (whether City, Town, Village,
Fort, Caftle, or Tower) fhall, as well as this remarkable Fortrefs,
draw towards a Period, and be entirely brought to

$$A\ N\quad E\ N\ D.$$

A N

I N D E X.

A.

ABbeys, a particular Account of the moſt remarkable ones in *England*, with the Names of their Founders, &c. .... *Page* 114

Abbey of St. *Mary, York*, a Proſpect of its Ruins, with a Sketch of an adjacent Multangular Tower, with ſome View of the Cathedral, between 116, and............................. 117

Abbot, George, Archbishop of *Canterbury*, High Steward of *Hull* 133

Alcock, John, Bishop of *Ely*, founds a Free-School, &c. 17

Alfred, King, bury'd at *Driffield*.. 10

Allybone, Judge, his threatning Speech to the Sheriff, &c. 183

Altar, a fine Piece, by whom portray'd.............................21

Anderſon, Nicholas, a Divine, his Epitaph 22

Antiquity a curious Plate, found, 197, 198. And, as I am compiling this Index, I hear, that, about the Beginning of *May*, 1735. above 100 Pieces of the *Romani Denarii*, or Pence, the neweſt of them are reckon'd to be more than 1600 Years old, (among which are very apparent the Buſts of *Julius, Auguſtus, Tiberius, Caligula* and *Claudius*, Emperors of *Rome*, with legible Inſcriptions) were found by a poor Man, working in a Lead Mine, near *Workeſworth*, in *Derbyshire* : Where (as a dignify'd Antiquary writes) " not only Lead, but " STIBIUM alſo, *a Mineral of a Metal-* " *lick Nature*, is found here in diſtinct " Veins ; us'd formerly in *Greece* by " the Women to colour their Eye- " Brows, upon which account the Poet *Ion* calls it OMMATOGRAPHON.

Aſſociation in *Hull* to defend Queen *Elizabeth* 126

B.

Baker, George, Eſq ; his Epitaph.. 23

Baker, Mr. call'd, *The Proteſtant Tinker*, compoſes an Addreſs to King *James* the Second 186

Barker, Captain, finds a *Groenlander* 38

Barnard, Sir *Edw.* his Character 183

—Eſq ; his Son, made Recorder 192

Barton Ferry, when founded.... 86

Battle, between the Archbishop of *York*, and the Mayor of *Hull*, &c. ..92

———— Betwixt the Sheriff of the latter Place, and the Prior of *Haltemprise*, &c. 107. Differences adjuſted. *ib.*

Bayliffs of *Hull*, that Degree aboliſhed, and Aldermen appointed 99

Bishops, Suffragan...............20

Blake, Dr. *Charles*, his Epitaph, 64, 65

Bloom, (the Worshipful, tho' unfortunate Mayor of *Hull*) travels into *Scotland*, and is there ſuddenly murder'd by a Native of that Country 173

Briefs, two different ones, their various Succeſs 131

Bruno, firſt Founder of the *Carthuſian* Order 66

Buckingham Duke of, ſtabb'd ..135

Burleigh, Lord, with the Lord Preſident, &c. viſit *Hull* and what happened thereon 129

Bush-Dyke finished 111

Bylt, Alderman, his Epitaph, a very antient one, and another over his virtuous Lady, with Paraphrases upon them both.....................25, 26

C.

Carlisle, Robert, Eſq ; reprehended by Lord *Langdale* 186

Carleton, Mr. loſt at Sea, his Epitaph, &c. 27

Caſtle at *Hull*, its Foundation ..112

Cathedral of *York*, fired by Lightening 103

Chain of Gold, enlarg'd by Sir *William Knowles's* Lady, with an Addition by Madam *Thurſcroſs*........122

CHARLES I. King, entertained at *Hull*, 138. Recorder's Speech, *ibid.* The King views the Town and Fortifications, 139. disbands the major Part of his Army, 140. his Death, 167

CHARLES II. aſcends the Royal Oak, 169. proclaim'd King, 172. his birth and Return ſolemniz'd in *Hull*,

173. the King orders a Citadel to be erected in *Hull*, 178. his Epitaph ..181

Charters, granted, &c. 11, 92.....98 new Ones granted, 100, 118, 129, 179. Charter feiz'd, 187. a new one, *ibid.*

Charter-Houfe demolish'd by *Henry* VIII. and refounded by *Edw.* VI...78 Hofpital and Chapel demolish'd, and afterwards rebuilt, &c. 72. deftroy'd by Gun-Powder, 146. a Battery rais'd upon the Ruins....................157

Cholmley, Hugh, Kt. delivers up *Scarborough* Caftle for the King's Ufe..150

Chriftianity's feeming Perfection in the Northern Parts, when........ 1

Church of *England,* in a declining Condition 184

Church, Holy Trinity, *Hull,* erected, 13. its Chantries, 15, 16, &c. three of which belong'd to *Gisburne* Priory, 18 the Church interdicted, 19. its Library, 21. a great Difpute amongft the Ladies about Seats, 128. South Profpect of the Church, between Pag. 12, and 13. Epitaphs in it, from Pag. 22. to 46. In the Church-Yard, from 46. to........56

Church, St. *Mary,* from 56 to 62. Church-Yard, 63. the poor State of both Churches, 119. their new Bells, when rung........................195

Common-Prayer-Book, when 'twas first introduc'd 19

Cloth-Hall, its antient Custom reviv'd, 120. an Act procur'd for an Incorporation 192

Conftable, Sir *Robert,* contrives to make himfelf Master of *Hull*......110

——Is hang'd in Chains over one of the Gates 111

Conventicles, when fuppreffed ..178

Convents of *Hull*.............78, 79

Corn, exceffive dear............196

Copper Farthings invented......132

Cromwell, Oliver, orders Capt. *Hotham* to be fent to Gaol, 153. is nigh being kill'd at the Battle of *Horncaftle,* 159. strange Fortune attends him, 161. gets the King into his Power, and (as he faid) the *Parliament into his Pocket,* thro' the Means of Cornet *Joyce,* a Taylor, 164. pretends to *feek God,* and is determin'd on his Majesty's Death, 166 call'd Protector, 170. takes little Notice of a Petition from *Hull,* and dies, ..171

Crowle, Alderman, Founder of an Hofpital, 29. his Lady, who was a Benefactrefs to the modern Library, her Epitaph, *ibid.* an Infcription over the Grave of Mr. *William Crowle,* Merchant, their Son...................51

Custom-House, Rooms agreed for 131

D.

Dalton, Alderman, begs Pardon..135 *Danes,* their Invafion of *England* 3 *Dobfon,* Alderman, his Epitaph ..58 Dooms-Day Book, why fo call'd.. 4 *Directory,* intruded instead of the Common-Prayer 162

E.

Earls of *March,* their Genealogy, 5 Earthquake, felt in *Hull*........129 *EDWARD* I. King, quells the Fury of the *Scots,* 9. vifits Lord *Wake* at his Castle at *Cottingham,* rides a hunting, [as defcrib'd on the left Hand on the Top of the first Copper Plate, &c.] and is mightily taken with the Situation of *Wyke,* 9. builds the Mannor for his own Ufe, and calls the Place *Kingfton-upon-Hull.* 10. gives a Charter, constitutes a Warden, 11. and dies..13

E D W. II. King, murder'd ....88 *E D W.* III. This King's Son's Effigy in *York-Minfter*..............*ibid* *E D W.* IV. crown'd at *York*..103 Election of Mayors, &c. when....196 *Ellefmere,* Lord, High-Steward..130 *Ellis,* Alderman, Founder of an Hofpital, his Epitaph ....30 *Empfon* and *Dudley,* two extortionary Lawyers, who had been us'd as Instruments by K. *Henry* VII. inform'd against in *Hull* ....106 *Exchange* built, 131. beautified..174

F.

Fairfax, Lord *Ferdinando,* Governour of *Hull,* defends the Town, when befieg'd, 157. affists at the taking of *York,* 160. dies...................163 *Fairfax,* Sir *Thomas,* takes *Leeds* 149 he and the Lord his Father routed 151 after many Dangers he meets his Father at *Hull,* 152. fignalizes himself at the Battle of *Horncaftle,* 159. fpreads about the Terror of his Arms, *ibid.* made the Parliament's General ....162 *Ferriby's* Mannor, in the East Riding of *Yorkshire* ....4 *Feribie, Richard,* proved to be Mayor in the Year 1378 ....91 *Field,* Alderman, his Epitaph ....31 Fire, a dreadful one.............194 Fish Garths pull'd up, 109......174 Fish, a prodigious large one, 20 Yards long, 119. another taken, call'd

A LITTLE SEA-HOG 127. more catch'd, but feiz'd by the Corporation 174

Floods in *Hull*, 90, 109, 123. the Country drown'd by the Sluices 147

Foxley, Alderman, fome of his Family bury'd at *Leeds* 175

Foster, Richard, and *Elizabeth* his Wife, dying in one Month, and both young, fome Lines written thereupon .. 52, 53

Frank, Alderman, the Generofity of the Corporation to him 173, 174

G.

Gee, Mr. *William*, his Will 84, 85

Gilds, how many, and why fo called 79, 80

Gisburne Priory, when founded .. 18

Goche, Sheriff, refufeth to stand .. 175 dies, A.D. 1679 32

Glandee, a Minister, an Account of his last Shift in Distrefs 180, 181

Glemham, Sir *Thomas*, made Governour of *Hull* 141

Gregg's Hofpital 15

Gregory, Sheriff, fined, &c. 120

Grimsby, Simon de, founds an Hofpital 79

H.

Hanson, Richard, Mayor, and a most valiant Captain, receives his mortal Wound at the Battle of *Wakefield*, fighting for his King 102

Harrison, Alderman, founds an Hofpital 117

Harvey, Mr. *Daniel*, the Infcription upon his handsome Tomb 64

Heneage, Sir *Thomas*, High-Steward of *Hull* 127

HENRY VI. King, vifits *Hull* and *Beverley*, 101. he escapes out of the Tower 103

HENRY VIII. vifits *Hull*, 112. and is afterwards entertain'd at the Monastery of *Thornton*, 113. dies .. 117

Heron, affifts the *English* at the Battle of *Floddon Field* 106

Hildyard, Henry, of *Wysted*, or *Winsted* Esq; (or rather a Knight, according to *Camden*) sells the Earl of *Suffolk's* forfeited Palace to the Corporation 73

Hildyard Henry, of *East Horseley*, Esq; makes a fresh Purchase of the said noble Palace &c. pulls down the antient Buildings, and erects other Habitations .... ibid

Hoar, Mr. *Daniel*, excluded from being an Alderman, thro' an Omiffion 175 lives a retir'd Life .... ibid

Hoar, Mr. *Daniel*, refigns the Sword and Mace a little before the Revolution 188

Hotham, Galfrid de, Knight, erects a Monastery, 78. his Son *Richard*, and the Corporation, &c. prove Benefactors to it 79

Hotham, Sir *John*, sent as Governour to *Hull*, 143. denies the King Enterance, 144. is proclaim'd Traytor, 146 invents strange stimulating Stories, 147 betray'd by *Saltmarsh*, a sly diffenting Parson, his Kinsman, 152. taken Prisoner at *Beverley*, and sent to *London*, 155. is try'd with his Son at *Guildhall*, 161. executed 162

Hotham, Captain, vilely insults the Earl of *Newcastle*, 144. proves (like his Father) an Incendiary, *ib*. is routed on the Woulds, 148. drove out of *Tadcaster*, ib. ravages the Country, .. 148, 149 forc'd to fly from *Scarborough*, 150 visits the Queen at *Bridlington*, ibid. committed to *Nottingham* Gaol, 153 escapes to *Hull*, and calls his former Friends very strange Names, 154. taken Prisoner, and sent to *London*, 155. reproaches the Parliament as he was upon the Scaffold, and couragiously suffers Death 162

Hotham, Sir *John*, a Descendent from the Family, made Governour of *Hull* by King *William* III. and dies 190

Howard, Sir *Edward*, takes in Forces at *Hull*, to withstand the *Scots* 106

HULL, its Origin, in the Reign of King *Edward* I. Pag. 1. Nature of its Soil, 2. built in Form of a Triangle, 10. Trade in Stock-Fish, 12. Fortifications, *ibid*. and 113, 134, 137, 139, 142. Roads about the Town, 13. Derivations of feveral Places in it, 14, 15, &c. Free-School founded, 17. the Town first paved, 14. grac'd with a handsomer Pavement, thro' the Means of Sir *Robert Hastings*, 87. newly paved, 131 the Town and Precincts made a County of itself, 100. Castle and Block-Houses, 113. deliver'd to the Corporation, 118. a noble Magazine made, 73, 137. the Garrison setled, 164. a Citadel order'd, 178. *Hull* vindicated, 172. in great Distress, 187. reliev'd by the Prudence and Courage of Captain *Copley*, and other Protestant Officers, &c at the Coming in of the Pr. of *Orange*, afterwards King *William* III. 189

Humber, why so call'd 10

Huntington

Huntington, near *York*, its Derivation 62

I.

JAMES II. King, called, *The Just*, his Speech to the Privy-Council ..182
Impiety, discover'd concerning a Taylor, and his Wife, *&c.*..........121
Insurrection, 109. quell'd, 110. other Risings ....122, 123, &c.
Johnson, Alderman, his Subtlety, 180 indicted of Baratry, 191. Epitaph ..33
Johnson, Dr. his Epitaph........198
Julius Cæsar's Expeditions into *England* 2

K.

Kingston-upon-Hull, why so called 10 Plan of it, between Page 84, and....85
Kingston, Earl of, unfortunately slain, 156. a different Account of the Circumstances of his Death 198
Kirby, Captain, kill'd 159

L.

Lamplugh, Dr. Bishop of *Exeter*, made Archbishop of *York*, and why 188
Lancaster, Duke of, deny'd Admittance into *Hull* 94
Lanes, Streets, *&c.* in *Hull*, 82. a Plan of the Town between 84 and 85
Land, sold to erect the Castle, *&c.* 91
Laud, Archbishop, beheaded 162
Lawson, Sir *John*, Admiral, an Account of him 198
Law-Suits commenc'd with *Beverley*, 119. with Q. *Elizabeth*, but dropt, 128 with *York*, concerning Foreign bought and sold, 132. with King *Charles* I. but dropt, 137. between the Ferry-Men of *Hull* and *Barton*, 177. with *Leeds* 178. with the Merchants of *Derbyshire, ibid.* again with *Leeds*, and *Beverley*, 183, and..................184
Legg, Captain, puts the Town into a Posture of Defence 137
Liberty of Conscience permitted 183
Lindsey, Earl of, his charming Behaviour, whilst bleeding and dying ..148
Lindsey, Colonel, reports that *Oliver Cromwell* made a *Satanical* Bargain! 169
Lister, Sir *John*, his Hospital, 35, 174
Long, Sir *Richard*, Governour....113

M.

Mace, the Rev. Mr. *Charles*, Senior, dies in his Pulpit 194
—— His Son made Vicar of *Hull, ib.*
Market-Cross erected 178
Marvell, A. Esq; Account of him 37
Marvell, the Rev. Mr. *Andrew*, Lecturer, drowned in *Humber*, along with

Madam *Skinner* of *Thornton*, and a young Couple who were on the Point of Marriage 142
Mawson, George, Chamberlain, barbarously used (in King *James's* the Second's Reign) 179, and 187
Mayor, a Priviledge granted, to make one free; in his Year, but revok'd, 127. a full Liberty given to keep Markets ....*ibid.*
Meaux Abbey, how begun to be erected........................ 6
Merchant - Taylors, dignify'd by Kings 80
Metham, Sir *George*, the Place of his Interment 63
Monk, Duke of *Albemarle*, High-Steward of *Hull* 174
Monasteries, with an Account of their Benefactors 66
——demolish'd by K. *Henry* VIII. with a more particular Relation of them, their Orders, Founders, and Manner of Worship......113, 114, 115
Money lent the King by the Town 108
Monmouth, Duke of, High-Steward 175
Moss, Dr. *Charles*, his Epitaph, *&c.* 60
Monuments, erected in Honour of the Family of *De la Pole* 72

N.

Neil, Richard, Archbishop of *York*, receives a Present from the Magistrates; and sends them another, 136. his Advice............................39
New-Hull, or **Sayer-Cryke**, what it was, &c.........................8
Newport, Earl of, and others take Arms from the Magazine, 137, 138. the Earl is shot into a Ditch by a Cannon Ball, but not mortally wounded, 147. he represents to the King the Impossibility of taking *Hull* 148

O.

Orders made, 100, 135..........176
Old-Hull 8

P.

Percy, Sir *Ralph*, his pretty Expression whilst valiantly dying 103
Penance perform'd by the Vicar of *North-Cave* 19
Pelham, Peregrine, Mayor, one of the wicked Judges, who assented to the Murder of King *Charles* I. 168
Persons executed at various Times, 109. 111, 123, 125, 126, 128, 183, &c.
Plague, very endemical in *Hull* and other Ports, 39. Other Visitations of it.........................104, 124
Plate, &c.

Plate, &c. belonging to *Hull*....124, and 198, 199
POLE, De la, a remarkable Account of their Origin and Family, 67. *William* of that Name, Merchant, in the *High-Street*, entertains King *Edward* III. who knighted him, and made him the first Mayor, 67. and 89. advanc'd him to be Baron of the *Exchequer*, 68. he lays the Foundation of a Religious House, dies, and the Building finished by his Son *Michael, ibid.* Translation of his Charter from *Dugdale's* Monasticon, 68, 69, 70, 71. Description of his Palace, &c. 72, 73. his Death, 74. *William De la Pole*, Duke of *Suffolk*, beheaded near *Dover*, 75. the Death and Epitaph of his Dutchefs, 157. the End of the Power of that Family in *Hull* 76
Pontefract Castle, an Account of its Towers from a Profpect in my Custody, 168. the Expence of its Demolishment from an authentick MS. *ibid.*
Port or *Haven*, in a bad Condition, but mended, 103. Ballast order'd to be taken from it....................175
Prison, order'd to be built for Thieves, 11. *Cold and Unquoth*, one fo called, 81
Pulpits, two of them, and two Reading-Desks in one Church 45
Pursglove Robert, Suffragan Bishop of HULL, his Epitaph paraphras'd, 20, 21

Q.

Quakers, their first Appearance .. 169
The Queen in Danger of being killed at *Bridlington*, 150. she fends Lord *Digby* to difcourse Sir *J. Hotham*..151

R.

Ramsden, John, Alderman, his exquifite Skill, 131. dies of the Plague, and is bury'd in *Holy Trinity Church:* Where the Rev. Mr. *Andrew Marvell*, not only ventur'd to give this Worshipful Magistrate Christian Burial; but also preach'd an excellent Sermon to the mournful Congregation, in that Time of Vifitation, 39. his Infcription......*ibid.*
Ramsden, William, Alderman, lays down his Gown, his Epitaph 40
Ranson, Chamberlain, refufes to receive one hundred Pounds, allow'd by the Town to affist him in the Office, to which he was elected 175
Ratcliff, Robert, founds an Hofpital 82
Ravenser, Richard, founds an Hofpital..........................46
Ravenspurn, a flourishing Town before the Building of *Hull* 67

Richard II. King, murder'd 95
Riots in the North 101
Riplingham, Dr. builds the Fish Shambles, 17. which were removed 131

S.

Saxons, poffefs the Kingdom 3
Scarborough, that Town's Agreement with *Hull*, 89. Addrefs to K. *James* II. upon News of the Queen's Pregnancy, 184, 185. Printing first practis'd there........................*ibid.*
Scots (Antient) having been declared Rebels, petition the King to revoke the Proclamation, 141. are invited to *England*, 160. their *Distemper'd* Loyalty, or Treachery difcover'd, *ib.* they affist at the Siege of *York*, *ib.* they deliver up the King, and leave *England*, 163
Scotch Wife, her over-pious Advice to her Husband to be hang'd 177
Sharp, Dr. *John*, Archbishop of St. *Andrew's*, slain by horrid Murderers ..177
Sheriffs fin'd for not feasting fplendidly 118
Ships fitted out, &c. 98, ...113, &c.
Sidney, Sir *William*, rewarded with the Estates that belong'd to the Family of *De la Pole*, 107, he fells them again to the King to build thereon Fortifications........................112
Siege of *Hull*, by King *Charles* I. 146 147. by the valiant Marquefs of *Newcastle*, 156, 157 158
Slingsby, Sir *Henry*, Prifoner at *Hull*, and beheaded at *London* 171
Smith, (Rev. Mr.) not waiting for the King's Re-Establishment of the Common-Prayer, reads it at the Market-Crofs 172
Society, Religious, when begun ..196
Some Differences faid to be reconcil'd, *ibid.* Society of Burgeffes, &c.....*ibid.*
Stage-Players, an Order pafs'd against them 128
Strafford, Earl of, beheaded 142
Strickland, a valiant Captain, slain 159
Styles, Rev. Mr. his Confternation 151
Swerde, Roger, Lands once belonging to him, when the Charter-Houfe was newly built, 70. a valiant Captain kill'd of the Name, whom I take to have been defcended from the aforefaid *Roger Swerde, Sward*, or *Swart*..75
Some Verfes on the Battle of *Floddon-Field*, where was slain the brave Sir *Bryan Tunstal*, mention one of his famous Ancestors, who fought for King *Henry* VII. when the Captain lay dead.
Most

Most fierce he fought in Blood-stain'd Field,
Where Martin Sward on Ground lay
slain ; -
When Rage did rage, he never reel'd,
But, like a Rock, did firm remain.

Sunday, a Prohibition against selling
Liquors thereon, *&c.* 98

T.

Tax upon Coals 133
Towers, Mr. [Sheriff] fin'd 192
Trees, why planted in Church-
Yards 16
Trinity-House, an Account of it .. 38
Tunnage and Poundage 135

V.

Velvet, a Declaration against it..124
Vice punished 118, 124, 125, 128
Usher, Archbishop, sprung from the
Nevill's Family, and how, 71. his
Saying of the Earl of *Strafford,* 142
his Death 170

W.

Walsingham, Sir *Francis,* High-Steward
of *Hull* 126
War, Preparation making for it, 137
Wards in *Hull,* a Description of
them...............................81
Wardens of *Hull,* their Power to put
Thieves to Death...................11
Water, a Dispute, about obtaining
and keeping it, between the Inhabitants
of *Hull* and the neighbouring Towns,
90, 91. a Battle concerning the Canals,
93. a Sewer begun to be cut from
Julian Well, &c. 93. the Workmen
oppos'd, 96. the Criminals punish'd,
ibid. the Waters polluted 97

an Instrument, which is said to have
prevented such Ill-Nature, Malice, and
Wickedness, *ibid.* the fresh Springs of
Anlaby granted to the Town, 108.
Water-Works begun, and finished, 130,
131. new Disputes, but adjusted, 176
Weigh-House, erected 93
Wetwang, John de, Benefactor to a
Monastery in *Hull* 79
Wetwang, Richard, Rector of St. *Den-
nis's, Walmgate,* YORK, ornaments his
Church in a beautiful Manner ....*ibid*
Whincop, Rev. Mr. *Thomas,* his Epitaph 44, 45
WILLIAM, Duke of *Normandy,*
his Conquest 6
William, Lord of *Holderness,* his Vow
to visit *Jerusalem* 3
WILLIAM III. King, the Inscrip-
tion on one Side of the Pedestal, that
bears the Equestrian Statue at *Hull* 200
the Portraiture of it is at the Top on
the Right Hand of the first Sheet taken
from a Copper Plate, curiously engrav'd by Mr. *Haynes* of *York.*
Willoughby, Lord, embarks at *Hull*
for *Denmark* 125
Work-Houses erected 192
Writing, sign'd by Pope *John,* a very
exhortatory one, to the Inhabitants of
neighbouring Towns to *Hull*........97
Writington, Sheriff, fin'd, &c.....134
Wyke, a poor Place at first........9

Y.

Young, Archbishop of *York,* visits
Hull, preaches, and confirms many Persons 121. he is much respected .. 125

BOOKS Sold at the Printing-Office in *Coffee-Yard,* near *Stone-Gate,* YORK ; by Mr. FERRABY, of *Hull;* and other Bookfellers in the Country, *&c.*

1. THE Antient and Modern History of the famous City of *York,* and in a particular
Manner of its magnificent Cathedral, commonly call'd *York-Minster.* As also,
an Account of St. *Mary's* Abbey, and other antient Religious Houses and Churches :
The Places whereon they stood ; what Orders belong'd to them ; and the Remains of
those antient Buildings, that are yet to be seen : With a Description of those Churches
now in Use ; of their curiously painted Windows ; the Inscriptions carefully collected ;
and many of them translated : The Lives of the Archbishops of this See : The Government of the Northern Parts under the *Romans;* especially by the Emperors *Severus* and
Constantius, who both dy'd in this City : Of the Kings of *England,* and other
illustrious Persons, who have honour'd *York* with their Presence : An Account of the
Mayors, and Bayliffs ; Lord-Mayors and Sheriffs ; (with several remarkable Transactions,
not published before) from different Manuscripts, down to the third Year of his present
Majesty

Majesty King *GEORGE* the Second. To which is added, A Defcription of the moſt noted Towns in *Yorkſhire*, with the antient Buildings, that have been therein : Alphabetically digeſted, for the Delight of the Reader ; not only by the Affiſtance of antient Writers, but from the Obſervations of feveral ingenious Perſons in the preſent Age. [*Price 4s.*]

II. **T**HE Antiquities of the moſt noted Places in the County, faithfully collected : As of

Beverley,	*Leeds,*	*Keighley,*	
Rippon,	*Knareſborough,*	*Skipton.*	
Pontefraet,	*Selby,*	With other remarkable	
Wakefield,	*Howlden,*	P L A C E S.	

Both theſe carefully collected by Mr. THOMAS GENT, *of* YORK.

Together with a Poem on *Studley-Park*, written by Mr. *Peter Aram ;* and another on the amuſing Delights of a Country Life, by a Young and Learned D I V I N E. [*Price, Bound in Calf Leather*, 4s. 6d. *in Sheep* 4s.]

III. *MISCELLANEA CURIOSA :* Or, Entertainments for the Ingenious of *Both Sexes*. Containing, I. E N I G M A ' S. II. P A R A - D O X E S. III. M A T H E M A T I C A L Q U E S T I O N S. Suited both to Beginners, and also to such as have made higher Advances in those S T U D I E S. Published Quarterly. Price Six Pence each Book.

Lately Publiſh'd, Price One Shilling,

IV. **C**Ritical R E M A R K S on the *EPISTLES*, as they were publiſh'd from feveral Authentic C O P I E S, by J O H N B E B E L I U S, at *Baſil*, in 1531. *N. B.* The Common R E A D I N G ſtands firſt. To which is ſubjoin'd *BEBELIUS*'s Text : Together with ſuch A U T H O R I T I E S as favour it : Which A U T H O R I T I E S, conſiſting of *Manuſcripts, Fathers*, and *Printed Copies*, near Forty in Number, are taken from Dr. *MILL*, and OTHERS.

By *BENJAMIN DAWNEY*.

V. **A** New General English D I C T I O N A R Y, calculated chiefly for the Young LADIES, in order to ſpell and write more correctly than uſual : And indeed is neceſſary for the Improvement of thoſe ingenious Readers, who do not underſtand the Learned Languages ; and uſeful for thoſe who do, ſince they may not retain in their Memory all the Terms made uſe of in

ANATOMY,	DIVINITY,	HUNTING,	MUSICK,
ARCHITECTURE,	GARDENING,	HUSBANDRY,	NAVIGATION,
ARITHMETICK,	GRAMMAR,	LAW,	PAINTING,
ALGEBRA,	HAWKING,	LOGICK,	POETRY,
ASTRONOMY,	HERALDRY,	MATHEMATICKS,	RHETORICK,
BOTANY,	HISTORY,	MECHANICKS,	SCULPTURE,
CHYMISTRY,	HORSEMANSHIP,	MILITARY,	SURGERY, *&c.*

To which is prefixed, a Compendious *Engliſh* GRAMMAR, with general Rules for the ready Formation of one Part of Speech from another : Together with a Supplement of the moſt proper Names of KINGDOMS, PROVINCES, CITIES, RIVERS, *&c.* throughout the known World : As also of the moſt celebrated Emperors, Kings, Queens, Prieſts, Poets, Philoſophers, Generals, *&c.* whether *Pagan, Mahometan, Jewiſh* or *Chriſtian*. The Whole Alphabetically digeſted ; and collected for the Uſe of ſuch Perſons, who have but an imperfect Idea of the *Engliſh* Orthography. [*Price Six Shillings.*]

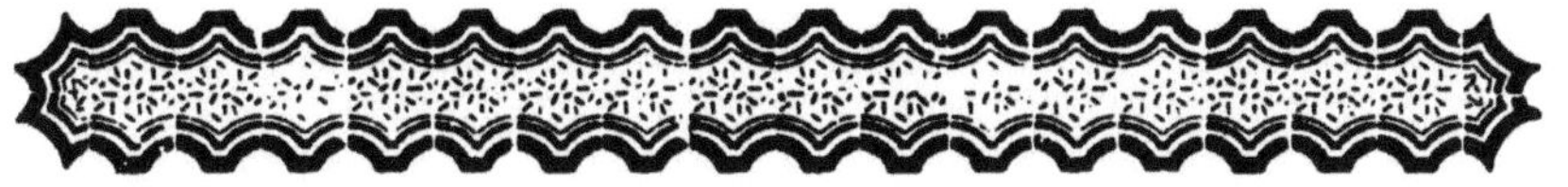

The following PIECES *coming into my Hands at various Times, I thought might not be unacceptable.*

LETTER I.

SIR, *Sheriff-Hutton*, 1733.

I Took Notice of you, when visiting our demolish'd Castle : Little can be said of it now, except that it is magnificent in its very Ruins : But as to our Church, dedicated to St. *Helen*, which you also internally view'd, I hope you regarded the Place of a Chantry on the North Side, (founded by Sir *Guy Fairfax*, to the Honour of the Holy Trinity, St. *Nicholas*, &c.) where there is an Effigy of a Knight Templer ; other remarkable Images of a noble Family, as appears by one of those being adorn'd with a Coronet ; and an antient Inscription, engrav'd on Brass, affix'd to a Stone, that is over the Bodies of Sir THOMAS WYTHAM, and his Lady ; the Feoffees of which Knight founded a Chantry within the Chapel of St. *Giles*, of *Cornborough*, the Town where the said Knight had in his Life-time resided. Before the Altar lies buried *John*, a Gentleman of the Family of *Ferrers*, with *Dorothea* his Spouse ; and another Couple, *Thomas* and *Anne*, of the *Dacres*, who dy'd near the latter End of the 16th Century. The Effigies of them are portray'd in Brass ; as also of Mrs. *Mary*, the most dear Wife of Mr. *Henry Hall*, once of this Parish, who dy'd the first of *September*, 1657. and is represented with her little Son *Edward* in her Arms. I am, Sir, a Well-Wisher, to all your Undertakings ; and,

Your humble Servant, &c.

LETTER II.

SIR, *Old Malton*, 1732.

ACcording to your Desire I send you the Inscriptions over the Graves in our venerable Church. Facing the Altar, upon a handsome raised Tomb, is this. "Here lieth the Body of "Mr. *John Bower*, late of *Newcastle*, "Merchant, who departed this Life "the 26th of *July*, 1715. aged 32 "Years." *And in the Middle Isle were these following.*

Richard, Son of *Richard Bielby*, dy'd *October* 11. 1730. aged 6 Years, and 6 *Months.*——(*Lionel Foster* dy'd 1609. *George Foster*, 1675. these lie before the Altar.)——*Mary Galloway*, dy'd *Dec.* 3, 1720. —— *John Luccock*, Mason, dy'd *May* 1, 1723, aged 49. *Judith* his Wife, *July* 31, 1727. aged 41. *John* their Son, *Jan.* 3, 1719. aged 11 Years. — *Hic jacet* Leonardus Richardson, *Generosus, qui obiit* 19 *Apr. Anno Domini* 1672. *Ætat. suæ* 64.—Here lieth the Body of *Elizabeth Usher*, who died the 20th of *June*, 1682. *James Usher*, of *New-Malton*, Gent. was buried *Feb.* 3. 1706. aged 58 Years. *Margaret* and *Mary* his Daughters ; the former dy'd *July* 27, 1683 ; the latter in *September*, 1697. —— In the Church-Yard are Inscriptions over *Percival Luccock*, who dy'd *July* 26, 1729, aged 60 ; over *William Brown*, who dy'd 1728 ; *Jane*, the Daughter of *John Story*, *Feb.* 24, 1726. and *Francis Hope*, who dy'd the same Year.

The Church, now much diminish'd, I take to have been that, which *Eustace*, the Son of *John* endow'd the antient Priory of *Malton* with ; which Monastery he had founded : Whose Son *William*, (being ripp'd out of his tender Mother's Belly, who was Daughter and Heir of *Ivo de Vescy)* when grown up, took the Name of *Vescy*, confirm'd to those *Gilbertine* Monks what his Father had given, and granted some Favours of his own : To them belong'd the Chapels of St. *Michael* and St. *Leonard :*

nard: But this Church, I fuppofe, was dedicated to St. *Mary.* It has a well-built Steeple ; and what elfe is ftanding, shew the Remains of antient curious Workmanfhip, fuch as Walks above to go formerly round it, and particularly a fine Stone † Gallery over the Altar. I am Sir, *&c.*

LETTER III.

The following Epiftle is a Copy from the Original of what was fent from Sir *John Lawson*, as mention'd Pag. 198. to *Luke Robinson*, Esq; which I had communicated to me by a Lover of Antiquity, near *Scarborough.*

From on Board the Common-Wealth Ship, near QUINBROUGH, *this* 18th *of March,* 1652.

HONOURABLE.

*Y*Our's *of the firft Inftant came to my Hand but Yesterday : Mr.* Coxmore *is not Secretary to the Honourable Commiffioners for the Admiralty ; therefore I fuppose it has laid in his Hands. I heartily thank your Honour for your great Expreffions of Affection mentioned towards me, as also of your great Love and Tenderness in relation to my dear Wife and Little Ones, by your writing to his Excellency and Mr. Speaker in their Behalf. Upon the Intelligence of my Removal hence, I muft take it as a greater Favour than can be done me in my Lifetime ; and therefore do acknowledge my felf engaged for it in the higheft Bonds of Gratefulnefs. The Almighty and my good God has renewed my Life to me ; and indeed has redeemed it from the Jaws of Death : His Name I defire with that Life to give (and bring) Glory to, the comfortable Iffue of our laft Engagements, who only ftruck Terror into the Hearts of our Enemies, and fent them away with Lofs and Shame. (Oh ! the* Lord *was* HE *the Author and Finisher*

sher *of it !) His Name therefore be magnified for it, the Honour and Praise of it is his : And truly I truft he will keep the Hearts of his Inftruments humble with him ; elfe they may juftly expect his withdrawing for the future. Honourable Sir, the Right Honourable Council of State Commiffioners of the Admiralty, and Generals of the Fleet, have appointed me Rear-Admiral of the Fleet : A very high Truft! I pray God enable me to discharge it : For of myfelf, I am not able ; it's too heavy : But I truft, that as the Lord, and their Honours, has called me to it, without any feeking of my own ; fo He will in fome measure enable me to answer that by Faithfulnefs and Diligence, which I want in Ability ; and that he will keep my Heart humble with Himfelf. I am forry to hear you have been fo ill : I shall not further become troublefome at prefent, but in the prefenting my moft humble and bounden Service to your felf, and good Mrs.* Robinfon. *My kind Love and Refpects to all, your's, all faithful Friends, I take Leave, but remain Honourable, Your Honour's and the Common-Wealth's Faithful Servant,*

John Lawfon.

I am removed out of the Fairfax *into the* George, *a gallant Ship, tho' I could have been content to have ferved in the* Fairfax *: But this is a more ftately Ship of about* 60 *Guns. I have not been at* London. *The* Fairfax *is gone to* Chatham *to be repaired. This Ship met me here. I shall be ready to fail within ten or fourteen Days ; but am commanded, when this Ship's fit to fail, to attend their Honours at* White-Hall. J. L.

LETTER IV.

SIR, *Robin Hood's Bay,* 1733.

I Took Notice in the Church-Yard of thefe following Infcriptions, *viz.*

Lotherington Bedlington, dy'd 1715, aged 22 Years.

My weary Days, and irkfome Nights, I've paft
With Sighs and Groans, which gave me Reft at laft.

Ann Boswick, dy'd in 1727, aged 40.

*Likewise, Father, and Mother dear,
Do lie beside me buried here.*

---

† *That Gallery, which appear'd like a Canopy of curious carved Stone over the Altar, was taken down, about the Year* 1734, *in repairing the Church, which was made more lightfome, and adorn'd with new Seats,* &c.

Roger Clerke, dy'd 1725. aged 83.

Begone, fond World! I've had enough of thee,
And do not care what thou can'st say of me :
Thy Smiles I hug not, nor thy Frowns I fear,
For now, behold, my Head lies quiet here.
What Faults thou find'st in me, strive thou to
    shun ;
And look at home, enough there's to be done.

Sir, I am juſt going into the Dominions of *Neptune ;* but am, Your's, *&c.*

LETTER V.

SIR,   *Whitby,* 1734.

OUR Church, (as you deſired an Account of it) is dedicated to St. *John.* 'Tis a large Edifice, cover'd with Lead, but of no great Altitude, and has a low flat † Steeple, with 4 Bells. The Motto on the leaſt is, *Repent in Time.* 1708. On that, of the next Degree, *JESUS be our Speed.* 1626. J. J. G. C. On the third, out of *Virgil,* (*Æn.* Lib. VI. *)* is, *Diſcite Juſtitiam moniti, & non temnere Divos.* 1590. And upon the largeſt, *Gloria Deo in Excelſis, et Pax Hominibus,* 1637. R. R. W. H. C. C. J. H. S. R. D. S. Within the Church are decent Galleries, adorn'd with Scripture Sentences : The Pulpit and Communion Table ornamented with red Velvet, fring'd about with Gold, *&c.* Theſe Inſcriptions I wrote down to oblige you. Here lieth the Body of *Nicholas Bernard,* who was interr'd the 13th Day of March, 1673-4. and *Anne* his Widow, 1689. Alſo *Richard Burrowse,* 1689-90. They lie buried in the N. Isle. And againſt the Wall within the Chancel on the South Side of the Altar, are these of the *Cholmley* Family.

Depoſitum Richardi Cholmeley Equitis Aurati, Henrici Cholmeley Equitis Aurati filij primogeniti, Richardi Cholmeley Equitis et Catharinæ Clifford filiæ Henrici Comitis Cumbriæ Nepotis, Rogeris Cholmeley Equitis Aurati Abnecotis, ab antiquâ Familiâ Cholmeleyorum de Cholmeley in Comitatu Ceſtrienſi oriunde, viri tam exteriori Corporis decorem ſpectabilis, quam potioribus animi dotibus adornati, Domini hujus Manerii : qui poſtquam per multos Annos in his partibus Eirenarcha deputatus, locum tenens Regis et Conſiliarius Domini Regis in partibus Borealibus ſub fere-
ſpirito

niſſimis Regibus Jacobo, et Carolo extitiſſet, Corpus ſuum huic ſepulchro, ſpirito vero ſuum immortalem patri pie placideque reddidit viceſimo tertio die Septembris Anno Æræ Chriſtianæ 1631. Ætatis ſuæ 65. ex Suſannâ priori Conjuge filia Johannis Ledgard Armigeri reliquit Hugonem Cholmeley Equitem Auratum, et Henricum Cholmeley præterea Richardum Equitem Auratum, et Urſulam Georgii Trotter Armigeri Conjugem. Ex Margareta filia Gulielmi Cob Armigeri Conjuge poſteriori reliquit Richardum et Gulielmum adhuc ſuperſtites. Margareta Relicta mæſtiſſima Conjugi amantiſſimo et bene merito poſuit.

Thus render'd in English.

The REMAINS of *RICHARD CHOLMELEY,* Kt. eldest Son of *Henry Cholmeley,* Knight, Grandſon of *Richard Cholmeley,* Knight, and of the Right Honourable *Catharine Clifford* Daughter of *Henry* Earl of *Cumberland,* Great Grandſon of *Roger Cholmeley,* Knight, deſcended of the antient Family of the *Cholmeleys* of *Cholmeley* in *Cheshire ; a* Man equally admirable as well for the Gracefulneſs of his Preſence and noble Mein, as for the nobler Endowments of his Mind : Who, after he had been many Years a Justice of the Peace, the King's Lieutenant, and of the Council to the Lord Preſident of the North under the most ſerene Princes James and Charles, at length devoutly and meekly reſign'd his Spirit to GOD the 23d Day of *September,* 1631. aged 65, and lies here buried. By *Suſanna* his first Wife, Daughter of *John Ledgard,* Eſq ; he left *Hugh Cholmeley,* Knight, and *Henry Cholmeley* and *Richard Cholmeley,* Kt. and *Ursula* Wife of *George Trotter,* Eſq ; By *Margaret,* Daughter of *William Cob,* Eſq ; his ſecond Wife, he left *Richard* and *William,* who ſurvived him. *Margaret,* his ſorrowful Relict, erected this Monument to the Memory of ſo affectionate and tender a Husband.——Above 'this Inſcription are repreſented three Hands joining, each from three different Coats of Arms having Rings on their Thumbs : Over them an Hour-Glass on an Angel's Head ; and on each Side two Angels, each having a Flambeau, with the lighted Ends down, as if they were extin-
guiſhed

---

† *A Sketch of the Church is in Page* 52. *with Mr.* Huntrode's *Epitaph,* &c.

guished them for Sorrow : With many other Ornaments finely done on Marble, or Alabafter. On the Top of all is a Pot of Incense, representing a clear burning Fire.—*Sir, I shall send you more Inscriptions in my next ; for in this I have exceeded the Bounds of an Epistle. I am, Your's, &c.*

LETTER VI.

SIR, *Whitby,* 1734.

ON the North Side of the Altar, near the Wall, is the following Infcription on a blew Marble Tomb. " Here " lieth the Body of *Nathaniel Cholme-* " *ley,* Esq; who marry'd *Mary,* Daughter " and Heir of Sir *Hugh Cholmeley* of " *Whitby,* Baronet, by the Right Ho- " nourable the Lady *Anne Compton,* " his only Wife. He departed this " Life the 20th of *April,* 1687. He " left by his faid Wife two Sons, and " one Daughter. *Hugh,* the eldeft ; " and *John. Anne* his Daughter was " born five Months after his Death."

Another large blew Stone, on the South Side of the former, has this. " Here lies the Body of Sir *Hugh* " *Cholmeley,* who departed this Life the " 9th of *January,* 1688. in the 57th " Year of his Age. He marry'd the " Hon. Lady *Anne Compton,* (Daughter " to *Spencer,* Earl of *Northampton*) by " whom he had two Daughters, *Mary* " the Eldest marry'd to *Nathaniel* " *Cholmeley,* Efq ; *Anne* the Younger " died four Years old. Likewife the " Body of the Right Honourable the " Lady *Anne Cholmeley,* interr'd the " 26th of *May,* 1705. the 68th Year " of her Age."——On a white Marble Stone before the Altar. " Here li- " eth the Body of *Anne Cholmeley,* " Daughter to *Nathaniel Cholmeley,* Efq; " by *Mary* his Wife, Daughter and " Heir to Sir *Hugh Cholmeley* of Whitby, " Bar. She was born *September* the " 21st, 1687. and departed this Life " *April* 28, 1691. being of the Age of " 3 Years, 7 Months, 7 Days."—Adjoining to this, is a lesser white Marble Stone with this. " Here lieth *Anne,* " Daughter to Sir *Hugh Cholmeley,* by " *Anne,* his Wife, Daughter to the Rt. " Hon. *Spencer* Earl of *Northampton.* " She was untimely born the 28th of " *May,* 1672, and died the 31st."—I will send you the remaining Infcrip-

tions within the Church at proper Opportunities ; and am, Sir, *&c.*

LETTER VII.

SIR, *Whitby,* 1734.

IN the Church Porch is this Infcription : Here lieth the Body of *Robert Constable* interred, who departed this Life the 6th Day of *April,* 1710. in the 33d Year of his Age.——*Between the Choir and the Pulpit is a white Marble Stone, with this.* Here lieth the Body of *Guy Fairfax* of *Steeton,* Esq, who departed this Life at *Whitby,* on the 10th of *August,* 1695.——*In the Church Porch.* Here lieth the Body of Mr. *Daniel Oughton,* who was Minister of *Whitby* 5 Years, interr'd here the 30th of *January,* 1704. aged 49 Years.—— *Within the Church, near the Chancel.* Here lieth the Body of *Charles Thomlinfon,* Gent. Son of *John Thomlinfon* of *Whitby,* Gent. both buried in one Grave. The faid *Charles* married *Esther,* the 2d Daughter of *Robert Ruffel* of *Rufwarp,* Gent. He died the 10th Day of *July,* 1690. aged 41 Years. Within the Choir is a blew Marble Stone, with this long Infcription. Here lieth the Body of *Hannah Wigginer,* eldest Daughter of Mr. *Will. Wigginer* of *Whitby,* deceafed. She was first married to *Luke Bagwith,* of *Whitby,* deceased, by whom she had seven Children. 1. *William,* deceased. 2. *Christopher.* 3. *Mary.* 4. *Jane.* 5. *William,* deceased. 6. *Thomas.* 7. *Luke.* After *Mary,* married to *Francis Connyn* of *Whitby,* Gent. and had 3 Children by him. 1. *Timothy,* deceased, who died within six Days after his Birth, and interr'd under this Stone. 2. *Margaret.* 3. *Katharine.* She died the 19th of *March,* 1670-71. Also *Timothy Bagwith,* Gent. Son of the above deceas'd *Luke* and *Hannah Bagwith,* aged 44 Years, *Feb.* 5, 1696. leaving a Wife and 4 Children.——In the North Part of the Church are 3 Folio Books. 1. A Defence of the Apology of the Church of *England.* 2. A Companion to the Temple. 3. A Book of Martyrs.—— There is a Memorial of Benefactions to the Church and Poor of *Whitby.*—— *Anno* 1657. Mr. *William Cleveland* gave 5*l. per Ann.* to put two poor Children Apprentices. —— 1668. Mr. *William Wigginer* gave a Silver Chalice to the Church.——1711. Mr. *Robert Fother-ley,*

ley, and his Sister *Elizabeth*, gave 50*l.* to buy Church Ornaments.——1712. Mr. *George Trotter* gave to the Church 3 Silver Salvers.——1702, and 1715. Mr. *Robert Norrison*, and his Wife *Elizabeth*, gave 40*l.* to the Poor of *Hawsker.*—1722. Mr. *William Pearson* gave two Houses to the Poor of *Whitby.*—1723. Mrs. *Margery Bowes* gave 6*l. per Ann.* to put 4 poor Children to Trades ; and 3*l.* 4*s. per Annum* to put 8 poor Children to School ; 12*d.* per Week to 12 poor Widows ; and one House for two poor Widows.——1723. Mr. *William Coverdale* gave 20*l.* to the Poor of *Hawsker.*——1725. Mr. *William Wigginer* gave to the Church a Silver Flaggon.——*I shall give you some of the Inscriptions in the Church-Yard in my next ; and am, Sir, Your's,* &c.

LETTER VIII.

SIR,   *Whitby,* 1734.

TO oblige you (because you urge Things to be effectually done) I shall take upon me to send the Inscriptions on the Tomb Stones, *&c.* in our Church Yard, which are many.

A.

Richard Alleson, Master and Mariner, dy'd 1711.

Elizabeth, Wife of William Addison, died 1720. aged 50.

A faithful, kind and virtuous Wife,
   While conversant in Earthly Things,
Has left the Toils of Human Life,
   To see th' Eternal King of Kings.

Mr. William Atkinson, dy'd 1702.

Thro' many various Tempests have I past ;
But a safe Harbour I have found at last.

Elizabeth, Wife of Andrew Atkinson, dy'd 1721.

Why should I unwilling be to die,
   Who liv'd so long in Pain, &c.

B.

Jacob Bean, dy'd A.D. 1688.

Robert Boultby, died 1721 ; and Hannah his Wife, 1728.

Jonas Boyes, died Dec. 4, 1691.

Jonas Boyes, 1691. and Barbara his Wife, 1705.

Elizabeth, Wife of Matthew Brown, dy'd 1722.

Why should I unwilling be to dye,
   Who liv'd so long in Pain ?
But rather chuse to go to Christ,
   And there with him remain.

Mourn not for me, my Husband dear,
   I am not dead, but sleeping be :
My Debt is paid, my Bed see here,
   Think what has past, then come to me.

C.

Mary, Wife of Richard Chapman, dy'd 1701 ; also her Husband, 1712.

Cornelius Clark, Master and Mariner, died 1723.

Who sail'd for Heaven the Port to gain,
In Hopes with Christ for to remain.

Mary Cowston, dy'd 1718.

D.

John Dent, *Jun.* dy'd 1719.

Francis Dickinson, dy'd 1705.

William, Son of William and Dorothy Dickinson, dy'd 1711.

F.

Robert Fotherley, 1686, and his Grandson. Elizabeth Wife of Robert Fotherley, 1665 ; and Robert her Husband, 1687.

G.

James, Son of James and Elizabeth Gildersleve, interr'd May 21, 1700. Also Elizabeth the late pious Wife of James Gildersleve, interr'd January 18. 1708. being the Day of her Birth.

Begone for ever Mortal Things,
   Thou Molehill Earth adieu, farewell!
Angels aspire on lofty Wings,
   Let me with JESUS ever dwell.

H.

Isabel, (Wife of Mr. Leonard Heart, Master and Mariner) dy'd in 1719.

Here lies entomb'd a dear and tender Wife,
Who was well-known to lead a pious Life:
Peace, Love, and Unity, did her inspire ;
And to relieve the Poor was her Desire.
With Worldly Care she is no more opprest:
No, no, she's gone to everlasting Rest.

Jane, Daughter of John Hill, 1701.

Jane, Wife of Francis Hill, 1674. And Francis Hill. Also Elizabeth Hill, 1720. all three under one Stone.

William Hobson, dy'd 1690.

William Hobson, *Jun.* 1703.

I.

John and Elizabeth Jackson.

A loving Couple here doth lie,
Who spent their Time in Peace and Unity.

Peter Jackson, *Sen.* 1635. and his Wife Susannah, 1683.

L.

On a Tomb-Stone is this written. Ruth, Wife of Thomas Lightfoot, Master and Mariner, 1719. aged 29.

O Lord, she was not puft in Mind,
   Nor had a scornful Eye ;

Nor did she exercise herself
In Things that were too high:
But as the Child that weaned is,
Ev'n from her Mother's Breast;
So did she, Lord, behave herself,
In Silence, and in Rest.
But now thou hast call'd her hence away,
Just in her Prime of Years,
Where I hope her Soul with thee doth dwell,
Without all Grief, or Fears.

William Long, died 1729. alſo his three Children, *viz.* John 1697. William, 1704. Jane 1704.

M.

Thomas Marshal, Master and Mariner, and his three Children, *viz.* John, 1697. William and Jane, 1704.

On a handsome Tomb is this Inscription.

Here lieth interr'd Mary the Wife of Robert Milner, Master and Mariner, who departed this Life *April* 6, 1722. aged 40. Alſo five of their Children buried by her.

A loving Wife, and tender Mother dear,
A faithful Friend, alas! lies buried here!
Return'd to Earth her late fair body is,
Till Christ more fair shall raise it unto Bliss.
Rest thou, whose Rest gives me a restless Life,
Since I have lost a kind and virtuous Wife;
Whose Charity procur'd her such a Name,
As is recorded in the Books of Fame.

Richard Marſingate, dy'd 1692-3.

N.

William, Son of Mr. Robert Noble, Minister of Danby, 1696.

Mary. Daughter of John and Jane Noble, died 1720, aged 18.

All you that come my Grave to see,
As I am now, so must you be:
I in my Youth was snatch'd away;
Therefore repent, make no Delay.

P.

William and Suſanna, Son and Daughter of William Parkins, 1710.

O cruel Death, that would not deign to spare
A loving Son and courteous Daughter fair:
Great is the Grief their Parents do sustain,
Tho' they in Heav'n will evermore remain.

Samuel Prudam, Master and Mariner, 1729. aged 33 Years.

Great is the loss to those that's left behind;
But he, no doubt, eternal joys will find.

John Potter dy'd 1727-8.

He hath left a Wife, and three Children dear:
I hope their Souls will meet in Heav'n, and their
[Bodies here.

Iſabel, Wife of John Proud, 1691.

R.

Here lieth the Bodies of Three Children of James and Hannah Reynolds, *viz.* James, dy'd 1721. James and Hannah, both in 1729.

Elizabeth, Wife of Stephen Rushel, who dy'd *Anno* 1713, lies buried here, with five Children.

S.

Leonard Smelt, dy'd 1724. aged 44.

A loving Husband here doth lie,
Who liv'd in Peace and Unity:
To Wife and Children sure the best,
Whose Soul's in everlasting Rest.

Elizabeth Stonnous, dy'd 1726.
Elizabeth, Daughter of Richard Stonnous, 1723.
Jane Steel of Ruſwarp, dy'd 1720. aged 69.
Henry Stonehouſe, Master and Mariner, dy'd 1722.

T.

Elizabeth, Wife of John Taylor, dy'd 1711, aged 26 Years.

O cruel Death! that would not spare
A loving Wife, and tender Mother dear:
Great is the Loss to those that's left behind;
But she, no doubt, eternal Joy doth find.

Robert Trewhit, 1724. aged 43.

W.

Esther, Wife of William Wainman, dy'd March 15, 1674. and two Children; and Mr. Wainman, 1690.

Remember, Man, as thou goes by,
As thou art now, so once was I:
As I am laid, so must thou lie:
Remember, Man, for thou must die!

Martha, the Wife of James Were, died 1729.

Elizabeth, Daughter of Mr. William Were, dy'd 1730.

Death's fatal Stroke hath brought me here to Rest;
My Soul with Saints and Angels now is blest:
I with my dear Friends longer would have stay'd,
But Death's great Power the Balance over-
Of Worldly Trouble I am eas'd, &c. [weighed:

Barbara Wigginer, dy'd 1658.
Lamont Wilkinſon, dy'd 1715.
John, Son of William Wilſon, died 1689. Alſo William his Son, 1696. and Robert, 1696. and Marmaduke Wilſon, 1703. *Anne*, Wife of *Isaac Wilson*, 173?.

Upon Mrs. Sarah Wilton.

She was a tender Mother to her Children dear,
Also a loving Wife, her Husband was her Care,
She ends this Life in Sorrow, Grief and Pain,
And hopes in lasting Joys for to remain.
She slighted Worldly Pomp, with sinful Pride,
And, having liv'd a pious life, she dy'd.

Barbara, Wife of John Wilton, dy'd 1728. aged 38, and lies buried with her Child.

A Wife she was both virtuous, chaste and kind ; Courteous to all, few such are left behind.

Anne, Wife of Joseph Wood, 1715.

Altho' her Body lies below,
I hope her Soul's in Heav'n above ;
In virtue's Path she us'd to go,
Her Joys will ne'er remove.

Y.

Daniel and Henry Yeoman, 1687.

Upon the Beadle's Staff, which is more than two Yards in Length, are the Arms of *Whitby*, (engraved upon the Head, which is of Silver) *viz.* Three Snakes in their Coile, or Wreaths, with the Names of the Church-Wardens.——Sir, This has prov'd a long Epistle : But I begrudge no Pains to serve my Friend, who doth his utmost to set forth the Glory of *Yorkshire*.

I am, with Respect, *&c.*

LETTER IX.

SIR, *Whitby,* 1734.

IF you have Leisure to consult the Writings of Mr. *Samuel Jones*, Author of W H I T B Y, a Poem, *&c.* you might find several Things, thro' the flowing Pen of that ingenious Gentleman, who has often employ'd himself upon the most exalted Subjects : He has shown the Virtues and Nature of the Waters, the Wholesomeness of the Air, and the Beauty of the Piers ; affording the sweetest view to the Ocean, which abounds with the finest Fish : You have given fome Account of the Town in your well-compiled History of *York*, Pag. 253, *&c.* with a remarkable Relation, how a pious contemplative Hermit was barbarously ·murder'd ; and the Penance enjoin'd for it, which yet continues every Year to be perform'd by the Successors of those cruel Homicides. I will only further tell you, That *Whitby* is in the N. E. Part of *Yorkshire*, 12 Miles N. from *Scarborough ;* is beautiful, and populous ; has two Fairs Yearly : The first, St. *Ilemass*, which I take to be St. *Bartholomew*, the 24th of *August :* The 2d, St. *Martin*, the 11th of *November ;* and the Inhabitants, tho' mostly Sea-faring Men, are of a mild, affable Temper, and exceedingly courteous to Strangers : The Market, which is on the South Side of the River, is kept on *Saturday.*——South East from the Church, at a little Distance, is the delightful Seat of *Hugh Cholmeley*, Esq ; (whose Ancestors I have so lately commemorated in my first Letter from this Place) which is S. W. of the Abbey.

The Church stands between the Abbey, and the Mouth of the River, from the Town : There is both a Foot and a Horse-way up the Hill ; the former consists of above 165 Steps from the End of the Town to the Church-Yard-Gate. There is a Chapel of Ease, on the North Side of the River, in which Prayers are read twice every Day ; and sometimes Sermons are preach'd therein, when the Weather is so bad, that People cannot easily ascend the Hill to the Church : East from which stands a Cross, (between the Church-Yard-Wall, and the Iron Gates in the Wall that incloses the Abbey) which is a firm stately Monument, formerly a Market-Cross ; And the antient Village *Strenshall*, to which the Church and † Abbey once belong'd, is said to have formerly surrounded it : But as the learned *Camden* writes concerning the Decay of *Headon*, near HULL, *ut Locorum non minus quam Hominum incerta est Conditio ;* so *Strenshall* is now no more : And *Whitby*, which formerly had been inhabited by poor Fishermen, is become at present an opulent Town, has near 130 Ships of 80 Tuns each belonging to it, and abounds with rich and expert Mariners. I shall write of the Ruins of our stately Abbey in my next ; in the mean time, I am, Sir, Your's, *&c.*

LETTER X.

SIR, *Whitby,* 1734.

YOU have, in your History of *York*, Pag. 254. mention'd how that our Abbey was founded by St. *Hilda ;* and, in that of *Rippon*, Pag. 63. given a small Sketch of its present ruinous Condition, only useful (like a *Pharus)* for a Sea-Mark. 'Tis erected upon a Hill, South of the River *Esk*, near the Ocean. No Remains of Tombs, or Monuments, (and but very imperfect Inscriptions) are to be seen : But there have been many Cells, or Vaults, in which were Stone Coffins, that contained Human Bones, and (as some report) antient Coins. Forlorn and [† *Dedicated to St.* ·MARY.] Roofless

Roofless appears the Edifice ; which is fo far demolish'd, that it's very perilous for any Person to enter therein ! To prevent which Danger, the Lord of the Manor, *Hugh Cholmely*, Esq; has inclofed it with a high Wall, adorn'd with a Pair of Iron Gates.

Concerning the Serpentine Stones found upon the *Scarr*, there have been divers Opinions. One will have it, that they proceed *thro' the meer Frolicks of Nature ;* a fecond Person afcribes it to *some occult Quality of the Earth ;* a third afferts, they are *but petrify'd Shell-Fishes of a* nautilus *kind,* like that of a Fish resembling a Ship at Sea, or any other Thing appertaining to the Ocean ; and the fourth says, they are *the spiral Petrifications which the Ground produces thro' a Fermentation peculiar to Alum Mines ;* for which they instance *Rome, Rochelle,* and *Lunenburg,* where such Stones are found. Since then each of these Opinions have been disputed, and no real Certainty given, as fully to satisfy the Curious ; accept, I beseech you, Sir, for Sake of Antiquity, the following antient, strange, yet pathetick Lines of St. *Hilda,* (which is said to have been carved on one of the Pillars in the Abbey, of which Part are to be feen) as tho' that celebrated Lady Abbefs would not have her Memory or Works forgotten, by this Address to the contemplative Readers.

A N Antient Building which you fee
Upon the Hill close by the Sea,
Was ‡ *STRENSHALL* Abbey nam'd by me.
I above-mention'd was the Dame,
When I was living in the same,
Great Wonders did as you shall hear,
Having my GOD in constant Fear :
When *Whitby* Town with Snakes was fill'd,
I to my GOD pray'd, and them kill'd :
And for Commemoration sake,
Upon the Scar you may them take :
All turn'd to † Stone with the same Shape,
As they from me did make escape :
But as for Heads none can be seen,
Except they've *Artificial* been.
Likewise the Abbey, now you see,
I made, that you might think of me ;
Likewise a Window there I plac'd,
That you might see me as undress'd.
In Morning Gown and Nightrail there,
All the Day long, fairly appear.
At th' West End of th' Church you'll fee,
Nine Paces there, in each Degree :

But if one Foot you stir aside,
My comely Presence is deny'd.
Now this is true what I have said :
So unto Death my Due I've paid.
[*She Died in* Dec. 680, *aged* 66.]
Sir *William Dugdale* writes, That this Monastery was ruin'd by *Inguar* and *Hubba,* the Leaders of the Danish Army : That *Titus* the Abbot fled with St. *Hilda's* Relicks to *Glastenbury* Abbey. When it was rebuilt by *Henry de Percy,* the Painting in one of the Cloister Windows shew'd, how the *Scots,* which dwelt near the Borders of *England,* were Man-Eaters, 'till the Time of *William* the Conqueror, who punish'd them with the Sword for their excessive Cruelty. 'Twas very well, that wholsome Correction made them better : For if fuch Wretches could make Meals of Peoples Bodies, certainly their Reputations would prove but as little Mouthfuls to those hungry Cannibals of Antiquity. The Words, in the *Monasticon,* are these : *Pictura vitrea quæ est in Claustro de* Streneshale, *monstrat Scotos, qui prope fines* Anglorum *habitant, fuisse vel ad* Gulielmi *nothi temporæ antropophagos, & hanc immanitatem a* Gulielmi *gladio fuisse punitam.* P. 72. I have nothing more to add of *Whitby* at prefent : I shall therefore conclude with my Wishes for your deserved Encouragement ; and am, Sir,

Your very humble Servant, &c.

† *I procur'd my Engraver to exhibit the Form of one of these Serpentine Stones (which I have not yet seen printed) in a Vacancy on the Copper-Plate, from which the following Prospect of* Scarborough *is taken off. The Originals, in my Custody, are in the Shape of Snakes in their natural Coil : Some of a Golden Colour representing Adders ; others more blue like Snakes, circling four or five times about. The Place, where they are found, is below the Cliff, in a blewish, or rather an Earth of a Slatish Kind, the Colour azure, more than Quarter of a Mile in Compass : Which, tho' call'd the Scar, yet is level with the Sands of the Sea Shore, and* But *overflow'd at every Tide.*

---

‡ *Ven.* BEDE *calls it* Streonef-halsh, *the last Syllable signifying a Hall.* LET-

LETTER XI.

SIR,   *New-Malton*, 1734.

I Observe, that, in the Preface to your History of *Rippon*, Page ix, x. you have given us that noble Inscription of the Gratitude of the Right Honourable the Lord *CARLISLE* to the Memory of one of his famous Ancestors. But as I happen'd to be at *Henderskelf* (or *Castle-Howard*) the other Day, I took Notice of the following Lines upon an Obelisk, which exceedingly pleas'd me, and will be acceptable in any succeeding Book of your Publication. I am, Sir, Your's, &c.

IF to Perfection these Plantations rise,
    If they agreeably my Heirs surprise;
This faithful Pillar will their Age declare,
As long as time these Characters shall spare :
Here then with kind Remembrance read his
    Name,
Who for Posterity perform'd the same.

CHARLES the Third Earl of *Carlisle*, of the Family of the HOWARDS, erected a Castle where the old Castle of *Henderskelf* stood, and call'd it *Castle-Howard*. He likewise made the Plantations in this Park, and all the Out-Works, Monuments, and other Plantations belonging to the said Seat. He began these Works in the Year MDCCII. and set up this Inscription *Anno Dom.* MDCCXXXI.

LETTER XII.

SIR,   *Malton*, 1734.

THE following excellent Lines, said to be written by a well-known Earl, as Advice to the young Lord his Son and Heir, I am sure deserves the Perusal of every ingenious Person. I shall be heartily glad, when such just and noble Thoughts will appear in your miscellaneous Collections, who takes such Pains to oblige the Curious in this County. I am, &c.

I.

IF in those *Lawns* and *Woods* thus form'd
    If in these shady Walks adorn'd,
    Thou takeft some Delight :
Let Him, who did perform the same,
With Peace of Mind, prefer'd to Fame,
    Stand present in thy Sight.

II.

To His long Labours, to His Care,
His Thoughts of Thee, who is His Heir,
    Some Thanks, perchance, are due :
If this His Wish thou would'st fulfill,
If You would execute His Will,
    The like Designs pursue.

III.

His Care of Thee in this he shows ;
He recommends the Life he chose,
    Where Health and Peace abound :
He did from long Experience find,
That true Content, a quiet Mind,
    Seldom in Courts are found.

IV.

Fly then from thence, the City leave;
Thy very Friends will Thee deceive,
    Virtue does there offend :
In this Retreat safe shalt Thou be,
From all those certain Mischiefs free,
    That do on Courts attend.

V.

Nor think, that in this lonely Shade,
For Ease and Quiet chiefly made,
    Inactive Thou wilt be :
Occasion often will present,
Whereby vile Deeds Thou may prevent ;
    Justice will call on Thee.

VI.

The bold Oppressor Thou shalt awe ;
And the Violator of the Law
    Shall feel thy heavy Hand :
To the Distress'd, Needy and Poor,
Thy ever charitable Door,
    Shall always open stand.

VII.

A gen'rous Kindness Thou wilt show :
Favours and Bounty Thou'lt bestow
    On those, who most deserve :
The * Innocent, thou shalt protect ;
The Modest, thou shalt not neglect ;
    In Safety all preserve.

VIII.

If thus thy Time thou dost employ,
True Peace of Mind thou shalt enjoy ;
    These Acts are Good and Just :
The poor Man's prayers will Thee attend;
The *Rich* thy *Works* will much commend;
    In Thee will put their Trust.

IX.

Then, think on Those who are to come ;
Think on thy blooming darling Son ;
    Thus for his Good provide :
Shew Him the Life that thou hast led ;
Instruct him in those Paths to tread ;
    Be thou his faithful Guide.

X.

If virtuous Thoughts his Soul endue ;
If this Advice he will pursue,
    Sure Happiness he'll find :
Nor can'ft thou, if great *Wealth* you leave,
Which often do the World deceive,
    To Him be half so kind.

* *His Lordship is universally pray'd for on this Account.*

XI. Thus

XI.

Thus for Thy Own, and for His Sake,
That His Abode He here may make,
  New Works for him prepare :
What then for Thee thy Sire hath done,
The like do Thou for thy dear Son,
  For Him shew equal Care.

XII.

The Times will come none can prevent,
From these green Shades we muſt be ſent
  To Darkness far below :
On yon green Hill a * Dome doth stand,
Erected by thy Father's Hand,
  Where Thou and He must go !

XIII.

To Thee, what Comfort will it be :
The same likewise 'twill be to me,
  When our last Breath we yield ; •
That ſome *good* Deeds we here have done,
A fruitless Race we have not run,
  When thus we quit the Field.

---

* *A new Church now erecting.*

LETTER XIII.

SIR,   *Towthorp,* 1734.

BEing a Lover of Antiquity, and hearing that the late Mr. *Anthony Addington* had bought (of Mr. *Smith,* Bell-Founder in *Micklegate, York*) an antient Mortar, that had been long in the *Fairfax's* Family, which once belong'd to St. *Mary's* Abbey ; I had the Curiosity to visit Mr. *Joseph Addington,* his Son, a Confectioner in the Minster-Yard, in whose Custody it is ; who courteously shew'd me the same, which I take to be about 11 Inches diameter, and the Inscriptions very remarkable. One is, *Mortarium Sancti* Johannis *Evangelistæ de Infirmaria Beatæ* MARIÆ *EBOR : But this is contracted after the

---

* *This Abbey was built about 12 Years after the Conquest ; and had 29 Abbots from that time 'till the Dissolution.* Stephen *of* Whitby *was the first.* Simon de Warwick *(the 10th) built a new Choir, inclosed the Monastery with a Wall, and dy'd about the latter End of the 13th Century. The 19th was* Thomas Spofford, *afterwards made Bishop of* Durham, *who was buried here. The last was* William Dent, *born at* Thornton : *He dy'd in the Year 1546, lies interr'd in* York *Minster, and on his Grave-Stone was once a Brass Inscription.*

---

the following Manner, with Stops between each Word, instead of Spaces. ✠*MORTARIU. SCI. JOH'IS. EWANGEL. DE. INFIRMARIA. BE. MARIE. EBOR.*—THAT IS, *The Mortar of St.* John *the Evangelist belonging to the Infirmary of Saint* MARY *at* YORK. And circling the Bottom is the Maker's Name, *&c.* as following : ✠*FR. WILLS. DE. TOVTHORP. ME. FECIT. A.D. MCCCVIII.*—*Fr. Wills.* are contracted for *Frater Willielmus :* And thus understood, the English will be this : *Brother* WILLIAM *of* Touthorp *made me in the Year of our Lord* 1308. For the Brethren, or Monks, who were then called with their Christian Names preceding the Places they were born in, us'd at certain Times to follow particular Occupations in their Monasteries : And so this was the Work of one of the Religious Men, who was born at (or came from) a little Town called *Towthorp,* in *Bulmer* Weapontake about 4 Miles N.E. of *York.* I observe, that antiently scarce any thing belonging to Religious Places, but what had some particular Inscriptions or Mottoes to distinguish them ; especially Bells of all Sorts, with *Sit Nomen Domini benedictum,* and such like, of which your History of *York* gives an Account, *Pag.* 28. 29. on the famous and tunable Ring of Bells in one of the beautiful Western Steeples of that Cathedral. I am, Sir, *&c.*

LETTER XIV.

SIR,   *Malton,* 1735.

WHEN I was at *York,* I had a Desire to see the Tomb of a once ingenious Friend, who lies buried in St. *Olave's* Church-Yard, near the venerable Ruins of St. *Mary's* Abbey. After I had paid a small Tribute of Sorrow to his Memory, contemplated of the Certainty of Death, and how uncertain we are as to the Time when our Bodies must be laid in the Dust ; I took Notice of two Inscriptions, on a handsome Tomb-Stone, near the East Window of the Church, which I took a Copy of, this that I now send you, if you please to insert it in any new Edition. I am, Sir, Your humble Servant, *&c.*

Hic

Hic fitus eft

Reverendus THOMAS MOSLEY, M.A.

Rector de Skelton, Vicarius de Overton,

Et hujus Ecclesiæ Curatus.

Pastor fuit fidus, & affiduus,

Non minus privatis Monitis,

Quam publicis Concionibus,

Ad veram Pietatem

Sibi Commiffos

Dirigens, adhortans.

Ita totus Minister Jesu Christi,

Ut Omnes agnoscerent Virum vere Primitivum ;

Et huic Muneri dum partes daret præcipuas,

Conjugis, Parentis, Vicini, & Hominis,

Officia haud neglexit ;

Sed omnium tale Se præstitit Exemplar,

Quale imitari neminem Pudeat,

Nunquam Pænitebit.

Obiit 26 Nov. An. Dom. 1732. Æt. 69.

Juxta Sita est

BRIDGETA, Uxor Ejus,

Digna tali Viro,

Cui Pulchra Forma, Conjugalis Amor, Domestica Cura,

Semper Charam, Semper Amabilem Præbuit ;

Ut illa privatus.

Quafi Sui Dimidio,

Vix duos Menses

Manserit Superstes.

Obiit illa 29 Sept. An. Dom. 1732. Æt. 59.

Concerning the TOWN of
S C A R B O R O U G H.

LETTER XV.

SIR,   *Scarborough,* 1734.

THE extraordinary Labours you have gone through of late Years merit the Encouragement of all ingenious Persons. As you was pleased to communicate to me your Design of printing the History and Antiquities of the Town of *Scarborough*, I send you the following Accounts as preparatory to it.

You are sensible, Sir, what the learned *Camden* writes of it, who is authentick as to its Derivation, that it is a Burgh founded upon a steep Rock: He has given you a very good Description from the famous WILLIAM, born at *Bridlington*, in King *Stephen's* Reign; but educated in the Abbey of *Newborough*, in the North Rid. of *Yorkshire*, where he became a Canon Regular of the Order of St. *Augustine.* The *Rock* (he tells us) *on which the Castle stands, is of a stupendous Height and Magnitude, inaccessible by reason of steep Crags, almost on every Side, and stands in the Sea, which very near surrounds it. On the Top is a delightful Grassy Plain of about* 30 *Acres, (tho' once accounted* 60, *or more) with a little Fountain of fresh Water flowing from a Rock. In the narrow Bit of Land, or Passage, which leads to the West, and to which on that Part it cannot be ascended without some Labour, is a stately Edifice. Underneath it, the Enterance of the Town begins,* spreading on † *both Sides, to the North and South, carrying its Front to the West, which is strengthen'd with a Wall; but from the East fenc'd with a Rock where the Castle is erected ; and on both Sides of the said Rock by the Sea. The noble Earl* W I L L I A M le Grofs *perceiving this to be a fit Place for him to build a Castle upon, increas'd its natural Strength by a sumptuous Work, which inclosed the Plain by a Wall ;* and

---

† The Streets, &c. are these. Castle Dyke-Lane. Key-Street. Smithy-Lane, and Hill. The two Peers, on the largest of which is Locker-House. Long-Greece, near which is the Town's Hall. Cuddy-Rood Lane. Peacock-Lane. Shill-Bottle-Lane. Castlegate. Paradise Close, and Garden. High and Low West-Gate. Tutthill-Lane and Street. Steeth-Bolt, near which is the Post-House and Custom-House. St. Mary's Street. Vicarage Garden, &c. near the Church. Sprite-Lane. Long West-Gate. Cook-Row. St. Sepulcher's Street, the Church-Yard, and Frieridge near it. Trinity-House. Sawton-Entry. Palace-Hill. Merchant-Row. Flesher-Street. Dumple-Street. High-Tolergate. Tolergate ; the Closes. Old-brough. Cart-Street. Market-Cross. Newbrough. Market-Place, and Newbrough-Bar, on the North Side of these 3 Places (or the Great Street) are St. Thomas's [the Martyr's] Church-Yard, St. Thomas's Hospital, St. Thomas's-Street, the Old-Bowling-Green, Black Fryer-Gate, and Oldbrough Bar. And on the South Side, towards the Ocean, are St. Nicholas's (or Long-Room) Street, where the ASSEMBLY is

and erected a Tower in the Enterance : Which, in Process of Time, having been decay'd ; King Henry II. commanded a large and beautiful Castle to be built on the same.

LELAND, in his *Itenerary*, mentions, That in the first Court of this Castle there were three Towers in a Row : betwixt each was a Draw Bridge, and an Arch ; under which, with some Expence, the Sea-Water might have been brought to flow. In the Second Square was the Queen's Tower, with noble Apartments : Not far from which was a beautiful Chapel. King *Richard* III. erected a Bulwark, which is gone to Ruin, thro' the Rage of the Ocean. Part of a Tower, with exceeding thick Walls, which had Common Necessary-Houses, with a Portal, and one of the Draw Bridges, are yet to be seen.

This Castle has had several Governours ; as *Roger*, Archbishop of *York*, that famous Prelate, who built the Choir of the Minster, and whom you have mention'd in your History, Page 72.——*Hugh Bardolf*, Son of Lord *William* of that Name.—*Brian Fitz-Alan*, High Sheriff of the County about the Year 1235.—*William de Dacre*, *A. D.* 1247.—*John de Vesci*, in King *Edward* the First's Time ; whose Widow, the Lady *Isabel*, possess'd 'till her Death : Then succeeded *John*, the Heir to her Husband ; and after him *William de Vesci*.—On his Decease came in *Henry de Percy*, in the Year 1322.—*Thomas de Oughtred* about 5 Years afterwards.— Sir *Thomas Lumley*, Anno 1444.—Sir *Ralph Evers*, in King *Henry* the VIIIth's Time.—Sir *Hugh Cholmeley*, in the Reign of King *Charles* the First ; and Sir *Jordan Crosland*, of *Newbie*, Knight, who was Governour also in that distressed Monarch's Reign, and in that of his Son King *Charles* II. as expressed in the Inscription over the Grave of the Knight, who lies buried in the Collegiate Church of *Rippon*, as you have made honourable Mention of in Page 124 of that History : These are all I can find mention'd as yet ; but I will make further Enquiry.

To this Fortress *Pierce Gaveston* (being accompany'd by King *Edward* II.) fled for Protection, who was afterwards beheaded on *Gaversley Heath*, near *Warwick*, the 20th of *June*, 1312. Here one Mr. *John Mercer*, a Scotsman,

was imprison'd by the Earl of *Northumberland* ; to revenge which, his Son enter'd the Harbour, making several Ships his Prey, 'till an *English* Fleet, set out by Alderman *Philpot* of *London*, recovered them from him, and his Assistants the *Spaniards*, who in 15 Vessels were made Prisoners. *Ask*, with his Train, in vain besieg'd this Castle : But Mr. *Thomas Strafford*, Son to the Lord of that Name, assisted by 30 Persons, valiantly took it ; from whom being recover'd, he was executed in Queen *Mary's* Reign. The Inhabitants of *Holland* and *Zealand* were wont to obtain Licence from this Place, in order to fish for Herrings. Here *Virac*, Envoy from *France* to *Scotland*, being in Queen *Elizabeth's* Time driven hither by a Storm, was seiz'd, and sent up to *London*. Sir *Hugh Cholmeley*, before-mention'd, both deliver'd the Castle up, and receiv'd it again, for the Use of King *Charles* the First, when he became sensible how much that unfortunate Prince was abused : Every one may guess how it came to be demolish'd, when they consider the general Destruction of such stupendous Buildings in those troublesome Times ; and of that Usurpation which follow'd the Death of the Royal Martyr. I am, Sir, Your's, &c.

LETTER XVI.

SIR, *Scarborough*, 1734.

OUR Church, before the Reformation, was adorn'd with three fair Towers ; two at the West End, and one over the Middle of the Cross Isle, like that which is now standing, if not the same. In this Edifice, which was dedicated to the Virgin *Mary*, was a Chantry, founded to her Honour, by the Bayliffs and Commonalty, which they endow'd with near five Pounds a Year ; another Chantry, in Reverence to St. *James*, was erected by Mr. *Robert Galand*, who endow'd it with near 6*l.* per *Annum* ; and a third to St. *Stephen*, (thro' the Piety of Mr. *Robert Rillington*) endow'd with Three Pounds a Year. No doubt but some, if not all of these, were then in the spacious Chancel, or East Part ; which is now Roofless, and has nothing to set it off, except a Pomp in Ruins, denoting its former Magnificence ; and the Tomb-Stones

Stones of the Dead, with which both it, and the Church-Yard, are almost fill'd. You may correct and supply what are wrong or wanting as to the Inscriptions, when you come hither your self ; but in the mean time I shall send you *some* Account, alphabetically digested after your easy and accustomed Method, which I doubt not but will prove acceptable Memorials to many of the surviving Kindred. I am, *&c.*

LETTER XVII.

SIR,   *Scarborough,* 1734.

ACcording to my Promise, I send you several Inscriptions, both in our Church and Church-Yard, which are as follow.

B.

Hic deponitur quicquid erat mortale Johannis Batty, nuper de Scarbrough, Gen. obiit decimo quinto Novemb. Anno Salutis 1719. Ætat. 58.

Sub hoc tumulo sepulta jacet Anna Boteler, Vidua Relicta Noelis Boteler, olim hujus Ecclesiæ Vicarii, tertio Die Januarij, Anno Dom. 1718-19. Spe Resurrectionis fælicis fatis ceffit. *This Gentlewoman lies buried in the Middle Isle.*

Isabel, Wife of Milborne Botteril, died 1728, aged 33.

Thomas, Son of James Boyes, died 1727. aged 9 Years.

Thomas Brackenbury, Gentleman, dy'd aged 47. *Buried in the Church.*

Milcah Uxor Christopheri Brown hic jacet, sepulta Jan. 17, A.D. 1676-7. Ætatis suæ 65. Virtus post Funera vivit.

Henry Burgh, died 1726. aged 47. Upon his white Marble Tomb is this.

All you that do behold my Stone,
O think how quickly I was gone !
Death does not always Warning give,
Therefore be careful how you live.

Mrs. Eliz. Burton, 1726. aged 59.

Mrs. Anne Burton, Wife of Mr. Richard Burton of Falsgrave, died A.D. 1719. aged 65.

C.

Elizabeth, Wife of Francis Clark, and their Daughters, all dy'd in 1727.

Elizabeth, Daughter of James Clavering of Greencroft, Esq ; died in 1714, five Years old.

Captain William Clement dy'd 1707, aged 81 ; and Isabel his Wife, departed in 1710, aged 85.

Mr. Thomas Cockerill, 1726. aged 40. I.I. *Cor.* vi. 2. *For he saith,* &c.

Jane, Wife of Thomas Cockerill, died 1712, aged 43. *Acts* xiv. 22. *We must through much tribulation,* &c.

John, Son of Thomas Cockerill, died 1713. aged 24.

Hic jacet Guliel. Cooper de Scarburg. Com. Ebor. Gener. qui obiit 27 Die Feb. 1695. Anno Ætatis suæ 54.

D.

Mr. George Davee, died Aug. 3. 1728 aged 34. *Lies buried in the Church-Yard, near the West Door.*

E.

Mr. Matthew Endick, died 1729. aged 62.

F.

Judith, Widow of Sage Fowler, died in the 48th Year of her Age.

When Sol *upon the* Centaur's *Back,*
 His circled Course apply'd,
And three Degrees therein had pass'd,
 Ev'n at that Time she dy'd.

John their Son departed this Life when he was three Years old.

G.

Alice, Wife of Francis Goland, 1725-6
GOD grant that all who on me cast an Eye,
May straightway go, and wisely learn to die.

H.

Jarvis Harden, died 1729. aged 37.

Margaret, Wife of John Harrison. 1702. aged 33. II. *Cor.* v. 1. *For we know, that if our earthly house,* &c.

Mr. Daniel Harwood, died 1727. aged 37.

William Holmes, dy'd 1717.
 Alas ! short was his Life,
  And sudden was his End :
 Reader, observe, so may your's be !
  Take Care how you it spend.

K.

Alice, Wife of Mr. John Kenyon, died in 1724. aged 40.
She was—but Room forbids me tell you what :
Think what a Wife should be, and she was that.

N.

William Norwood, *of* Filey, Ship-Carpenter, departed 1729. aged 51.

Hic deponuntur Cineres Johannis Nunwick Gener. qui 12mo Die Januarij Diem clausit supremam, A. D. 1717. Ætatis suæ 61.

O.

Christopher Owston, 1725. Aged 63.

R.

Against the Wall, at the West End of the Church, is this. Hunc juxta Locum
reponuntur

reponuntur Cineres Roberti filii Roberti Kaine, Chyr. qui 21 Martii supremam clausit Diem 3tio fuæ Ætat. Anno. Dom. 1722.

Mr. John Robinson, died An. 1702. Mrs. Jane, 1703. Thomas and Timothy Robinson, 1680, 1681.

Mary, Wife of Mr. John Robinson, departed in 1722, aged 52.

O Death inflexible ! that would not spare
A loving Wife, and tender Mother dear :
Great is the Loss, &c.

Hic deponuntur Cineres Gulielmi Robinson, Generofus, qui diem clausit fupremam octavo die Menfis Martij Anno Ætatis fuæ quadragefimo quarto Annoq ; Dom. millefimo feptingentiffimo et decimo quinto.

Nicholas Rowe, dy'd 1713. aged 19. *Buried within the Church.*

S.

Mr. William Scriven, died 1727. aged 67.

Hic deponuntur Cineres Richardi Shepherd, qui obiit 8vo Junii, Anno Dom. 1711. Ætatis fuæ 56.

Hic jacet fepulta Elizabethæ Uxor Richardi Shepherd, quæ obiit 29 Julij, A.D. 1715. Ætatis fuæ 55. *Interr'd in the Church.*

In fpe Resurrectionis gloriofæ prope petram fepulta eft Anna Sinclare Uxor Gulielmo Sinclare, Chyr. obiit 25 Decembris Ann. Salutis 1723. Ætat. 60. fuit pia & probitate micans, fponfoque fidelis.

Hic requiefcit in Spe Refurrectionis Domini noftri Jesu Chrifti Francifcus Sollit, qui obiit nono die Menfis Novembris Anno Ætatis fuæ 62, 1680.

Hic requiefcit in Spe Refurrectionis Domini noftri Jesu Christi Rebecca Sollit, uxor Francisci Sollit, hic fita ; quæ obiit 12mo Die Mens. Martij, 1681. Ætat 60.

Mr. Samuel Springall, of Great-Yarmouth ; who, having received a mortal Wound Aug. 14, 1709. in defending his Ship against a French Privateer bore the Anguish, with the Courage of a Christian, 'till October the 24th, when he refigned his Soul to God, about the 40th Year of his Age.

M.S. Elizabethæ nuper Uxoris Gulielmi Stockdale, quæ (Menfibus fexdecim Connubio nondum peractis) diem clausit fupremam xviiivo. die Novembris, Anno Salutis Humanæ 1714. Ætatifq ; fuæ 33. Cujus exuvias in læ-

tam et fælicem Refurrectionis diem moeftiffimus Maritus curavit hic reponi.

Omnia debentur fato paulumq ; morato,
Serius aut oitius sedem proper amus ad unam .

Thus rendered.

To the Sacred Memory of *Elizabeth,* late Wife of *William Stockdale* ; who (fcarcely enjoying a Marriage-State for 16 Months) fubmitted her mortal Body to Death the 18th of *November,* in the Blessed Year of our Redemption, 1714. and of her Age 33 : Whose Remains her ' sorrowful Husband here interr'd, until the joyful and happy Day of Refurrection.

All Things are subject to a ling'ring Fate,
Sooner or later to the Earth we fall,
That gen'ral Grave, both for the Poor & Great
Just as inexorable Death shall call.

T.

Hic jacet Stephanus Thompson, Gen. qui obiit 3tio Decemb. Ætat. fuæ 63, A.D. 1698. vicinis vixit charus, jucundus amicis, moribusq ; bonum fe præstitit exemplar.

William Tindall, dy'd 1715, aged 65. Vir apprime procus, omnibus amicus, flendus omnibus.

W.

Hic requiescit Jacobus Wilson, Generosus, partis hujus olim Telonarius, qui diem clausit supremam 23 Maij Anno Dom. 1708. Ætatis fuæ 55. *Buried in the Church, near the Font.*

Martha Wilson, Daughter to James Wilson, dy'd 1716. *Buried in the Church.*

The Rev. Mr. Peter Withington, late of Bolton in the Moors, Lancashire, died in 1722. aged 34. *I shall be satisfied when I awake with thy Likeness.*

Rebekah, Wife of Thomas Woodcock, died in 1728, aged 25.

She like a Lilly, fresh and green,
Was soon cut down, and no more seen !

Thus, Sir, I have given you the greatest Part of the Inscriptions : But there are so many yet remaining, that I shall but just exhibit the Sir-Names of the Deceased, which are as follow.

Allatson, Allenby, Allison, Arnold, Armstrong, — Baynes, Beswick, Bird, Brathwaite, Bridday.—Chapman, Coal, Colsey, Cook, Cooper, Cottrel, Coulson, Crow, Cowley.—Dale, Dickinson, Disbrough, Dobby, Dobson, Dusbrey, Dunslay. —Emlinton.—Fletcher, Ford. —Gamble, Gofton, Gole, Grainge.—Hall, Hallden, Harper, Hart, Henderson, Hind, Hodgson, Holland,

Holland, Hovington, Hudson, Huntriss.—Jackson, Johnson.—Kendal, Kitchen, Knaggs, Knowsley.—Lambert, Lindsey.—Maling. Maxwell, Millenar. Meggin, Megson, Mokdin, Moor, Morwen.—Naylor.—Ouram.—Parr, Pearson, Peat, Pender, Polgate, Porret, Potter.—Ranwick, Read, Rickinson, Robinson, Ross, Rump, Russel.—Sawdon, Scafe. Seller, Sherman, Simpson, Skelton, Slee, Steel, Stephenson, Sterriker, Story, Strotton, Sunlay.—Taylor, Tindall, Tocket, Torr, Topcliff, Thorp, Tristram.—Walker, Waind, Williamson. Wilmington, Wilson, Wood, Woodall, and *Woolfe.* I conclude, (having exceeded the Bounds of a Letter) Sir, Your humble Servant, &c.

LETTER XVIII.

S I R ,   *Scarborough,* 1734.

UPON the Rock, (near the *Assembly-Rooms)* which leads down to the *Spaw,* was formerly a Church, dedicated to St. *Nicholas,* of which scarce remains the Foundation. There was also *S. Sepulchre's* Church, near *Cook-Row;* of this, the Limits of the Yard are perceivable. The Church of St. *Thomas* was near *Newborough-Bar,* on the North Side : The Hospital, called by that Saint's Name, was founded by the Burghers in the Reign of King *Stephen;* for which pious Intent the Land was given by *Hugh de Bulmere :* The Appurtenances belonging to it were afterwards used in common by the Brothers and Sisters of St. *Nicholas's* Hospital, not far from the Church. The antient Benefactors, both to *Scarborough,* and other Places, were as follow. 1. *Americk,* of this Place, help'd to supply *Rosdale* Nunnery with Oyl. 2. *Halden,* also of this Town, bestow'd his Favours on *Malton* Priory. 3. *Aylmar* de *Cliffland* gave liberally to St. *Mary's* Altar at *Scarborough,* with Money for Oblations, and 3 Priests to officiate. 4. A Toft was bestowed by *Osbert de Hansard.* 5. A great House on the Rock given by *Walter,* Son of *Gunner.* 6. Money was given by his Brother *Richard.* 7. One *Alan* granted Lands and allow'd Fish, &c.—Other Benefactors were these : *Emera,* a beautiful and religious Virgin, the Daughter of *Robert de Filey,* Anno 1219. *Laurence* and *Juetta* his Wife, of *Newburgh : Goddard* and *Bogard* their Sons : *William Mailcake, Tho. Fitsen,* and *John de Hansard ; Galfrid de Lutton : Galfrid de Oroom,* who

also gave Lands to *Kirkstall-Abbey* and *Keldholme* Nunnery ; Some Land under the Cliff was bestow'd by *William de Harton ;* and *Thomas Hardin* gave fome of his own that was in the Town.

As to the *Carmelite* Fryery, it was suppress'd in the Reign of K. *Henry* V. A Benefactor to this was *William Tothole,* a Knight Hospitaller, who gave a Meffuage, &c. which lay between the Lands of *John Blake,* (then held by *William de Harun.)* from the South, and the Street which is called *le Dumple* on the North, &c. Dated at *Meltheburn, June* 11, 1300. The Wood under *Cropton* Castle belong'd to the Fryers Minorites. The Black-Fryers resided in the Lane that comes Northward into the Middle of the Market-Place, facing *Helperby-Lane* on the South. *Speed* writes, That King *Edward* II. *Henry* Earl of *Northumberland,* and Sir *Adam Sage,* were their great Benefactors. In my next, I shall give you the Heads of some of the Town's Charters. In the mean time, I am your's &c.

LETTER XIX.

S I R ,   *Scarborough,* 1734.

KIng *Henry* II. (of whom it's said, that he gave *New-Burgh* without the Walls to another of his own creating call'd the *Old-One,* from which Time the Burghers possess'd *Walsgrave,* now call'd *Falsgrave)* by his Charter granted to the Town the same Priviledges and Customs that *York* enjoy'd : But for those Houses, whose Sides were turn'd towards the Highway, 6d. each Yearly was to be paid ; and if their Ends were that way placed, then 4d. each. King *John's* Charter was much to the same Effect : *Et quod ipsi de unaquaque domo de* Scardeburgh, *cujus Gabulum est turnatum adversus viam, nobis reddent singulis annis quatuor denarios ; & de illis domibus, quorum lateræ versa sunt erga viam sex denarios per Annum,* &c. And then follows his Command, That the Inhabitants shall peaceably enjoy the Woods, Plains, Pastures, Ways, &c. belonging to them. *Henry* III. his Successor, granted Liberty to build Tenements as they thought convenient ; those of Scot and Lot to be exempted from other Taxes : That, for the future, the Burghers, or their Heirs, should answer for their Town's Farm every *Michaelmas* at the *Exchequer :*

quer : None to be impleaded out of the Burgh, except as to Tenures that are not within it ; and that a Fair might be kept on the Assumption of the Blessed Virgin *Mary*, to the End of St. *Michael*, if it did not prove to the Damage of Provifions. In another Charter, the same King granted Freedom of Pontage throughout his Dominions : That the Inhabitants might take Distress for their Debts, and defend themselves from all Claims, (except the King's) by the Oath of 26 Freemen, upon paying 66*l.* a Year ; and the Penalty of 10*l.* was to be laid on any Person that should disturb them in their Priviledges. On the 25th of *May*, 1229. the same Monarch granted to them the Manor of *Falsgrave*, with Liberty of Free Passage thro' *Pickering* Foreft, for Wood *gratis*, which they might carry away, without Hinderance from the Verderers, except on the forbidden Month. Again, in the Year 1255, he gave 'em the Mills and Pools of *Falsgrave*, with 60 Acres in the Fields of *East-Scarborough*, paying 25*l.* Yearly for the Freedom, whereby they were to have free Warren. I have little more to add at present, but that in King *Henry* the VIIIth's Time an Act of Parliament was obtain'd for repairing the Piers. Sir *William Strickland*, Bart. and *William Thompson*, Esq ; Members of Parliament for this Borough, in the 5th Year of his present Majesty obtain'd another for their Enlargement. Our present Bayliffs are Mr. *Cockeril* and Mr. *Hepden ;* Mr. *Harrison*, our Town-Clerk ; and we have 2 Coroners, 4 Chamberlains, and a Council of 36. We have alfo proper Officers, fuch as are at *York*, from which City we are diftant 30 Miles N. E. I am, *&c.*

LETTER XX.

SIR, *Scarborough*, 1735.

I Sent you, the last Year, what I really thought material, relating to the Antiquities of our Town. Every one, who has been here, knows that we frequently abound in Plenty of the finny Train, (which fupplies the Country for 30 Miles) such as Cod-Fish, Fluke, Haddock, Herrings, Ling, Mackrel, Whiting, *&c.* The Sweetness of the Air from the Ocean, the Beauty of the Pros-

pect, and the Diversions of the Town, might demand a Visit from the most curious Persons at the extremest Parts of the Realm, and other Countries : But, above all, the sovereign Vertues of the SPAW (discovered about 115 Years ago by Mrs. *FARROW*, then an Inhabitant of *Scarborough*) attract the Nobility and Gentry, who extend their Charity to the afflicted Poor. The happy Discoverer, whose Memory ought to be for ever precious, one Day walking along the pleasant Strand, and observing in the Streams a russet Tincture, she made an Experiment with Galls, which converted the Water to a purple Colour : Afterwards drinking a fresh Quantity, and at several times as she thought convenient ; the Consequences were so visible and wonderful, that with Joy she communicated their Excellency to the World. Dr. WITTY tells us, That this ever-flowing Spring (which in an Hour yields more than 24 Gallons) proceeds from a Participation of Alum, Iron, Nitre, Salt and Vitriol : The last gives the Water a sharp Taste; the Smell is like that of Ink ; and the Colour azure, much resembling the Sky. 'Tis this, (this justly celebrated SPAW, which is the Preservative of Health, the greatest of all earthly Blessings) that generally draws some Company hither from *May* to *September*, makes the Town to flourish, and consequently the stately Buildings continually increase, even to Admiration.

But I shall conclude at present, with acquainting you, That if ever you design to publish a more ample Account of this Place, and let me know, I shall endeavour to procure for you (what you once desired) sufficient Materials for the Purpose. In the mean time, I wish you the greatest Success, as to your extensive Design in setting forth, *The HISTORY of that Great* Emporium *of* KINGSTON-upon-*HULL*. In a Manuscript I find, that in the Reign of King *Edward* III. *Anno* 1354. *Gilbert de Berkin* and *Roger de Swerde* were Members of Parliament for that important Place. May Happiness attend you in your laudable Undertakings. I am, I assure you, Sir, Your Well-Wisher, and very humble Servant,

PHILOTHEOROS.

SOLI DEO GLORIA.

POSTSCRIPT.

Tho' this Book was compleated according to my first Design, and ready to be sent to the Binders : Yet as the following Additions relating to the Town of SCARBOROUGH' *with an Account of* BRIDLINGTON, *came to Hand; in Gratitude therefore to my generous Subscribers, and to oblige the Publick more and more, I could not find in my Heart to omit them.*—— NOTE, *The Inscriptions and Epitaphs are within the Churches, except those mention'd to be in the Church-Yards.*

LETTER XXI.

SIR,   *Scarborough, Aug. 8, 1735.*

I Have sent you some Additions to my former Accounts ; and am

Your Humble Servant.

Within the Church, at the West End, on the Wall, near the Stairs, is the following Inscription and Epitaph.

A.

HIc jacet clariffimus Vir Dominus ANDREAS AINSLIE, a *Black-Hill*; Natione *Scotus*, Urbis *Jedburgeæ*, fæpiffime Conful, Juris *Scoticani* peritiffimus : Qui obiit xii *Augusti* MDCLXXXVIII. Ætatis suæ LII.

PIETAS TUTISSIMA VIRTUS.

This was the Motto of this pious Man,
Which he by holy Practice did maintain :
Whether his Love to God you shall consider,
Or that great Love he paid unto his Brother,
Here he doth dye a Stranger; and we know
No other Reason why it happens so,
Than that our God hath for his Sake this Aim)
Ev'n by his Death abroad to spread his Fame,)
Who took such Care to glorify his Name.)
Stop, Christian Reader, and here lend one Tear,)
As Earnest 'till his Country once shall hear,)
Then thousand thousand will be payed there.)

B.

HEre lieth the Body of Mr. PAUL BATTY, who departed this Life the 24th of *April, Anno Domini* 1705. aged 70. His Text was the 39th Pfalm, 4th Verfe. "LORD, make me to know "mine end, and the Meafure of my "days, what it *is*: *that* I may know "how frail I *am*." —— Hic jacet PAULUS BATTY, Generosus, Vir apprime probus et amicorum per quam optimus, nullis corumpendis, non proprio fed publico femper confuluit commodo ; Nautarum Propogator fpontaneus. Obiit 24 Aprilis, Ætatis suæ feptuagefimo primo Annoq ; Dom. 1705.

HEre lieth the Body of Mrs. CLARE BATTY, late Wife of Mr. *Paul Batty,* who departed this Life the 2d Day of May, 1714. aged 79 Years and 10 Months : Her Text was the 88th Pfalm, 1st and 2d Verfes. "O Lord "God of my Salvation, I have cried "day and night before thee : O let my "Prayer enter into thy Prefence, in-"cline thine ear unto my calling."

HEre lieth the Body of *Mary*, Wife of *Richard Beilby*, and their Sons. She departed Sept. 1713. aged 36.

HEre lieth the Body of *John Bracken-bury*, Gent. who died *Anno* 1712.

C.

HEre lieth the Body of Mrs. *Elizabeth Clark*, Wife of Mr. *Francis Clark*, and their two Daughters. *Elizabeth* died the 2d of *April*, aged 6 Years: *Mary, June* 23, aged 17: Mrs. *Clark, Aug.* the 27th, aged 51: All in the Year 1727.

HIc jacet *Catherina Constable*, filia Marmaduci Constable de Wassam, Armigeri, denata 6 Apr. 1666. Reliquiis juxta Sororem repositis.

HEre lies the Body of *Henry Cottrell*, who died A.D. 1731. *Buried in the Church-Yard.*

HEre lieth the Body of *Anne Coulson*, Wife of Edward Coulson, who departed this Life the 27th of April, A. D. 1714. aged 36 Years

NEar this Place lies the Body of *Elizabeth*, Daughter of Mr. *John Craven*, late of this Town, She departed this Life in *Sept.* 1692.

D.

HEre lieth the Body of *Robert Dighton* who departed this Life the 25th of May, 1729 aged 60.

HIc deponuntur Cineres *Gulielmi Dodsworth*, filius Gulielmi & Janæ Dodsworth de Scarburgia: Qui obiit IImo Die Decembris An. Dom. 1704. Ætat. suæ 24.

HEre lieth the Body of *Alice Dods-worth*, who departed this Life, July 26, 1710. aged 25 Years.

HEre lies the Body of *William Dunslay*; who died August 25, 1732. Lies buried in the Church-Yard.

Tho' Boreas' *Blasts, and,* Neptune's *Waves*
Have tost me to and fro ;
Yet still, by God's divine Decree,
I harbour here below :
Where I do now at Anchor ride,
With many of our Fleet ;
But once again, I must set Sail,
Our Admiral CHRIST *to meet.*

E.

HEre lieth the Body of *Sarah Elding*, Wife to *Richard Elding*, who died February the 6th, 1733-4. aged 30 Years. *Buried in the Church-Yard.*

F.

M. S. Hic deponuntur Cineres *Adami Farside*, Gen. Corporationis Scarburgesis, bis Consulis : Qui placide requiescens in Domino, obiit decimo quarto die Junij, Anno Dom. 1701. Ætatis suæ 45.

M. S. *Gulielmi Farside*, Generosi, cujus Reliquiæ, (una cum Maternis in hoc Tumulo, Annos abhinc xxv tumulatis) in lætum & felicem Resurrectionis diem hinc sunt repositæ. Domini *Adami* et Dominæ *Annæ Farside* filius fuit unicus. Consulatumq ; agens. supremum clausit diem ; obiit xxiv Julij Die, Anno Salutis Humanæ MDCCXIII. Ætatis fuæ xxv.
Humana cuncta, Fumus, Umbra, Vanitas,
Et nihil hic Orbis, quod pereret possidet.

M. S. Sub Pedibus in Avi sui *Tristrami* Tumulo complures inter Proavos sepultus jacet *Timotheus Fish*, Generosus. Obiit 23 Die Decembris Anno Ætatis suæ 55, Annoq ; Dom. 1727.
Non omnis moriar.

MEmoriæ Sacræ DANIEL, filius minimus natu GULIELMI FOORD de *Scarborough*, Generosi, natus Octob. undecimo 1637, denatus Martij 23, 1682. Cujus Exuvias mærens mæstaque Vidua curavit hic reponi.

SEpulta hic jacet ANNA FOORD, Generosa, quæ Charitatis & Annorum plena diem clausit supremum vicesimo die Maij 1717. Ætatis suæ 66.

HEre lieth the Body of *Richard Ford*, Mafter and Mariner, who died Aug. 11. 1730. *Bur. in Church-Yard.*
Awake, arise, behold thou hast
Thy Life a Leaf, thy Breath a Blast :
At Night lie down, prepare to have
Thy Sleep thy Death, thy watry Grave.

G.

HEre lieth the Body of Mrs. *Elizabeth Gidne*, who died Septemb. 27, 1727. aged 70.

HEre lieth the Body of *George Goland*, who died in the Year 1733.

MAry, Wife of *Francis Goland*, departed this Life the 15th of August, 1734. aged 41 Years. *Buried in the Church-Yard.*

H.

HEre lieth the Body of *Mary Hodgson*, who departed this Life 1696.

HEre lieth the Body of Mr. *Francis Hodgson*, who departed this Life the 22d of February, 1707. aged 61.

I.

IN hoc Tumulo requiescit Corpus *Josephi Jenkinson*, de Scarburgia, Pharma-copei, qui decimo 4to Januarij,

arij, Annoq ; Ætatis tricesimo sexto fatis cessit, Anno 84.

Diciq ; beàtus
Ante obitum nemo, supremaq; funera debet.

HIc jacet *Jana Jenkinson*, quondam Josephi Jenkinson Conjux charissima : in cujus pietatis erga Deum, indigis munificentiæ, erga omnes charitatis, et illi præter morem amoris, curæ & indulgentiæ memoriam ; ut vivi qua possint defunct æmulentur virtutes, utq ; suam Gratitudinem letaretur, hæc inscribi curavit mæstissimus nepos ROBERTUS NORTH : Obiit 1mo Octobris, A.D. 1722. Ætat. suæ 69.

K.

HEre lies the Body of * WILLIAM KITCHINGMAN, of *Pontefract*, Esq ; who departed this Life the 6th Day of August, *Anno Dom.* 1732. in the 32d Year of his Age.

* *He was Mayor of* Pontefract *in the Year* 1729, *as a Manuscript of that Town informs me.*

L.

HIc jacet LOVELL LAZENBY, Generosus, qui xxxmo Septembris MDCXC, hujus Municipij Scriba cooptatus, et postquam per spatium xxi Annorum munus inculpate sustinuit, fatis cessit xmo Januarij MDCCXII. Ætat. XLV.

HEre lieth the Body of HANNAH, Daughter to GEORGE LLOYD of *Manchester*, Merchant, born August 22, 1605. buried July 11, 1701. aged 96.

P.

RObert *Pollet*, died A. D. 1681. Buried in the Church-Yard.

HEre lieth the Body of Mrs. *Sarah Porret*, who departed this Life *May* 16, 1711. aged 16 Years.

R.

HIc reconduntur Ossa
JOHANNIS ROBINSON,
Qui,
Vir eximius,
Hujus Municipii multoties Præfectus,
Leges Juraque Fidei suæ commissa
Usque servavit ;
Communitatis Decus Ordinem et Concordiam
Rite sustinuit ;
Omni quæ ad Cultum Divinum
Aut Societatem Humanam pertinet,
Virtute præcelluit.
Continenter & sobrie vivendo
Octoginta & quatuor Annos complevit
Obiitque 8°. Februarij 1732°.
Memoria Justi debet extolli, Injusti abolerit

In the Ruins of the Chancel, upon a handsome Tomb, is the aforesaid Inscription.

HIc requiescit *Jacobus Rickinson*, Generosus, qui diem clausit supremam vicesimo primo Aprilis Annoq ; Dom. 1711. ætatis suæ 55.

Diciq ; beatus
Ante obitum nemo, supremaq; funera debet

HIc jacet fepultus *Jacobus* filius Jacobi *Rickinson*, Gener. qui placide requiescens in Domino obiit vicesimo quarto die Mensis Octob. A. ætat. suæ 20. A. D. 1711.

HIc jacet *Sara Rickinson*, filia Jacobi Rickinson, Gener. quæ obiit primo die Novembris A. D. 1711. ætat. suæ. 15.

S.

HEre lieth the Body of THOMAS SIMPSON, who died the 6th of March, 1734. aged 51 Years.

HEre lieth the Body of *Mary Skelton*, who departed this Life *April* 1726.

T.

P. M. S. Hic jacet Elizabetha, uxor Francisci Thompson de Scarborough, Armigeri, quæ clausit extremum diem 4 Aprilis 1666. Cujus Exuvias mæstissimus Viduus curavit hic deponi.

Sic ibant omnes; sic ibimus, ibitis, ibunt.

HEre lieth the Body of *Stephen Tristram*, a Child of a Year and two Days old, who died in 1730.

To screen him from all Earthly Charms,
Death took him from his Mother's Arms,
Happy's the Change, he's free from Care,
And dwells where Blessed Angels are.

[Buried in the decay'd Chancel.]

On a Table, North Side, in the Church.
12 Nov. 1714.

THOMAS SEDMAN, of *Scarborough*, Gentleman, devis'd to the Bailiffs of *Scarborough*, for the Use of the Poor, an House and Garth, (being three Tenements) in *Cargate*, for an Hospital for six poor People, and a Close with a Piece of Ground adjoining to the same, near the ‡ *Segg-Garth*, the Rent whereof was to be paid on the First Day of *May*, at the Church Door of St. *Mary's*, to all such Poor as frequent the same, except 20s. which was to be for Repairs of the Hospital if needful ; and if not, then to be paid to the Poor of the Hospital.

‡ *Some Ruins, in or near this Place, feem to indicate, that there had been a Religious-House there in former Times.*

Another Table near the former.

GREGORY FYSH, in the Year 1640. gave unto Mr. *Simpson*, then Vicar, and to his Successors for ever, one Close, lying in a Street called the *Market Gate;* the said Vicar paying out of the same Ten Shillings Yearly to the Church-Wardens for Repairs of the Window where the Lead is cast, being the * Burial-Place of the Family : And also the Vicar of *Scarborough*, and his Successors for ever, one Parcel of Ground lying at *Sprite-Lane-Head;* and also to the Grammar-School one Close, lying in *Worlington-Grave*, for the teaching of four poor Scholars ; and also to the Hospital of St. *Thomas* one Parcel of Ground called by the Name of St. *John's House*, lying near *New Dike-Bank* ; and also several other Bequests in Money.

* *It is at the North West End.*

On a Table, in a Place on the South Side, where formerly had been a Chantry.

REMEMBER THE POOR.

SIR *John Lawson* gave 100 Pounds, the Interest thereof being 6*l. per Annum*, to be distributed Yearly on St. *Thomas's* Day to the Poor of the Town for ever.——Mr. *Thomas Farror* of this Town, Merchant, by his Will gave two Hospitals near the *Low-Conduit*, in a Place call'd *Cook-Row*, adjoining the *Quakers Meeting-House*, for the Habitation of as many poor Widows, as the same can conveniently entertain for ever.

ANOTHER TABLE.
For GOD loveth a cheerful Giver.

MR. *Conyers* by his Will gave 40*s. per An.* to be distributed on St. *Thomas's* Day to the Poor of this Town for ever.——*Elisha Trott* by his Will gave an Hospital in *Tanner-Street* for an Habitation to the Poor ; and also an Acre of Ground, lying in *Burton-dale*, to repair and maintain the same, if needful ; or to be distributed to the poor Widows there for ever.——*Alice Chambers*, late of *Scarborough*, Widow, by her Will gave 20*l.* the Interest to be distributed Yearly, upon St. *Thomas's* Day, by the Minister and Church-Wardens to the Poor for ever.

Between the two preceding Tables, is this Inscription upon a Brass Plate.

THis Window was wholely rebuilt, in the Form it now is, at the pro-

per Charge of Mrs. *Clare Batty*, Widow, (whose Body lies near hereto) *Anno Dom.* 1714.

On the East Side of the Steeple,

FRancis Thompson, } *Bailiffs* 1669.
Thomas Oliver,

THUS, Sir, I have given you an Account of *Scarborough* as well as I was able : And, in order to get a List of the Mayors, as it was formerly govern'd by such, and also of the Bailiffs, who ruled before the Rise, and since the Decline of that Office ; I apply'd myself to an ingenious Gentleman for that Purpose ; who courteously told me, *That no certain Account could be had from their Original ; or tho' there might be Hopes to find it, yet the Attainment seem'd Difficult, by Reason that the last Mayor had gone off with the Records.* The Occasion of which, (if another sensible Person has inform'd me right) was thro' the following Transaction. Most English Historians relate, That *Scarborough* had signaliz'd its Loyalty to King *James* II. in a very high degree, by a most eloquent * *Address* to that unhappy Prince, upon his Majesty's Declaration for *Liberty of Conscience.* And so zealous was the Mayor, that he order'd the Curate of St. *Mary's* to read it in the Desk, or Pulpit ; which the conscientious Divine refusing to do, that Magistrate basely struck the Minister, or *Caned* him, even in the Place of Divine Worship. Such unparallel'd Usage was resented by many ; and particularly by a Captain of the Army, who not long after sent for the Mayor to the *Old Bowling Green :* But the Magistrate slighting the Message as impertinent from a military Officer, the Captain made no more ado, but by a File of Musketeers forc'd him to come, and then oblig'd him to undergo *Sancho Pancho's* rude Discipline of being *Toss'd in a Blanket.* Soon after the exasperated Mayor took Post for *London*, in order to make his Complaint to the King ; and the Captain rode another Way, to avert the dreadful Punishment intended against him by his highly affronted Adversary. But the Revolution happening, and the King

---

* *The Substance of which Address is set forth, by Way of Note, at the Bottom of the Pages* 184 *and* 185 *of this Book.*

King abdicating his throne, a Period was put to the Officer's Fear ; and the Mayor had no opportunity to glut his Revenge. Then follow'd a Succession of two Bayliffs each Year in *Scarborough*, as they now happily continue ; and, with great Prudence, Justice and Honour, govern an honest, active, thriving and most courteous People.

LETTER XXII.

SIR,

ACcording to your Desire I have visited *Bridlington*, or *Burlington* ; and herewith I send you the following Inscriptions I could find within that antient Edifice, St. *Mary's* Church, which once did belong to the demolish'd Priory of the *Augustinian* Order.

A.

HEre lieth the Body of *Ruth Aclam*, Wife to Thomas Aclam, who died the 19th of July, 1722. aged 23 Years. *Buried in the Church Yard.*

B.

HEre lieth the Body of *Mary*, Wife of James *Backhouse* of Bridlington, who died July 23, 1716, aged 38 Years, 9 Months, by whom she had 7 Children, whereof 4 are dead, and lie here. *Buried in the Yard, facing the S. West End of the Church.*

HEre lieth the Body of *Marmaduke Ball*, who died A.D. 1696. *Buried in the Church-Yard.*

HEre lieth the Body of *Charles Barton*, of Bridlington, who departed this Life May 29, 1718. He was marry'd to Barbara, the Daughter of George Crosyer, 7 Weeks and 6 Days.

HEre lieth the Body of *William Bower* of Bridlington-Key, Merchant, who departed this Life the 26th of June, 1657.—— Also *Thomas* Son of Edward *Bower*.

HEre lieth *William Bower* of Bridlington-Key, Merchant, who departed this Life the 23rd of March, 1671. in the 74th Years of his Age ; and *Thomasin*, the Wife of the said *William*, departed the 14th of Sept. aged 59. He did in his Life-time erect at his own Charge at Bridlington a School-House ; and gave to it 20*l. per Annum* for ever for maintaining and educating of the poor Children of Bridlington and Key in the Art of Carding, Knitting and Spinning of Wool.

HEre lieth the Body of *Edward* Son of *John Bower* of Bridlingtom-Key, who departed this Life March 8, aged 7 Months, and *Thomasin* Daughter of the said *John*, who departed the 11th of March 1669, aged 10 Months, and lie buried here. [*All within the Chancel.*]

HIc jacet hoc tumulo Corpus *Gulielmi* filii Gulielmi *Buckle*, qui obiit tertio Octobris, Anno Dom. 1712, ætatisque suæ vicesimo primo. *Interred in the Church-Yard.*

AT the Foot of this Pillar lies interred the Body of Mr. *William Bower*, of Bridlington-Key, Merchant, who departed this Life the 9th Day of May, 1702. in the 53rd Year of his Age. He had 2 Wives ; the first was Sarah the Daughter of Robert Belt, Esq; of Bossal, by whom he had 7 Children, and 6 by the latter, who is Catherine the Daughter of Edward Trotter, Esq ; of Skelton-Castle in Cleveland, at whose Charge this Monument is erected. *Mr.* Bower *lies buried N. in the Chancel.*

HEre lies the Body of Mrs. *Elizabeth Bowlton*, Wife of William Bowlton of Bridlington, who died Dec. 1, 1717. and of William their Son, Octob. 17, 1717, aged 1 Year, 7 Months, and 21 Days. *Buried in the Church Yard.*

C.

HEre lieth the Body of *William Corbet* of Bridlington, Gentleman, who died in the Lord the 12th of February, 1637. aged 48 Years. Mrs. *Anne Corbet* died in 1636.

HEre lieth the Body of *Richard Cammel* of Bridlington, who departed this Life Nov. 2, 1721. *Richard* his Son, 1706. *John Cammel*, 1722. Buried in the Church-yard.

O Death, how bitter is thy Sting,
That Youth and Age to Earth do's bring !

HEre lieth the Body of *Henry* Son of Thomas *Carter*, who died July 26 1715. aged 13 Days.

HEre lieth the Body of *Matthew Cornwell* of Bridlington-Key, Mafter and Mariner, who died Aug. 7, 1733. *Buried in the Church-Yard.*

HEre lieth the Body of Mr. *William Cocke,* Son of Mr. *Samuel Cocke* of Newcaftle.

HEre lieth the Body of *Elizabeth,* Wife of Henry *Cowton* of Bridlington, Merchant, one of the Daughters of John Bower, late of Bridlington-Key, Merchant, deceafed, who departed this Life the 16th Day of December, A.D. 1695. in the 28th Year of her Age. And with her two Sons ; *William,* who was born the 11th Day of December, 1694. and died the 13th Day of the same Month ; and the other abortive.

D.

HEre lieth the Body of *John Darley,* of Swerby, Sen. who died March 3, 1728. aged 78 Years. *Interred in the Church-Yard.*

HEre lieth the Body of *George,* the Son of Richard *Deale* of Bridlington-Key, who died *Dec.* 1710. aged 8 Years. *Buried near the Passage to the South West Door of the Church.*

HEre lieth the Body of *John Dodsworth,* Son of John Dodsworth, late of Scarborough, who was born the 14th Day of October 1647, and died the 8th of Sept. Anno Dom. 1685.

G.

HEre lieth the Body of *Melchior Gibson,* Son of Thomas Gibson, who was born at Bridlington in the Year of our Lord MDCXL. and deceas'd the first of September in the LXXI. Year of his Age, *Anno* MDCCXI. *Mors mea Vita mihi.*

HEre lieth the Body of *Robert Greame,* who died March 17. 1708. aged 78 Years, 2 Months, and 4 Days : And of *Barbara* his Wife, who died Oct. 29, 1706, aged 66 Years, 7 Months, and 15 Days.

H.

HEre lie the Bodies of *James* and *Joseph,* Sons of Thomas *Harrison* of Bridlington-Key, Master and Mariner : The former died Dec. 23d, 1714. aged 2 Years, and 14 Days ; the latter died Jan. 1715. aged 10 Weeks and 2 Days.

HEre lie the Bodies of *Jane* and *James* the Daughter and Son to Thomas (and Catherine) *Hawsom* of Bridlington Key, Master and Mariner : The former died March 6, 1722. aged 15 Months ;

the latter died May the 9th, 1722. aged 3 Years and 11 Months.

HEre lieth the Body of *John Hodgson,* of Bridlington, one of the Patentees, who died in the Lord.

P. M. *Francisci Holdsworth,* A.M. et *Christianæ* Uxor ejus. Hic ob. 29. Jun. 1687. ætat. 52. Illa 9 Jun. 1712. ætat. 65. P.O. imitemur. *Upon the Stone are 5 Hearts interwoven.*

Here lies in——————
Which Nature in the World——
But sheath'd, and put it up again.

HEre lieth the Body of *William Hildyard,* Son of Hugh——————
of Christopher *Hildyard* of Wystead in Holderness, Kt. Which said *William* was born the 14th Day of September, 1659 ; and departed this Life the last Day of December—— in the——
Year of King Charles the Second's happy Reftoration. *Buried near the Altar.*

HEre lieth the Body of *Thomas Howdon* of Bridlington-Key, Master and Mariner, who died July the 15th, 1717, aged 40 Years, 5 Months, and 7 Days.

HEre lieth the Body of *Jane Howdon,* Wife of William Howdon, who died Dec. 29, A.D. 1712, aged 56 Years.

HEre lieth the Body of *John Holden,* of Martin, who departed this Life the 15th of September, 1707. aged 74 Years. As also *William Holden,* Son to the said *John Holden,* who died the 10th of January, 1705-6, aged 20 Years.

HEre lieth the Body of *Thomas Hood* of Bridlington-Key, Mariner, who died Jan. 25, 1720. aged 28 Years.

I.

HEre lieth the Body of *Richard Jackson,* who died July 7, 1692.

L.

QUod mortale fuit *Elizabethæ Lamont,* Jun. 24, 1714. *Mariæ Lamont,* Jul. 16, 1719. et *Thomæ Lamont,* Octob. 31, 1722. in lætam refurrectionis diem Parentes hic repofuerunt.

HEre lieth the Body of *Edward Lawson* of Newcastle, Anchor-Smith, who deceased Jan. 29, 1640.

HEre lieth the Body of *Hicres Lister,* Son to Thomas and Frances Lister of Key, who died Feb. 2, 1727. aged 5 Months. Mrs. Lifter had by her former husband 3 Children, who were interred here.

HEre lieth the Body of *Hannah Luck,* Wife of William Luck of Bridlington-Key, ton-Key, Mafter and Mariner, who departed this Life Octob. 22, 1722, aged 64 Years and 9 Months. *Buried in the Church Yard:*

M.

HEre lieth the Body of *Thomas Marshall* of Bridlington, who died Anno 1712. *Buried in the Church Yard*

HEre lieth the Body of *Hannah Matchon*, Wife of William Matchon of Bridlington, Woollen Draper, who departed this Life the 9th day of Auguft, in the 36th Year of her Age, A. D. 1681.

HEre lieth the Body of *Dinah Medforth* the Wife of William Medforth of Bridlington-Key, Master and Mariner, who died June 29, 1717. aged 28 years, 2 months, 6 days. Alfo *Samuel* their Son, who died the fame Year.

THOMAS MYERS de Allerthorpe, Gen. Ob. xx DecembrisMDCCXVIII.An. Æt. 58. *Eliz. Myers* uxor ejus 6 ejusfd. Menf. Anno Ætat. 63. *Jerem. Myers,* fil. 12 Octobris MDCCXXIII. Annoq; Ætat. 30. *Bur. in the N. W. Isle.*

N.

HEre lieth the Body of *Katherine Newton,* the Daughter of Eliazar Newton of Bridlington Key. Baptized Nov. 10, 1663, and died Sept. 14, 1690.

HEre lieth the Body of *Samuel Nicholfon* of Bridlington-Key, Mafter and Mariner, who died March 19, 1715. aged 31 Years, 6 Months, 2 Days. Alfo *John Nicholfon* his Son. *Buried in the Church Yard.*

P.

HEre lieth the Body of Mr. *Robert Palmer,* of Bridlington-Key, Merchant, who departed this Life the 26th of Dec. 1640. As alfo *Jane Palmer,* Wife to him above-named, being interred October 15, 1629.

HEre lieth the Body of *Francis Palmer* of Bridlington, who died in the Lord the 24th of Feb. 1639, aged 62.

HEre lieth the Body of *Robert Parkin,* who died the 11th of December, 1718, aged 66 years : Nigh unto whom is interred the Body of *Alice* his Wife, who departed this Life the 2d of Feb. 1693. aged 38 years, and alfo nine of their Children.

HEre lieth the Body of *Sarah* the Wife of John *Parfon* of Bridlington. *Buried in the Church Yard.*

HEre lieth the Body of *Emanuel Peritage,* who died A. D. 1699.

HEre lieth the Body of *John Pierson,* of Bridlington-Key, Mafter and Mariner, who departed this Life the 5th of July, 1728, aged 37 Years.

R

HEre lieth the body of *John Rickaby,* Son of *John Rickaby* of Bridlington-Key, who deceased June 25, 1634.

HEre lieth buried the Body of *Thomas Rickaby,* who died An. Dom. 1665. Alfo here interred *Elizabeth Rickaby,*

HEre lieth the Body of *John Rickaby,* the Elder, of Bridlington, Merchant: A Man true to his Truft, just in his Dealings, and one that with wonderful Patience fubmitted to the Will of GOD in all thofe unaccountable Difpenfations of Divine Providence to him in his latter Years. Obiit the 25th of Dec. 1701. Æt. fuæ 68. Alfo the Body of *Giles Rickaby,* Merchant, Son of the above John Rickaby, who died the 27th of July, 1729. in the 54th year of his Age. *Bur. at the W. End.*

HEre lieth the Body of *Emma Rickman,* Wife of Richard Rickman, of Bridlington, who died Oct. 15, 1720. aged 64 years, and 10 months.

S

HEre lieth the Body of *Jane,* Wife of John *Sanderfon*; who died in 1717.

HEre lies interred the Body of Mrs. *Jane Skinner,* fecond Daughter of Alderman *William Skinner, Merchant of Hull : She died the 19th of July, 1727. in the 68th year of her Age. *Buried within the Rails of the Altar.*

HEre lieth the Body of *John Stabler,* of Bridlington.Key, Master and Mariner, who died May 13, 1708, aged 61 Years : Also his Children, *Elizabeth* and *John*; the former died March 17, 1687 ; the latter Jan. 24. 1692.

HEre lieth the Body of *Solomon Stephenson,* of Bridlington, Woollen-Draper. Obiit the 31ft of February, 1710, Aged 63 years.

Bonus Ecclefiæ Anglicanæ filius.

HEre lieth the Body of *Dorothy Sur,* Wife of Robert Sur, who died the 1st of Dec. 1698. aged 69 years, who had *Twenty Three Children of her own Body born.*

W

HEre lieth the Body of *Faith,* Daughter of Thomas and Sufanna *Walker,* Obiit Octob. 24, 1710. aged 7 Months and 13 Days.

⁎ See his Epitaph, Pag. 42 of this Book.

NEar this Place lie the Bodies of *Thomas Wilfon*, Merchant, and *Lucy* his Wife, who had Iffue 6 Sons, and 2 Daughters. He was defcended from a worthy Family of Thirsk in this County: Was a tender Husband, a kind Father, and a true Friend ; juft in his Dealings, which defervedly intitled him to the Character of an honeft Man. She was a Daughter of Edward Harrington, Efq ; of an antient and noble Family in the County of Rutland, and by her Mother's Side Great Grand-Daughter of Sir Walter Alexander of Scotland, Kt. Cup-Bearer to King James the First. She was a dutiful Wife, a tender Mother, and endued with all other amiable Qualities. He died 24 Feb. A. D. 1718. *Ætat.* 74. And she 7 Aug. 1723. *Ætat.* 59.—Near the fame Place is alfo depofited the Body of *Elizabeth Hickman*, Daughter of the faid Edward Harrington, Efq ; who was first married to Francis Bowes, Efq ; eldest Son of Sir Francis Bowes of the Bishoprick of Durham, Kt. and afterwards to John Hickman, of Warwickshire, Efq ; She was an obedient Wife, had an agreeable Perfon, and a fine Understanding, improved by a polite Education. She died 31 July A. D. 1732. aged 71. To the Memory of thefe dear Friends, J A N E H A R R I N G T O N, their furviving Sister, hath erected this Monument.

HEre lies the Body of *Jane*, the Wife of Richard *Wilfon*, of Bridlington-Key, who departed this Life on the 13th Day of Nov. 1730. aged 36 years.

M. S. *Prifcillæ* nuper uxoris Rogeri *Woodburn*, quæ diem claufit fupremam x° die Augusti Anno Salutis Humanæ 1715. Ætatifque fuæ 26. Cujus Exuvias in lætam & felicem refurrectionis diem mæstiffimus Viduus curavit hic reponi.

Omnia debentur fato paulumq; morato,
Serius aut citius sedem properamus ad unam.

HEre resteth the Body of *Hannah Woolfe*, the late beloved Wife of Richard Woolfe, Jun. Daughter of Mr. *John Rickaby*, who departed this Life the 12th Day of July, A. D. 1712. aged 40 years, 6 months, and 12 days.

Under this Stone doth lie, bereav'd of Life,
An indulgent Mother, and a tender Wife;
A kind Relation, and indearing Friend,
Belov'd in Life, lamented at her End :
In doing Good, Time wisely did employ; [Joy"
From whence (she said) "There sprung a secret

An Epitaph's too short by much to tell
The Worth of her, who liv'd and dy'd so well.
Then why should we lament ? It is in vain :
To her to live, was Christ ; to die, was Gain.

HEre lieth the Body of *Mary*, Wife of Mr. *Richard Woolfe*, and Daughter of Mr. John Bower, both of Bridlington Key, Merchants. She departed this Life the 19th Day of Octob. 1723. in the 35th Year of her Age ; had Iffue 4 Sons, and 3 Daughters ; *Henry, William, & George,* deceased ; and near hereunto interred.

Y.

HEre lieth the Body of *John Yates* the Elder, late of Bridlington, who departed this Life the 12th day of September, and in the 77th Year of his Age, A. D. 1680.

On the Back of the King's Arms the following Words, *&c.* are painted.

Thomas Walker, Minifter. *Gilbert Mainforth, Thomas Hill, Richard Hardy* Church-Wardens, 1713 ——The Gallery, N. of the Chancel, was erected by *John Walker*, Church-Warden, in the Year 1716.

I think, Sir, I have sent you every thing that I could poffibly collect by transient Observation. I need not write much further, since you have (in your first Vol. at the End of the History of York, *Pag.* 243*) given a general Account of both Church and Town. When the Monastery of the Regular Canons flourish'd, it was noted for* John *the Prior, a pious Man ; but, as it is reported of him, strangely given to rhiming Prophecies, who dy'd Anno* 1379, *aged* 60. *Sir* John Ripley *was another Canon of the Place. 'Tis said, that having been excellently learned, studying* 20 *Years in* Italy, *he found out the Philosopher's Stone ; and expressed his Joy thereat in these rapturous Words,* Inveni quem diligit anima mea. *Returning to* England, *he left the Convent, and became a* Carmelite *Anchoret at* Boston, *where he wrote several Books, particularly of* Alchimy : *But so modest was this contemplative Man, that he desired them to be burnt, as being his own Opinion, which he thought afforded no certain Proof ; and departed this Life, with a perfect Resignation in the Year of our*

Lord

Lord 1492. *Another of the Canons was called* Robert the Scribe, *who was buried before the Cloyster Door. He was a swift Penman, and wrote several learned Books. But what need I discourse of a Monastery, or the Worthies of it, when there is no such thing, except the venerable Church, in Being? However, one may gness where the Priory stood, (by the breaking off of the Church Pillars, and the stopt-up Arches) that it was on the South Side thereof: And if fine Ground, a pleasant Country round about, and a sweet reviving air from the Ocean, may be the Means to inspire Mortals with a happier Genius; it is little to be wonder'd at, that* Bridlington *should have produced such famous Gentlemen, being admirably blest with a delightful Situation.* Walter de Gant *was the Founder of the aforesaid Priory, which became worth near* 700 l. *a Year.* Gilbert, *his Son, who was Earl of* Lincoln, *confirm'd what his Father had done, and desired to be buried amongst them. In King* Henry *the First's Time,* William de Percy *was a Benefactor. King* Henry II. *confirmed to the Canons their Lands and Possessions.* Walter de Ven, *King* Stephen, Hugh *and* Ralph de Nevill, *added to their Happiness: But the last Prior, named* William Wolde, *opposing the Designs of King* Henry *the Eighth, that unfortunate Gentleman suffered Death at* Tyburn, *near* London, A. D. 1537. *The Key is about a Mile South of it, and seems a very beautiful Town, having Houses fronting each other like a Street. South of this is the Sea, in which two Piers are built of a considerable Length, forming a narrow Entry for Ships to pass into a Place of Safety. On the East Side is pleasant Strand to walk or ride upon for* 3 *or* 4 *Miles to a Promontory (forming a Creek) called* Flamborough-Head; *and Westward, one may ride, as I hear, for* 10 *or* 12 *Miles together, with a pleasant Prospect of the Deep, and frequently of Ships under Sail.* Bridlington *has likewise a long Street and several Lanes. At some Distance, Westward of the Church, is a fine Gate-House, which I am not certain whether or no might not have belong'd to the dissolv'd Priory, and terminated their Boundaries on that Side: But now it is called the* Old Bail, *in a part of which Malefactors are confin'd 'till such time as they can be convey'd to* York *Castle. In this Building is a spacious Court-Room; and Stone Steps to ascend to the Top, which is flat, and I suppose covered with Lead.* Mr. William Hustler *was a great Benefactor to a Grammar School in this Town. The present glorious Ornament to* Bridlington, *is the Earl thereof, the* Mæcenas *of Learning, the Encourager of Arts, and the Comforter of all good Men. There is a fine Spaw near the Town, and another at* Filey, *on the Sea Coast betwixt here and* Scarborough: *So that almost every Place along the Shore even charms the Traveller into Excess of Joy, and affords inconceivable Delight, Health and Recreation. I am, S I R,*
Your's, &c.

PHILOHISTORICOS.

A LIST

OF THE

Names of the *Subfcribers*.

A

MR. Jofeph Addington
   The Reverend Mr.
James Addifon.
Mr. William Anderfon
Mr. Peter Aram, *Author of*
a Poem on Studley-Park
Mr. Eugenius Aram
Mr. Samuel Afcough

B

Mr. Thomas Bakewell
Mr. Edmond Barker
Mr. Cornelious Barker
Mr. Thomas Bedell
Mr. Stephen Beverley
Mr. Jofeph Boddington, *Sta-*
tioner, of London
Mr. Henry Boddington
Mr. Robert Bollans
Mr. George Bourne, *Station-*
er, of London
Mrs. Barbara Bradley
Mr. John Brennand
Mr. Marmaduke Bullock
Mr. Jofeph Burton
Mr. Joseph Bull

C

Mr. John Care
Mr. John Clark
Mr. A. Clark
Mr. Edward Coats, *Painter-*
Stainer, of York.

Mrs. Magdalen Conyers
Mr. John Coffins

D

Mr. John Davidfon
Mr. Benjamin Dawney
Mrs. Rebekah Deacon
Mr. James Dewitt
Mr. James Dickinfon
Mr. Thomas Dickinfon
Rev. Mr. Tho. Dowbiggin
Mr. John Dowbiggin

E

Mr. Thomas Ellis
Mr. E. Ellis
Mr. Richard Eggleston, *Spec-*
tacle-Maker in the Minster
Yard, YORK

F

Henry Fairfax, *of* Towlston,
near Tadcaster, *Efq* ;
Mr. Jofeph Fenner, 2 *Books*
Mrs. Mary Fenner, 2
Mr. George Ferraby, 100
Mr. John Fryer, *Verger of*
York-Minster

G

Mr. Edward Geldard
Mrs. Sarah Gent
Mrs. Mary Gent
Mr. Thomas Green, *of* Lon-
don, 17 *Books*
Mr. Emanuel Gregson.

Mr. Jofeph Gray
Mr. Richard Guy

H

Mr. William Haberjamb, *at*
the Elephant and Castle,
(*or the* Old Post-House) in
Skeldergate, YORK
Mr. Roger Hall
Mr. Jeremiah Hall, *Merchant*
Taylor and Draper, in
Jubbergate, YORK
Mr. Thomas Hammond, 6
Books.
Mr. Thomas Hawerth, *Mer-*
chant
Mr. John Haynes
Mrs. Anne Haynes
Mr. Thomas Hays, *Grocer*
Mr. Roger Hopditch, *Gar-*
dener, at Clifton
Mrs. Mary Heptinstall
Mr. John Hildyard, 25
Books
Mr. Henry Hindley, *Clock-*
maker, in Petergate,
YORK.
Mrs. Mary Howlden
Mrs. Sarah Hoyle
Mr. Henry Hoyle

I

Mr. John Jackfon

NAMES of the SUBSCRIBERS.

Mr. Thomas James, *of* London, *Letter Founder*
Mr. John Jewitt
Mr. Edward Johnson

K

The Rev. Mr Thomas Kaley
Mr. Tho. Kaley, 2 *Books*.
Mr. Thomas Keregan
Mr. Thomas Knowlton

I.

Anonymous
The Reverend Mr. Lambert
Mr. John Lambert

M

Mr. Rupert Mace, *Attorney at Law*
The Rev. Mr. John Màwer,
Mrs. Anne Michill
Mr. John Moore
Mr. John Morton.

P

Mr. Charles Parkinson *Officer in the Army*

Mrs. Elnor Parson, 2 *Books*
Mr. Thomas Pattison
Mr. Robert Peacock, *Gardener to* Thomas Duncomb, *Esq*
Mr. William Prest, *at* Sessay

R

Mr. George Reynoldson, *Upholder, in* Stonegate, YORK ; *also the Maker and Seller of Looking Glasses,* &c. at London *Prices.*
Mr. Christopher Reynoldson
Mr. George Rhodes
Mr. Robert Richardson
Thomas Robinson, *Esq* ;
Mr. Thomas Robinson
Mr. Edward Routh

S

Mr. Hugh Savile
Mr. Thomas Sedwick
Mr. William Skinner
Mr. Francis Smyth

The Rev. Mr. John Standish
Mr. John Strangways
Mr. J. Steel
Mr. Jonathan Symonson

T

William Tatham, *Esq;*
Mr. Samuel Taylor
Mr. John Turner

V

Mr. John Vanner

W

Messieurs Ward *and* Chandler, *Booksellers at* Scarborough, 6 *Books*
Mr. Richard Ware, *of* London, 6 *Books*
Mr. William Warrin
Mr. Thomas Williams
Mr. Richard Wilkinson.
Mr. Robert Willsthorpe
Mr. John Willis, *Stationer, in* Tower-street, London
Mr. David Wood

1869 :
REPRINTED BY M. C. PECK AND SON, 10 MARKET-PLACE,
HULL.